The Story of Modern Skiing

The Story of Modern

Skiing

JOHN FRY

UNIVERSITY PRESS OF NEW ENGLAND

HANOVER AND LONDON

Published by University Press of New England,
One Court Street, Lebanon, NH 03766
www.upne.com

Title page photograph: Jim McConkey at Alta, Utah, 1960. *Photo by Fred Lindholm.*

Library of Congress Cataloging-in-Publication Data

Fry, John.
    The story of modern skiing / John Fry.
        p.   cm.
    Includes bibliographical references and index.
    ISBN-13: 978–1–58465–489–6 (cloth : alk. paper)
    ISBN-10: 1–58465–489–9 (cloth : alk. paper)
    1. Skis and skiing—History. I. Title.
    GV854.1.F78   2006
    796.93—dc22   2006013869

 University Press of New England is a member of the Green Press Initiative. The paper used in this book meets their minimum requirements for recycled paper.

To my loving wife and children,
and to Serge Lang who encouraged me to write this book.

Contents

Preface

The Story of Modern Skiing is about the period after World War II when change came rapidly to the sport of alpine skiing. Especially in the period between 1950 and 1972, many of the sport's enduring innovations arrived. Metal and fiberglass skis, plastic boots, and lightweight poles opened the way for revolutionary advances in technique. Major international races came to be held in North America every winter. Starting from a 1955 base of only 78 ski areas, over the next ten years the United States and Canada gained 580 new resorts having chairlifts and T-bars. Giant base lodges presaged the arrival of pleasure domes, dramatically different from the dark, dank, low-ceilinged base huts of the 1950s. The construction of the interstate highway system and the arrival of jet passenger planes gave rapid access to better, bigger, more distant terrain. Visits to U.S. ski areas soared from four or five million per winter to almost forty million. Spending on travel, equipment, and clothing rose above one billion dollars annually.

All of these things were in place by 1972. Thereafter came a decline in the number of young people entering the sport. New resort construction slowed in the wake of the oil crisis and environmental legislation strengthening the influence of groups opposed to development on public land. Mass participation in cross-country skiing peaked at the end of the 1970s, and never recovered. Wintertime alternatives to skiing arrived: cheap jet vacations in the Caribbean, Disney World, indoor tennis, the first arcade game from Atari, and pay cable television. In Michigan, the Brunswick Corporation began to make tens of thousands of toy-like "Snurfers" . . . a kid stood on a single board and rode downhill on the snow.

The changes in the sport, familiar to long-time skiers, can now be viewed in judgmental perspective. Who left indelible marks on the sport? Why did one innovation endure, another disappear? I was in an advantageous position to observe. For most of the second half of the twentieth century, I edited national magazines for skiers and wrote extensively about the sport. I contributed to launching *Ski Life* magazine in 1959. In 1964, I became editor-in-chief of *SKI*, the nation's oldest ski magazine. For the next sixteen years, I oversaw *SKI* and its related trade magazines. I started a magazine about cross-country skiing. In 1988, I was the founding editor of the New York Times Company's *Snow Country*, which over the next ten years attained a circulation of more than 450,000.

In editing special interest magazines (I also served as editorial director of *Golf* and of *Outdoor Life*), I took the view that a magazine's editorial mission should extend beyond creating informative, entertaining content. I believed in fostering reader action. And so I played a direct role in launching programs such as the National Standard Ski Race (Nastar), skiing's equivalent of par in golf. I invented the Nations Cup of alpine ski racing, and helped to introduce the Graduated Length Method (GLM) of teaching. As my interest shifted to a concern about the impact of unrestrained development in the mountains, I helped to organize conferences about this troubling challenge to the environment.

I knew many of the notable people in the sport, and this book is as much their story as mine. Among them are triple gold medalists Toni Sailer and Jean-Claude Killy; double gold medalist and environmental champion Andrea Mead Lawrence; the first winner of the women's World Cup, Nancy Greene; 1970 World Alpine champion Billy Kidd; and the Sarajevo gold and silver slalom medalists, the Mahre twins, with whom I wrote a book. I often interviewed resort and ski equipment pioneers, such as Squaw Valley's Alex Cushing, Vail founder Pete Seibert, metal ski designer Howard Head, plastic boot inventor Bob Lange, and ski pole innovator Ed Scott. I enjoyed a career, which happily fused with the love of a sport.

The Story of Modern Skiing embraces every aspect of the sport's modern development—resorts, equipment, technique, teaching, and competition. I've written it from the perspective of someone who is both American (by citizenship and length of residence) and Canadian (by birth and schooling). It's unlikely that my history will be entirely satisfying to an Austrian or a Norwegian, or to someone in Japan, which for a brief period counted more skiers than any country in the world. A Swiss or a Swedish historian's account of the sport's past obviously would be different than mine. But I would argue that no one is better suited than a North American to write a balanced skiing history. Through immigration, the United States and Canada became home to leading skiers from around the world, who attained their greatest successes here. America produced many of the innovations that transformed the sport—including the chairlift, the metal ski, the plastic boot, the modern ski pole, snowmaking and grooming, professional head-to-head racing, the waxless cross-country ski, the freestyle movement, and snowboarding. *En passant*, I'm tempted to remark that Scandinavians often opposed innovations, such as the use of skating in cross-country racing. The Austrians tended to support advances that would narrowly benefit Austria. The Swiss did all of these things, and ran the International Ski Federation as well. Meanwhile, Americans went from change to change, largely ignorant of the past, a neglect that inspired me to write this book.

How tiresome it is for the young to hear their elders proclaim the glory of things past. Skiing—and one may say fishing, golf, movies, indeed life itself—has never been as good as it was in 1940. Or was it 1950? Or 1960? No mind. The facts in this book speak for themselves. If you are a veteran, you can enjoy this trip into a past that I share with you. If you happen to be a younger skier, read on. You will learn a lot about your sport's heritage.

John Fry, 2006

When It Happened

Events and innovations appearing in *The Story of Modern Skiing*

1945 10th Mountain Division de-activated.
1947 Aspen opens with world's longest chairlift.
U.S. government encourages ski area development in the National Forests.
Two-seater chairlift introduced.
Commercial debut of plastic ski bottoms.
1948 Winter Olympics resume after World War II.
World championships are made biennial.
Ski Magazine consolidated and re-launched.
Rocky Mountain Skiing Magazine launched.
First dual-course slalom in sanctioned competition.
1949 Squaw Valley opens.
1950 Commercial snowmaking.
Howard Head, successful aluminum sandwich construction ski.
Major international alpine races in North America—world championships at Aspen.
Giant slalom becomes third alpine discipline.
Warren Miller movie premieres.
1951 Early snow grooming: Bradley Packer-Grader.
Average lift ticket price, $2.50.
1952 Andrea Mead Lawrence, 19, wins 2 of 3 Olympic gold medals.
Heel and toe release binding by Cubco.
1953 Amputee ski school in America, Big Bear, California.
Ski industry trade show, New York City.
1954 Stretch pants.
Fiberglass skis.
Founding of the U.S. National Ski Hall of Fame.
Mount Snow opens with wide trails.
1955 Short swing (wedeln), official Austrian technique.
Buckle boots.
Polyethylene base for skis.
Ski charter flight to Europe.
100-mph speed barrier unofficially broken at Portillo, Chile.
1956 Olympic Winter Games at Cortina, Italy, are televised.
Toni Sailer wins all 3 alpine Olympic gold medals.
1957 Freestyle tricks taught by Doug Pfeiffer.
1958 First U.S. gondola lift, Wildcat, New Hampshire.
Slopes iced for competition.

1959   Introduction of lightweight, strong, tapered aluminum ski pole.
        Buddy Werner wins Hahnenkamm, world's most difficult downhill.
        Jet airline service shortens time to reach European and western North
            American ski resorts.
1960   Olympic Winter Games, Squaw Valley, California.
        Racing live on national TV in the U.S. (CBS).
        Olympic downhill won on metal skis.
1961   Professional racing with cash prizes.
        Professional Ski Instructors of America founded.
        Official American ski technique.
1962   National Ski Areas Association founded.
        Opening of Vail, Colorado.
        World Championship medals won on epoxy fiberglass skis.
        Full-time coach for U.S. Ski Team, Bob Beattie.
1963   Ski brakes on bindings.
        Ski ballet, created by Phil Gerard.
1964   Kidd, Heuga—first U.S. men to win Olympic alpine medals.
        Kennedys vacation at Aspen.
        Easy-to-repair polyethylene running surface on skis.
        Giant base lodge at Hunter Mountain, 45,000 square feet.
        Skiing starts November 1 at Killington.
        I-80 interstate highway opens between San Francisco and Tahoe basin.
1965   Plastic boot by Lange.
        Polypropylene, moisture wick-away underwear.
        Magazine testing of skis.
        Uniform national symbols designating trail difficulty.
        Made-for-TV international team race, Vail.
        Average lift ticket price, $4.18.
1966   GLM—Graduated Length Method of teaching.
        Exhibitions of freestyle stunts by pro racers.
        Jackson Hole Teton resort opens.
        FIS World Championships, Portillo, Chile. Only championships ever
            held in Southern Hemisphere.
        Man wins women's downhill.
1967   First World Cup of alpine skiing, won by Jean-Claude Killy, Nancy
            Greene.
        Nations Cup: 1. France; 2. Austria; 3. Switzerland; 4. Canada; 5. USA
        Groundbreaking book, *How to Ski New French Way*, by Georges Joubert.
        Double aerial flip by Hermann Gollner, Tom Leroy.
        The Incredible Skis, first film popularizing freestyle.
        Real estate–based ski resort, Snowmass.
1968   Jean-Claude Killy wins all 3 alpine gold medals at Olympics.
        Killy is first skier to be represented by sports agent, Mark McCormack.

International Congress of Ski Instruction (Interski), Aspen.

Nastar, national standard race.

55-degree couloir descended by extreme ski pioneer, Sylvain Saudan.

Helicopter skiing lodge opens in Bugaboos, British Columbia.

1969 Mineral King ski area development is blocked by Sierra Club.

Over-the-boot pant, with elastic inner cuff.

1970 National Environmental Policy Act (NEPA) requires Environmental Impact Statements (EIS) for ski developments and expansions in National Forest, including public hearings.

Anti-fog double-pane goggles.

No wax fishscale bottoms for cross-country skiing.

Fiberglass ski purchases exceed metal.

Anti-friction pad improves binding safety.

The film *Downhill Racer*, with Robert Redford.

1971 Custom fit boots by foaming.

National Championship of Exhibition (freestyle) competition.

1972 International Olympic Committee (IOC) ejects Karl Schranz from the Olympics for being a professional.

1976 Olympic Winter Games opposed by Colorado voters.

France wins Nations Cup for last time.

1973 Eisenhower Tunnel to Colorado western slope resorts, bypassing 12,000-foot Loveland Pass.

Technique book *How the Racers Ski*, by Warren Witherell, defines the carved turn.

1974 4-wheel drive Subaru wagon.

1975 Rear-entry boot, by Munari.

Women-only ski clinics.

Hearings on failed senate bill to fortify state and local government control of ski development on federal land.

President Ford on Vail ski vacation.

1976 Franz Klammer's spectacular Olympic downhill is the televised sports highlight of the year.

Bill Koch, first American to win Olympic cross-country medal.

Average lift ticket price, $8.52

1977 Injured skier wins $1.5 million jury award.

Inner skiing emphasis on mental aids to learning.

1978 Telemark skiing with specialized equipment.

200-kilometer/hour speed barrier broken by American, Steve McKinney.

Vermont, New Hampshire legislate skier's personal responsibility codes.

1980 Grooming of steep slopes by winched snowcats.

Snowboarding competition.

Hinged slalom pole used in World Cup race.

1981 World Cup introduced in nordic skiing.
      Skating technique speeds up cross-country skiing.
1982 Super G added as fourth alpine discipline.
      Bill Koch wins cross-country World Cup in its second year.
      Beginning of rapid growth in cable-detaching, high-speed chairlifts.
      Beaver Creek and Deer Valley, last destination ski resorts built in U.S.
          before millennium ends.
1983 Tamara McKinney, Phil Mahre win overall World Cup titles.
1984 U.S. Ski Team wins three, or half, of alpine gold medals at Olympics.
1985 Exaggerated sidecut, shaped ski patented.
1986 Average lift ticket price, $20.37.
1987 Snowboarding popularity grows.
      U.S. lift capacity up 56% in a decade; skier-visits fail to grow.
      Population in 19 ski counties grows five times faster than U.S.
          population.
1988 Freestyle is a demonstration sport in the Olympics.
      Extreme skiing movie by Greg Stump, *Blizzard of Ahhs*.
1989 Ingemar Stenmark retires after record 86 World Cup victories.
1991 Luxury mountain-top day lodges: Two-Elk and Keystone.
      First extreme skiing competition, Valdez, Alaska.
      Ski website, on AOL.
1992 Fat skis for deep snow.
      Freestyle moguls added as Olympic medal event.
1993 Average lift ticket price, $31.00.
1994 Freestyle aerials added as Olympic medal event.
1995 Record 49 fatalities of skiers, snowboarders in U.S.
      Hunter Mountain base lodge over 100,000 square feet.
1996 Olympic gold medalist Picabo Street joins Nike athlete panel with
          Michael Jordan.
1998 Snowboarding enters the Olympics.
      Norwegian cross-country skier Bjorn Dahlie wins record eighth Olym-
          pic gold medal.
      Four resort companies control 28 percent of American skiing.
      Renegade environmentalists burn down lodge, damaging lifts at Vail.
      $700 season pass for 4 persons.
      353,600 vertical feet in one day of heliskiing.
      End of professional racing tour.
1999 Norway's Lasse Kjus wins record two gold and three silver medals in a
          single world championship.
      Ballet (acro) ski competition ends.
2000 Average weekend lift ticket price, $45.97.
      Austria's Hermann Maier wins 2,000 World Cup points in a single
          season.

Speed skiers near 250 kilometers per hour (155 mph).
Slovenia's Davo Karnicar skis from Mt. Everest's summit.

Caveat: Years in which discoveries and inventions occurred are often shrouded in controversy and dispute. Where in doubt, I have listed the year when a product or service generally became available or known to the skiing public.

Where It Happened

European locations of events in *The Story of Modern Skiing*

Sites of Olympic Winter Games (OL) and FIS World Alpine Ski Championships (WSC)

1948	St. Moritz, Switzerland	(OL)
1950	Aspen, Colorado	(WSC)
1952	Oslo, Norway	(OL)
1954	Are, Sweden	(WSC)
1956	Cortina d'Ampezzo, Italy	(OL)
1958	Bad Gastein, Austria	(WSC)
1960	Squaw Valley, California	(OL)
1962	Chamonix, France	(WSC)
1964	Innsbruck, Austria	(OL)
1966	Portillo, Chile	(WSC)
1968	Grenoble, France	(OL)
1970	Val Gardena, Italy	(WSC)
1972	Sapporo, Japan	(OL)
1974	St. Moritz, Switzerland	(WSC)
1976	Innsbruck, Austria	(OL)
1978	Garmisch, Germany	(WSC)
1980	Lake Placid, New York	(OL)
1982	Schladming, Austria	(WSC)
1984	Sarajevo, Yugoslavia	(OL)
1985	Bormio, Italy	(WSC)
1987	Crans Montana, Switzerland	(WSC)
1988	Calgary, Alberta	(OL)
1989	Vail/Beaver Ck., Colorado	(WSC)
1991	Saalbach, Austria	(WSC)
1992	Albertville, France	(OL)
1993	Morioka, Japan	(WSC)
1994	Lillehammer, Norway	(OL)
1996	Sierra Nevada, Spain	(WSC)
1997	Sestrieres, Italy	(WSC)
1998	Nagano, Japan	(OL)
1999	Vail, Colorado	(WSC)
2001	St. Anton, Austria	(WSC)
2002	Salt Lake City, Utah	(OL)
2003	St. Moritz, Switzerland	(WSC)
2005	Bormio, Italy	(WSC)
2006	Torino, Italy	(OL)
2007	Are, Sweden	(WSC)
2009	Val d'Isere, France	(WSC)
2010	Vancouver, British Columbia	(OL)

North American locations of events in *The Story of Modern Skiing*

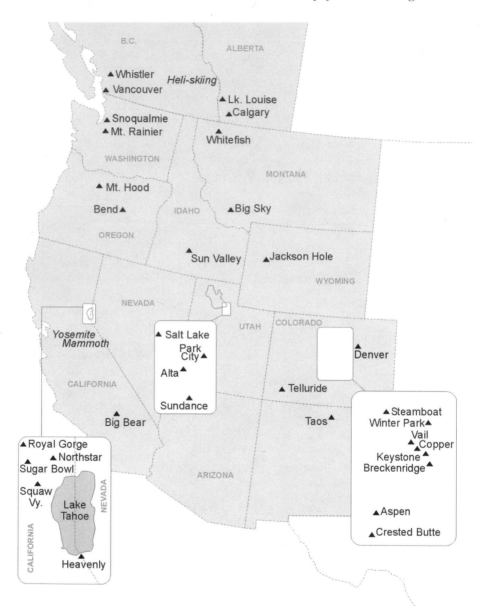

Ski Areas and the Winter They Opened

ROCKY MOUNTAIN WEST

Alberta

Lake Louise	1931

Colorado

Aspen	1947
Breckenridge	1961
Copper	1972
Crested Butte	1962
Keystone	1970
Steamboat	1963
Telluride	1972
Vail	1962
Winter Park	1940

Idaho

Sun Valley	1936

Montana

Big Sky	1974
Whitefish/Big Mtn.	1947

New Mexico

Taos	1955

Utah

Park City	1963
Sundance	1969
Alta	1938

Wyoming

Jackson Hole	1964

FAR WEST

British Columbia

CMH Heliskiing	1968
Whistler/Blackcomb	1965

California

Big Bear Lk./Bear Mtn.	1946
Heavenly	1955
Mammoth	1955
Northstar-at-Tahoe	1972
Royal Gorge	1971
Squaw Valley	1949
Sugar Bowl	1939
Yosemite/Badger Pass	1935

Oregon

Bend/Mt. Bachelor	1958
Mt. Hood/Timberline	1937

Washington

Snoqualmie	1937

NORTHEAST

Maine

Sugarloaf	1951
Sunday River	1959

New Hampshire

No. Conway/Cranmore	1937
Waterville Valley	1966

New York

Hunter Mountain	1959
Lk. Placid/Whiteface	1958

Quebec

Mt. Ste. Anne	1965
St. Sauveur	1934
Tremblant	1937

Vermont

Jay Peak	1955
Killington	1958
Mad River	1949
Mt. Snow	1954
Okemo	1955
Stowe	1937
Stratton	1962
Sugarbush	1958

MIDWEST

Michigan

Boyne	1947

Minnesota

Buck Hill	1954
Lutsen	1948

I

People and Place

Genesis

From herringboning to rope tows, telemark to stem christie.
The story of how skiing started before World War II.

In an odd dream that I experience occasionally, I glide effortlessly down a mountainside with no skis attached to my feet. I am floating on the snow. On a 1980 visit to the remote hills of northeastern China, the dream was eerily enacted for me. A small boy sped down a broad open slope, looking like a speed skater bent elegantly at the waist with bare hands clasped behind his back. As he accelerated, the flaps of his Manchurian winter hat extended from the sides of his head, like the ears of a donkey in full flight from some terrifying pursuer. Believing that I'd failed to catch sight of the boy's skis, I blinked and looked again. But there were none. Then he fell, and the mystery was revealed. Lashed to the soles of his crude boots were two small, crudely carved wooden blocks mounted with wire runners.

In its purest form, the act of skiing is as appealingly simple and effortless as the Chinese boy's demonstration. Moving downhill, a good skier turns by playing the force of gravity against the resistance of the snow. The action is akin to holding an arm out the window of a moving car, and by redirecting the force of the wind, cause the hand to swoop and turn like a glider. It's a series of balletic movements—twisting, flexing, balancing, pressuring one foot and sometimes two. Executed on a trampoline in a gymnasium, the movements, requiring superior eye-foot coordination, would be unremarkable. Performed while speeding in a space where the snow-covered earth meets the sky, the action is intoxicating. So intoxicating that people have abandoned conventional, practical lives to work for meager wages at resorts in return for the opportunity to be on the mountain on every good snow day that the resort has to offer. The thrill is no less intense for the affluent leisure class. Sliding down a

mountain on skis, to paraphrase Thorstein Veblen, may be a costly, con-
spicuous act of no social usefulness.[1] But it is somehow irresistible to the
person who has everything else in life he or she needs.

The Earliest Skiing

Skiing as a means of winter travel, of hunting, and of waging war evolved
before the written word or the pyramids. Wooden skis were made more
than six thousand years ago in Siberia and possibly as long ago in Scandinavia, and in China in the second century B.C. Herodotus, Xenophon,
and Tacitus all describe snowshoes and skis as a way of moving around
in wintertime, specifically in Lapland. The first printed images of people
on skis appeared in the 1555 *Historia de Gentibus Septentrionalibus* [*History
of the Northern People*] written by a Swedish cleric, Olaus Magnus. Slove-
nians as early as 1689 rode downhill on 150-centimeter skis, using a single
pole, their feet held to the ski with a leather toe strap and braided willow
shoots.[2] In the middle of the nineteenth century, Norwegian skiers in the
Telemark region invented the first heel strap to hold the foot more securely in place. In Norway, skiing was less a sport than an element of the
nation's culture, and an important one, known as Idraet. When Norwegians voted to re-institute the monarchy in 1905, they brought in a Dan-
ish king and queen to occupy the throne, a consequence of Norwegian
royal blood having died out. One of the king's first acts was to visit the
Holmenkollen jumping hill.[3] Most European royalty wouldn't be caught
dead at such a sports event, but the new king needed to demonstrate the
seriousness of his intention to become a true Norwegian, and the way to
his subjects' hearts was through skiing. He was later succeeded by King
Olav, who actually went off the world-famous jump, virtually a national
monument. The court made sure there were plenty of pictures showing
him doing it!

No one better exemplified Ski-Idraet's spirit, nor believed more in its
antagonism toward timed competition and distance records, than the intrepid explorer Fridtjof Nansen. In 1888, Nansen had excited the imaginations of millions of people by crossing the Greenland ice cap on skis.
His book *On Skis Across Greenland*, published two years afterward, excited the world's imagination about what could be done on skis, so much
so that tens of thousands of people took up skiing in countries that had
scarcely known of it previously. And so the decade of the 1890s brought
about changes as momentous as the technical innovations that revolu-

First Book. The earliest published images of people on skis, soldiers or hunters, appeared in the 1555 book *Historia de Gentibus Septentrionalibus* [*History of the Northern People*] by the Swedish cleric Olaus Magnus. *Mammoth Ski Museum, Beekley Collection*

tionized skiing seventy years later in the 1960s. Skis and bindings were designed differently. The first formal technique of skiing downhill appeared, along with the first literature on how to ski, and the formation of ski clubs. Thousands of utilitarian years of skiing as winter transportion suddenly gave way to skiing as winter diversion, a sport.

Early American Skiing

The first people to ski on the North American continent were Siberian fur traders who employed skis to cover their Alaskan trap lines in the eighteenth century.[4] In the second half of the nineteenth century, a few rural postal workers and itinerant preachers—usually of Norwegian heritage—used skis to bring letters and spiritual messages to remote, snow-bound communities. Snowshoe Thompson, a Norwegian immigrant from Telemark, carried mail across Sierra Nevada mountain passes to California mining towns. A popular wintertime sporting event in the mining towns in the 1860s were 60-mile-an-hour straight downhill schusses, performed on 12-foot-long skis made speedier by coating the running surfaces with beeswax and spermaceti.[5]

Schuss! The world's earliest high-speed downhill races were staged at mining camps in California's Sierra Nevada mountains in the 1860s. A group of skiers, early in the twentieth century, simulated the miners as they would have started together in a race-to-the-finish on 12-foot-long skis. The simultaneous "ge-schmozzel" start was abandoned but was revived at the beginning of the twenty-first century in ski and snowboard cross races, which put a half-dozen competitors simultaneously on the course. *Courtesy of the California History Room, California State Library, Sacramento, California.*

Skier cross race, 2005. *Photo by Scott Markewitz.*

Scandinavians popularized jumping in Michigan, Minnesota, Wisconsin, Illinois, and British Columbia. Like the California miners' races, the jumping tournaments often awarded cash prizes. On the frozen, windswept shores of Lake Superior, on Michigan's isolated Upper Peninsula, immigrant Scandinavian jumpers in the town of Ishpeming in 1891 created one of the nation's oldest enduring ski clubs, one that in a few years would spawn the National Ski Association.[6] Across the nation, clubs like Ishpeming in Michigan, and like the even more venerable Nansen Ski Club in New Hampshire and the Aurora Ski Club, which was founded in 1886 in Minnesota, supplied the foundation for organizing the sport and recruiting new skiers.

In 1907, tens of thousands of spectators bought tickets to Barnum and Bailey's Circus in order to see the sensational act of a man on "skees" roaring 75 feet through the air, "across a yawning, death-defying chasm. An act of a thousand thrills! Seen for the first time this side of Norway's snow-capped peaks."[7] At the time, the "perilous Scandinavian sport of skee-ing" was little known to Americans. The circus appearance of a ski jumper was guaranteed to make it known, because traveling circuses such as Barnum and Bailey's and Ringling Brothers—moving on railroad cars with hundreds of performers—constituted the biggest entertainment and populist cultural force in the nation at the time.[8] The man who performed "the fateful falcon flights on skimming skees" for Barnum and Bailey's in New York's Madison Square Garden was Carl Howelsen, a thirty-year-old immigrant and Norwegian cross-country and jumping champion. Howelsen eventually made his way to Colorado, where he introduced jumping as a feature of winter carnivals and where he settled in Steamboat Springs. (The town's Howelsen Hill today is the oldest continuously operated ski area in Colorado. A jewel of a municipal park, it has produced fifty-four Olympic skiers, the most of any U.S. town.)

The British Influence

The sport cross-fertilized around the world. In 1868, for example, when a Swiss who had been digging for gold in California's Sierra Nevada saw his first skis, he ordered a pair made for himself upon returning home. Skis in Switzerland at the time were rare.[9] In 1864, the Swiss hotelkeeper Johannes Badrutt persuaded adventurous but skeptical British summer clients to come to St. Moritz at Christmas.[10] After exhilarating weeks of sun and snow, the English got hooked on the idea of a winter snow vacation, and they continued to return. Toward the end of the nineteenth century, the British travel agent Henry Lunn and his son Arnold further popularized Swiss skiing at Grindelwald, Mürren, and Wengen. Austria's Kitzbühel was popular with Germans. Gstaad in Switzerland, Chamonix in France, and Garmisch in Germany offered skiing.

In the Alps, the earliest downhill races—some long descents, some merely sprints—were held in the late nineteenth century. By 1905, Mathias Zdarsky, who brought Norwegian skis to Austria and who published the first book on alpine ski technique, staged a slalom-type competition on a slope above his hometown of Lilienfeld.[11] In 1910, Hannes Schneider, using his version of the sliding stem turn—the famous stem christie—won the Swiss national championships. The next winter, travel agent Henry Lunn organized a downhill race at Montana, Switzerland. Lunn asked Lord Roberts of Kandahar, the victorious Victorian general who had famously lifted a siege of the Afghanistan town of Kandahar, if he would, as a favor, lend his illustrious title to the name of the race.[12] The general consented, and the Roberts of Kandahar race was born in 1911. The competitors all started down the mountain together in what was called a geschmozzel start. There was no piste, or trail. Struggling through unbroken snow, the first man took sixty-one minutes to reach the bottom, 5,000 vertical feet below.

Henry Lunn's son, Arnold, was mad for skiing. At Mürren, a small gem of a resort with a spectacular view of the Jungfrau, at the age of thirty-three, he made his mark on ski history in 1922 when he organized the first race called a "slalom."[13] Two years later, Lunn founded the British-members-only Kandahar Ski Club, borrowing the name from the Roberts of Kandahar race. Four winters after that, in 1928, he joined with Hannes Schneider, now Austria's most famous skier, to organize a new alpine competition. Since Schneider was from the Arlberg region, and Lunn wanted to memorialize his beloved Kandahar club, they named the competition the Arlberg-Kandahar, known as the "A-K." It involved a downhill and a slalom race, with the outcome determined by combining the competitor's times for the two races in a single result.*

---

*After World War II, when the world championships were no longer staged annually, the A-K also served as a kind of world alpine championship in the years when there were no Olympics or FIS Championships. The A-K is still a designated downhill and slalom combined event on the World Cup schedule in most winters. Jean-Claude Killy has won it. Karl Schranz holds the record of six victories. North American winners have been surprisingly numerous, including Jimmie Heuga, Nancy Greene, Tyler Palmer, Marilyn Cochran, and Phil Mahre.

Big baskets, small flags. Bob Livermore of Boston's Hochgebirge Ski Club exhibits advanced technique of the 1930s as he flies through the gates in a slalom race on Mount Rainier. He was vying for a berth on the 1936 Olympic ski team that went to Garmisch, Germany. *From the archives of* Ski Racing Magazine

Even though they had successfully launched the Arlberg-Kandahar races, Lunn and Schneider and other alpine enthusiasts, mostly Brits and Swiss, had been unable to persuade the twenty-year-old Fédération Internationale de Ski (FIS), dominated by tradition-bound Scandinavians, to accept downhill and slalom officially as disciplines in the sport of skiing. The Norwegians, in particular, clung to the belief that the nordic competitions of cross-country and jumping were the only true tests of skiing. The new alpine races were seen as possibly impure . . . alien to Idraet. But Lunn, persistent as the proverbial English bulldog, finally prevailed, and in 1931 the first official FIS World Championship of Alpine Skiing was held at Mürren, Lunn's winter home.

The world championships were held annually until 1940 when the onset of World War II halted international competition (see chapter 7). During the same pre-war period, the Arlberg-Kandahar alternated between St. Anton and Mürren. Unlike the FIS Worlds, it served as an annual open championship, since anyone—pro or amateur—could enter. The sites of the annual A-K eventually expanded to Chamonix in France, Sestrieres in Italy, and Garmisch in Germany. It became the world's most recognized alpine competition, and the name Kandahar spread across the ski world, like McDonald's. Scores of hotels and restaurants were named Kandahar. There was a Kandahar binding, ski, and boot, and Kandahar parkas. Kandahar races spread to Norway, Scotland, Chile, New England, and California. At Mont Tremblant, Quebec, the first Kandahar held outside of the Alps was organized by the Red Birds Ski Club, a creation of skiers from Montreal's McGill University.

The Laurentians: Place of Innovation

In 1908, the famous Montreal winter carnival attracted Dartmouth College student Fred Harris to come up from Hanover, New Hampshire. The experience must have made an impression on Harris, because a year later he founded the Dartmouth Outing Club, which proceeded to organize its own Winter Carnival. The first intercollegiate competition in North America—an 8-mile cross-country relay race between teams from Dartmouth and McGill—was held on February 22, 1914, at Shawbridge in the Laurentians.

It was in the Laurentians that the sport of alpine skiing, created in Europe, established its first enduring North American roots, where the first formalized downhill ski teaching was taught, where the template for the commercial ski area was made, and where the first popular ski train rolled down the tracks.

The Laurentians are not among the world's great mountain ranges, which typically can be seen from afar. From Denver, for example, the white-capped Rockies stretch across the western horizon, but over the same distance from Montreal, the Laurentians are hardly visible. It's not only because they are more like hills than mountains, but they also are concealed by the flat, upward-tilting apron of one of Earth's oldest geological formations, the Laurentian Shield, so that traveling north toward them from Montreal, it's as if you were climbing a slightly raised drawbridge. Then you are down among the mountains before you have a sense of even having arrived. Suddenly, rugged hillsides and sharp little valleys surround you, and you are conscious of a place alive and utterly different from the featureless plain that brought you here from the city.

Montreal itself was a fertile place for the transplantation of a sport like skiing. North America's first organized winter sports club, the Scottish-dominated Montreal Curling Club, was founded in 1807. In 1874, at Cambridge, Massachusetts, Montreal's McGill University and Harvard

Jackrabbit

The man who singularly captured the early spirit of the sport was Herman Smith Johannsen, who was born in Norway in the nineteenth century not long after the American Civil War, emigrated to the United States, and lived most of his life in Canada's Laurentians, until he died late in the twentieth century. Johannsen's Methuselah-like life, centered around skiing, spanned the invention of the stem turn and of downhill and slalom, the first formal teaching of the sport, the rope tow and the chairlift, the beginning of Olympic and World Championship skiing, the arrival of snowmaking, trail grooming, fiberglass skis and plastic boots, down parkas and stretch pants, and ski villages built from the ground up.

Johannsen was born in Norway in 1875 near Christiania, which later became Oslo. Learning to ski as a child, he would have employed the traditional christiana and, of course, telemark turns, his feet secured by the first flexible heel strap made of woven root shoots, recently devised by Sondre Norheim of Telemark. At around the age of fifteen, he would very likely

have used the first skis made with side curvature—narrower at the waist than at the tip and tail. As a schoolboy, Johannsen met Fridtjof Nansen, who in 1888 electrified millions of people by crossing the Greenland icecap on skis. Nansen's book, *On Skis Across Greenland*, made much of the world aware of a sport previously little known outside of Norway.

In 1910, during the course of a trip selling machinery in northern Ontario, Johannsen stopped long enough to demonstrate to the Cree Indians how much faster he could move on skis over long

His 111-year lifetime paralleled modern skiing. Herman Smith "Jackrabbit" Johannsen, born in 1875 around the time of the first christie turn, died in 1986 at the dawn of shaped skis and high-speed chairlifts. Piedmont, Quebec, November 1971. *Photo by Michael Drummond*

distances than they could on their snowshoes. They later called him Oka-macum Wapooes, "Chief Jackrabbit." In the early 1920s, Jackrabbit moved his family to New York's Adirondacks. At the exclusive Lake Placid Club, he cut cross-country ski trails and took movie star Tom Mix on a bushwhack through the forest. Later he laid out the first downhill trails on Whiteface Mountain. When the stock market crashed and the Great Depression took his business down the tubes, he moved with his Cleveland-born wife and their children into a wood-heated cabin in Shawbridge, Quebec. They had little money. "I had time for the things which enriched my life," he told William Lederer (co-author of *The Ugly American*), "being with my family, cross-country skiing, exploring the wilderness, enjoying nature, and teach-ing these pleasures to others."[a]

With piercing eyes and a lean, hard frame, Johannsen looked like a wind-torn Norwegian pine as he bent over his skis. In 1930, he led the first group on skis to the summit of Mont Tremblant, offering proof to those who came later that the terrain would be suitable for a major resort. During the de-scent, wrote Bill Ball in his book *I Skied the Thirties*, "The party half slid, half rolled down the mountainside. It was here that the old master (Johannsen) fully exploited his bag of bushwhacking tricks—pole-riding, grabbing a spruce tree and sliding its length to grab the next one, dragging a ski . . . al-ways through bush that would have been difficult even on snowshoes."[b]

Johannsen was paid a modest fee to blaze and cut much of the 80-mile Maple Leaf cross-country ski trail that runs from north to south, paralleling the rail line through the Laurentians. He had a poor regard for lifts, prefer-ring to climb. He camped out in winter. "February and March are the best time of the year. You can build a fire way back in the bush and sleep in your sleeping bag in the snow."[c] Competing as a cross-country racer in the Stowe Derby in Vermont at the age of seventy-two, four times older than the youngest competitor, he placed third.[d] At the age of a hundred, he could still manage an outing on cross-country skis. He died of pneumonia in his native Norway in 1986. He was 111 years old.

College played a hybrid game of English rugby, from which U.S. and Ca-nadian football rules evolved.[14] The continent's oldest golf club, founded in 1873, is in Montreal. James Naismith of McGill had the idea for the game of basketball. Montreal is the birthplace of hockey.[15] It's a sports anthropologist's dream town. My own Red Birds Ski Club is North America's oldest downhill club, founded in 1928. A team of Red Birds produced the first North American skier to win an international race in Europe (see page 128).

Ski Train. The first North American railroad service bringing skiers from the city to the mountains commenced in 1927. This ski train from Montreal was making its way into the Laurentian mountains, 50 miles north of the city. *Nicholas Morant ~ Canadian Pacific Railway Archives ~ M611*

The Ski Trains

A pair of railways—the Canadian Pacific and the Canadian National, running from Montreal to the Laurentians—offered the earliest North American train service designed for skiers.[16] Over the winter of 1927, eleven thousand people and their wooden skis regularly journeyed north on special ski trains to the north. Four winters later, in January 1931, the first U.S. ski train ran out of Boston, some of its seats occupied by members of the Appalachian Mountain Club who had already ridden on trains to the Laurentians.[17] By the mid-1930s, tens of thousands of enthusiasts, captivated by the novelty and excitement of the new form of winter vacationing, were reaching hills by rail. New Yorkers and Bostonians filled weekend trains traveling to Maine, New Hampshire, and Vermont, the Berkshires and the Poconos, disembarking at stations that sometimes were only a walk, or a cross-country ski, away from the hill. The Chicago and Northwest Railway ran ski specials to Wisconsin and Michigan. Salt Lake City enthusiasts took the train to Parleys Summit and the hills of Park City. Beginning in 1932, San Francisco skiers rode The Snowball Express to Truckee in the Lake Tahoe basin. At the end of the 1930s, Denver skiers were traveling through the Moffat Tunnel to Winter Park, and Alaskan skiers from Anchorage to Curry. (Ski trains serving these locations were still running almost seventy years later.)

During the Presidential holiday weekend of February 22, 1936, under ideal weather conditions, transportation experts estimated three hundred thousand people in New England and New York went skiing.[18] In the first three months of 1936 alone, almost seventy thousand skiers entrained from New York City for the mountains of the northeast. The intrepid, ski-toting train travelers were a spectacle to behold. In Grand Central Station, otherwise sophisticated New Yorkers gathered to gawk at the exotically dressed skiers departing on the Friday night trains to the north country.

The train riders were a raucous, romantic bunch. Parties raged through the night, as revelers ranged up and down the aisles, singing. Falling in love could begin in a tangle of skis redolent with pine tar and paraffin. The more sedate tried to find seats in other railroad cars. I recall as a child traveling from Montreal through plowed canyons of snow so high that passengers stared for a mile out the window at a wall of snow, a journey through whiteness. Reaching the station, amid the eerie, sub-arctic air of nightfall, the steam locomotive hissed and groaned. Along the platform, horse-drawn sleighs waited to transport us to inns or to second homes in the hills. It was a familiar scene, depicted in railroad company promotional posters and on *Saturday Evening Post* covers.

People were attracted to the new sport after attending ski shows at the Boston Garden and at New York's Madison Square Garden. The 1936 New York show drew eighty thousand people who watched jumpers hurl themselves off a wooden ramp covered with shaved ice. They thronged exhibits of equipment manufacturers, sporting goods dealers, hotels, clubs, and resorts. That same year, Saks Fifth Avenue store had an indoor slide covered with Borax, on which customers could practice how to ski. John Allen, in his book *From Skisport to Skiing,* tells of an encounter between two women at a resort in Quebec's Laurentians. "Where did you learn to ski?" asked one. "At Saks Fifth Avenue, my dear," her companion replied.

Birth of the Ski Area

Americans who took their first winter vacation in the Laurentians by-passed their own Adirondacks, Green Mountains, and White Mountains for Quebec's more reliable northern snow. After changing trains in Montreal, their first stop was Shawbridge, a village of wooden houses and of

Ready to go—

with an engine that defies the cold

Golden Texaco flows—flows at zero—flows *freely* when many oils lag dangerously.

Brief starting seconds—the short time you spend "warming up" a cold engine—may cause more harm than hours of high-speed driving. For motor oil must flow and feed *instantly*, else pistons ride cylinder walls rough-shod, and metal grips metal harshly—destructively.

Only an oil as alert as Texaco—free of paraffin wax, of tars and cylinder stock, free of all cold-sluggish substances—can give instant protection. *No matter how cold the engine may be, Texaco Motor Oil never hesitates.*

Stop at any Texaco Service Station—the Red Star and Green T identifies it. Insist upon the *correct* grade of Golden Texaco Motor Oil.

THE TEXAS COMPANY, 17 Battery Place, New York City
Texaco Petroleum Products

TEXACO
CLEAN CLEAR GOLDEN
MOTOR OIL

Love at First Sight: The Automobile and Skiing. As early as the 1920s, the automotive industry discovered a powerful way to sell: Surround a car with society's hip new people—skiers. This motor oil ad appeared in the December 1927 issue of *The Country Gentleman. Mammoth Ski Museum, Beekley Collection*

lanes made as deep as canyons with plowed snow. It was the home of the Laurentian Lodge Club, started in 1923 and maybe the oldest residential ski club in North America. Known familiarly as the Shawbridge Club, it radiated a bonhomie characteristic of ski clubs in the period between the two world wars. Writer Corey Ford, in a 1929 issue of the *New Yorker*, offered an amusing account of being invited to Shawbridge to ski. Ford and his friends seem never to have left the clubhouse, as they consumed brandy, Canadian whiskey, and ale, and carefully resisted any temptation to venture into the sub-zero air.

Outside of Shawbridge, on "The Big Hill," a Montreal ski jumper named Alex Foster, after experimenting for a couple of years, established the first rope tow operation in the winter of 1931.[19] Foster's invention consisted of a four-cylinder Dodge sedan car jacked up on two low cement blocks, with 2,400 feet of hemp rope running around one tireless rear wheel rim and along pulleys. The latter were hung on telephone poles set in a straight line up to the top of the Big Hill. The intrepid skier grabbed the swiftly running rope with thick leather mitts and hung on until he released his grip at the top. A ride cost 5 cents; a day's ticket, 25 cents. At the bottom of St. Sauveur's Hill 70, the base lodge was a log shack heated by a wood-burning stove, with a unisex outdoor toilet—a drafty one- or two-hole crapper—dug over a pit.

The first U.S. rope tow—erected on Gilbert's Hill, near Woodstock, Vermont—was a copy of Foster's, just as the first ski train out of Boston had been a copy of a service already existing in the Laurentians. People were seduced by the luxury of grabbing a rope and being pulled uphill without having to climb. Across the Vermont's Green Mountains and New Hampshire's White Mountains, over the hills of Michigan and California's Sierra Nevada, and in Ontario and Quebec, rope tows came to lace the white-hilled landscape. At the bottom of the hills, entrepreneurs built warming huts, from which they sold hot dogs and hot chocolate. Thus was born the ski area in North America.

Notwithstanding the discomforts and the droughts when no snow covered the ground, the nascent resorts multiplied as fast as car dealerships. Milwaukee beer heir Fred Pabst thought there would be a synergy in operating more than one rope-tow hill, and so he leased the land for a number of operations in Michigan, Vermont, and Quebec. Among them was Hill 70 at St. Sauveur in the Laurentians, where the numbered hills—70, 71, 69—corresponded to battlefields on which Canadian soldiers fought in World War I. The know-how acquired in managing one mountain, Pabst believed, could be applied profitably to another. It didn't work out. Pabst abandoned his scattered rope-tow operations, and he eventually used the J-bar drag lifts he owned and his brewery inheritance to expand the Bromley ski area in Vermont, which briefly boasted the largest uphill capacity in the nation.[20] (Pabst's experiment in multi-ski-area ownership was mirrored fifty years later in the 1990s when investors and banks poured money into ski area conglomerates.)

All across the United States and Canada, people thronged to community rope-tow hills. The proliferation of ski areas to virtually every town with a hill and a decent, reliable snowfall had no counterpart across the European subcontinent—a consequence of climate and geology. European ski resorts were concentrated in the Alps, and in a lesser way in the Vosges, Harz, Jura, and Tatra mountains, and in the Black Forest region. In the Alps, there was a tradition of villages catering to summer mountaineers and tourists in the nineteenth century. Consequently, they possessed not only hotel rooms next to the slopes, available and ready to cater to skiers, but also cog railways and funiculars that could be adapted to transporting them to higher elevations. They didn't much need rope tows. When they did build lifts on ski slopes, they generally eschewed the rope tow in favor of steel-cabled surface-drag lifts like the J-bar and the Pomalift.

Italian prime minister and dictator Benito Mussolini was an enthusiastic booster of skiing. The first Alpine resort specifically designed and built for skiing was Sestrieres in Italy's mountainous northeastern corner, started in 1930 by the wealthy Agnelli (Fiat) family.

Americans who crossed the Atlantic on steamships and entrained for ski vacations in the Alps came back impressed by what they'd experienced, and were ready to respond to anyone who might have the idea of building a European-type winter vacation resort in America. Averell Harriman was the first to gratify their desire in a grand way. Inspired by the European model, he used his Union Pacific Railway to create Sun Valley in Idaho, the first North American destination ski resort built from the ground up. To be sure that he got it right, Harriman hired an Austrian, Count Felix von Schaffgotsch, to advise him. Only a European, after all, would know how to build a proper ski resort. But it was an American who had the idea that eventually swept all others before it. James Curran, a Union Pacific engineer, knowing how the company transported bananas, hooked a chair onto a moving cable and plopped a skier, rather than a banana bunch, onto it. In a blaze of publicity orchestrated by promoter Steve Hannagan's office in New York, Sun Valley opened in 1936 with three chairlifts. Within a couple of years, chairlifts went up at Gunstock in New Hampshire, and at Alta, Utah. The first aerial tramway in the United States accessing ski trails was erected at New Hampshire's Cannon Mountain in 1938.[21]

Mont Tremblant, after Sun Valley, was the next North American destination ski resort to have a chairlift. Tremblant was begun in 1938 by Joseph Bondurant Ryan, the scion of a wealthy Philadelphia family, who was encouraged by the impassioned ski enthusiast, radio broadcaster Lowell Thomas, to create a resort that may qualify as the world's coldest. Frigid winds coming down from Hudson Bay scour Mont Tremblant, the highest mountain in the Laurentians. Little wonder that Ryan oriented his first runs toward the sun. He started by putting a single chair up the south-facing lower half of the mountain called the Flying Mile, under which he built a wooden platform so that acrophobic riders would never feel that they were far from the ground. At the base of the lift, he constructed a charming little resort of lodges and small houses that bore the graceful rooflines and pastel colors of old French Canadian country homes.

The Laurentians were filling with wonderful and quite sophisticated resorts: Tremblant was by no means the first catering to skiers. There were the Lac Ouimet Club and Gray Rocks at St. Jovite, Far Hills Inn and Country Club, the Alpine Inn, a sprawling wooden inn Chalet Cochand, and the luxurious Chantecler. Affluent Canadians and Americans were taught to ski during the day. They socialized at night. Unlike the skiing, the après-ski was not a skill that the naturally boisterous, hard-drinking guests needed to be taught.

Alex Cushing, Squaw Valley's founder, received his skiing baptism in the Laurentians under quaint circumstances. He was chasing a debutante who had boarded a train in New York to go skiing. When she reached St. Sauveur in the Laurentians, she went to the guest house and rope-tow hill operated by the Marquis della Albizzi. The Marquis was an émigré of aristocratic lineage, a war hero, who had taught skiing at Peckett's in New Hampshire and at Lake Placid, and who attracted guests from as far away as exclusive Newport and Long Island's north shore. Cushing, still garbed in evening clothes he'd worn at the Manhattan debutante ball, entered a race organized by the Marquis. "I'd never skied before," Cushing recalled, "but I sneaked a pair of the Marquis' skis and went out on the hill in my dinner pants. In the race I went so fast I was too scared to fall down. I crossed the finish line in the air. The Marquis was furious. Just before I crashed, I heard him cry, 'Cushing, you're disqualified!' I landed in a crumpled heap, his skis broken."[22]

Early Teaching, Racing

In the 1930s, European skiers were ahead in every way: racing, resort management, and—essential to the sport's development—teaching people how to ski. Just as the earliest golf teachers in North America had been Scottish and English, the best ski instructors available to Americans and Canadians were Austrians, Swiss, and Norwegian. The first rudimentary ski teaching in North America was at the Lake Placid Club. For the winter of 1904 to 1905, the club imported skis from Norway for the use of its members. Later, it imported instructors to teach the members how better to use them. Most of the focus was on cross-country and jumping. In the Laurentians, when the champion Swiss skier Emile Cochand arrived, he brought with him several dozen pairs of skis.[23] In 1911, at the Laurentide Inn at Ste. Agathe des Monts, Cochand taught beginners to do scissor-like christies and telemark turns . . . the first alpine ski school in North America.

The earliest ski teaching in the United States modeled after Hannes Schneider's ski school in St. Anton was undertaken by immigrant Otto Schniebs in 1928. Certified in Schneider's Arlberg Technique, Schniebs operated a traveling ski school that taught members of the Appalachian Mountain Club to ski. He followed Schneider's model of organizing students into classes. In 1929, Katherine Peckett hired Sig Buchmayr to operate a Schneider-inspired resort school on Sugar Hill outside of Franconia, New Hampshire, at an old farmhouse that she had converted into a sophisticated inn. At Peckett's, socially upscale Bostonians and New Yorkers came to learn the snowplow and stem turn from instructors who had been trained by Schneider in Austria. His St. Anton school thus exercised a profound influence over the way Americans learned to ski, and not only at Kate Peckett's Inn. Schneider instructors crossed the Atlantic to work at resorts from Quebec to California. The urbane, brilliant Benno Rybizka taught in New Hampshire, and headed the ski schools at Mont Tremblant and Lake Placid. In 1936, Sepp Ruschp opened a ski school at Stowe, Vermont. Otto Lang, who later would direct movies in Hollywood, went to Mount Rainier in Washington. Hannes Schroll, who would marry Maude Hill, heiress to the Hill railroad fortune, went to Yosemite and the Sugar Bowl in California. He was succeeded by two more Arlberg instructors, Luggi Foeger at Yosemite, and Bill Klein at the Sugar Bowl. Adonis-like Hans Hauser taught at Idaho's Sun Valley Ski School, which he briefly headed. Hauser famously married Virginia Hill,

Hat Trick. At a 1940 banquet in the Sun Valley Lodge, the legendary Dick Durrance celebrated his third winning of the Harriman Cup alongside Averell Harriman, who created what was American skiing's most coveted trophy for twenty-eight years. *Courtesy of the Durrance Collection*

the former Las Vegas girlfriend of mobster Bugsy Siegal. At Sun Valley, he was succeeded by another Schneider-trained instructor, Friedl Pfeifer, who would go on to co-found the ski school at Aspen.

There was a notable exception to the superiority of European skiers—Florida-born Dick Durrance. As a boy, between 1927 and 1933, Durrance had gone with his mother and siblings to live in Bavaria. At Garmisch Partenkirchen in the shadow of the Zugspitze, Germany's highest mountain, he actually won the 1932 German National Junior Championship. Before returning to America the following year, Durrance learned a marvelous new, feet-together racing turn, which he copied from two-time world slalom champion Toni Seelos of Austria (see page 94). Back in New England at high school, Durrance, now seventeen, outclassed every native-born American skier, senior as well as junior. In 1936, now a student at Dartmouth, he led the first U.S. Olympic alpine ski team to race in the Winter Games at Garmisch where he had lived as a child. The team's Olympic results were disappointing, but the next winter Durrance won the first Harriman Cup competition at brand new Sun Valley.

As at the 1936 Winter Olympics and the Arlberg-Kandahar, the Harriman Cup recognized the best combined performer in downhill and slalom. Though he was an amateur collegiate racer, Durrance managed to out-ski seasoned European professionals, including 1933 World Downhill Champion Walter Prager. Durrance won the Harriman again in 1938, and completed the hat trick in 1940. By that time, he had won seventeen national titles and four collegiate championships. (After training World War II paratroopers to ski at Alta, Durrance eventually moved to Aspen where he successfully persuaded the International Ski Federation (FIS) to hold the 1950 World Alpine Ski Championships, the first held in North America.)

Just as World War II broke out, Hannes Schneider himself arrived in America as a result of a chain of events that started back in St. Anton, where he'd been arrested by the Nazis. Schneider was extricated from their grasp through the influence of North Conway, New Hampshire, native Harvey Gibson, who headed a consortium of U.S. banks that were owed money by Germany. Freed from house arrest, Schneider quit Europe and sailed for America—specifically to North Conway, where Gibson owned the ski area and where the banker invited him to settle down with his family, and to take over the eponymous ski school that Schneider's disciples had built.

The Ski Area Owners

Gibson, Harriman, Ryan, Pabst, Agnelli, all wealthy men, dabbled in ski area ownership as a kind of hobby. Possibly it was amusing to mention at a cocktail party in New York or London that you happened to own a ski area. Steel heir and publisher Jay Laughlin bought the Alta, Utah, ski area (see page 260). Roland Palmedo, a gentle, patrician New Yorker who founded the exclusive Amateur Ski Club of New York and who worked for Brown Brothers Harriman on Wall Street, solicited investors to build the first Stowe chairlift. In the Canadian Rockies, Sir Norman Watson, a wealthy Englishman, owned Skoki Lodge near Lake Louise, where fields of alpine flora—Indian paintbrush, anemones, arnica, and mountain daisies—bloom in summer. In later years, he built a gondola lift for summer sightseeing that came to be used for alpine skiing.

The Sugar Bowl near Lake Tahoe and the Badger Pass ski area at Yosemite lured a scintillating mix of San Francisco society and movie VIPs, including Walt Disney and Charlie Chaplin. San Francisco society—Hendersons, Chickerings, Gregorys, the banker W. W. Crocker, plus Disney—invested in the Sugar Bowl, not far from where the Donner Party starved to death. In the 1930s, California surpassed New England and much of the Laurentians, except Alta, in the quality of its ski runs.

Aspen's future came into view in 1936 when Joe Ryan's cousin Ted

Ryan and his friend, bobsled champion Billy Fiske, hired the Swiss avalanche expert Andre Roch to study the building of ski-lift-served slopes. They built the first out-and-out ski lodge in the environs of Aspen, the Highland Bavarian, which they saw as a base for the future. Four years later, Fiske was the first American pilot killed in World War II combat

Rapid Growth, Ended by the War

"All the facets of modern skiing were in place before the outbreak of the war," observes historian John Allen.[24] Around the time of Pearl Harbor, the United States had about two hundred, perhaps as many as three hundred, rope-tow-equipped hills, and by 1943, nineteen chairlifts. There were still almost as many jumping hills as rope-tow hills.

When skiers broke a leg or twisted an ankle, they were rescued by the new National Ski Patrol System, founded in 1938 by C. Minot "Minnie" Dole. In 1941, Dole succeeded in persuading Army Chief of Staff George C. Marshall that the United States needed troops specially trained in mountain warfare, capable of moving on skis. The Army eventually recruited fourteen thousand men, and a few women, to serve in the illustrious 10th Mountain Division.

In Europe, one measure of skiing's pre-war popularity surfaced in Germany when the Nazi government in 1940 demanded that citizens surrender their skis so that they could be sent to troops on the eastern front. No fewer than 1,567,000 pairs were donated, and as many more skis probably remained hidden in German attics and cellars.[25]

In America, recreational skiing, having started slowly, exploded in the Northeast in the late 1930s. There was a $10 million-plus industry of skiwear and hardware manufacture, wholesale, and retailing. Northland, Strand, and Groswold produced skis of ash, maple, and hickory— laminated in the better models. Peter Limmer, Bass, and L.L. Bean, and Tyrol in Montreal made leather boots. Dovre made bindings. Seattle's Hjalmar Hvam invented the release binding in 1939. The U.S.-made products were supplemented with goods imported from Switzerland, Austria, France, and Norway. The public flocked to buy the gear at ski specialty shops. The clothing floors at Saks, Abercrombie & Fitch, B. Altman's, and Filene's were swathed with fashionable two-tone parkas and pleated gabardine pants.

During the war, between 1941 and 1946, the building of lifts and resort infrastructure was virtually shut down, as resources like steel were dedicated to munitions and to building ships and planes. Gas rationing severely limited people's ability to travel to ski hills. Sun Valley was converted to a Navy recuperating hospital. Valiant men in the 10th Mountain Division sat in foxholes dreaming of the ski areas they one day would build and ski schools they would direct. When the war ended, the sport they loved hadn't changed much from what it had been when they left to fight in Europe.

2

A Way of Life

*The rich and the threadbare lived together. "He and She
sticks." The myth that skiing was ever cheap.*

The most widely quoted missionary for the sport, before and after
World War II, was Otto Schniebs. A 1927 German immigrant, Schniebs
began his life in America teaching the sacred stem turn to Appalachian
Mountain Club ski classes, to Dartmouth and other Ivy League college students, and to Lake Placid Club members. He was an enthusiastic schmoozer and natural-born salesman. "Skiing is not a schport,"
Schniebs informed the phonetically correct *New York Daily News* in
1948, "it is a vay of life." What Schniebs meant by his now-famous remark was that the committed skier doesn't just ski; he or she enters into
a culture, an ambiance of comradeship and a transcendent love of the
mountains.

The influence of foreign instructors like Schniebs on American skiing was as profound as that of the Bauhaus immigrants on American architecture. (Coincidentally, the Bauhaus designer Herbert Bayer moved
in 1948 to Aspen where he skied when not drawing plans for buildings.) The Austro-Bavarian alpine lifestyle filled a need. Lacking a native high-mountain culture, the American skier enthusiastically adopted
a jolly ersatz culture of yodeling, wearing a loden jacket and boast-
ing about *schussing* and *wedeling*. A ski vacation in the Alps was a rite
of passage. In St. Anton, guys who skied hard and played hard typically
stayed at the Old Post Hotel, perhaps hoping to have a liaison with a
beautiful countess down on her luck. Just across the mountains in Garmisch Partenkirchen, a U.S. Army R&R facility enabled thousands of
GI's on leave to learn to ski. If 10th Mountain Division veterans created the post-war ski industry, Garmisch surely created many of its
customers.

Hardiness Required

Skiing enjoyed its most rapid growth when it was full of brutal discomfort. After World War II and through much of the decade of the 1950s, it was a macho sport that called for resolute participants willing to endure waiting times of forty-five minutes in order to board a chairlift or T-bar. Tips of fingers and noses commonly were speckled white with frostbite. To keep warm during the long upward passage on a slow-moving single chair, the rider wore coarse woolen underwear layered-over with a flannel shirt and two sweaters under a nylon wind jacket. At the bottom of the mountain, you could warm up in the base lodge—a dank, dark shack filled with eye-stinging smoke emanating from a wood-burning stove and the unfiltered cigarettes of the occupants.

Outside, you ascended the hill by clinging to an arm-wrenching moving rope, and descended through deep, chopped-up snow concealing edge-ripping rocks. Occasionally, the 7-foot-long wooden skis lost a section of steel edge, or were warped. Leather boots alternately shrank and swelled. Bindings earned the name "bear traps." The fixed toe irons held the foot in a vise-like grip. If your ankle wasn't badly sprained or your tibia didn't break in a leg-twisting fall, it was because your ski had broken first. Slope conditions were whatever nature provided, including patches of grass and bare gravel. On the hill beside the rope tow, there was no machine to groom snow. Tow operators often were willing to trade a ticket to anyone willing to pack the snow for an hour by sidestepping the hill first thing in the morning.

To reach a ski area on the weekend, the eager participant started from home, shouldering skis, and walked the gray, frozen streets to the railroad station. The snow trains were relatively cheap and could be made even cheaper after boarding by hiding while the conductor gathered tickets. The alternative to the train ride was getting a ride in someone's car and sharing the gas expenses. The trip to Stowe, Vermont, from New York City, or to Michigan's Boyne from Chicago, or to Lake Tahoe from San Francisco on a Friday night required as many as seven hours of driving on two-lane roads. If there had been a thaw, a skier leaving the mountain at the end of the day could find his car stuck up to its hubcaps in mud in the parking lot. As late as 1953, it was a matter of pride for a New England ski area to be able to say that it had replaced its outdoor johns with flush toilets.[1]

Weekend warriors slept in farmhouses, through whose lath and plaster walls -20-degree night air leaked, and a glass of water left on the dresser at night was a block of frozen ice by morning. The faucet in the bathroom was made to dribble continuously to prevent the pipes from freezing. A wood-burning cooking stove heated the interior, but by morning the fire had died. The day's first chore was to place kindling on the night's embers and blow them to life. Thawing boots involved a complex strategy of placing them close enough to the stove to warm their interior, but not so close as to damage the leather by over-drying.

Skiers were undeterred by the hardships of flawed equipment and lifts, frostbite, rain, ice, and blustering winds. Paradoxically, the discomforts seemed to give them a sense of camaraderie and adventure.

Frugality and Singing

At the end of each winter, after writing exams, college students from across New England and eastern Canada motored to Tuckerman Ravine on Mount Washington in New Hampshire's White Mountains. Car racks were piled with skis and tent and sleeping bags. The car radio blared the big-band music of Harry James, Glenn Miller, and Artie Shaw. Arriving at Pinkham Notch, the springtime skiers parked their cars, and donned backpacks filled with clothing, food and beer, skis and boots lashed to the pack frames, and began the climb up the Fire Trail, a long, tortuous jumble of rocks, mud, and snow patches. In April, when the sap in the trees thaws, the aroma of the forest—red spruce and balsam fir—filled the air. A brook, swollen to a torrent by the melting snow, roared like distant automobile traffic. Skiers camped in lean-tos and tents pitched around the Tuckerman Ravine Shelter that had been built by the Civilian Conservation Corps in 1937 to give temporary shelter to hikers and skiers.[2] It was comically named the Howard Johnson Hut. Forking off the Fire Trail was a path that led to the smaller Harvard Hut. While it was under the care of the Harvard Mountaineering Club, the hut in winter was occupied mostly by McGill, Dartmouth, and Middlebury skiers. The compact interior contained a half-dozen hard-surfaced wooden bunk beds. A simple cast-iron box stove served for heat and cooking. Hut occupants lived off of oatmeal, powdered egg mix, boxes of raisins, tinned fruit and beans, and cans of pemmican that often turned out to be horsemeat. The place smelled of drying clothes and of molten paraffin wax. In an icy brook outside, skiers washed the cooking utensils and bodies coated with sweat from climbing. The sounds produced by melting snow were cease-

No Lodge. Skiers enjoyed an alfresco self-cooked lunch in the 1940s. *Nicholas Morant ~ Canadian Pacific Railway Archives ~ M720*

less. Rivulets of water gurgled under the frozen crust or laced the surface of the firn, and the melt dripped from the hut's eaves.

At night, after backpacking beer up the Fire Trail, skiers made themselves hoarse singing. This chorus was sung to the tune of the "Man on the Flying Trapeze":

> Some ski the Arlberg and some the Allais,
> While others the Swiss on the mountains display.
> But we ski Elliptical, give it a test;
> The Elliptical Technique's the best![3]

Ski songs like "The Elliptical Technique" were at the core of the ski culture. When *The Ski Song Book* was first published in 1950, *SKI Magazine* gave it a two-thumbs-up review: "For those skiers who don't know any ski songs—can there be any?—this book is a must."[4]

Immediately after World War II, a day's rope-tow ticket cost $1.50 to $2.00. At Aspen in 1948, a bed and three meals could be had for $6 a day at Fritz Benedict's.[5] At St. Sauveur in Quebec's Laurentians, a shack could be rented for $140 for the entire winter season. In the center of St. Sauveur stood The Pub, a sturdy wooden building with low ceilings and cigarette smoke so thick that you couldn't see the piano player across the room. On a Saturday night, beer-swillers gathered to sing Quebec favorites, such as "Alouette" (pronounced alooetta). There were English-language songs as well.

> My skis are of hickory, my harness of steel, my
> poles are made of bamboo!

or

> If you're out of control, running wild down the trail
> It is simply not done to sit down on your tail,
> You must get your weight forward, all experts agree
> Till your line of descent coincides with a tree.[6]

At Stowe, Vermont, the cheapest places to stay were Ma Russell's and Ma Moriarty's. At Ma Moriarty's dinner table on Saturday night could be found future Olympic silver medalists Penny Pitou and Betsy Snite, and wild Rip McManus, U.S. Ski Team mates of her son Marvin, for whom Mrs. Moriarty created a unique woolen hat. Another Stowe boy, Billy Kidd, wore it, and so did Jean-Claude Killy. It became famous as the Moriarty Hat, the official hat of the U.S. Ski Team. In the late 1960s and early 1970s, canny Ma employed fifty-five home knitters who were scattered about the Green Mountains, loom-knitting a hundred thousand copies annually of Marvin's original hat.[7]

The other Ma, Ma Russell, operated a boarding house, which at one time was the nation's oldest continuously operating ski lodge. It first took in skiers in 1932. During the winters between 1943 and 1962, for $5 a day, you could sleep in a bunkroom at Ma Russell's *and* eat two gargantuan meals cooked by Ma herself. Overflow guests could be found in sleeping bags on the living room floor. Breakfast started at 6:30 A.M. because most of the guests, including U.S. Ski Team racers, wanted to make the first lift ride up Mount Mansfield in the morning. In the evening, as many as twenty skiers sat on ladder-back chairs around a table groaning under the weight of Ma's soups, pot roasts, and pies. Instructor and future freestyler "Iron Mike" Hughes, who boarded at Ma Russell's for fourteen winters, recalls a dinner conversation. "It was about the length of ski poles," said Hughes, "and it went on in installments over three days."[8]

The most expensive place to stay in Stowe, at a sky-high $25 a night, was the Lodge, a favorite of DuPonts and the ubiquitous Kennedy clan. The food matched the best of any Manhattan restaurant. Guests were expected to wear jacket and tie at dinner.[9] The *maître d'hôtel*, Ivor Petrak, would go on to run the Canadian Pacific hotel chain. In front of the hearth in the Lodge's lounge, instructors from Sepp Ruschp's Mount Mansfield Ski School, including Olympic medalists Pepi Gabl and Othmar Schneider, gathered for après-ski drinks with their clients, whose number invariably included worshipful, radiantly beautiful women.

"Restricted Clientele"

Of twenty-six hotels, inns, and ski lodges in Stowe during the winter season of 1947–1948, no less than eighteen were listed as "restricted."[10] Advertisements bearing the code words "Restricted clientele" meant the lodge didn't welcome Jewish guests. As late as 1955, the New York State Commission Against Discrimination investigated the Lake Placid Club because of its exclusion of Jews and Negroes from membership, starting as early as 1904 when the club first offered skiing.[11] The Lake Placid Club was more or less ruled by Godfrey Dewey, the son of the inventor of a phonetic system of spelling, whose legacy still can be seen in local place names, such as the Adirondak Loj. In the Catskills, Jewish resorts, perhaps retaliating, made it clear which religious followers might feel uncomfortable staying there, with code words such as "Dietary rules observed."

At Mont Tremblant, Joe Ryan, a blustering, hard-drinking bon vivant and outdoorsman, with a flash-point temper, ran his lodge with an iron hand and an implicit anti-Semitism. "You're not welcome here," Ryan would inform a perplexed Mr. Goldstein or an outraged Mr. and Mrs. Rabinovich, after he learned that they were about to register as guests. "Take your bags elsewhere."[12] The guests who were permitted to stay included Doris Duke, the tobacco heiress, broadcaster Lowell Thomas, Nelson Rockefeller, the actor Cliff Robertson, and the world-famous neurosurgeon Wilder Penfield. During Christmas vacation week in 1947, at Tremblant, Ethel Skakel of Greenwich, Connecticut, first met Bobby Kennedy, a student at the University of Virginia.[13]

Exclusion and discrimination were exceptional, though. Most skiers thought of themselves as belonging to an open community, not restrictive like a golf club. At the lodge where they stayed, they were served by young waiters and chambermaids—college students earning $30 a month plus tips—who typically were the social equals of the guests. Dining was at communal tables—a tradition that has been kept alive over the years at places like Taos in New Mexico, Alta in Utah's Wasatch Mountains, and at British Columbia's heliskiing lodges.

Sport of the Stars. At Sun Valley's Dollar Mountain in 1946, actors Gary Cooper (center) and Clark Gable (right) worked to learn the basic traverse. The instructor was Sigi Engl, who later headed the resort's ski school. *Photo courtesy Sun Valley Resort*

Thorner House, near New Hampshire's Cannon Mountain, attracted guests such as Bette Davis, Zsa Zsa Gabor (then Conrad Hilton's wife), the news commentator Eric Sevareid, and the architect Walter Gropius. The place was operated by Hans Thorner, a Swiss, who had followed a trail familiar to foreign-born operators in America. He had taught skiing at Lake Placid and at Mount Rainier, ran a ski shop in Hollywood, taught indoor skiing at Saks Fifth Avenue, and sold skis and dog leashes at Abercrombie's in Manhattan. A creative fellow, he collaborated with the sports writer Grantland Rice in 1941 to make one of several ski movies, which he filmed not long after he had opened Thorner House. He could be acerbically witty. In the late 1940s, the fashionable eastern skier wore pants made by Andre of New York, or by the Montreal haberdasher Irving, who made an early gabardine wool stretch-like pant that sold for $25 at Saks Fifth Avenue where Thorner had worked. The back of the pant extended in a straight line down to the heel, like the tailfin on a vintage Cadillac. Of skiing, Thorner observed, "Where else can you dress like a circus clown and still be admired for it?"[14]

Ski for $10 a Day

In the 1950s, a one-day excursion to a ski area—including lift ticket, lunch, and gas for the car—could still be had for as little as $10. Many people "brown-bagged," bringing their own sandwiches to eat in the base lodge, a custom that survives today. *SKI Magazine* published what may have been the first authentic survey of skier habits in November 1950. It found that almost three out of four skiers were under thirty-five years of age. Among them were doctors, lawyers, housewives, artists, carpenters, schoolteachers, and registered nurses. The publisher—marking what was perhaps the earliest effort to demonstrate to the world's advertising community the wisdom of marketing to skiers—celebrated the affluence of the magazine's upscale readers. Two out of five subscribers, it claimed, earned more than $5,000 a year. Half were single. Fifty-seven percent of them belonged to ski clubs, sixty-three percent drank whiskey, and forty-three percent smoked cigarettes. They used a car for weekend skiing, a train or plane for longer trips. Three out of ten regularly skied in Canada. They typically skied slightly more than ten weekends a winter. Their daily budget for skiing was $12.65 (equal to about $90 today, adjusted for inflation). Half of the money was for food and shelter. The balance covered lifts, transportation, instruction, and incidentals. The less affluent expected to pay $6 a day to sleep in a bunkhouse offering three meals. The more affluent could buy an entire learn-to-ski week at Sun Valley, Idaho, for $75, including accommodations, all meals, six days of lifts and lessons, plus swimming and dancing.[15]

Skiing was a perfect milieu for boy-meets-girl. Four out of seven men and three out of four women were single. The prime daytime socializing took place in the lift line, where skiers routinely waited for thirty minutes and as long as an hour on a holiday weekend—plenty of time to talk, observed Morten Lund, "to meet a member of the opposite sex, get infatuated, engaged and plan the wedding."[16] The chances for agreeable encounters were enhanced with the switch from rope tows to T-bars, known as "he and she sticks." The trouble with the T-bar occasionally proved to be its blessing. The trouble was simply that if a tall and a short person were paired, their unequal heights would cause one or the other to fall off. Consequently, the lift attendant sought to pair people of equal height. The notoriously short Dr. Ruth Westheimer, who skied at Belleayre in New York's Catskill Mountains, was waiting in the liftline one day while the attendant sought a suitable rider to go up with her.

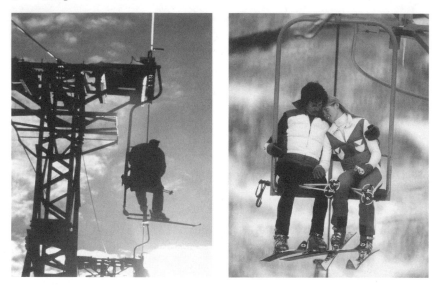

Technology Enables Romance. The arrival of two-seater chairlifts, starting around 1950, turned what had been a lonely uphill ride into a boy-meets-girl opportunity. *Single chair picture at Mad River, Vermont, by Martin Griff. Double chair photo at Vail by Barry Stott*

Eventually, a shortish man showed up, and they rode up together. He later became Dr. Ruth's husband.

The boy-meets-girl opportunities absolutely shot ahead in the 1950s with the switch from single to double-seater chairlifts.[17] Instead of sitting silently alone wondering how to meet the gorgeous gal he had seen in the liftline, a fellow could now actually sit next to her on the chair. Or the lift rider could enter into a lively dialogue about politics and the shortcomings and peccadilloes of the current White House incumbent. (In later years, the opportunities for intimate conversation lessened as the lift riding time shortened and the number of chair occupants grew from three to four, to six, and even to eight.)

More Amenities, More Cost

One by one, the resorts and the equipment and clothing makers devised ways to overcome the sport's discomforts. Cable lifts replaced rope tows. Civilized, enlarged base lodges served food more varied than hot dogs and hot chocolate. The down parka and the foot-warming inner ski boot arrived (see pages 81, 82). Release bindings reduced the risk of injury. But the improvements—at least, some of them—came at a cost. Between 1951 and 1965, the price of a weekend and holiday lift ticket, nationally, increased from $2.51 to $4.18, or 66 percent—triple the rate of inflation.[18] In 1955, Head's cheapest ski, the Standard, cost 85 dollars, the equivalent of more than $500 dollars today. A premium leather boot from Switzerland cost $85. A pair of the best steel ski poles cost $13, equal to $78 in 2000. A two-week European ski vacation for one person, including air fare, was advertised at $688, equal in inflation-adjusted dollars to more than $4,000 in the winter of 2000 when, in fact, a skier could purchase a similar trip for half that amount.[19]

In 1954, when a week of lifts, lessons, and lodging was advertised for as little as $50, it was an amount equal to one one-hundredth of the annual income of a *SKI Magazine* subscriber. The amount may seem small, but historically it was comparatively high. In future years, the cost of a ski week, relative to a person's income, actually would decline. Skiing was not a blue-collar worker's sport. In 1962, the average skier made $8,550 a year—more than three times the income of a typical American.*

Because there were relatively few other wintertime diversions, however, people did not regard the sport as expensive, as they would later, since they concentrated their disposable income for four snowy months on a single activity, skiing. In the year 1958, the average American skier spent $60 for equipment, $60 for lifts, $15 for instruction, $170 for lodging, $90 for travel, and $40 for "living it up"—a total of $435 for a season of skiing.[20] A new car at the time cost $2,200, and the median American household income was $4,650.

In the two decades of the 1950s and 1960s, participation in skiing grew at 15 percent annually, which is to say that the sport was doubling in size every five or six years. In the winter of 1962–1963, one of every five people on the slopes was skiing for the first time, and three out of five had skied for fewer than five years.[21]

The engine of skiing's expansion in the 1960s was driven by demographics. The sport was inundated with young people born during the post–World War II baby boom. On average, downhill skiers were twenty-four years old, twelve years younger than they would be by the end of

---

*In 1990, a *Snow Country Magazine* survey found that the median household income of its subscribers, $68,000, was only 75 percent more than the U.S. median household income of $39,000. In 1962 it had been 300 percent more. At the end of the twentieth century, skiers spent less on their vacations as a percentage of their income than they did forty years earlier. An advertised $500 ski week in 2000 accounted for 1/150th of a *SKI* subscriber's average annual salary of $75,000, compared to 1/100th in 1954.

Hurry Up and Wait! At ski
areas, long weekend liftlines
persisted in the 1960s and
1970s, and were not much
shorter than the 45-minute
waiting times of the 1950s.
This was the scene at mid-
Vail before the installation of
fast-moving chairlifts in the
1980s. *Photo by Barry Stott*

the century.[22] Here was an activity of speed and risk perfectly matched
to the age of the population bubble. It also helped that society perceived
skiing as a socially desirable, positive, and healthy outdoor activity. It was
a welcome escape in a society gloomy over the Vietnam War and the as-
sassinations of the Kennedys and Martin Luther King.

Tens of thousands of kids traveled to ski areas on buses, organized by
clubs and schools. Families heading for the mountains on weekends included the Thomas J. Watsons of Greenwich, Connecticut, who, if they
didn't fly, packed into the station wagon on Friday night after Mr. Watson
had completed a busy week running IBM. The Watsons resembled 45
percent of all U.S. households in 1960, in that they consisted of a married
man and woman living with their children. (By the year 2000, that percentage would drop to 23.5 percent of households, and half of all marriages would end in divorce—statistics unfavorable to fostering young
ski families.)[23]

Being a skier was a badge proudly worn, even by the rich and powerful. In 1968, Canada's Prime Minister Pierre Trudeau, the American
Ambassador to India and economist John Kenneth Galbraith, and the
president of the World Bank Robert McNamara told *SKI Magazine*'s
readers about their favorite trails. Trudeau picked historic Ryan's Run

at Tremblant, Galbraith a run at Gstaad, and McNamara the Big Burn at Snowmass.[24] It didn't seem odd to these busy men, nor to their aides, occupied with the affairs of the world, that they should take the time to choose and comment on a trail for a ski magazine.

In 1964, the Kennedy family descended on Aspen for their Christmas vacation. The arrangements were facilitated by the Aspen Skiing Corporation's Jim Snobble and Tom Corcoran. A member of the 1960 U.S. Olympic Ski Team, Corcoran was a quick-laughing, voluble fireplug of a guy. A nephew of Thomas G. "Tommy the Cork" Corcoran (advisor to President Franklin D. Roosevelt), he had recently graduated from Dartmouth and the Harvard Business School and had come to Aspen to work for the head of the Skiing Corporation, Darcy Brown, who gave him a job as a kind of all-purpose manager and strategist. Corcoran later built the Waterville Valley ski area in New Hampshire and worked on Robert F. Kennedy's New York senatorial campaign.

The Kennedy family spending Christmas at Aspen included Bobby, Ethel and their seven children, and newly widowed Jacqueline Kennedy

In-Sport of the Sixties. Recently widowed Jackie Kennedy, with her children John and Caroline, vacationed at Sun Valley in 1965, besieged by the press. The Kennedy clan skied at Stowe, Aspen, Waterville Valley, and other venues. *Photo courtesy Sun Valley Resort*

with Caroline and John-John. Local photographer Joern Gerdts took an exquisite picture of Jackie and the children trooping through the snow, only thirteen months after JFK's assassination in November 1963.[25] The Christmas entourage included Robert McNamara, an early Snowmass homeowner; Kennedy family friend Chuck Spaulding; Snowmass developer Bill Janss; and Denver University ski coach Willy Schaeffler. *SKI* ran a cover featuring a winsome head shot of twelve-year-old Kathleen, the Kennedys' eldest daughter (later, lieutenant governor of Maryland). Corcoran organized a race that was won by his and Jackie's team. Bobby skied aggressively and liked to make long, non-stop runs. He led his children—Bobby, Jr. and seven-year-old Michael—down the slopes. (Returning to the same Aspen Mountain thirty-three years later, Michael was killed when he fell and hit a tree.)

RFK liked to ski at Sun Valley, where he preferred to stay with his family in the cottage owned by U.S. Ambassador-at-large Averell Harriman, Sun Valley's founding owner.* Harriman annually called Sun Valley Ski Company President Harry Holmes to remind him that if Kennedy called to request the cottage, that Holmes should tell him that he must make his request to Harriman personally. He wanted Kennedy to remember who was doing him a favor.[26]

The Kennedy family's enthusiasm for skiing garnered an extraordinary amount of press coverage for the sport. Bobby attended a glittering, black-tie New York City Ski Ball, which raised $40,000 for the U.S. Ski Team. He and his brother Ted were considered so integral to the ski culture that they appeared in *SKI Magazine*'s 1964 list of the hundred most influential people in American skiing.[27] The list of equipment makers, resort builders, journalists, and instructors included Aspenites Friedl

---

*Sun Valley was not the only ski enterprise undertaken by Averell Harriman. Twenty years later, as governor of New York State, he endorsed the building of the Whiteface Ski Area in the Adirondacks. Mountains such as Whiteface, and Belleayre and Gore Mountain, located on state land, could not be operated privately under New York's constitution. As a result, the state had to build and operate them. The government-owned ski areas were promoted enthusiastically by Arthur Draper, an Exeter Academy and Harvard graduate, whose love of the mountains had caused him to quit his *New York Times* reporter's job in order to become a forest ranger with the State Conservation Department. Draper built Belleayre Mountain ski area under Governor Thomas Dewey. Then, befriending Democratic Governor Harriman, he persuaded Sun Valley's founder, now New York State's chief elected official, to shut down the ill-conceived Marble Mountain ski area outside Lake Placid. In its place, the new Whiteface area opened in 1957, later becoming the venue for the alpine races of the 1980 Lake Placid Winter Olympics. Financially, the government-operated ski areas fared poorly. In 1968, Governor Nelson Rockefeller had to propose a bill to relieve the Adirondack Mountain Authority of $10 million in debt incurred in building ski area facilities. *SKI Magazine* (Spring 1968): 90.

Pfeifer, who in 1961 had launched the ski-for-cash professional racing circuit, and the wisecracking Steve Knowlton, who had paid $1,000 to buy a corner lot where he built a ski shop over his Golden Horn bar. Considered as members of the Establishment were C. Minot (Minnie) Dole, who'd founded the National Ski Patrol System; ski manufacturer Howard Head and White Stag skiwear maker Harold Hirsch; retailers Don Thomas in Michigan, Buzz Fiorini in Seattle and Harry Vallin in New York City; racing coaches Bob Beattie, Chuck Ferries, and Dave McCoy; *SKI Magazine*'s publisher David Rowan and *New York Times* ski writer Mike Strauss; and area operators Pete Seibert of Vail and Damon Gadd of Sugarbush.

Slope Chic

Damon Gadd had started Vermont's Sugarbush in 1959, partnered by Jack Murphy, a veteran ski area operator. Heir to an Hawaii fortune, Gadd enjoyed strong connections to New York and Boston society, which were reinforced by his popular, handsome ski school director Peter Estin. The resort became popular with East Coast socialites and statuesque women wearing tall fur hats and stunning Bogner suits. Bogner's new stretch pants were sexy, if not outright erotic. For the first time in winter, a woman's hips, thighs, and buttocks were highly visible. Public demand almost overwhelmed the family's small factory. Within three years, Bogner was turning out thousands of pairs of pants in shocking new colors never previously worn by skiers—colors such as mauve, fuschia, and chartreuse. The pants sold at an unheard-of $40 and more. Marilyn Monroe, Ingrid Bergman, the Shah of Iran, and Stein Eriksen wore them. Henry Ford ordered fifteen pairs.

The press, in a not altogether friendly way, labeled Sugarbush "Mascara Mountain." At the base of the mountain, couturier and society maven Oleg Cassini and his celebrity-worshipping brother Igor (the pseudonymous gossip columnist known as Cholly Knickerbocker) and their café society friends established the exclusive Ski Club 10.[28] Members included Kennedys, Shrivers, and Heinzs, shipping magnate Stavros Niarchos, Fiat chief Gianni Agnelli, the bandleader Skitch Henderson, aristocratic Michael Butler, and ski racer Doug Burden. Inside Club 10, the manager, a Frenchman named Olivier Coquelin, created a dance floor illuminated by flashing lights—a primitive discotheque. (A group of Sugarbush skiers, led by Coquelin, put up the money to create the first discotheque in

Did Skiers Ever Look as Good? Bogner model Sandra Heath shows off an early form-fitting stretch suit in 1961. Stretch, the classic ski look of the 1950s and early 1960s, was displayed here with the world's classic mountain as a backdrop. *Courtesy of Sandra Heath*

America, Le Club in New York.) Armando Orsini opened a restaurant. Photographer Slim Aarons, who was to high society what Ansel Adams was to wilderness, chronicled the scene, taking pictures of society beauty Nan Kempner and super-model Cindy Hollingsworth skiing. Stein Eriksen was the ski school director for several seasons; his handsomeness and social suavity perfectly suited to the glamorous Sugarbush clientele.

A rather soignée, chi-chi bus service to Sugarbush was started by Buddy Bombard, founder of the Chalet Ski Club. The round trip fare of $25 included cocktails, wine, and dinner. Asked by travel editor Abby Rand what kind of skiers used his service, Bombard replied, "We don't want rude people, drunks, slow payers or terribly unattractive people."[29] The comfortable, fashionable buses served the function performed by ski trains in the 1930s. J. J. McKeever, a New York patent attorney, launched a Manhattan-to-Stowe bus service because he hated to drive himself to northern Vermont and back every weekend. Among McKeever's passengers were bankers, brokers, designers, models, editors, and ad men. On board were Princess Elizabeth of Yugoslavia, the Baroness Afdera (Henry Fonda's former wife), and football star Kyle Rote.[30] They skied on Mount Mansfield's trails by day, and twisted on the dance floor of the Baggy Knees at night.

A New Après-Ski Style

In 1967, a third of America's dozen best après-ski places were in Vermont: the Wobbly Barn at Killington, the Blue Tooth at Sugarbush, Sister Kate's at Stowe, and the Five Flys in Manchester.[31] A new après-ski zeitgeist reigned, reported *SKI*'s fashion editor, Pat Doran. Gone were guys and gals singing "Down by the Old Mill Stream" around a cast iron stove under wet socks drying on a line. The future of after-skiing glittered on a psychedelically lit dance floor. Powerful electronic guitars and sitars heated the atmosphere. Doran wrote about the new lifestyle with the breathless, chaotically phrased exuberance that only fashion editors can bring to the English language: "It's off with the ski clothes and on with spotless après-ski outfits. metal colored hostess pants and stovepipe slacks, $45 après boots which can double on the dance floor. Spontaneous combustions of energy fling inhibition to the corners and the world becomes one Big Beat. Pairs push off, still tingling, to selected rendezvous with a Bob Dylan backing; by Beatle Time, Lucy in the Sky with Diamonds puts a soaring finish to the evening, as a tinge of dawn touches up the horizon."[32]

A mildly libidinous humor suffused the sport. A *SKI Magazine* cartoon showed a handsome instructor and a beautiful girl in ski school, while a curious bystander asks mockingly, "Why doesn't he move her up to the next class?"[33] Instructors were traditionally male and attuned to coaching men. Bronzed and handsome, often with an exotic foreign accent, they treated the female pupil as athletically challenged and easily dominated. Of course, if she chose to play the game, the woman became a desirable object of flirtation. In a briefly published series of Ann Landers–styled columns in *SKI Magazine*, "Girls' Rules," Abby Rand advised women about how to deal with challenges on and off the slopes.

> Beware of the gorgeous guy who leaps over moguls and whose every turn creates a plume of flying snow. Equally visible are his girlward lunges. If you can't wriggle free, look up into his eyes and ask how he does those perfectly perfect turns. He'll feel obliged to answer and, to do it, he'll need both hands up where you can see them.[34]

On weekend ski trips, women took wig cases containing falls, ready to sport a fresh, pre-made hairdo for Saturday night. They wore turtleneck shirts and ski sweaters. The ski look caught the nation's eyes at the same time as rock 'n' roll music caught its ears. Soon more ski parkas were being worn by non-skiers than by skiers. By the late 1960s, the original stretch pant of the 1950s had metamorphosed into a svelte, coordinated ski look that seized the imagination of the fashion world. Skiwear designers exploited new "smart" fibers, varied weavings, and needle punching to flatter the human shape outdoors in every conceivable way. Under slim jackets and contour-clinging stretch pants, skiers learned the trick of wearing layers of thin apparel to keep warm on sub-zero days. Windshirts, pants, turtlenecks, sweaters, and stretch inserts were color-matched, and as seamlessly coordinated as formal eveningwear. The dramatic ski look even showed up in the 1969 James Bond film, *On Her Majesty's Secret Service.* The clothes looked so good that it was sufficient just to stand around in them, behavior not unknown in Europe where half of resort visitors don't ski, and where the act of skiing is integrated with hotel life, food, drinking, and tea dancing.[35]

From Utopia to Dissidence

Aspen served as a model of what a ski town should be in the years after World War II.[36] It was a place of boisterous living and of passionate skiing. Like a Phoenix risen from the ashes of its defunct silver mining past, the town became world famous. Yet it was a small-town utopia, populated by people who loved skiing above all else. The rich and the threadbare lived together, deliberately and blissfully oblivious to their economic and social differences. "No one came to Aspen to make a bundle," wrote Leon Uris. "They came because there was a certain way they wanted to live their lives."[37]

The writer Martie Sterling operated Aspen's charming, chaotically run Heatherbed Lodge, where guests like author Uris mingled with the boarders, several of whom were fresh-off-the-boat-from-Europe instructors. Also in Aspen, Mary Eshbaugh Hayes raised five children and began to write a column about the comings and goings of movie stars and local ranchers; the column went on for fifty years. Photographer Franz Berko was building a rich, immense iconography of black and white pictures. Billy Marolt, who would come to run the multi-million-dollar U.S. Ski and Snowboard Association (USSA) at the end of the century, attended the local high school.

In the 1960s, Aspen changed. The tension in the community came to mirror the nation's tensions. America was entering the Vietnam War, and the Los Angeles Watts riots were just ahead. While brave people marched in Selma, Alabama, to protest civil rights violations, people marched in Aspen to protest the cost and availability of lift passes. The town became a place of dissidence, rife with as many opinions as there were ranchers, waiters, developers, ski patrolmen, writers, painters, shopkeepers, and coupon-clipping retirees who'd moved there. Long-haired hippies hung about. Gonzo journalist Hunter Thompson would run for the office of Aspen Sheriff on a ticket of fighting "greedhead" land speculators and developers. The bonds of community were strained to the limit.

When writer Morten Lund went to Aspen in 1969 to investigate the scene, he reported that the beautiful things had become hair, peace, dogs, and pot. Un-beautiful were uptight, goal-oriented, problem-solving, aggressive people.[38] Also un-beautiful were the officers of the ski corporation and of organized competition. The antipathy was mutual. The sport's establishment no more liked the barbaric new American young than did the college professors who barricaded themselves in their offices at the time. In après-ski hangouts, the acrid smell of stale beer and nicotine now mingled with the sweet smell of marijuana. On the slopes, guys with long hair on ultra-short skis brought the psychedelic rebelliousness of the tumultuous sixties to a shocking new culture: freestyle.

Clubs, and Changing Choices

By the 1970s, ski clubs—originally organized to hold competitions—were organized principally to run ski trips, from weekend bus trips to European charter flights. In early summer, at travel marketplaces, dozens of ski area marketing and airline reps began to meet with as many clubs to negotiate packaged trips for the next winter. In the winter of 1973, the largest USSA Division, Far West, offered its members the choice of no fewer than twenty-seven trips to North American resorts and four to Europe. A one-week trip to Aspen, including air fare, lifts and lodging, cost $233.

An estimated 116,000 people in 1974 belonged to clubs associated with the regional divisions of the United States Ski Association; another 150,000 belonged to unaffiliated clubs.[39] A club in Houston, Atlanta, or Washington, D.C., attracted a thousand or more members. In addition to travel, the clubs offered membership benefits that included price discounts and autumn ski equipment swaps, discounted lift tickets and good insurance buys, as well as continuing to organize competitions. The traditional ethnic clubs—German, Swiss, and Norwegian—were augmented by clubs made up of black skiers.

Jet passenger planes that could transport people to winter vacations in the Rockies and the Alps also could transport them to beaches on the Caribbean, where the only equipment they needed was a snorkeling mask and a bathing suit. The arrival of the 1970s saw the ominous appearance of alternatives to sliding down snow-covered slopes. Why freeze outdoors when now you could play tennis indoors? Disney World opened in Florida in 1971. The first computer game, "Pong," debuted in 1972. So did the first pay cable television service, HBO. Skiing participation began to level off. The baby boomers, who as children and teenagers caused the huge surge in ski participation in the 1950s and 1960s, were entering their twenties. After reaching a record high in 1972, the population of young people fell. The gene pool of U.S. skiers—from families who could afford to ski, whose heritage was Nordic and European and acculturated to skiing—actually shrank after 1972. By 1999, the school population contained 7.3 million fewer non-Hispanic white students than it contained in 1972.[40] There had been an almost 20 percent decline in young people belonging to the ethnic group that traditionally fueled the sport's growth.

The Response to Risk

Possibly more people are keen rather than disinclined to ski precisely because it *does* involve risk. One has only to look as far as the amusement park roller coaster for evidence that folks are readily drawn to activities that at least offer the patina of risk. Flirting with speed and danger is a deeply rooted instinct in skiing.

The shared feeling among skiers of risk's consequences found its highest, altruistic expression in the National Ski Patrol System (NSPS) formed in 1938 (see page 22). It has been a gem of an organization within the sport. Thousands of men and women have volunteered their time to perfect the skills of getting injured fellow skiers down the mountain to medical care. By 1964, they had already tobogganed a quarter of a million ankle-sprained, shoulder-separated, leg-fractured victims off the slopes.[41] Over the next forty years, NSPS membership grew from 10,000 to more than 25,000, including paid professional patrollers whom the big resorts needed to employ to care for the burgeoning numbers of midweek ski vacationers.

Contrary to the beliefs of cautious resort marketers and worry-mongering lawyers, there's no strong evidence that even the possibility of fatal injury has deterred people from skiing. During the 1960s, a young man seeking to save his life by evading service in Vietnam might have ended it in seeking pleasure on a steep ski slope. Death suffered as a result of following another's command is different from death suffered as a result of following one's own. In the winter of 2000–2001 when forty-seven people died in skiing and snowboarding accidents in the United States, and three winters after Michael Kennedy was killed at Aspen and Congressman Sonny Bono at Heavenly Valley, visits to the nation's ski areas climbed to a record high of 57.3 million.[42]

Despite more padding of lift towers, wider slopes, and a barrage of safety-awareness propaganda, and the increased wearing of helmets, fatalities at U.S. ski areas remained at about the same level—between a low of twenty-four and a high of forty-nine—over twenty winters from 1984 to 2004.[43] Half of the fatal collisions with trees and other objects—including collisions with other skiers and snowboarders—happened to charged-up males, aged twelve to twenty-five. They weren't as proficient as they thought. Young men tend to ski beyond their ability, and they're more inclined to neglect basic safety measures.

Neither risk nor demographics account for another change that occurred after 1970. A single culture of skiing gave way to an assortment of splinter sports (see part IV). Interest became focused less exclusively on alpine. Skiers turned to specialties: telemarking and cross-country skiing, racing, freestyle stunts, bump skiing, off-piste mountaineering and, eventually, snowboarding. The variety of magazines about the sport increased (see page 270). All of these shifts occurred against a background of tumultuous change in equipment, technique, and teaching, beginning in the 1950s.

3

From Rope Tow to Resort

The boom that happened, and how it faltered.

Immediately after World War II, banks and investment houses weren't especially eager to supply scarce capital to every genius entrepreneur itching to build a ski area. Resources like steel wire rope were in demand for post-war construction, and so the building of chairlifts and T-bars, begun before the war, did not take off immediately. But there was no shortage of hemp, pulleys, and used truck engines with which to build rope tows. By 1948, no fewer than 850 rope tows were operating in North America, perhaps three times as many as had existed before 1940.[1] As little as one lift slanting up a field of snow constituted a ski area. California's Sierra Nevadas and New Hampshire's hills could claim to have more "ski areas" than they had fifty years later in 1998. Often in pristine mountain settings, they were the seeds of future resorts.

The rope tow itself, however, had no more chance than the electric streetcar or the coal-burning home furnace of enduring into the second half of the twentieth century. To the hordes of new participants beginning to ski, the rope tow was uncomfortable and tiring to use, and especially difficult for beginners to master. Few sights were as comic as a tangle of pathetic weekend athletes hanging desperately onto a fast-moving woven strand of hemp that twisted agonizingly in their hands. The unwitting comics furnished filmmakers John Jay and Warren Miller with an endless, eye-boggling supply of visual gags for their movies (see page 278). Wherever possible, skiers were happier riding up the mountain comfortably seated or dragged uphill by the seat of their pants.

Lifts were the key to the spread of the sport, but there had to be some place to put them, and the higher and more beautiful the place the better. The best locations were almost entirely on government land in

The Ascent Grew Easier. A 1933 skier firmly grips the first tow rope on the Big Hill at Shawbridge in Quebec's Laurentians— 5 cents a ride. A half century later, skiers rode effortlessly uphill in modern gondola cabins—this one at Mt. Ste. Anne, Quebec. *Rope tow photo courtesy of Emile Cochand, Sr. Gondola picture supplied by Mt. Ste. Anne*

mountainous high country of the West.* The United States Forest Service (USFS), eager to promote uses of the national forests other than logging, encouraged qualified people to apply for permits to build ski areas. The government encouraged ski area growth as vigorously as it later came to discourage it (see page 294).

Immediately after the war, relatively few ski areas could boast of offering skiers a comfortable ride on a chairlift, or a half-sitting ride on a drag lift like a T-bar, J-bar, platterpull, or Pomalift. There were perhaps three dozen such places. Over the next ten years, they tripled in number, propelled partly by the work of Ernst Constam, the Swiss inventor of the J-bar, which evolved into the T-bar. After he'd built a couple of dozen such surface cable lifts in Europe, Constam quit Europe early in World War II, emigrating to the United States where he set about building T-bars at a rapid pace, especially during the 1950s.[2] But by the winter of 1955–1956, North America still had only seventy-eight ski areas equipped with steel wire rope lifts—forty-one chairlifts and sixty-two drag or surface lifts.[3] The great growth lay ahead.

The Resort Builders

From the beginning, the typical North American ski area was operated and promoted by a single entrepreneur. Resorts in the Alps, by contrast, typically are governed by various lift owners, hotel and restaurant owners, the instructor-owned ski school, and taxpayers, coordinated by an Office of Tourism. Skiing is more of a community enterprise in Europe. In America, the ski area operator usually owns the lifts, ski school, and on-mountain restaurants, and he dictates the marketing, often with only minimal input from the community.

It has long been an item of faith that veterans of the U.S. Army's 10th Mountain Division established the ski industry. And they did, although they were typically guys who didn't have two nickels to rub together. The men who were not casualties of the bloody battles in Italy's Apennines, and who had learned to love skiing, built lift towers on mountains

---

*One of the few eastern ski areas in a national forest is Wildcat Mountain in New Hampshire's White Mountains. Opened in the winter of 1957–1958, it was the first large ski area developed on federal land in the East, according to Jeff Leich of the New England Ski Museum. Located in Pinkham Notch, next to Mount Washington, Wildcat started with a gondola, long trails, and 2,000 feet of vertical drop, but without private land on which to build a real estate–based village. As a result, the area has struggled financially.

like Aspen and Vail. They operated shops. They eventually founded, managed, or directed no fewer than sixty-two ski schools.

The ski area founders came from varied backgrounds—gnarly blue collar and bluestocking, homesteader and land baron—sharing a passion for skiing. They were a dynamic, risk-taking lot, unlike the conventional, uptight executives depicted in the classic book of the 1950s, *The Organization Man*. The ski area guys wore denims, not gray flannel suits. They were tough and determined, brash in the face of possible failure. They looked for the premium mountains, the north and east slopes facing away from the sun that melts and from the wind that scours. They sought a recorded history of deep, measured snowfalls. Against this background of private enterprise, often undertaken on public land, the North American ski resort industry began to gain serious traction.

Among the destination resorts—places involving travel and a vacation—Stowe, Sun Valley, and Mont Tremblant were the preeminent trio that had been started before World War II. By the 1950s, Stowe declared itself to be the capital of eastern skiing, and for a while it really merited the description. Operating on Vermont's highest peak in the Mount Mansfield State Forest, Stowe boasted the best trails east of the Mississippi—the National and the Nosedive. The latter was famous for seven treacherous turns that snaked a steep, narrow cut down through the trees. C. V. Starr, who made his fortune in Shanghai and who was the chairman of what would become the huge AIG insurance company, poured money into the expansion of the Mount Mansfield Company. His general manager was the capable ski school director Sepp Ruschp. With Starr's money and Ruschp's organizing skills, the two made Stowe the focus of international racing—as prominent as Vail and Beaver Creek became in the 1990s. They paid the expenses of the top stars—among them Toni Sailer, Anderl Molterer, and Adrien Duvillard—to come to Stowe for the American International Races. In 1954, European officials fumed when the stars didn't show up at the historic Arlberg-Kandahar in the Alps. They were racing in Stowe, courtesy of Starr and Ruschp.[4]

In Aspen, Walter Paepcke, the wealthy Chicago industrialist and patron of Bauhaus art, and his brother-in-law Paul Nitze provided the seed money for the Aspen Skiing Corporation in 1946. Former racers, led by Friedl Pfeifer and Dick Durrance, cleared the trails and built on Aspen Mountain what was, at the time, the world's longest chairlift.[5] Two years later, Paepcke succeeded in establishing a cultural and musical base of summer tourism for Aspen by organizing the Goethe Bicentennial. Albert Schweitzer and a host of intellectuals and musicians descended on the town. The following year, Aspen hosted the 1950 Federation Internationale de Ski (FIS) World Alpine Ski Championships, the first international alpine skiing championships ever held outside of Europe. Aspen now rivaled Sun Valley and Stowe as a destination resort. It took off in 1958 when Friedl Pfeifer opened Buttermilk, an area designed for intermediates, and millionaire Whip Jones opened spectacular terrain at his new Aspen Highlands area next door.

California's two largest ski areas—Mammoth Mountain and Squaw Valley—were launched by two strikingly different characters. Alexander Cushing, who built Squaw Valley, came from aristocratic Boston and Newport stock. Dave McCoy, who built Mammoth Mountain, was a gritty, determined, self-made man, a working stiff. McCoy's struggle to lay out trails and build Mammoth's lifts in the national forest mirrored the struggles of dozens of pioneering, boot-strapping ski area builders around the country after World War II. He started with rope tows. Saving every penny, occasionally extracting a loan from the bank, oiling the lift gears, serving hot dogs, he painstakingly built Mammoth into a Mecca for Los Angeles skiers.

Alex Cushing, a Harvard man and Newport, Rhode Island, blueblood, built Squaw Valley with profits from a Tahitian coconut plantation investment and with crucially needed funds from Laurance Rockefeller. His discovery of Squaw Valley was the unintended consequence of a winter trip to the Laurentians. Arriving at Mont Tremblant, he found that a rainstorm had washed away the snow, destroying any possibility of skiing. It was Sunday. Sympathetic to his client's disappointment, the resort's millionaire founder, Joe Ryan, cashed a check so that Cushing could take a train to Chicago and find a place to ski in the West.[6] During the trip, Cushing met Californian Wayne Poulsen, an airline pilot and a skilled skier who had been looking for someone just like the seemingly affluent Cushing to raise the money to build the ski area he had long dreamed of at Squaw Valley in the Lake Tahoe Basin. The two quickly formed a partnership, which just as quickly broke up. Cushing was not an easy sort to deal with. Squaw Valley opened in the winter of 1949 with a twin-seater (double) chairlift and a rope tow. Revenue from the first year of operation was $28,000. "We were broke the day we opened," said Cushing.[7] The place didn't really develop as a resort until he won the 1960 Olympic Winter Games for California, a tale recounted in chapter 8.

Dozens of future destination resorts were started as ski areas in the decade of the fifties: Heavenly Valley in the national forest above azure Lake Tahoe; 9,000-foot-high Mount Bachelor in the Deschutes National Forest outside of Bend, Oregon; and Taos Valley Ski Area high in New Mexico's Sangre de Cristo Mountains, carved out of the forest by immigrant Ernie Blake, who ten years earlier had been interrogating high-ranking German war criminals in Europe. Amos Winter pioneered rugged Sugarloaf in Maine. Jay Peak opened in Vermont in 1955 on the United States–Canada border.

Mount Snow in southern Vermont was founded by Walt Schoenknecht, a tall, stuttering ex-Marine with a serious crewcut. Schoenknecht started Mount Snow in 1954 with two lifts on land that had been owned by a farmer, Reuben Snow. Schoenknecht's vision shaped the resort: Boca Raton in the snow. He built a heated swimming pool in front of the base lodge, tropical pools and gardens inside the hotel, and a monstrous 300-foot-high fountain in the middle of man-made lake, across which soared an aerial cable car connecting his Snow Lake Lodge to the mountain's lifts. He dreamed of having a village perched high on a cliff, with a cable car connecting hotels, shopping areas, and ski slopes. He envisioned a stadium for watching slalom races, a mountaintop observation tower and natural history museum, and a radiant-heated, glass-sided outdoor boardwalk for strolling. A theatrical stage would float on a man-made lake. He even had the idea, happily never realized, that he could persuade the Atomic Energy Commission to give him access to an atomic bomb, the detonation of which would create a vast skiing amphitheater on one side of the mountain. Few of Schoenknecht's ideas materialized. But his widening of trails designed for intermediate skiers was ahead of its time in the 1950s, and was quickly copied by other area operators, who admired his creativity.[8]

They were a strong-minded, individualistic lot, these ski area founders. Preston Leete Smith was an economic libertarian and a conscientious objector from a Quaker family, whose salient qualities, wrote Morten Lund, were "straight talk, bullheadedness and a slight case of monomania."[9] Smith chose Killington Peak, Vermont's second-highest mountain, as the site of what would become the Northeast's largest ski area. Smith's partner was Joe Sargent, a Hartford, Connecticut, stockbroker, a climber and outdoorsman. Sargent recruited investors for the proposed ski area, then drove to Vermont on the weekends to help Smith chainsaw trees and brush. The two men, both twenty-six, persistent, frugal, and stubborn, built Killington against formidable obstacles. They lacked rich investors, and the mountain had no ski history or even a viable town at its base. Nor did the place possess the panache of Sugarbush to the north, a favorite of New York café society, described in the previous chapter.

Smith opened Killington in 1958 with a secondhand Pomalift, and as winter succeeded winter, battling thaws and recessions, he added T-bars, double chairs, a gondola, and high-speed quadruple chairlifts. By building his uppermost lift to the summit, he offered skiing 320 feet higher than Stowe, whose uppermost lift was well below Mount Mansfield's higher summit. Smith's manner of marketing the place reflected his own asceticism. The discomforts of sleet, fog, or arctic winds were merely part of the sport of skiing. Killington's marketing department insisted that if you were a real skier, you should not be bothered when it rained, for example; skiers weren't given partial rebates on their lift tickets, but rather plastic garbage sacks that they could pull over their heads to stay dry. Killington's snow reports—the newspaper and radio reports of ski conditions—were notoriously shy of accuracy. Ice was called "hardpack." Snow was measured at the top of the mountain, not at the bottom where unmentioned rain might have melted everything to the bare ground. Thanks in part to Killington, three out of five New England skiers, questioned in a 1974 survey, came to disbelieve the snow reports issued by ski areas.[10]

Explosive Growth in the Number of Ski Areas

Starting from the 1955–1956 base of 78 U.S. ski areas, 580 resorts were added in the next ten years. Many were hills, originally equipped with one or two rope tows, which sprouted into statistical existence as full-fledged ski areas when they installed cabled (wire rope) lifts. By the winter of 1965–1966, North America counted 662 ski areas.[11]

Places to go skiing emerged at a dizzying pace. In a typical year, fifty new ski areas with chairlifts and T-bars opened across the continent. More than one of every four of today's Midwestern ski areas were created in a five-year burst of construction between 1959 and 1964.[12]

In the ten years between 1956 and 1965, 1,392 new chairlifts and overhead-cable drag lifts were constructed. In 1964 alone, North American ski areas installed a remarkable total of 247 lifts, including 93 chairlifts and a gondola.[13] The lifts were made by a homegrown industry of wire rope and steel fabricating companies—American Steel & Wire, Roebling, Borvig, Riblet, Heron, and Hall Lifts.*

Development reached a peak of intensity in 1962 and 1963, when at

---

*Thirty years later, domestic ski areas became almost totally dependent on Austrian and French companies for their lifts.

least a half-dozen future destination resorts opened: Vail, Crested Butte, and Steamboat's Mount Werner in the national forest in Colorado; Teton Village at Jackson Hole; Park City on a former mining site in Utah's Wasatch; and Stratton in Vermont. Despite the massive lift construction, the supply of chairlift seats heading uphill in the Northeast, where more than a third of the skiers lived, was unequal to the weekend demand to ride on them. Lift lines were choked with waiting skiers. So intensely popular was New England skiing that a lift ticket at Vermont's Mount Snow ($8.50) in 1967 cost 30 percent more than one at Aspen ($6.50).[14]

The number of U.S. skiers grew from an estimated half-million in 1956 to 1.5 million in 1962–1963 to 3.0 million in 1968–1969.[15] The growth coincided with three notable Olympics (Squaw Valley in 1960, the first U.S. men's skiing medals in 1964, and Jean-Claude Killy's spectacular triple gold win in 1968). The conventional wisdom for a long time was that the Winter Games increased the public's desire to ski. And quite possibly they did. The reality, however, is that the Winter Olympics and ski growth may be little more connected than the famous rise in the stock market after a Super Bowl victory by an NFL team. Skiing's growth, rather, is linked to the weather and to the economy. Between 1962 and 1968, a series of mostly good snow years combined with an 85 percent rise in the stock market.[16] There's nothing like the sloshing around of extra money in the pockets of the wealthy to induce discretionary investment. Money poured into building new ski areas. By 1968, there were more ski areas than would exist at the end of the century.

The growth was accelerated by powerful, innovative developments: the near-completion of the Eisenhower interstate highway system; the creation of massive base lodges for dining and après-ski; the realization by operators that they could fill the need for beds at their resorts by selling condominiums; and the refinement of machinery to make and to groom snow.

Snowmaking and Grooming

Snowmaking's achievement was to guarantee to skiers that they would have a surface to ski on when they arrived at a ski area. The ability to manufacture snow is based on a highly energy-consumptive process by which rapidly cooled water spray is converted into snowflakes. The world's first snowmaking systems were installed in the winter of 1950–1951, first as a test at Mohawk Mountain in the Berkshire Mountains, and commercially at Big Boulder in Pennsylvania's Poconos, and the Grossingers ski hill in New York's Catskill Mountains.[17] By 1964, fourteen years later, 140 areas in the eastern United States and Canada were able to cover their slopes, at least partly, with man-made snow.[18] Most bought their systems from Larchmont Engineering's John Mathewson, a ruddy-faced New Englander who was the Johnny Appleseed of artificial snow. His customers were typically low-elevation areas that believed they couldn't survive without installing ponds, water pumps, and air compressors to make snow. Mathewson initially experienced difficulty in selling to the bigger, higher-elevation resorts, which counted on natural snow. The timing of winter is anything but predictable, however, and so the higher resorts came to realize that snowmaking would give them a business advantage, too. By installing it, they were able to guarantee skiing on their published opening day. It effectively increased the number of days that people could ski in a season. Stowe, for example, eventually was able to advance its opening date from December 17 to November 17, adding 25 percent more days to the ski season. No longer was winter from Christmas week to Easter. Now it lasted from November to Easter. For the first time, Thanksgiving became an important ski weekend. It was an occasion, commented Morten Lund, when the necessary ingredients came into play: "air and water under pressure and vast numbers of single guys and gals. The former are combined in pipes to guarantee snow; the latter are combined in long-haul buses and gemütlich inns to assure the love making and good fun traditionally associated with long ski weekends."[19]

Giant grooming machines now refurbished the snow, both machine-made and natural. Attempts to smooth the snow's surface, using tractors and snowcats dragging chain-link mat and agricultural harrows and rollers, pre-date World War II. Steve Bradley, a Dartmouth skier who traveled widely, had undoubtedly witnessed such attempts.[20] In 1951, now manager of Colorado's Winter Park ski area, he invented a lighter, more maneuverable grooming device requiring no engine. It was a 400-pound roller, led downhill by a single skier who was under constant threat of being "groomed" himself should he stumble or fall. Called the Bradley Packer-Grader, it was hauled back up the hill by hooking it to a T-bar. Bradley recognized the limitations of his invention, and later he challenged engineers and agricultural machinery makers to design equipment specifically to meet the needs of the ski areas.

The new grooming machines were of a different order and size, more like the monstrous, hydraulically controlled tillers used in commercial

Winter Extender. Compressed air and water producing machine-made snow lengthened the ski season by 25 percent. *Photo by Stuart Bratesman*

farming. They vanquished the ice, crust, bumps, and choppy broken snow that had plagued a generation of skiers. The resulting surface was wonderfully easy to ski on, enabling people to learn the sport faster. Beginners were no longer limited to bunny slopes; they could access smooth terrain all over the mountain.

The old, winding trails, cut in the 1940s, were not suited for machine grooming. Designers and ski area consultants, like New Hampshire–based Sel Hannah and Jim Branch of Sno-Engineering, urged ski areas to retro-fit their terrain with not-so-steep, wide, straight-sided trails following the fall line—more cost-efficient and easier for snow cats and groomers to operate on, and suitable for intermediates to ski on. The new wide, ribbon-like runs lacked individuality, though. One wide, straight slope seems to be almost like another—so similar that a person skiing in Colorado at Breckenridge, for example, might be excused for thinking that he or she is on a trail next door at Copper Mountain![21]

Erasing Bumps. Fleets of grooming machines smooth slopes once riddled with huge moguls. The steep Outer Limits slope at Killington, seen at left in the 1970s, was eventually groomed by machines suspended on cables. *Outer Limits, Killington Photo by Bob Perry. Snow grooming machines From the archives of* Ski Racing Magazine

About the only surfaces the new machines couldn't manipulate were steep slopes. The problem was solved at Killington, Vermont, in the early 1980s by using an old construction trick—attaching a cable to another snow cat or to a fixed anchor upslope, and winching the grooming machine up and down on it.

Bringing the City to the Mountain

After 1957, at least a half-dozen new areas opened within a couple of hours drive of Manhattan. Camelback brought a bigger scale to skiing in Pennsylvania's Poconos, where the resort began in mid-November to pile 6 feet of man-made snow on its trails before opening them for Christmas. Butternut Basin modernized Berkshires skiing, not only with snowmaking, but subsequently with an award winning base lodge. Windham, Scotch Valley, and Hunter Mountain opened in the Catskill Mountains, three thousand feet above the Hudson River Valley to the east.

Metropolitan New York natives drove to Hunter Mountain as much to party in its huge base lodge as to ski on its machine-made snow. Hunter at one time had been owned by Jimmy Hammerstein, son of the composer Oscar Hammerstein, who sold the place to a couple of alternately genial and cranky Catskill general contractors, Izzy Slutzky and his brother Orville. The Slutzkys dynamited trails out of a mountainside originally unsuited to skiing. Then they proceeded to build the largest base lodge in American skiing. At the time, 1964, day lodges were mostly oversize Quonset huts or inexpensive post-and-beam buildings to warm up in, sit down, buy a hot dog, and change out of ski boots for the drive home. The new Hunter structure was as different as an enclosed shopping mall is from a general store. It had 45,000 feet of space devoted to a huge bar, a monstrous cafeteria-style restaurant, piped-in music, and soaring ceilings.[22] It especially attracted young urban singles who might otherwise have spent their weekends in the city connecting with one another in rock 'n' roll discos. Now they could ski during the day, and rock 'n' roll the night away at the mountain base. To shocked ski area operators everywhere, the massive scale of the Hunter day lodge showed what the future looked like, and it looked like it was going to cost a lot to satisfy the urban lifestyle of the oncoming hordes of customers.

Because of snowmaking and grooming, ski area developers came to believe that northern metropolitan regions would be encircled by ski areas. In 1969, *SKI Magazine* published a special feature predicting an exciting future for what the magazine called "Metroski."[23] Illuminated slopes at Great Gorge, New Jersey, for example, could be reached easily by car by several hundred thousand skiers in the New York metropolitan region.* Hills around Los Angeles, Chicago, Seattle, Toronto, and Philadelphia were destined for a brilliant, snow-filled future. But the ideal was rarely realized. Neighbors complained about the noise from snowmaking, if snowmaking was even possible. Global warming eventually made it acutely expensive to make snow on the low-elevation hills closest to large, heat-generating population centers.

Condos Create a Base of Beds

In the distant mountains, away from the cities, the expanding resorts could no longer rely on the willingness of skiers to sleep in the farmhouses, summer inns, and ski clubhouses that once had served as overnight accommodations. Few entrepreneurs were willing to build inns, and even fewer were willing to build hotels. But the budding resort operators found a solution. They could build guest rooms next to the slopes without taking on tens of millions of dollars of long-term debt by persuading skiers to pay for the construction through the purchase of condominium units. The condo apartments, when not occupied by their owners, could be rented out. Time-sharing, imported from the Caribbean, followed. For the investing skier, it was like owning a seat in a cinema, then paying MGM and Paramount to see their movies.

Earlier, California's Sugar Bowl and Vermont's Okemo had grown up around ski homes. The pioneer of the new real estate–based ski resort— Snowmass, 15 miles outside of Aspen—opened in 1967. The project was spearheaded by the Janss Corporation, which had experience in California land development. The corporation was headed by two skiers, Ed Janss and his brother Bill, a member of the never-to-compete 1940 U.S. Ski Team. Together with Janss Corporation president Victor Palmieri, they began with not one, but two ventures. In late 1964, for $10 million, they purchased Sun Valley from Averell Harriman's Union Pacific Railroad. The Janss brothers' first acts were to add condominiums adjacent to the renovated Sun Valley Lodge and to build lifts opening ski terrain on Bald Mountain's Warm Springs side. Meanwhile, at Snowmass, they set about creating a resort resembling Harriman's original 1936 Sun Valley in

---

*Great Gorge, New Jersey, survived as Mountain Creek, owing to the success of real estate sales generated by the area's owner, Intrawest.

that it was built new, from the ground up. Darcy Brown's Aspen Skiing Corporation (ASC or "Skico") was a perfect partner for the Janss Corporation. Brown did not believe his Skico should be engaged in lodging or retailing. It would, however, erect and operate the lifts, leaving Janss to create slopeside lodging, restaurants, shops, second homes, and condos.[24] Initially, Brown's skiing proved more profitable than Janss's real estate, which had required a huge investment in infrastructure. Bill Janss, the company's energetic spokesman and visionary, left to focus on the Sun Valley Company, which he purchased in late 1967 by trading his Janss Corporation shares.

In the wake of Snowmass, condominium ownership boomed. Between 1965 and 1970, fifteen condo buildings containing apartments with two thousand beds appeared in and around Aspen.[25] Condos proliferated at Vail, Steamboat, and Park City. In California's Lake Tahoe basin, two new real estate–based areas opened at Kirkwood and at Northstar, a visionary car-free village. Condo-equipped Big Sky, Montana, was completed in 1974— a post-retirement project of NBC television anchorman Chet Huntley.

The skiers who bought condos or timeshares were educated to believe that it was cheaper than renting a room at an inn. In one respect, they were wrong. Year-round mortgage and tax payments, maintenance, and repairs on a condo typically exceeded the cost of renting a first-class room for a vacation. Even income from renting a condo unit often didn't close the gap for owners. Nevertheless, they believed they were skiing inexpensively because the market price of their unit was going up. And they were right! Second homes doubled, tripled, and even quadrupled in value. Nor was condominium ownership the only way to imagine one was enjoying a cheap vacation. Doctors and professionals, with the assistance of accountants and clever travel packagers, could transform a ski trip into a tax-deductible vacation. For the inconvenience of spending après-ski time listening to a lecture on renal dysfunction or the implications of *Roe vs. Wade*, a professional could deduct the cost of his hotel room and lift tickets from his gross income.

Go West!

To the improved experience of skiing as a result of plentiful condo beds, snowmaking and grooming, and more lift capacity, was added another convenience: accessible, faster transportation to the slopes. By the 1970s, the main interstate highways were open:

- I-91 and I-93, penetrating the Green and White Mountains—
  eventually all the way to the Canadian border;
- I-90 going into northern Wisconsin, and I-75 into northern
  Michigan;
- I-70 from Denver as far as Vail Pass;
- I-80 out of Sacramento and San Francisco to the Tahoe Basin.

At the same time, jet flights, costing less than they did when they were introduced in 1959, allowed a skier to fly from New York to Denver in fewer hours than it took to drive to Stowe. And after the Eisenhower Tunnel pierced Colorado's Great Divide in 1972, bypassing avalanche-prone Loveland Pass, a Chicago skier, by plane and Interstate 70, could be on the slopes at Breckenridge or brand-new Keystone or Copper Mountain as quickly as he could drive his VW Beetle or the family's station wagon to Boyne, Michigan.

The improved airline service to the Rockies did more: It introduced eastern skiers to the pleasure of skiing powder and of escaping the boilerplate ice created in the Green Mountains and the White Mountains by rain and ice storms followed by freezing temperatures and scouring winds. It was a revelation from which New England never recovered. Nationally, vacation skiing shifted to the Rockies, and new resorts created after 1962 in Vermont—Ascutney, Burke Mountain, Timber Ridge, Bolton Valley, and Magic Mountain, for example—struggled financially in later years.

The slopes of the Central Rockies, at altitudes between 7,000 and 12,000 feet, create a benevolent combination of temperature, air, and moisture that produce light powder. Colorado and Utah's Wasatch Mountains have ideal climates for ski-based tourism. The sun shines with a consistency not found in the Alps. East-coast skiers, who once enjoyed a winter ritual of vacationing at Gstaad or St. Anton, now turned 180 degrees and flew west. Not only was the snow better and the sunshine more abundant, but you avoided Europe's crowded, shoving, disorganized lift-lines. And North American ski areas groomed snow, a benefit not yet widely available in the Alps.

After 1968, the nature of skiing's growth began to change. No longer did fifty or seventy new areas open annually. Rather, they began to grow more in size than in number. At an existing resort, a terrain expansion— such as Vail's China Bowl, Winter Park's Mary Jane, Heavenly Valley's Nevada slopes, or Killington's Skye Peak—often exceeded in size an entire Berkshire or Midwestern ski area.

An existing resort also could add to its terrain by buying or building another area. The Aspen Skiing Company sought to deal with the rising tide of Colorado skiers by acquiring the Breckenridge area as a kind of overflow valve. Michigan's Boyne Mountain added the Boyne Highlands ski area. The resorts' growing revenues attracted the attention of new-business strategists at corporations. The Ling Temco Vought Corporation bought the burgeoning Mount Werner ski area at Steamboat Springs. Weyerhaeuser owned Jay Peak in Vermont. The Ralston Purina Company, better known as a purveyor of animal feed, expanded the Keystone ski area, located below Loveland Pass, where it sold second homes to skiers. Fortunately for the executives involved, the shareholders of these public companies didn't seem especially curious about whether it was a prudent investment of their money.

The Boom Falters

By the winter of 1970–1971, the number of chairlifts in North America—nineteen at the end of World War II—had risen to more than a thousand.[26] New lifts were no longer mostly double chairs, but four-seater chairs and gondolas. As a result, even though the number of new lifts built annually was halved between 1967 and 1977, North American ski areas more than doubled the number of skiers they could carry uphill.[27] In fact, all together the lifts installed in that ten-year period had a capacity greater than all of the lifts that existed before 1967!

Beginning in the 1970s, however, ominous challenges to ski resort growth began to appear. One was the enactment of the National Environmental Policy Act (NEPA), signed by President Nixon in 1970, requiring environmental impact statements in connection with building or expanding on public land. It affected the expansion plans of existing resorts such as Vail, and the starting of new mega-resorts, such as Adam's Rib west of Vail. NEPA's passage into law worried resort investors, from the mountains to the canyons of Wall Street. Why invest in a ski area if it took years of uncertainty to discover whether the expansion could actually happen? (The effects of environmentalism on resort development are discussed in detail in the book's final chapter.)

A second reversal of fortune for ski areas took place at the beginning of the winter of 1973–1974, when OPEC imposed an oil embargo on the United States. Gasoline prices shot up from 30 cents to $1.20 per gallon. Gas stations were asked to hold their sales to a maximum of 10 gallons per customer, and President Nixon successfully proposed a ban on Sunday gas sales. Resort owners worried that weekend skiers would be unable to reach the mountains. Okemo in Vermont even built its own filling station so that patrons could be assured in advance that they'd have enough gas to drive home on Sunday. The situation was not helped by the fact that eastern skiers suffered their third snow-starved winter in a row.[28]

As if the energy crisis and an environmentalist rein on expansion were not enough, the sport was experiencing a continuing loss of small local hills that historically had brought youngsters into skiing. Even before the number of areas peaked at 650 in the mid-1970s, small community hills were in decline. The infrastructure needed to operate a ski area attractive to skiers wanting varied terrain and entertainment had come to exceed any reasonable return on investment. Areas went out of business when they couldn't afford more lifts, a bigger base lodge, a restaurant, and snowmaking, and when they were unwilling to pay for the rising costs of insurance and of meeting more stringent environmental standards. Consequently, a host of convenient, inexpensive places to go skiing disappeared.[29] When kids grew to an age when they could ski, their opportunities to do so were diminished. The exact loss has never been quantified, but it was magnified by the fact that although leading-edge baby boomers—frequent skiers—were getting married and beginning to have children, they were having fewer than their parents had. And when the infants were too young to ski, parents stayed away from the slopes.

Insurance Costs Rise

Ski areas faced yet another challenge. On February 10, 1974, a twenty-one-year-old novice, James Sunday, on his fourth day on skis at Stratton Mountain, Vermont, was gliding along a cat track and suffered a fall that paralyzed him from the waist down. It would confine Sunday to a wheelchair for the rest of his life. He sued Stratton Mountain, blaming his accident on the negligence of the resort in not removing underbrush growing out of the snow.

Concern about injured skiers litigating against resorts had existed at least twenty years earlier. "There has been a growing number of unscrupulous skiers," reported *SKI Magazine* in March 1953, "who are a discredit to the sport. After suffering a sprain or break, they rush to the nearest 'ambulance-chasing' type of lawyer, who tries to prove negligence on the part of an area lift operator and then collect unreasonable damages."[30] In 1951, the courts had taken the view that people knowingly assume a risk when they go skiing. But after 1977, the legal environment changed. A Burlington, Vermont, judge and jury awarded James Sunday $1.5 million in damages as a result of his Stratton accident. The judgment was unexpected and unprecedented. Here was a judge saying, "The novice ski trail of today is a far cry from the stump and rock strewn slashes on mountains in 1951. Now the stumps and rocks are removed with bulldozers and the holes are filled in."[31]

Among long-time skiers, there was anger over the Vermont jury's verdict. There were rumors about Sunday. He must have fallen into the hands of the worst sort of shysters. Perhaps a lack of sobriety had caused him to fall. "Real skiers," unlike Sunday, surely would never blame the sport for their demise. Foster Chandler, the top marketing executive at Killington, called the jury decision favoring Sunday "unreal. It assumes we can control the elements and turn everything into a nice, neat sandbox. Hell, that's nature out there."[32]

To a non-skiing jury, however, the Stratton decision was clear. The modern ski area—by promoting groomed, manicured slopes—was enticing people to believe that the sport was easy and safe. But their marketing, it turned out, was attracting litigators as well as customers. If a skier like Sunday could successfully sue for a million-and-a-half dollars, an army of contingency-fee lawyers must be waiting in the wings. The operators faced paying higher insurance premiums or they could increase their deductible—in effect, insuring themselves or "going bare."

The areas so far had managed to keep a reasonable lid on the cost of insuring themselves, particularly after 1962 when they organized as the National Ski Areas Association (NSAA). The association came to unite four hundred ski areas, enabling their owners to share information, to lobby the U.S. Forest Service in Washington, to establish lift engineering standards, and to schmooze with one another each spring at annual conventions held at warm-weather resorts. In one of its earliest actions to improve safety, the new association in the winter of 1964–1965 standardized signs across the United States indicating to skiers the degree of difficulty of the terrain below. Green signified easy skiing. The color maroon (later changed to a black diamond) designated a difficult slope.[33]

The new association came into being, in part, so that ski areas could leverage their bargaining power with insurers. For a while, the giant AIG Company was the industry's principal insurer, possibly for the reason that it was likely the only insurance company in the country that actually owned a ski area—Mount Mansfield at Stowe. After the James Sunday trial, Maurice "Hank" Greenberg, the head of AIG, insisted that he would no longer extend insurance to Vermont ski areas if they didn't take steps to persuade the state legislature to enact a statute defining the responsibilities of people when they ski. Skiers should recognize the risks inherent in going fast, of steep terrain, of trees that naturally line the trails. Common law, to say nothing of common sense, long ago established that a person undertaking to ski, or to dive into a pool or scale a mountain, does so at his or her own risk. What had been absent were written statutes or codes protecting ski areas specifically from unreasonable claims of negligence, except in cases such as chairlift accidents and negligently operated equipment where the ski area was at fault.

Spearheaded by Rutland attorney David Cleary, the Vermont statute was enacted, and in 1978, guided by Cleary, the NSAA drafted model legislation used by state ski associations across the country. Local lawyers and lobbyists went to work, and by the next year skier responsibility statutes or codes had been enacted or were pending in a dozen states, alongside similar statutes already in place.[34] Thereafter, plaintiffs' lawyers faced far greater obstacles in recovering damages for injury.

Friction with Neighbors, Competitors

While they collaborated with one another on insurance, American ski areas were less collaborative when it came to connecting their lifts and trails. The ability to journey on skis from one village to another on a single pass, valid on dozens of lift networks, is enjoyed throughout Europe's Alps, where resort operators have had no difficulty solving the rather elementary accounting challenge of how to credit a lift ride to the lift's owner. The American resort operator, by contrast, looked at the same phenomenon and saw a competitive loss of business.

An interesting exception, in that he was chairman of one of the nation's largest corporations (IBM), was Thomas Watson, Jr., who owned Madonna Mountain several hundred yards distant from the summit of Stowe's Spruce Peak. In the 1960s, Watson wanted to sell a lift ticket that would allow people to ski both areas. The Mount Mansfield Company and Madonna could market themselves as a single massive linkage of trails, the largest in the East. Mount Mansfield's board, however, rejected Watson's idea, seeing no financial benefit.* Like Killington and Pico in

---

*Watson wearied of losing money and sold Madonna, which later survived, not by building high-speed lifts, but by establishing itself as the best skiing resort in America for families and children, renamed Smugglers' Notch.

Vermont, and Park City and Deer Valley in Utah, the Mount Mansfield people were more interested in protecting their own market share than in enlarging the pie. They were not alone. The American ski area operator typically saw his neighboring area as a competitor to take business away from, not someone to unite with. The Aspen Skiing Corporation ("the Skico") spent hundreds of thousands of dollars in legal fees to defend the principle. In 1977, after fifteen years of cooperation in selling a joint lift ticket valid at all four Aspen areas (Aspen Mountain, Buttermilk, Snowmass, and Aspen Highlands), the Skico reversed itself and refused to include Aspen Highlands, which it didn't own. The area's owner, Whip Jones, accused the Skico of monopoly and restraint of trade, and sued. Over the next eight years, through the Skico's ownership by the Twentieth Century Fox movie studio, the case made it all the way to the United States Supreme Court.* Aspen Highlands won and was awarded $11 million.[35] Aspen never did build lifts connecting its four ski areas despite the obvious benefit not only to guests, but to workers and to the environment. Aspen guests still move around in air-polluting cars and buses. In Europe, they would be able to travel from one area to another on quiet, clean-operating, inter-connecting lifts.

While most ski areas enjoy cordial relations with the communities in which they operate, the potential for friction always exists. The goals of the mountain town are potentially in conflict with the commercial goals of the ski area operator, especially if the resident population doesn't see skiing's expansion as central to the community's interests or environmentally sustainable. The sour notes of community–ski area disharmony sounded loud in Aspen, where the mountain company clashed with the editor of the town's award-winning newspaper. Darcy Brown ran the Aspen Skiing Corporation and how he ran it, he argued in his gravelly, sometimes squeaky voice, was none of the town's goddamned business. The editor and owner of the *Aspen Times* was Bil Dunaway, a miniature of the tall sinewy Brown. A former racer and a hardened mountain climber, Dunaway was perhaps the best small-town newspaper editor in America. Principled and determined, he believed that what happened on Brown's ski hill was not a private business matter as Brown thought, but a matter of community concern. Dunaway's editorials angered Brown as they jabbed at his Skico. The verbal combat between the two set the tone

---

*The U.S. Supreme Court determined that a monopolist, which it perceived the Aspen Skiing Company to be, cannot refuse to deal with competitors. It was a landmark decision and to this day the court's decision in *Aspen Skiing Co. vs. Aspen Highlands Skiing Corp.* is relied upon in the lower courts to protect businesses threatened by monopolies.

for the town. Dissident locals began referring to incoming tourists as "turkeys," arguably damaging the economic interests of their neighbors operating lodges and shops. Aspen's communal bonds weakened as property prices soared and workers could no longer afford to live in town. It did not help that a narrow majority of voters rejected the idea of restoring an old railroad line that could bring in commuting down-valley workers and relieve air pollution.

At Stowe, the Mount Mansfield Company was the town's largest employer and taxpayer, commonplace among mountain communities across the country. The company ran the lifts, the ski school, the lodge, and restaurants and shops at the mountain. The community supplied the rooms needed to accommodate skiers, entertaining them at night and plowing the roads so they could get to the lifts in the morning. Each party thought the other should do more to attract skiers. In the end, neither community nor mountain thought the other did enough. In the town, a merchant-dominated ruling cadre failed to create a pedestrian core of the kind that Vail had created in 1962 and that later was emulated by downtown Aspen and by resorts such as Whistler in British Columbia. Absence of a larger vision contributed to Stowe's gradual decline as a national destination ski resort after 1970.*

Tough Road to the Bottom Line

The health of ski areas frequently was undermined by their over-optimistic financial projections. "You want to make a small fortune in the ski business?" joked skeptics. "Start with a large one." Banks and investors, who initially supplied capital to the area operators, encountered dismaying financial statements stained in red. The ski area operators themselves were frustrated. "It's the worst business in the world," proclaimed Hans Thorner, the fiery owner of Magic Mountain, located in a beautiful part of the Green Mountains near Londonderry. "Anyone who goes into it has rocks in his head." Thorner recalled a meeting that he and his fel-

---

*At Stowe, the open-handed Neil Starr ultimately was succeeded at AIG by the tight-fisted Maurice Greenberg, once listed by *Fortune Magazine* as one of America's toughest bosses to work for and removed from his chairmanship of AIG in 2005. Greenberg badgered a succession of ski area managers to make the Mount Mansfield operation profitable. Investments in snowmaking and better lifts were deferred. Eventually, the money was found by selling expensive condominiums and homes on the south-facing Spruce Peak, creating a separate mountain village.

low area operators held with representatives of banks making loans to them. He jumped to his feet, his face nearly purple, his eyebrows bristling outward. "Yeah, it's fine for you people to sit there in your conservative suits," leveled Thorner at the bankers, "and tell us broken down-and-out operators that you want us to put up the first 90 percent and kill ourselves doing it. Well, I've got news for you. We want the 90 percent from you to start with!"[36]

Despite his concerns about the weather and the banks, Thorner was confident of his own resort's future. And why not? His Magic Mountain, Vermont's newest resort, would grow and eventually prosper—wouldn't it?—like all the ski areas he had seen built since he'd arrived from Europe in the 1930s. Yet twenty-five years later Thorner's ski area, in financial collapse, shut down.

John Kenneth Galbraith once supplied a perspective in his 1959 essay, "The Pleasures and Uses of Bankruptcy."[37] Galbraith habitually spent his summers living in an old Vermont farmhouse that he owned. He believed the state's economy was sustained by a succession of capital losses. Here's how it worked, explained Harvard's emeritus professor of economics: Investors flee the city and buy old inns, ye olde shoppes, and ski areas; they lose money operating them; then they sell them to the next idealistic investors, who continue the cycle. Among the examples of resorts tracing Galbraith's cycle of investment, loss, and rebirth—spiraling downward as assets, and being re-purchased at lower prices—were Crested Butte in Colorado, Stratton Mountain and Ascutney in Vermont, Mont Tremblant in Quebec, Snowshoe in West Virginia, Schweitzer in Idaho, Bear Mountain in California, and Snow Basin and Snowbird's Cliff Lodge in Utah. Mount Snow in Vermont was another example.[38]

At Mount Snow, flamboyant visionary Walt Schoenknecht's inability to contain his spending forced the resort's sale. In an ironic fulfillment of his prediction that ski areas some day would come to be owned by public corporations, Mount Snow was taken over in 1977 by the Sherburne Corporation. The new corporate owner, personified by its CEO Preston Leete Smith, Killington's founder, was unapologetically and unsentimentally bottom-line. To cut costs, it removed Schoenknecht's aerial car, his 300-foot fountain, the outdoor heated swimming pool at the base of the slopes, and the tropical garden. It did improve the skiing and the lifts, even as the exoticism of Mount Snow's quixotic, flamboyant founder, a futurist, receded into the past.

Pres Smith proceeded to pursue Fred Pabst's chimerical belief (see chapter 1) that synergistic efficiencies arise from operating multiple ski areas. He launched S-K-I Ltd., a Nasdaq-listed public company, and used the proceeds from the sale of shares to add to his ownership of Sunday River and Mount Snow. S-K-I bought Waterville Valley in New Hampshire, Haystack and Carinthia in Vermont, Bear Mountain in California's San Bernardino Mountains, and half of Sugarloaf in Maine. In California, S-K-I lost millions at Bear, where its vaunted eastern snowmaking was unsuccessful, and its aggressive marketing failed to generate sufficient revenues to recapture the millions it had invested. Meanwhile, Smith had put a young manager, Les Otten, in charge of the Sunday River Skiway in Maine. Having succeeded in giving the impression that the place was unprofitable and that it needed a commitment of funding to expand, Otten persuaded S-K-I to sell him Sunday River. He rapidly developed it into a formidable competitor for Killington. But his hubris got him into financial trouble, as we shall see.

The Last Big Resorts Are Built

The construction of large new ski areas slowed as the 1970s progressed. Energy supply was now a worry. The economy was in a state of stagflation—inflation with little economic growth. There was a dwindling supply of accessible, developable big mountains having really good terrain for skiing. By the time the 1980s arrived, only three major North American destination resorts were on track to open. One was Blackcomb and the Whistler resort village in British Columbia. Another was Deer Valley in Utah. The third was Beaver Creek, Colorado, an outgrowth of the most successful new ski area after World War II, Vail.

The story of Vail Mountain's discovery and its development has been iterated in magazines and newspapers, and has been chronicled profusely in books.[39] Pete Seibert, a 10th Mountain Division veteran, secured the land, sweet-talked investors, and laid out the trails for what became America's largest ski resort. He even convinced the Denver Organizing Committee for the 1976 Olympic Winter Games that they should hold the alpine ski events at an as yet un-built ski area, Beaver Creek, to the west of Vail (see chapter 8). But Seibert never completed his vision. By the mid-1970s, when the Goliad Oil Company acquired financial control over Vail, confidence in the ability of men like Seibert to manage resorts was already waning. Increasingly, investors came to believe that ski companies needed more than the enthusiasm and intuition of 10th Mountain Division veterans like Seibert to manage their affairs. Resorts, they believed, needed men with an MBA and financial savvy at the helm, not ex-sergeants who could climb mountains and tell whether or not a slope would hold snow. A manager's relationship with a ski area owner is as insecure as that of a baseball manager with his team owner. Seibert refused to hand over his title of chairman of the board to Vail's owner, Goliad Oil chief Harry Bass. A dozen years after Vail's 1964 opening, he quit.

Harry Bass, a taciturn and unemotional fellow, soon demonstrated that his business credentials were no more a defense against financial failure than Seibert's lack of them. It was on Bass's watch that Vail Associates in 1980–1981 opened Beaver Creek, the ski area that Seibert had envisioned. With its blend of Tyrolean and Pyrenees architecture and free of automobiles, it was arguably the best ski village ever designed in the United States. Its base slowly filled with luxurious, nicely landscaped, spacious condo buildings, in which a typical unit cost a half-million dollars or more. The price of the real estate proved to be a problem, however. Bass failed to anticipate that people who could afford to buy such costly second homes in the mountains didn't need the income from renting them to transients. Owners and their friends occupied them for only a few weeks during the winter. The trails on the mountain were gloriously un-crowded, while by night, Beaver Creek's beds remained largely empty, and the place was as populated as a highway underpass. Merchants were unwilling to open shops and restaurants. For the man who had dislodged Pete Seibert as Vail's CEO, the financial losses kept piling up. By 1985, Bass cried uncle, and he sold Beaver Creek.

Fortune was not much kinder to Harry Bass's brother, Dick Bass, who in 1971 began to invest heavily in the Snowbird ski resort in Utah's Little Cottonwood Canyon, next door to Alta. An ebullient, irrepressible Texan, powerfully built, dark-haired, of middle height, Dick Bass possessed super-human lungs that took him to the top of Everest at age fifty-five. He became famous as the first man to reach the summits of the highest mountains on all seven continents. Speaking in a staccato Dallas voice that seemed perpetually hoarse (not surprising in that he talked almost non-stop), he self-deprecatingly referred to himself as "Largemouth Bass," adding that he was not a member of the super-rich Texas Basses—a mere pauper by comparison. Indeed! His financial losses in Snowbird reached $75 million after the building of the resort's trophy ten-floor Cliff Lodge. In a variation of economist Galbraith's thesis, he regained ownership of the place for less than the cost of his original investment.

Ski Area Ownership Concentrates

Vail itself suffered the pains of bankruptcy a few years after Bass's Goliad sold it to meatpacking and television station owner, George Gillett. Gillett's financial failure did not arise directly from his ski operations, which were universally lauded. He improved guest conveniences and led the American resort industry in installing high-speed chairlifts. He pushed to bring the World Alpine Ski Championships to Vail in 1989. His financial failure stemmed from his inability to pay the interest on tens of millions of dollars that he had borrowed on the advice of junk-bond guru Michael Milken. He was forced to sell Vail's operations to the vulture capitalist Leon Black of the New York–based Apollo Management LP.

Les Otten traced a path similar to Gillett's. To bankers, Otten initially appeared so successful that in 1996 his American Skiing Company (ASC) could lay its hands on $106 million in order to take over Pres Smith's S-K-I. The acquisition seemed like a triumph of Otten over Smith, between whom no love was lost. Smith left or was ousted. Yet he may have enjoyed the last laugh. Otten's hubris propelled him to borrow tens of millions of dollars to buy Heavenly Valley in California and Steamboat in Colorado, and to build what was a virtually new resort, the Canyons, outside of Park City, Utah. The debt generated by the acquisitions was unsupportable, and Otten lost part of a personal fortune when ASC stock fell to less than a dollar a share. The company wound up as the virtual caretaker of seven resorts.*

Otten's path to financial ruin apparently raised few doubts about the wisdom of multiple ski area ownership. George Gillett, after losing Vail, had no difficulty persuading banks to help his new company, Booth Creek Holdings, purchase a half-dozen ski areas from New Hampshire to California.† Gillett's former domain—Vail Resorts, now under Apollo—bought up Breckenridge and Keystone in Colorado and California's Heavenly Valley, which it purchased from Otten's former ASC. Canadian headquartered Intrawest came to own or operate ten ski areas.‡

*The seven American Skiing Company–owned resorts in 2005 were Steamboat, Colorado; the Canyons, Utah; Killington and Mount Snow, Vermont; Attitash Bear Peak, New Hampshire; and Sugarloaf/USA and Sunday River, Maine.

†Booth Creek in 2005 listed its ski resort holdings as Northstar-at-Tahoe and Sierra-at-Tahoe in California; Waterville Valley, Cranmore Mountain Resort, and Loon Mountain in New Hampshire; and Summit at Snoqualmie in Washington State.

‡Starting originally with Whistler/Blackcomb in British Columbia, Intrawest went on to buy and rebuild Mont Tremblant in Quebec. It did the same for Stratton in Vermont and

By the turn of the century, about one of every four dollars that ski-ers spent on lift tickets was going to just four companies—ASC, Booth Creek, Vail Resorts, and Intrawest. In 1998 alone, they installed 43 per-cent of all the new lifts at ski areas.[40]

Faster Uphill

The resorts hugely increased their uphill carrying capacity after 1985, partly with expensive gondolas, but mostly with high-speed chairlifts having twice the speed of old fixed-grip lifts. The new lifts, which allow the chair to detach and re-attach to the fast-moving tow cable, were an instant hit with skiers. Forty years after chairlifts came into widespread use, you no longer had to suffer from being slammed in the back when boarding. Rather, the chair—detached for a few moments from the fast-moving tow cable and moving at a snail's pace—allowed the rider to be seated comfortably before accelerating uphill. The detaching technol-ogy made it possible to double cable speed, so that a new fast-moving quadruple or six-seater lift could convey many more skiers uphill than a fixed-chair lift once did, if the resort operated wanted to. During the last five years of the twentieth century (1995–1999), North American resorts installed about 250 lifts capable of carrying more skiers uphill than all of the 1,496 fixed grip lifts that existed in the winter of 1965–1966![41]

The increasing capacity to carry more skiers uphill, ironically, coin-cided with decreasing growth in their visits to ski areas over the twenty years leading up to the end of the twentieth century. Consequently, at many resorts liftline waiting, even on weekends, vanished, virtually elim-inating the sport's oldest and most irritating inconvenience. Additionally, the large resorts opened hundreds of acres of new terrain. It was now possible to ski black diamond (difficult) trails without bumps, thanks to advances in grooming. And thanks partly to Skier Responsibility Codes, the resorts were able to open special terrain parks, satisfying young ski-ers and snowboarders who enjoy risk.* The dream of interconnected

---

Copper Mountain in Colorado. It acquired an ownership interest in Mammoth Mountain, where it built a new base village. It also built a long-needed base village at Squaw Valley, Cali-fornia. It operates Winter Park in Colorado. It owns and operates Snowshoe Mountain in West Virginia, Mountain Creek in New Jersey, Panorama in British Columbia, and Blue Mountain in Ontario. Intrawest also is an owner of Canadian Mountain Holidays, the world's largest heli-skiing operation, in British Columbia.

*States began in the 1990s to update the Skier Responsibility Codes to include snow-boarding and snow tubing.

villages—common in Europe's Alps, where valleys are narrower and the mountains more tightly packed—was finally realized when the lifts of Beaver Creek, now a hugely successful resort, were linked to two satellite villages, Bachelor Gulch and Arrowhead.

A remarkable turnaround occurred in the first few years of the twenty-first century. Season-pass holders, who were frequent skiers, came to account for more than a quarter of all downhill activity. Visits to small and medium-sized ski hills grew once again.[42] Nationally, U.S. ski area visits (a skier-visit is one skier or snowboarder participating one day at a ski area) reached a record 57 million in the winter of 2000–2001 — 7 million higher than the average in the decade of the 1980s.[43] The special people who caused the regrowth in skier-visits were young, baggy-panted snowboarders, who shocked resort operators, as if they were aliens from another planet. Actually, they had been around before. The boarders were another version of the early alpine skiers who'd rebelliously reveled in the sport as a way of life. But how that way of life had changed! It had gone from rope tows and warming huts to heated gondola cars and multi-storied condo hotels. Nor had it been the only revolution experienced by skiers. Their gear and clothing changed radically as well.

II

Technique and Equipment: Partners in Progress

4

A Revolution in Equipment

The metal ski, the plastic boot, and the lightweight pole changed how people skied, and stretchable synthetics changed how they looked.

Skiing's challenge has proven irresistible to inventors. Typically they've been enthusiasts, fervent in the belief that their clever new device, whatever it may be, will save people from mediocrity on the slopes, and cause skiing to soar in popularity. Scores of ingenious Rube Goldberg ideas have invaded the sport. There was a ski whose performance could be altered by pumping air into it. Another ski contained rods that you could tighten and loosen to adjust flex and camber. Still another contained oil that allegedly caused the ski's performance to alter in relation to snow surface and temperature. There were bizarre little devices to prevent skis from crossing, and a pair of swiveling rods to keep the skis parallel at all times, so that the skier would never suffer the embarrassment of being seen vee-ing them in a stem. A parachute-like sail pulled a cross country skier uphill when there was a following wind. One invention, which varied in design details over the years, was a ski pole having a hollow space to hold brandy or your liquor of choice. Poles could be used for sitting. A sling, suspended on the handles of two ski poles planted in the snow, created an *al fresco* seat on the slopes. It was a good idea, as long as you were prepared to carry the sling around with you all day.

Dozens of indoor devices attempted to simulate skiing. The most famous in the 1950s was the Bongo Board. It was a short board placed atop a cylinder. Standing on the board, upper body still, the Bongo rider angulated his or her legs outward from side to side, as if going from one turn to another on snow. It was superb for practicing how to recover from near-falls and how to go quickly from edge to edge.

Skiers groped their way through snowstorms until Bob Smith of

Sun Valley, after years of experimentation in the 1960s, introduced the double-lens ski goggle. It allowed air to circulate behind two hermetically sealed, amber-colored plastic panes, drastically reducing the fogging that had bedeviled skiers' vision for years.

Leather and Wood

Before 1950, the accoutrements of skiing were short on efficiency and long on discomfort. The insulating value of air in the loft of a jacket was still not well understood. Hands froze easily. Leather boots were without interior padding or insulation, and toe frostbite was common. Skiers spent hours screwing and gluing steel edges back onto their wooden skis to replace the sections that had been torn off when they hit rocks. Steel edges came in small lengths, which you could buy and install. The replacement work was intricate. If the ash or maple or hickory had softened, making the screw hole too large, it was necessary to shove wooden shards into the hole and fill it with glue before driving in a new screw.

Before the general introduction in the mid-1950s of polyethylene P-Tex and Kofix that prevented snow from clinging to the running surface, a day on the slopes could be ruined as a result of not applying the right wax.[1] Waxing was messy work. It started with impregnating the base with klister or pine tar, then applying over it a running paraffin wax suitable for the day's snow conditions: warm or cold, powder or corn. Some waxes were mixed with graphite powder to add speed. A-X from Switzerland was a popular wax for wet snow. Sohm's red and blue were favorites. They could be rubbed on directly with a warm hand or with a hot iron and a cork block, or the wax could be melted and layered on with a brush. You could paint a lacquer like Faski on the raw wooden base. The lacquer also helped to protect the ridged top surfaces—a critical sealant, or a pair of $10 ash skis could become waterlogged in spring skiing. Breaking a ski was commonplace. Specialist woodworkers in ski shops knew how to insert laminations and splice and glue the fractured ski back together.

Soft leather boots, a couple of inches higher than the ankles, were held in place by the Kandahar binding, made up of steel toe plates and a spring cable. The cable wrapped around a groove in the boot's heel, through hitches or hooks on the ski's sides, attaching to a lever in front of the toe. Pressing forward on the lever tightened the cable. The heel was held down via the side-hitches for downhill skiing. Detaching the cable from the side-hitches loosened the heel, so that you could lift it upwards for cross-country skiing on level terrain.

Warfare often produces advances in technology, but the skis made during World War II for the 10th Mountain Division troops did nothing to advance the efficiency or pleasure of recreational downhill skiing. Made-in-America Northland wooden models, they were built stiffly so that they wouldn't break under the weight of a 200-pound soldier carrying a 100-pound pack. After the war, equipment was pretty much what it had been before. The skis were torsionally weak—that is, they twisted too easily, and so didn't hold a turn well. To maintain the skis' camber during summer storage, a two-inch-thick wood block was positioned between the skis' midsections, and short slats with nuts and bolts clamped the tips and tails together. It also prevented them from warping. Skiers shopping for a new pair were advised to sight down the length of each ski to make sure it wasn't warped. To select the correct length, the skier reached up so that he or she was just able to grasp the tip. Matching two skis into a pair was difficult, because wood—unlike metal or plastic—isn't uniform in construction. The solution, agreed engineers, was to replace an organic material, wood, with metal—or more specifically aluminum alloy sheet, perfected in aircraft manufacture during the war.

First, the Metal Ski

Skill in tennis is governed by the quality of the contact between the racquet strings and the ball. In golf, the flight distance and path of the ball are governed by how the clubhead face strikes it. In skiing, the turn is governed by the interaction between the snow surface and the ski's tip-to-tail curvilinear edge, known as its sidecut. How the edge interacts with the snow depends on the *ski's* properties of flexing, twisting, and the damping of its vibrations. The way the skier pressures the edge comes through the *boot*. The timing of the turn comes from the planting of the *pole*. Beginning in the 1950s, three men—Howard Head, Bob Lange, and Ed Scott—revolutionized skiing through the use of dramatically new combinations of materials to make skis, boots, and poles. As a result, skiing skill progressed more rapidly than at any time in the sport's history.

Attempts to make a metal ski began in France in 1928 and continued in England.[2] In America the Chance Vought company held the U.S. patent on the lamination of aluminum to wood for the manufacture of airplane wings, skis, and other products. In 1948, three former Chance

Their Inventions Altered the Way People Skied. At left, Howard Head flexes a 1957 black Vector ski, descendant of his first aluminum-alloy Head Standard, introduced commercially seven years earlier. Called "the Cheater," the Head metal ski made turning dramatically easier for recreational skiers. At right, Bob Lange celebrates one of many victories achieved by racers wearing his plastic boot, which he successfully began selling to the public around 1965. Having durable lateral rigidity superior to leather, it leveraged the skier's power to edge the ski. *Howard Head photo courtesy of Martha Head. Bob Lange photo by Barry Stott*

Vought engineers made twelve thousand pairs of Truflex skis, designed with aluminum top and bottom sheets, a hollow core, and a celluloid strip for a running surface. The product, reacting to the snow like an uncontrollable spring, was a failure.

Howard Head ultimately succeeded where his predecessors had failed. Head successfully assembled into a single ski aluminum alloy sheets, steel edges, plywood cores, phenolic running surfaces, topskins, and sidewalls, and most especially the flexible adhesives needed to hold them all together. The work of combining such disparate materials demanded enormous persistence. Head shucked off the notion that he was a brilliant, creative genius. "Inventing is only about ten percent of it." he snorted. "The rest is sheer dogged persistence."[3]

Bald with penetrating eyes, and six foot four inches in height, Head looked like an overgrown gnome. An un–athletic casual skier, he began to design a ski, not with the European idea of a product that would give racers a winning advantage, but of one that would make it easier for himself and other recreational skiers to make a turn. Starting in 1947, he built a few pairs, then tested them. Unfortunately, the adhesives failed, and the skis bent or delaminated. At the time, Head was working with moonlighting colleagues in a garage that he rented for $35 a month in Baltimore. He was thirty-four years old and, despite his failures, certain that he was on the right track. Roby Albouy, an engineer and Aspen instructor who worked briefly for Head, told about sleeping on a couch in the inventor's home. "I woke up in the middle of the night," Albouy recalled, "and I heard Howard in the next room talking in his sleep. 'I know I'm right, you're wrong! I'm right, you're wrong!'"[4]

Unlike the wooden ski, Head's aluminum alloy sandwich construction resisted twisting. The ski held a turn more efficiently, and yet it was forgiving. People called it the "cheater." You could initiate the turn easily. It was easy to get on and off the edges in transitioning from one turn to the next.

Head saw—as his predecessors did—that a ski, like an airplane wing, is a flexing beam. Its strength, and the way it acts, depend on the flexing of the top and bottom skins. The ski's performance can be altered by varying the gap between the two layers sandwiching the core, usually made of wood. The design became the basis not only of the first Head metal skis but later of fiberglass skis and surfboards.

Over the 1950–1951 ski season, Head fabricated three hundred Standard models available only in black and in three lengths—6'9", 7' and 7'3" (205 to 220 centimeters).[5] The skis sold for $85 a pair, an unheard-of price at the time—more than a week's salary for most skiers. It didn't discourage demand. By the mid-1950s, the Head Standard was America's most popular ski, and for the first time an American-made ski was being sold widely in Europe.

The potential of the recreational market seemed to Head to be huge. But at the time, a ski's credibility with the consumer depended on its ability to race and win world championship medals. Head was perceived as having created a Volkswagen, not a Porsche. No one sensed the situation better than pre-war world champion Emile Allais, who had spent the years between 1946 and 1954 in North America, teaching skiing and coaching U.S. and Canadian racers, and was thus fully aware of what Head had accomplished by the time he returned to France in 1954. There he designed for Rossignol a riveted aluminum ski, later called the Allais 6. With Allais's ski, Jean Vuarnet won the downhill gold medal at the 1960 Squaw Valley Winter Olympics. Although an American had perfected the metal ski, a European made it credible among racers, coaches, and dealers.

Head improved his skis by finding ways to dampen vibrations in the metal. He made a high-speed model that he called the Vector, and a Deep Powder model that became the favorite of deep snow enthusiasts. He finally broke through in racing when the Swiss National Ski Team began using Head skis in 1963. Along with sales of his black metal Standards, Head by then was so successful that he controlled almost 40 percent of the U.S. market. But there were already omens that he would be unable to sustain the growth. Head's sales people warned him that the metal ski probably would be replaced by fiberglass, and soon. But Head was stubbornly convinced that metal was the superior material for ski-making. The Head Ski Company was sold in 1970 to the conglomerate AMF, about the time it set about selling a fiberglass ski, endorsed by Jean-Claude Killy. Head himself retired to his house in Timonium, an upscale Baltimore suburb, where he worked on the idea of making a revolutionary new tennis racquet. His over-size Prince racquet came to revolutionize the game of tennis as much as his skis had revolutionized the sport of skiing.

Fiberglass Skis

The use of fiberglass to make skis was underway in 1954 when Dale Boison in Santa Monica, California, produced and sold the Dynaglas ski.[6] Most of his early models were composed of fiberglass strands reinforcing hickory. Indeed, throughout the 1960s, skis marketed as fiberglass often were composed of wood and epoxy glue, with little actual glass. Nevertheless, in icy conditions, the new skis were better; they didn't chatter like metal. A breakthrough comparable to Jean Vuarnet's Olympic win on metal occurred in 1962 when Karl Schranz won two gold medals on Kneissl's White Star epoxy fiberglass skis at the FIS World Alpine Ski Championships at Chamonix, France. At the time, pole vaulters were beginning to set new records with fiberglass poles.[7] By the time of the 1966 World Ski Championships, more than half of the racers had switched to fiberglass skis.

With the advent of a ski truly built around the engineering properties of fiberglass, the designer was able to vary torsional flex independently of longitudinal flex. If he wanted, the designer could create a ski that was stiff along its length and soft across. Or he could make it soft longitudinally and firm torsionally. It also became possible to craft a shorter ski that rode like a longer ski. By the early 1970s, adult men were on skis

Revolution in Running Surfaces. In the Sun Valley Lodge's ski room in 1938, ski school director Hans Hauser and resort discoverer Count Felix von Schaffgotsch apply the wax of the day before heading out on the slopes. A half-century later, sophisticated machinery structured a ski's base to perfect flatness, enhancing its ability to initiate a turn and to run true on the snow. *Waxing photo courtesy Sun Valley Resort. Ski tuning machine picture: John C. Russell*

as short as 180 centimeters. With a shorter length, the skier could pivot more easily in order to start the turn.

Lightweight Pole Triggers Change

An aid to starting the turn is to plant the pole in the snow to trigger the action. Instructors often describe it as a deft flicking of the wrist that sets the pole tip subtly on the snow. The action is difficult to perform unless the pole in your hand happens to be light, like a well-balanced tennis racquet with a pleasant swing weight. Prior to the 1960s, poles were anything but light or easy to swing. Made with bamboo, or with steel shafts used in manufacturing golf clubs, and often with clumsy baskets, they were whippy and almost impossible to flick in a quick, accurate plant. All that changed in 1959 when Sun Valley ski shop owner Ed Scott, forty-four, designed the first tapered aluminum-alloy ski pole strong enough to resist breaking.

"Poles were designed stupidly or unimaginatively at the time," Scott wrote in a fourteen-page autobiography, penned in longhand, which he sent to me in 1986. "I had the idea to use large-diameter, thin-walled aluminum tubing. I tapered the shaft and added a light basket. The poles were a sensation because everyone wanted to make short linked turns initiated by a pole plant."[8] The poles were a cinch to sell, according to Scott. He would go into a shop and ask the dealer, "What's the best pole that you carry? Invariably," Scott said, "it would be Eckel, a nicely finished steel pole with a slender, buggy-whip-like shaft that was as heavy as a croquet mallet. I would ask him to hold the Eckel in one hand and two of my poles in the other, them flick them back and forth. Their eyes would bug out because it felt like two of my poles weighed less than one steel pole. Mine also felt twice as stiff. So I'd say, 'Okay, how many do you want?' They were that easy to sell."[9]

Scott was a tall fellow, with a rough red complexion and watery eyes behind glasses as thick as the walls of a brandy decanter. He hated falsity and pretense. At a time when manufacturers commonly paid racers under the table to use their poles, he refused. Like Sir Arnold Lunn (see chapter 8), he saw the payments as hypocritical. Because his poles had such a clear performance advantage, the racers had to have them anyway. Later, when competing pole factories were able to match Scott in sourcing light, tapered shafts, the racers switched to sponsoring brands that paid them. It deprived Scott of his advertising claim that most of the world's best racers used his poles, but he stubbornly refused to pay the racers.[10]

Thirty years after Scott's invention, aluminum alloy came to be replaced by carbon fiber shafts in expensive, high-performance poles. Releasable handles reduced wrist and hand injuries. However, improved skis and poles on their own could not enable the skier to produce a more perfect turn. To tilt the skis on edge in order to etch a skid-less track on the snow, something else was needed.

The Birth of the Modern Boot

The ski boot sits like a gearbox between the engine and the wheels. In the period immediately following World War II, skiing's gearbox—the single-shell leather boot—was miserably inefficient.

An improvement, at least in comfort, occurred around 1950 with the introduction of the double boot, a soft, lace-up boot inside the hard outer shell. The inner boot held the foot in place without subjecting the skin to the harsh pressures of rubbing up against the harder outer boot. Klaus Obermeyer, a young German instructor who had migrated to Aspen, imported the first inner-laced boots to America. Tens of thousands of feet immediately warmed up.

Obermeyer sprang from the Germanic alpine culture that was the fertile ground of many of the sport's innovations in the 1950s. The most popular boots were made in Austria by Koflach, Humanic, and Kastinger. The first buckle-closure boots, by the Swiss/German company Henke, appeared in 1955. Skiers needed such a convenience. The number of lacing hooks, especially on better boots, had multiplied in the prior hundred years, and they virtually doubled around 1950 with the introduction of the laced inner boot. The digitally challenged skier could spend as long as ten minutes lacing the equivalent of four boots before setting out on the slopes. Time wasn't the only inconvenience. Tightening the laces of the hard, stiff outer boot, unless you used a hook-like device to draw them taut, caused raw, sore fingers.

The time-saving buckle boot surely would be the answer. "Are you still lacing while others are racing?" asked Henke in its advertisements.[11] But in 1955, when Henke's salesmen began to show their new Speedfit boot to ski dealers, they often were laughed out of the shops. At the time, buckles were associated with the galoshes worn by folks to walk through slushy streets. "Who would want to wear galoshes to ski?" asked skeptical shop owners.[12]

Nor did skiers invade shops demanding the new buckle convenience of getting in and out of boots faster. They were reluctant to give up the comfortable close fit of the laced boot, especially when it had a soft, separately laced inner. The infinite, intimate adjustability of a couple of dozen lacing hooks offered skiers the most sensitively accommodating fit they would enjoy until the arrival of custom-foamed liners twenty years later. Indeed, racers—usually the first to seize on new technology—didn't begin to adopt the buckle boot until the early 1960s, when hand-lasted inners and better-designed tongues evened out the pressure. Even then, a top racer would wear out a leather boot in a few weeks. The leather was never stiff enough, even when it was hardened with epoxy. Nor were boots high enough. The skier relied a lot on his ankles to turn, twisting his upper body in a tortured angle to get the skis up on edge. What the performance-oriented skier awaited was the replacement of leather with indestructible, stiffer plastic.

What was needed was a boot sufficiently high and stiff laterally so that the lower leg could pressure the side of the boot to edge the ski, while still allowing the knee to flex forward.

Fashion and Technology

While designers searched for fabrics and colors to make skiers fashionable (see chapter 2), they were engaged in a constant struggle to make them warmer. Fashion had to co-exist with technology.

After Klaus Obermeyer warmed feet with an inner boot (page 81), he realized that he'd solved only half the problem. Observing his classes on the mountain, he remarked that they weren't responding well to his teaching because their bodies were cold. They were shivering. To keep them warm, Obermeyer designed a parka with two vinegar-waterproofed cotton gabardine layers, between which was stuffed insulating material. At first, in 1948, he used the factory's sweepings of thread and cotton fragments, because goose down was scarce or non-existent. The early version failed. "The insulation fell to the bottom of the parka," Obermeyer recalled. "So we criss-crossed the stitching to keep the sweepings from dropping."[a] Obermeyer initially had his quilted parka made in Munich in his native Bavaria. Then he opened a facility in Aspen, which ultimately mushroomed into one of the nation's largest skiwear manufacturers. A smiling, outgoing fellow, who has yodeled on the Jay Leno show, Obermeyer seemingly has waded through life giving little hint of whether he is playing or working—a useful lesson for those who may be frustrated by lack of success in business.

In Munich in the winter of 1952–1953, another Bavarian, Maria Bogner, began to make ski pants of wool blended with Helanca, a Swiss nylon yarn that had an amazing ability to stretch to four times its length. The result-

Robert B. Lange's initial effort, before and after 1960, to create a better boot paralleled Head's development of the metal ski ten years earlier. Successive failures did nothing to discourage either man. Like Head, who incidentally was also a Harvard graduate, Lange was not particularly talented athletically. "It took me weeks to graduate from stem class," he confessed. Lange wanted to create a boot, as Head had conceived his easier-to-turn aluminum alloy ski, which would make it easier for people like himself. Before he could conjure up the boot, Lange toyed with dozens of different manufacturers' leather models. He cut them apart to understand their construction. He experimented, as did others, with stiffening the boots by applying polyester resin and fiberglass to the leather. "I don't know how many ovens, toasters, and irons Bob ruined, making prototype boots," recalled his wife Vidie.[13] Lange worked weekends, holidays, nights at his home in Dubuque, Iowa, supporting his family by selling insurance and by turning out plastic hula-hoops, doorknobs, and miniature Corvette cars. Finally, in 1957, he said, "I skied in my very first

---

ing fabric could pull up and down and sideways, and return to its original shape. It stretched and tightly contoured the wearer's body. And the wool made it warm. The stretch pant changed the look of skiing.

The original stretch pant's shortcoming was that the pant leg went inside the boot, where the stirrup ruined the boot's fit, making ankles painfully uncomfortable. Snow also could seep inside, where it melted. The problem was solved by elasticizing the pant cuff and having it cover the boot shaft.

The stretch pant eventually was abandoned. The post-1970s ski pant was no longer a contour-hugging design, but more like a padded warm-up pant. Trim jackets gave way to bulkier and warmer parkas, with multiple snaps and Velcro closures and pockets, and high neck coverings. Polypropylene and breathable waterproof fabrics, such as Gore-tex, wicked moisture away from the skin and inner garments. In the 1990s, authentic New Zealand wool for fleece wear was replaced by spun polyester fiber made from discarded plastic soft drink bottles—more affordable than wool and better because it helped the environment.

In the 1990s, a harried-looking seventy-year-old widow and grandmother, Gert Boyle, produced apparel to benefit people who were stretching their budgets to ski. Her family's Columbia Sportswear Company made a million practical and affordable parkas with zip-out liners that could be worn separately. Practicality came to influence skiwear designers as much as fashion.

plastic boot. The conditions were icy, but after I'd made only two turns I knew I had a boot better than anything ever made before."[14]

It wasn't true.

Actually, it wasn't until 1962, five years later, that he made his first molded boots.[15] Lange's statement was a prelude to exaggerated promises that he came to make over the years in order to wring money from investors, or to make dealers believe that boots would be delivered on time. Even then, the boots were stiff, hard clunkers. But in 1963, Lange switched to a new DuPont polyurethane plastic, adiprene, which—warm or cold—possessed the pliability of good leather boots. But like Head's early skis, the boots were unable to meet the most important criterion of the time: They weren't good enough for racers.

Dave Jacobs, who years later would innovate children's skiwear and create revolutionary Spyder skiwear, was coaching the Canadian National Ski Team in January 1966, when he wrote to Lange, mentioning at least fifteen things the inventor should do to make the boot work properly.[16] By the time Jacobs and his Canadian racers showed up in June for races at Mount Hood, Lange was there with five pairs of custom-made boots, incorporating the changes the racers wanted. "It was amazing what he had accomplished in such a short time," Jacobs said. "The boots were the most unbelievable racing machines I'd ever seen in a lifetime of competing and coaching."[17] When the World Alpine Ski Championships took place two months later in August 1966 at Portillo, Chile, a dozen racers—Canadians and a few U.S. Ski Team members—wore Langes. Curious racers and coaches from different countries crowded around the forty-year-old American inventor in order to study his creation. By the time of the Grenoble Olympics a year-and-a-half later, the Europeans were ready to jettison their own national boot brands in order to ski in the superior performing U.S.-made plastic boot. Five gold medals were won in Langes. In the next four years, seven out of ten of the world's leading racers would switch to Lange. The inventor loved nothing more than to see racers mount the medal winners' podium in his boots, and afterwards, to pour the celebratory champagne. Lange—or RB, as he was called—adored parties, either hosting or attending them. His voice would crackle like lightning, his hazel eyes lit up with a feverish craziness. If après-ski hadn't existed, he would have invented it along with the plastic boot.

One last obstacle remained before Lange could market his boot successfully. He had not found a way to make people's feet comfortable within the boot's harsh plastic interior. He was convinced that the solution lay in a putty-like synthetic flow material, whose patent was held by a prominent chemist named Alden Hanson. The "flo" material would conform to a person's foot. It would absorb shocks and cushion skin and bone from the harsh abrasiveness of the hard vinyl boot liner. The flo would also be capable of changing shape—essential since a person's foot changes shape and size; for example, a foot generally is smaller in the morning than it is later in the day.

Without testing, Lange ordered flo's installation in the colored vinyl liners of all the company's 1970 boots, as many as a hundred thousand pairs. A couple of months after the boots were shipped, the liners cracked and the flo oozed out like toothpaste. Angry shops sent twenty thousand pairs back to the Lange factory, demanding that new liners be installed. Removing the faulty glued-in liners cost at least a million dollars. The company's recently issued public shares, once at $26, plummeted. Lange's personal stake—perhaps as much as $15 million on paper—was reduced to nothing. The Garcia Company, a ski and fishing tackle distributor, took over the company, and Lange left not long afterwards.[18] Almost twenty-five years—half of his life—had passed in developing the plastic boot. He would never share in its commercial success. His original design—a lower shell riveted to a hinged clamshell overlap or cuff—is basically the same design that millions of skiers were wearing forty years later.

Boot makers—primarily centered in the northern Italian town of Montebelluna, the world capital of ski boot manufacture—rapidly switched to plastic, and Langes came to be made in Europe. By the early 1970s, a million and more skiers were wearing plastic boots.

During the decade of the 1970s, the boot top gradually rose up the back of the leg. If what the manufacturer provided wasn't high enough, you could buy a boot-back attachment called a Spoiler, popular with racers and newly arrived freestyle skiers. The high back allowed the skier to pressure the ski tails and create the feeling of jetting the skis forward into a turn (see next chapter).

The Rosemount Engineering company built an ingenious fiberglass boot with movable pads to conform to the wearer's foot shape, cants to alter the angle of the leg to the boot shaft, and changeable springs to alter its flex. In 1969, as many as 350 ski shops were fitting skiers with the Rosemount boot. But its complexity doomed it as a business.

The rear-entry boot was invented in 1975. The entire back of the boot hinged back so that you could easily slide your foot into it, and within a few years it became hugely popular. But a coterie of testers and manufacturers decreed that the rear-entry design didn't offer adequate

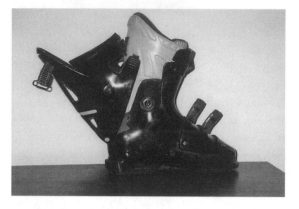

Convenience Lost. Rear-entry and mid-entry boots in the 1980s, like this Salomon model, made it easier and faster for recreational skiers to get in and out of boots. Millions of rear-entry boots were sold, but the design was dropped after critics contended that it didn't supply adequate performance. *Photo by the author*

performance, even though hundreds of thousands of recreational skiers couldn't sense the inadequacy. A hybrid, the mid-entry boot, attempted to solve the problem by combining an overlap lower shell for accurate fit with a hinged upper cuff that opened wide for easy entry and exit. No matter. The insistent demand for better-performing boots from the manufacturers' own racing-oriented staffs and from critical magazine product reviewers forced a return to the more difficult to get-in-and-out-of, conventional top-entry buckle boot.

Binding Safety Improves

The earliest, commercially sold release binding was invented in 1939 by an American, Hjalmar Hvam. Release bindings, however, didn't come into common use until after World War II, when they mercifully started a decline in lower leg injuries. New Jersey inventor Mitch Cubberly led the way. An engineer, Cubberly correctly believed that metal-to-metal contact would provide more reliable release than leather-to-metal contact. With a Cubco binding toepiece, you needed a corresponding metal piece screwed onto the toe of your leather boot. Cubberly was an ascetic, no-nonsense fellow, who designed his binding so that all its springs and inner workings were exposed, enabling mechanically minded males (like himself) to see the mechanism's inner workings. The Cubco offered upward as well as torsional release. By 1957, with his combination of heel release and toepiece, Cubberly had effectively created the world's first convenient step-in binding.

Cubco's advertising today would make a product litigation defense attorney wince. Next to a photograph of a man sitting in a wheelchair, with leg encased in plaster and propped up on the footrest, appeared the headline:"DON'T LET THIS HAPPEN TO YOU!"Above the headline, Cubberly mounted fake testimonials from businessmen and housewives, assuring readers that the Cubco would save them from the kind of leg-disabling injury suffered by the unfortunate basket case in the picture.[19]

At Garmisch Partenkirchen in the Bavarian Alps in the late 1940s, Hannes Marker perfected a binding that made it easier for the skier to adjust the tension regulating how much force would cause the toepiece to release in a twisting fall. Marker and Tyrolia and France's Look bindings, with their greater elasticity, eventually came to dominate the American market.

Gordon Lipe, an upstate New York engineer, invented a handy little device, the Release Chek, which he began to sell to shops and to skiers in 1965. It was calibrated for the user's weight and skiing ability, and made it possible to check whether the toepiece would twist out successfully in a fall. Beginning in 1979, cooperation among manufacturers and people like Lipe led to a single international system (DIN) for calibrating the force required to release in a fall. As a result, today anyone can easily adjust binding tension with a screwdriver, using a one-to-ten scale visible on the binding.

Lipe was ahead of his time in showing how the friction between a rough boot sole and the ski's top skin impeded binding release. It led him to the idea of an anti-friction pad—a small Teflon pad mounted on the ski under the boot toe, which increased the certainty that the binding would release in a twisting fall.

So that the ski would not take off down the hill and endanger other skiers, skiers for a long time wore a retaining strap that attached the ski to the boot. The trouble was that it retained the flailing ski dangerously close to your body after the binding released. The solution was the spring-pronged brake, which Earl Miller claimed to have invented in 1963. It separated ski from skier, yet the prongs prevented the ski from sliding out of control down the hill. Miller, an earnest, rather humorless fellow, was the all-time champion of ski inventing. He came to hold no fewer than seventy patents, including the first strapless pole, a fat soft powder ski, and a releasable snowboard binding.

Metal plate bindings—Spademan, Gertsch, Besser, and Burt—flourished between 1965 and 1970. Like the earlier Cubco, the plate binding employed metal-to-metal contact. It didn't need an anti-friction pad. Boot and binding plate released together. Burt Weinstein's binding consisted of a metal platform worn on the boot sole, which performed the entire function of releasing, whether by twisting or forward thrust. There was no need for a releasing toepiece; nor the need to align the foot and to step back into the binding after a fall. When a skier fell and the Burt binding released, the boot didn't come off the plate; rather a retracting cable snapped the plate and ski back together. Like Sony's video-cassette format and Apple's operating system, however, the plate binding eventually lost out to an inferior technology promoted by superior distribution and funding.

In the 1980s, skiers were frustrated when they bought new skis and discovered that the shop, under pressure from lawyers, would not mount them with the used, perfectly functional bindings that were on their old skis. They were told that they had to buy new bindings costing upwards of a hundred dollars. The reason given was that their old bindings— which may, in fact, have only been used for only one or two winters— no longer conformed to new safety standards. If a skier were injured, an attorney could sue the shop for not having installed a state-of-the-art product. The added cost of updating bindings became a giant turn-off for people who skied only a few days a winter.

While skiers may have complained about having to buy new bindings, there were good reasons to do so. Technological advances in binding release had succeeded in reducing tibia fractures by 86 percent in a fifteen-year period before 1985. Then, however, a new kind of injury emerged, one that could not be cured by a better binding. The problem was that the rigid plastic boot now rose higher on the lower leg while pitching it about 15 degrees forward, and people skied with a wider stance and with more independent leg action. The result was analogous to what happened when football performance was advanced with the introduction of a superior helmet: an unintended side-effect was created. In football, it was a tripling in the incidence of neck and spine injuries. In skiing, the unintended side-effect was a serious increase in knee injury. What was once an ankle injury or a tibia fracture rose up the leg to become a more costly injury to the anterior cruciate ligament, famously known as an ACL tear. The trend so alarmed Olympic gold medalist Toni Sailer, the chairman of the Alpine Committee of the International Ski Federation, that he warned that advances in modern boot and ski design were destroying the knees of a whole generation of young racers.

Another hazard arising from good intentions came with the realization that raising the foot higher off the ski allows the skier to edge it more powerfully. It led to the elevated binding platform. Coupled with more exaggerated sidecut of the shaped ski, the elevated binding increased the chance of knee injury. For a while it did. But in the 1990s, competitors—followed by recreational skiers—began to use dramatically shorter skis. The shorter the ski, the less it leveraged the injurious twisting of the leg in a fall.

The Shaped Ski

Before the new ski of the 1990s shortened, it first became shapelier. Snowboarding was responsible for the change. On packed surfaces, the snowboard can make a turn that leaves an arced line on the snow's surface, as if it had been carved by a bread knife. The sensation was difficult to replicate on skis, whose turning radius before 1992 was much larger than that of a snowboard. So why not make a ski to perform in the same manner—with a smaller turning radius, wasp-shaped with wider tips and tails, like a snowboard? The Olin Ski Company patented and tested just such a ski in 1986, and not long afterward the Elan Ski Company in Slovenia began work on a giant slalom ski with a deep sidecut.[20] Within a few years, skiers almost universally adopted the shaped, or parabolic, ski. Its sidecut looked positively elliptical compared to the relatively straight side of traditional skis. It was wider at the tip and tail, and it would soon become shorter. Now the skier, like a snowboarder, could lay down a crisp, clean arcing track on the snow.

The wide snowboard also had an advantage over the narrower ski in deep snow. Its greater surface area allowed the rider to float on the snow and a snowboarder of no special competence could turn in unbroken powder better than a skier. It occurred to a designer at the Atomic Ski Company that a snowboard, split longitudinally in half, would create a running surface area for two skis equal to that of a snowboard, capable of producing the same flotation that a snowboarder experiences. Thus was born the fat ski in 1992.[21] It enabled any decent advanced skier to enjoy the pleasure of making turns down a virgin slope of fresh powder. Back-country and helicopter skiing, already popular, got a further shot in the arm.

Ski Testing Controversy

As more technology invaded the sport, a ski came to seem like a product, such as a car or a power boat, piloted by its owner. The notion that gear was primarily responsible for how well people skied gained traction, particularly after plastic boots leveraged the mechanical power of the lower leg to make the ski's edge carve. Marketers and ski magazines encouraged the notion. In 1967, *SKI Magazine* touted the idea that the skis did the carving of the turn (see page 104). *Skiing Magazine* began to test skis in the way that its publisher and owner Bill Ziff's other magazines tested automobiles and hi-fi equipment (see page 267). At first, the test reports gave the reader ratings of products the testers had liked, with no negative reviews. Unlike *Consumer Reports*, the ski magazines were not keen to condemn products manufactured by the magazine's major advertisers. Their tests resembled the stock evaluations done by investment banks, whose analysts must consider what a negative rating may do to the bank's business. As for the ski companies, the test reports were a mixed blessing. Companies exulted at the chance to use an approving quote from a report in their promotional brochures. On the other hand, they squealed like stuck pigs if a magazine gave the slightest indication that a ski was anything less than superb.

The skis tested by the magazines were typically prototypes; they weren't necessarily the skis available in shops. They did not come off a factory production line, nor had they cured over months of shipping and sitting on racks, as happened with store-bought skis. The magazines were unable to monitor the ability of manufacturers to deliver to consumers large numbers of skis, for example, free from concavity in the running surface. Also, the magazines were unable to obtain the skis in time to evaluate them on mid-winter snow. Testers skied on them in April, when snow became soft and mushy by mid-morning. That was just one problem. The magazines also subjected their readers to a kind of high-tech jargon used by the engineering departments of the ski companies, which was virtually incomprehensible to someone who was just taking up skiing. For example, a report on 1984 models in *SKI Magazine* told bewildered readers about skis having "a torsion-stiffener of diagonally oriented bidirectional fiberglass roving running along the top of the lower core."[22]

Later, the language of the laboratory was replaced by the language of marketing. "Brings out a smile and the smile just gets bigger with every turn."[23] "The Fred Astaire of the slopes. Makes you feel light on your feet, yet strong enough to take on the world."[24] The enthusiasm eventually was justified. By the late 1990s, quality differences among skis became less pronounced. The magazines did not have to equivocate about whether certain models were good or bad. Skis uniformly performed better.

Poet Laureate of Ski Testers. Magazine reviews of ski performance attracted readers and occasionally irked manufacturers. Former freestyler and Yale cum laude grad Jackson Hogen wrote vividly about skis, including one model whose "spirit sagged at the sight of a short turn." © *Tom Lippert. Quote from* Snow Country Magazine *(October 1995)*

Materials invented for space exploration and the military had utterly transformed skiing. Complex alloys and plastics, which engineers could control, replaced organic materials like wood, leather, and bamboo. Just as Toyota created small cars that rode like limousines, ski manufacturers created shorter skis that rode the snow like long skis. Beveled steel edges and sintered running surfaces gave a smoother sensation of skiing. The long-suffering recreational skier was even given back the opportunity to buy softer boots. The technology actually enabled people to ski better as they grew older. When 1964 Olympic slalom winner Pepi Stiegler turned fifty, he confessed that "modern" skis and boots allowed him to make better turns than when he won his Olympic gold medal at the age of twenty-six.[25]

Baby boomers, as they aged into their forties, may not have been as fit, but in many cases they skied better than they did when they were young. The improved equipment opened the way to techniques that enabled people to ski with greater efficiency and less effort.

Technique: From Stem to Carve

How ski technique, embroiled in controversy, went from snowplow and stemming, to parallel skidded turns, to carving.

Skiing is a graceful fusion of gravitational and muscular force, modulated by twisting, flexing, balancing, on one foot or two. The action is magical, full of freedom and inventiveness. Gravity carries the skier downhill. Leg muscles redirect the force of the snow against the skis to change direction. An expert skier, skilled in the coordination involved, makes a turn of a given radius and speed with far less effort than a novice does. The free access to the power of gravity is why the sport ranks with sailing, soaring, and surfing in deeply satisfying man's need for play in nature, and coincidentally why it's a favorite sport of the disabled.

The early technique pioneers necessarily restricted the promise of boundless freedom. Their job was to clarify and codify the forces involved in turning skis so that tourists could be taught and racers coached. They were idealists, not ideologues, and the skier owes them a debt of gratitude for their strenuous efforts to turn ignorance into knowledge. The trouble started with the disciples of the official technique religions. Or as Sigmund Freud once mischievously observed, "I am not a Freudian myself."

A wonder it is that a sport expressive of freedom so often came in conflict with narrowly defined doctrines of how people should ski. As regional and national instructor-certifying organizations arose around particular techniques, each tended to describe those who were not followers as heretics to be cast out or, at the very least, denied a higher level of certification. The battles raged: Arlberg stem against French parallel, rotation against counter-rotation, up-unweighting against down-unweighting. Advocates of carving turns denied the reality of skidding them. The end and the beginning of the turn became a point of confusion; for a split second, they are effectively one and the same.

From Stem to Parallel

Technique is about defining efficient and even graceful ways to manage terrain, with the turn having two purposes: to change direction and to govern the speed of descent. The earliest authentic edged turns were made possible by the improved foot control that came from the invention of the first elastic free-heel binding in the 1860s by Sondre Norheim of Telemark, Norway. Further improvement came when the Telemarkers began to make skis that were no longer straight-sided. When the new skis were tilted on edge, their curved edge, later called sidecut, made it easy to turn them.[1] It was an important historical lesson. For 130 years after Norheim, ski technique would progress in tandem with changes in equipment design.

As the end of the nineteenth century neared, technique made its next big advance: the stem or snowplow turn. By bringing the skis tip to tip, and fanning the tails out in a Vee configuration, the beginner could control his speed downhill more easily. A braking and turning maneuver, the

Mother of All Turns. The basic snowplow, or stem or wedge turn, never died despite efforts to remove it from teaching. The pyramid-like formation of the legs offers a stable base under the upper body, and the skis automatically go up on edge, enabling the novice to control his speed. Even expert racers use the position to gain better feel for their ski edges and boot fit. Two Austrian instructors in the 1960s demonstrated the edging of the outside ski to turn either left or right. *Photo by Franz Hoppichler from the collection of Verein Tiroler Skigeschichte, St. Christof, Austria*

stem turn was invented by Mathias Zdarsky, a native of Lilienfeld, Austria. Zdarsky featured it in one of the most important how-to-ski books ever published—his 1896 *Lilienfelder Skilauftechnik*, which ultimately went into seventeen editions.

The ability to turn progressed further with the introduction of stiffer heel bindings such as the Bilgeri, which prevented the heel, previously loose, from sliding off the ski to the right or left. Now the world was ready for the parallel turn, or at least the partly parallel turn. Called the stem christie, it was Austrian Hannes Schneider's masterpiece. The skier started the turn with a stemming action, and brought the skis parallel to one another as the turn progressed. Schneider incorporated the technique into a disciplined stem-to-parallel progression, which he and his disciples taught in organized classes at St. Anton, starting in the 1920s (see chapter 6).

The introduction of slalom and downhill races in the 1920s shifted the emphasis in technique from braking to finding ways to go faster. In racing, it was no longer desirable to retain the cumbersome, decelerating Vee stem shape, but rather to speed the turn by keeping the skis parallel at all times. Again, progress in technique needed progress in equipment, and in 1929 the steel edge came to the rescue. It allowed the skier to adopt a more erect, athletically superior stance. With steel edges, more supportive boots and bindings, and the curvilinear ski, you could make a hundred percent parallel turn! In the 1930s, the acknowledged architect of linking pure parallel turns down the hill and through the gates was the master slalom skier, Austria's Toni Seelos, 1931 silver medalist and 1933 gold medalist in the World Alpine Ski Championship. Seelos's Tempo Turn served as a model for at least two famous skiers who copied it.

Dick Durrance, when he was a teenager growing up in Bavaria, saw the Seelos turn and brought it back with him to America where, while he was a student at Dartmouth, he became the nation's dominant native-born racer of the 1930s (see page 20). The other beneficiary was Emile Allais, who hired Seelos to coach the French national team and as a result went on himself to win the 1937 and 1938 world championships. Allais amended Seelos's turn and presented it as a French technique in the 1937 book *Ski Français* (by Emile Allais and Paul Gignoux), and in Allais's *How to Ski by the French Method*, published in 1947.

In the Allais turn, the upper body was cocked in a windup motion. Led by the arm, the upper body then projected forward and around in a powerful rotary action. When Allais blocked the rotation at the hips, the turning force was transferred to his skis, which were kept parallel to one

Father of Parallel. France's Emile Allais demonstrated a pure parallel christie turn without stem in 1937. The uphill shoulder was held back, preparatory to Allais rotating it swiftly around in the direction of the turn. His legs and skis would turn as a result of his blocking the upper body rotation at his hips. *Photo from* Ski Français, *par Emile Allais et Paul Gignoux, Grenoble, France: B. Arthaud, 1937*

another throughout the turn. Once again, the new technique could not progress without an advance in equipment design. To enable the skier to steer the parallel turn with his feet, the loose-heeled binding was replaced by one with a powerful cable that pulled the boot into the iron toepieces. When the cable hooked onto the sides of the skis under the ankle, it clamped down the heel so that the boot could not move up or sideways. Such a binding wasn't enough for Allais. He saw that the weak link in the turn was the boot itself. The leather wasn't sufficiently stiff to hold the foot and ankle firmly. To correct the deficiency, he wrapped a leather thong or *lanière* around the ankle and over the front of the foot. While the leather thong wasn't a new idea, Allais moved the point of attachment farther back so that it truly anchored the ankle and heel. The thong attached through fixed steel rings at the sides of the wooden skis, or through a hole drilled through the ski underfoot.

The leather thong had a couple of notable drawbacks. Wrapping and threading and tightening it on a cold day with bare fingers was an experience comparable to that possibly felt by the explorer Robert Falcon Scott penciling his dying thoughts in Antarctica. And while the thong improved performance by locking the foot inside the boot as if it were held by an alligator's jaw, it also removed the possibility of the boot releasing by even a fraction of an inch from the ski. Sprained ankles were common.*

With the thong tightly wrapped around the boot, Allais expanded his technique repertoire to include the ruade, a change of direction accomplished by the skier planting both poles ahead and kicking the tails of the skis in the air.[2] The turn was made by thrusting the tails from side to side, pivoting around the tips. It was important to keep the upper body facing down the hill at all times. With the ruade and the *lanière*, said Allais, "raw rotary power wasn't needed any more in the turn."

A Twist Comes to Parallel: Wedeln

Animals supplied the imagery for different techniques. Allais' *ruade* is a French word suggesting the kicking of a horse. It was not to be confused with *wedeln*, a German word meaning "wagging" — as in a dog wagging its tail. Wedeln emerged in the early 1950s when slalom skiers found that they could race faster through a series of tight gates in the fall line if they simply turned their legs and skis against the massive inertia of the upper body. The shoulders rotated in a direction counter to the twisting of the skis. It was a much quicker action, and it shortened the line of descent through the flags by enabling the racer to turn close to the inside pole of the gate. The effect of the inside shoulder leading the turn and of having the upper body laterally at an angle to the legs also put the skis on a high edge to cut the turn aggressively. Wedeln was superior to the ruade in that it was a sinuous action on the snow, and had less wasteful up and down movement.

Wedeln's twisting, pretzel-like movements represented a radical change from Zdarsky's and Schneider's rotation turn, and wedeln attracted the attention of Austrian Professor Stefan Kruckenhauser, a physical education teacher. Kruckenhauser, who was also a skilled photographer, proceeded to analyze the movements of wedeln — he preferred to call it *kurzschwingen* (short swing) — on film. He was in a powerful position to bring about change, since he headed the state-owned Bundesheim, the center of Austrian ski instruction. The Bundesheim was located at St. Christof, a tiny village above St. Anton, where, a quarter century earlier, Kruckenhauser's pre–World War II counterpart, Hannes Schneider, had reigned as the pope of ski instruction. Now Kruckenhauser was the pope.

---

*The history of twisting injuries in skiing is their upward migration from the ankle in 1945 to the knee in 1985, noted on page 88.

Counter-Rotation. In a slalom course in the mid-1960s, Austrian racer Anderl Molterer reversed his shoulders in relation to the twisting of his legs. The extreme movement allowed the racer to get his skis as close as possible to the slalom pole, shortening his line of descent and gaining precious fractions of a second. *Peter Miller (petermillerphotography.com)*

Krucky, as he was familiarly known, was a thickset man, with a bronze face as wrinkled as a sharpei's pelt. He was aided by his daughter's husband, Franz Hoppichler, who for years labored in the shadow of his father-in-law's carefully cultivated fame. Krucky was a garrulous, gifted promoter; Hoppy, the crown prince, a somewhat autocratic sophist, blessed with a wry sense of humor. The two of them dispatched images of the correct way to ski to nations around the world—in books, films, and magazine articles. Both superb photographers, they made a virtual art form of ski technique with their exquisite black and white pictures, which they shot using a tripod-mounted Leica, filters, and slow 16 ASA film.[3] To show how a turn developed, they didn't fire off rapid-sequence pictures of a single demonstrator. Rather, they took pictures of precision-trained instructors dressed in the same clothes—each demonstrating a phase of the turn. It worked because they had so perfectly disciplined the instructors in their movements. Kruckenhauser wrote a book on the final forms of skiing, which first came to the attention of the English-speaking ski world in 1958 when New Yorker Roland Palmedo translated it into English as *The New Official Austrian Ski System.*

Reverse Shoulder. The correct 1960s stance for traversing a slope on 7-foot skis was uphill arm and shoulder ahead, hips thrust into the hill. The body's resulting angulation causes the skis to go up on their edges, allowing the skier to maintain the line of traverse. The stance is identical in both directions, as demonstrated by a pair of instructors from the famed Bundesheim in St. Christof, Austria. *Photo by Franz Hoppichler from the collection of Verein Tiroler Skigeschichte, St. Christof, Austria*

America's best racer, Brooks Dodge, first demonstrated wedeln for Americans in 1956 after returning from Europe and the Olympics.[4] Dodge took a photographer up into Mount Washington's Tuckerman Ravine above his family's home in order to demonstrate the Austrian-developed wedeln for *SKI Magazine*'s readers. Curiously, his turn sequence didn't look a whole lot like the reverse shoulder and wedel turns demonstrated in the approved Austrian technique of Kruckenhauser. It looked more like a short-turn sequence that might appear in a magazine published twenty, thirty, or even forty years later. It was breathtakingly modern. Dodge's body, seen from behind, is facing directly downhill. His feet are turning under him. There's little body contortion. It wasn't a turn anyone was typically doing. It was something of the future. The picture caption read, "Top U.S. Olympic skier Brooks Dodge demonstrates wedeln on steep Hillman's Highway."

How did he do it?

The explanation originates with the fact that a skier makes a turn by edging the skis at an angle to the slope. The flatter the slope, the greater the effort required to set the skis at an angle to the slope. A steeper slope, on the other hand, naturally cants the skis at an angle to the snow. Hillman's Highway is extremely steep, so that Dodge didn't need to contort his body much to set his edges. He could rotate his legs under a stable upper body in a natural stance, and easily swing the skis around in the direction of the new turn without having to work very hard to make the skis edge. The steep slope did it for him. Dodge's turn was a beautiful thing to watch and, in fact, a similar sequence of Austrian triple gold medal winner Toni Sailer, appeared the following year under the headline, "Wedeln the relaxed way!"[5] Not coincidentally, Sailer was skiing the National, Stowe's steepest trail at the time.

On intermediate terrain, skiers couldn't come close to emulating the way Sailer and Dodge skied in the pictures. The slope didn't provide enough edge angle. Moreover, their leather boots, which weren't stiff or high enough above the ankle, didn't provide good lateral leverage. It was as difficult to edge a ski as it was to skate effectively in a loose hockey boot. But it could be done by tilting the upper body laterally downhill and extending the legs at a severe angle to the upper body in what was called the comma position, and that was just the stance that wedeln promoted.

It wasn't long before Kruckenhauser found it necessary to modify wedeln. The feet-glued-together, extreme reverse shoulder stance didn't work well in the increasingly common bumps freckling the slopes at winter resorts. At Interski, the international congress of ski instructors, which was held in 1959 at Zakopane, Poland, Kruckenhauser proposed a more open stance with less reverse shoulder. In doing so, he introduced another animal into the lexicon of technique, the marmot turn, or *murmel-schwung*.

The arrival in North America of wedeln, branded with Kruckenhauser's authority, meanwhile, had stirred confusion. Did it mean that ski schools should abandon Hannes Schneider's old Arlberg technique of rotating the upper body in the direction of the turn? Or should pupils now be taught to reverse their shoulders in relation to the turn? A compromise was a French turn "split rotation," promoted by Mt. Tremblant ski school director and racer Ernie McCulloch, by ex-racer and magazine columnist Tom Corcoran and others.[6] At the turn's beginning, the skier anticipated the direction of the turn by rotating, then he completed the turn with reverse shoulder. Split rotation, by the way, was neither a formal technique nor a teaching system. It was the way that really good skiers and giant slalom racers skied at the time. They didn't need an official association of ski instructors to tell them it worked.[7] McCulloch took it further. As early as 1958, when rotational body action was still considered the engine of the turn, McCulloch advocated making a turn simply by placing the curved edge on the snow. Pressure the edge, and the ski would turn by itself, he said. "With proper edging, and the aid of the side camber or curve built into the ski, a turn may be started with very little movement."[8] McCulloch thus anticipated a technique that would revolutionize skiing twenty years later.

Theories Abound—and a Resolution

The late 1950s and early 1960s were a bewildering period in ski technique. Terms such as snowplow, stem, and wedge sometimes described almost the same thing. It took an expert to discern that *abstem* was a slight fanning of the uphill ski prior to the turn, not to be confused with *schritt-bogen*, which was a stepping of the uphill ski. The term *counter-rotation* was not to be confused with the more fixed position of *gegenschulter*, meaning reverse shoulder. On the other hand, the French technique of *projection circulaire* demanded that the skier rotate his whole body in the direction of the turn. The arguments, often nationalistic, raged fiercely. There was something in ski technique that attracted a didactic or an authoritarian strain of thinking. But in 1961, hope for agreement on the basics of ski technique—at least in the English language—was raised with the publication of an article in America concerning the work of Professor Hugo Brandenberger, a Swiss physicist and mathematician.[9] Brandenberger had scrutinized the pure physical laws underlying the act of skiing. His analysis, *Ski Mekanik*, translated into English by Paul Valar, ski school director at Cannon Mountain, New Hampshire, proclaimed that the basis of all skiing lay in Newton's laws of motion. The skier's body when in action, Brandenberger said, operates with three units:
- The upper torso—shoulders, chest and arms;
- The lower torso and pelvis;
- Legs, feet, and skis.

When an action takes place in one of these body parts, Brandenberger said, Newton's third law of motion requires that an equal and opposite reaction take place in another part. If you unweighted your skis, the split second you were in the air freed your feet and skis to pivot in a new direction. If you pivoted the skis to the right, your action found its equal and opposite reaction in your shoulders twisting to the left. For stem-christie traditionalists, who believed at the time that the new reverse shoulder turn was an unnatural body movement, here was hard evidence that they were wrong. Brandenberger said it was absolutely natural for the shoulders to rotate in a direction opposite to the turning of the feet and skis. Wedeln was as logical as rotation.

But how could skis also be turned by the classic rotation of the shoulders, chest, and arms in the direction of the turn? Easy, answered Brandenberger. In classic rotation, the skier steers the skis around without unweighting them from the snow. To make them turn, the skier contracts his abdominal and gluteal muscles. Like a clutch, the muscles grab the rotary force of the upper body and use it to rotate the legs, feet, and skis. A common fault among skiers, over-rotating, is actually a failure to capture the rotary force generated by the upper body.

Which technique was best? All of them, answered Brandenberger. The choice of technique depends on how one wants to ski. Counter-rotation was ideal for slalom racing because it quickened a turn. But it demanded precise skill and timing, since the movement must be synchronized with the split second of unweighting the skis. Ordinary rotation was easier for beginners to learn, because it allowed more time for the turning moment of the upper body to be transmitted to the skis.

Serpents and Eggs

Notwithstanding the hundreds of German-speaking instructors and racers who dominated the American ski culture, a mere trio of Frenchmen were almost as influential. The three were Emile Allais, superstar Jean-Claude Killy, and Georges Joubert. Unlike the many Austrians, Bavarians, and Swiss who became Americans, none of the three Frenchmen settled here permanently. Allais coached a generation of North American racers, and then went home to France (see chapter 6). Killy was in the U.S. off and on over a dozen years, his image so dominating that people temporarily forgot who Stein Eriksen was (see page 226). Joubert's new technique ideas were like Dior dress designs, regularly wafted across the Atlantic to fashionable acclaim.

In 1955, Joubert introduced the French version of wedeln, called *godille*, and over the next twenty years, from his home in Grenoble, he assembled the text and pictures for at least a half dozen learn-to-ski-better books. Several were co-authored with Jean Vuarnet, the 1960 Olympic down-hill gold medalist. The books were read by tens of thousands of skiers in France, Italy, Japan, Scandinavia, and North America.

A short, perpetually tanned fellow, Joubert was distinguished by a high-bridged nose and smallish eyes that darted about. He spoke extremely rapidly, scarcely moving his lips, sounding as if he might be talking out of the sports pages of a newspaper. As he did with magazine editors in other countries, Joubert bombarded me across the Atlantic with manuscripts, sent on onion-skin paper, typed single space, accompanied by dozens of sequence photos of racers in action. From their stances and turns, Joubert was able to divine messages, like a soothsayer reading tea leaves. Born of his creativity, snakes (*serpents*) and eggs (*oeufs*) became images of the most efficient ways to make a sequence of turns and to streamline your-self to go faster. In 1967, thanks to Joubert, *SKI* published a cover that was one of the most provocative that the magazine ever carried. Up to that time, generations of skiers had been admonished by instructors to get their weight forward and to never sit back. *SKI*'s cover, however, showed a skier back on his skis, or more accurately projecting his feet forward into a turn, his upper body lagging behind. "Look! They're sitting back!" shouted the cover line, "Introducing avalement, the new technique that demolishes a sacred cow."[10] *Avalement* is a French word that means "low-ering down" or "swallowing." Joubert had discovered it in the stances of top racers—captured in thousands of sequence photos he took. Rather than have the body rise or drop in order to unweight the skis and allow them to turn, avalement asked the skier to swallow the forces of terrain and of rebounding pressure. The knees were retracted upwards to swal-low the force, and the feet shot forward, projected into the next turn. The skis remained in contact with the snow as much as possible. The skier ap-peared to be sitting back, but the position was only momentary.

In 1966, Joubert and Vuarnet wrote *Comment se perfectionner à ski* (How to improve your skiing). Dial Press in New York published it under the title *How to Ski the New French Way*. On receiving the news of the title change, a disappointed and annoyed Joubert, with his translator Sim Thomas, vigorously challenged its logic. "To suggest a peculiar French way of skiing is incorrect," Joubert wrote. "There are no longer national differences in the way the best skiers ski. In fact, there is an astonishing similarity in the movements of champions of all nationalities."[11] In the disagreement over the book's title, oddly enough, both Joubert and Dial were right. The division of techniques by nationality, as Joubert argued, was an archaic idea, as everyone in Europe knew. Nationalistic differences in technique were rapidly dying. Austrian instruction czar Stefan Kruckenhauser agreed. "There is no Australian crawl, just swimming, yah?" said Krucky. "There is no Austrian technique or American or French, only skiing, yah? The way we all ski."[12] Only in America did the legacy of the Austrian influence remain so powerful that a New York publishing house would see the value of shocking readers with the title *How to Ski the New French Way*. The book came to exert a huge influence over instructors and coaches. Joubert convincingly showed that the new international common denominators of technique were angulation; feet acting independently, not locked together; keeping the upper body quiet; and anticipating the direction of the oncoming turn.

For his articles and books, Joubert filmed his own photo sequences of skiers demonstrating technique. Rather than face the demonstrators as they headed down the hill, he went up the hill and photographed them from behind. The resulting sequence pictures were easy for the reader to follow because a right turn literally became a turn to the right on the page. The same logic compels instructors to ask pupils to follow them down the hill. The unfortunate consequence, as anyone who has taken a ski lesson can attest, however, is that the instructor cannot see what you are doing.

Joubert seemed to find a new technique every winter. Along with the godille and avalement, there was *glissement* or sliding—the skier's mastery of contact with the snow. *Glissement*, akin to the sailor's feel for wind, was once described by Jean-Claude Killy as "the intelligence of the feet." Joubert would find the sources of his new techniques, which he sold to readers, in frozen photo frames of Killy in action. To Killy, it was dishonest. He detested the sequences of his turns in Joubert's books. No single position of an athlete can represent his total technique. It would be as erroneous to show Jack Nicklaus's sand shot as representative of his golf swing. Avalement, especially, was misinterpreted. Skiers adopted it as a way to ride the tails of their skis, wearing a spoiler, an attachment used to heighten the back of the boot. But sitting back was a momentary action of the racer, and a bad example for recreational skiers to pursue.

Arrival of the Carved Turn

By 1970, with the invention of the stiff plastic boot that reduced lateral ankle play, it finally became possible for Everyman to put a ski on edge without contorting his body. After that, national differences in technique rapidly disappeared, as Joubert had predicted. The use of extravagant up and down motion to unweight the skis, and the use of the upper body to power the turn—whether by rotation or counter-rotation—mostly disappeared. Emphasis turned to stabilizing the upper body and using it as an anchor to twist the legs and feet. In steadily facing downhill, the upper body anticipated the direction of the turn. Then, when the pressure of the skis on the snow was released by subtle unweighting, the skis twisted naturally into the turn, like the releasing of a coiled spring. The skier almost fell into the turn to initiate it, catching the snow with his edges to complete it.

As the public became more aware of the influence of equipment on technique, instructors were more inclined to explain to students how to employ the ski's sidecut—its curvilinear edge. The higher, laterally rigid plastic boot, after all, made it easier for the skier to pressure the edge. "A small but growing nucleus of the world's best skiers are talking about something called the pure carved turn," reported *SKI Magazine* in early 1967. "The skier senses the moment when the edge of the outside ski takes over the powering of the turn. He consciously surrenders to its external force. The result is a feeling that the skis are literally carving the turn for you."[13]

The most prominent promoter of the carved turn was Warren Witherell. A prodigious athlete—world water-skiing champion at age eighteen, captain of his college hockey team, all-American swimmer, soccer player—Witherell didn't start to ski until he was twenty. Applying his remarkable athletic skill to snow skiing, he quickly built a detailed knowledge of technique, partly by coaching teenage racers. He savagely criticized ski schools, calling them places that failed to teach students properly. His ideas were conveyed with a bulldog persistence, pained by the knowledge of the deprivations suffered by those who neglected his advice.

In 1972, Witherell wrote *How the Racers Ski*, a book that for a long time exerted a powerful influence over American coaches and instructors. It was the first attempt to sell the public on the idea of a pure carved turn, "without skidding or sideslipping." For such a turn to be made, its radius would have to correspond with that of the ski as the skier pressures it. That was the theory. Witherell, however, was honest enough to admit that some skidding and pivoting were involved—a disclosure that carved-turn advocates typically neglected to mention at the time. Truthfully, it was necessary to pivot, drift, and maybe skid the skis in order to

The Hinge that Opened the Door to a Radically Different Slalom Turn

One equipment invention—not a ski or a boot—dramatically changed the technique of racers. It was the hinged slalom pole.

From the earliest days of slalom in the 1920s, the racer's aim has been to ski as closely as possible to the turning pole of the gate, made up of two wooden or bamboo poles stuck in the snow. For years, the repeated impact of hitting rigid wood or bamboo bruised arms and shoulders. There was also a problem of equity. After the first three or four racers, the poles became less upright and easier to turn around. Racers in the middle of the first group, before the snow surface became rutted, enjoyed an advantage.

If a pole came entirely out of the snow, there was a further problem. The gatekeeper had to run downhill and retrieve it, bring it back up, and jam it back into its hole in the hard snow—hopefully the hole originally drilled by the course setter. Even with replacement poles, the work interrupted the competition and prolonged slalom training. An especially aggressive racer could leave a hill strewn with half-fallen poles. If there wasn't time to make the pole upright, it became a dangerous hazard. In 1965 at Val d'Isère in France, Australian racer John O. Edgar impaled himself—a slalom pole pierced his thigh into his intestines and stomach, almost killing him. Splintering wood and bamboo occasionally punctured legs, arms, hands, and lungs. The injury risk was mitigated in 1969 by the introduction of a flexible plastic pole. Yet the challenge remained: how to make a pole that would remain upright throughout a race and not come out of the snow.

In 1979, Peter Laehy and Stefan Dag of the Aspen-based Rapidgate, Inc. patented a pole that bent on contact and sprang back into place. A Swedish pole, the Snow Feather, which hinged at the snow line, already existed. The safe, new poles were an instant labor-saving success, appreciated by hard-working trainers and gatekeepers. And they were eventually a boon for recreational racing, such as Nastar and coin-operated courses, since they reduced the manpower needed to run the races, and they reduced the potential liability for ski areas worried about the injuries that could be caused by the old-style poles.

The hinged pole made its debut in international competition in the 1980 World Cup races at Waterville Valley, New Hampshire, using the Reliable Racing Company's Break-A-Way pole. With the spring-back pole, racers no longer brushed the pole aside with their shoulders and hips. Now they aimed their upper body directly at the turning pole, slashing it out of the way. Still the poles occasionally came out of the snow. The problem was finally solved in 1987 by the Austrian-born U.S. coach Herman Gollner. A skilled climber, Gollner saw that the ice screw used in glacier climbing could be made to work as the slalom pole's tip. Twisted into the hole drilled in the snow, the threaded tip held the pole firmly in place. Gollner also patented a new kind of disc-like hinge (more on him in chapters 12 and 16). The International Ski Federation (FIS) adopted Gollner's pole as the standard, and it made its World Championship debut at Vail in 1989. Safety in giant slalom was enhanced with the introduction of a flag panel that broke away if a ski got caught.

When the hinged pole first came on the scene, racers used their inside arm to brush it aside. But with the introduction in the 1990s of shorter, shaped skis, carving a virtually non-skidded line, racers switched to using the outside arm to knock the turning pole aside. Almost the skier's entire body was now outside of the gate; only the feet and ankles were inside. There was little shoulder action. Arm and hand quickness became as important as legs, described by Gollner as "like skiing and playing tennis at the same time."[a]

The new slalom technique did not impact recreational skiing in the way, fifty years earlier, that the revolutionary reverse-shoulder slalom technique gave rise to popular wedeln, which dramatically altered the way people skied in the 1950s. The new arms-and-hands slalom technique has had virtually no influence on the way recreational skiers make their turns.

set up the one-third of the turn that was carved, because the turn-radius built into the ski's sidecut did not correspond to shorter radius turns on the snow.

Of course, if skiers wanted to carve the entire radius of the turn, it may be asked why manufacturers weren't making the sides of skis *more* curved? It took until the 1990s for the shaped ski to enter the sport's mainstream.[14] Witherell had been more prescient than he could have imagined. Advances in ski design now made it possible for recreational skiers to increase the amount of the turn they can carve in a way that was all but impossible for them in 1972 when he wrote his remarkable book. By the end of the twentieth century, slalom racers were making tight, one hundred percent pure carved turns on severely shaped 155-centimeter skis. The need for rotational and counter-rotational body action to turn the skis disappeared from discussions of technique, as did up and down body movement to unweight the skis. Old technique controversies vanished. Emphasis shifted to pressuring the ski fore and aft, and to transferring weight onto the outside turning ski early in the turn.

Just as newly designed skis and bindings enabled Sondre Norheim and the Telemark skiers to perfect the Christiana, so a hundred years later the shaped ski and the elevated binding platform revolutionized technique. Brandenberger, and Stefan Kruckenhauser in his New Official Austrian Ski System, and even Joubert, had been obsessed with body mechanics as the source of power for turning the skis. In golf, this would have been as negligent as attributing the ball's flight exclusively to the golfer's swing, unrelated to the clubhead, the club's shaft, or the dimpling of the ball's surface.

In the 1990s, intermediate and advanced skiers imagined they were making better turns as a result of having shaped skis. Mostly it wasn't true. They turned more easily because the skis were shorter and therefore easier to pivot, but they continued to make skidded turns, the way they always had. To truly carve a turn on the new shaped ski—that is, to arc an unskidded turn like the one made by snowboarders—it was necessary to change the way you skied. Good skiers adopted a slightly lower stance, projecting legs outwards so that the skis went up on edge, allowing their shape to induce the turn. It was a different way to ski, and first-time owners of the new skis needed to take lessons to learn it. Regrettably, the marketers of the "shaped ski revolution" neglected to tell them. It was as if Nike—comparable in size to the entire ski equipment industry—scrapped all of its models of running shoes and ordered up a new design, neglecting to tell customers that they needed instruction in order to run in them. Of course, the marketers could be forgiven. They may have been unaware that in any given winter 86 percent of skiers don't take a lesson.[15]

6

New Ways to Learn

From graduated classes to graduated length skis to graduate school psychology.

Ski teaching ebbs and flows. For a while, an accepted, uniform method of teaching may hold sway. Then it's determined that instruction needs to be saved from the death of stale orthodoxy. A tidal wave of change bores in. New gear, such as shaped skis and higher boots, demands the teaching of new movements. Or resorts cry that ski schools need to do more to attract and retain guests. The sport sprouts brilliant, surefire, exotic "new" ways for people to learn better, faster. Reformers appear, selling direct-to-parallel skiing, graduated length method, instant carving. They open special schools and traveling clinics. Their ideas invariably are fertilized in the pages of the ski magazines. But then the tide ebbs. It's determined that the new learning approaches don't work any better than those that they replaced. After trying them, the public loses interest. The organized instruction establishment, victorious again, takes the learning process back to the tried, if not necessarily the true.

Early Ski School: A Place of Discipline

The history of skiing is littered with teaching systems that have come and gone, including Arlberg, Swiss, Natural Skiing, new Official Austrian, American Teaching Method, French school, GLM, Natur Teknik, Inner Game, Centered Skiing, Center Line, Primary Movements, and more.

The first ski school to organize pupils systematically in classes, in which they learned a progression of skills, was created after World War I by Hannes Schneider at St. Anton in westernmost Austria, at the en-

Bend Zee Knees, Five Dollars, Pleez. The ritual of the group lesson has changed little since Hannes Schneider operated his pioneering ski school in the 1920s. This was the scene around 1978, as neophytes were herded into classes of eight to a dozen students for two-hour sessions. *Photo courtesy of United Airlines News*

trance of the Arlberg railroad tunnel used for many years by people traveling between eastern and western Europe. Schneider's Arlberg teaching system was in ascending order of difficulty.[1] The pupil first had to master the snowplow or double stem. Then came the single stem—a turn made with one ski. Then the stem christie, in which the skis are brought parallel to one another in the turn's final phase. A few progressed to where they could keep the skis parallel to one another throughout a turn, the mark of the expert. Schneider's genius was to have created a ladder of skills, each turn requiring a little more tolerance for speed.

Because his disciples had spread the Arlberg gospel far and wide in North America, Schneider's arrival at North Conway, New Hampshire, in 1939 did not especially expand his influence (see chapter 1). The Arlberg method was already solidly established. But it was not the only teaching method. The Swiss had perfected a solid teaching method, starting with Schneider's stemming, but also using sideslipping exercises to hasten the pupil's advance to parallel. Although it had American admirers as early as 1940 the superior Swiss system failed to gain a foothold . . . a loss for skiing in North America.

Just after World War II, in 1946, France's Emile Allais, world champion of 1937 and 1938, arrived in Quebec City, a couple of hundred miles north of where Schneider was teaching. Since 1939, a Swiss, Fritz Loosli, had been in Quebec City baptizing guests of the Chateau Frontenac in Allais's parallel turn. Now, lo, parallel's messiah had arrived! Allais was a superb ski school director. With his stylish hair and a deeply tanned face, wearing a foulard, Allais looked like a popular painter who might have a following of affluent buyers. Short and slim, he possessed a disarming modesty and intelligence. As for Allais's ideas, they were considered important enough that *Life Magazine* put him on the cover of its January 24, 1949, issue, with an illustrated article inside showing how to make the French parallel turn. Allais's ideas, however, failed to spread widely. Unlike Schneider, he left few disciples to proselytize for him after he returned to France in 1954.

Not that Schneider's influence prevailed either. By the time he died in 1955, the slow torquing action of Schneider's rotated stem turn didn't fit with the advances in binding and ski design that allowed wedeln — rapid, faster-paced turns made by quickly torquing the legs (see previous chapter). Furthermore, fewer vacationers were content to accept the idea that they must perfect skills at one stage before progressing to the next, as Schneider's system had insisted. Skiers wanted to ski parallel, to roam on the trails, and to enjoy a vacation without being micro-disciplined in the kind of school the Austrian maestro had invented. Anyway, why perfect a turn, the stem, that you were only going to discard later? After all, you don't learn to paddle by perfecting the action of rowing. Why not accelerate learning by starting right away with parallel turns?

Direct-to-Parallel: Getting Rid of the Stem

Vermont in the late 1950s was the spawning ground of two controversial systems of learning to ski that bypassed the stem turn and started pu-

Skip the Stem. Alternative teaching systems, starting in the 1950s, offered the beginning skier the chance to bypass the stem. The direct-to-parallel approach was difficult with 7-foot skis. Clif Taylor solved the problem by starting pupils on 32-inch skis. They could be turned by simply swiveling or twisting the skis with the feet. *Photo by Kim Massie*

pils immediately with their skis parallel. In the far northeastern corner of the Green Mountains, virtually on the Canadian border, Walter Foeger operated a unique direct-to-parallel ski school at Jay Peak, where he arrived in 1956. An affable sports teacher and tennis champion, the stocky Foeger had been influenced back in his native Austria by compatriot Toni Seelos, the man who perfected the first pure parallel turn. At Jay Peak, Foeger proceeded to teach beginners to ski with a system he called Natur Teknik, and he persuaded a dozen other ski areas to adopt it as well in their teaching. From the beginning, students learned to change direction by hopping the skis as they held them parallel to one another. Natur Teknik instructors were required not only to pass an on-slope examination, but also a long written exam, and God help any instructor who was seen stemming his skis!

Meanwhile, at the other end of the Green Mountains in the south, between Brattleboro and Bennington, Clif Taylor was teaching pupils at the Hogback ski area to turn with skis parallel. But they did it more easily than Foeger's pupils. Taylor's pupils used shorter skis, which were easier to pivot.

Taylor's idea was not new. Short-ski teaching began in the early 1950s at Karl Koller's Kitzbühel school in Austria, where learners started on 5-foot 5-inch skis. When they became skilled enough, they graduated to longer skis. When he started his own teaching in the winter of 1959–1960, Taylor claimed he was unaware of Koller's prior work. At any rate, the skis on which he started beginners were much shorter than Koller's skis—under 3 feet in length. The novice could turn them, not by stemming or hopping and body rotation, but by simply pivoting or twisting the skis with the feet.

At the time, the conventional 6-foot-plus ski was far more difficult to turn than today's shaped ski. A person needed to rise, or hop, in order to unweight them from the snow and turn them in a new direction, an act of coordination that the messianic Taylor believed was easier to perform with short skis.

With his 32-inch Shortees, Taylor advertised that "You can learn to ski in one day, the instant skiing way, safely under control, making parallel turns."[2]

In nearby Woodstock, Laurance Rockefeller was so enthused that he supplied Taylor with a loan of $30,000 to expand his Shortee ski company. Taylor traveled across America selling Shortees, teaching people on snow and on dryland decks.

Taylor was a veteran of the 10th Mountain Division fighting in Italy during World War II. Taylor survived. His face perpetually weatherbeaten, he had a laugh that was barely audible, a kind of wheezing "huh huh," accompanied by a broad smile and twinkling eyes, the whole effect of which was hilariously contagious. He was a born salesman who never met a ski hill or a girl he didn't like. His compulsive, exclusive interest in the subject of short skis led him into odd encounters. A story—perhaps apocryphal—has it that he and Howard Head once faced off at an industry trade show, each touting the virtues of his skis: Taylor's Shortees versus Head's Standards. Frustrated at his inability to dent Taylor's argument, Head brandished one of his 7-foot-long black metal skis, eyed the short ski Taylor was holding, and allegedly announced: "The trouble with your skis, Clif, is that they suffer from penis envy."

Taylor's proselytizing for ski shortness was reinforced by his ghostwriter Morten Lund, who focused attention on the idea that the pupil, while starting on short skis, ultimately should graduate to longer skis as his or her skill progressed.[3] But Taylor and Lund had the same problem that Foeger had: they lacked third-party, proven evidence that people could learn faster with length progression. In 1966, *SKI Magazine* decided to become the third party evaluating Natur Teknik and what was called the Graduated Length Method, or GLM.[4] At Killington, Vermont, the magazine compared experimental test groups of GLM-taught novices with students of similar age, sex, and athletic ability who learned via the conventional progression approved by the Professional Ski Instructors of America. The GLM group was found to progress faster than the conventionally taught skiers.[*]

As for Foeger, *SKI Magazine* conducted a study comparing his system with conventional classes taught at Sun Valley. The Natur Teknik pupils were found to be no more proficient at the end of a week than Sun Valley's regular pupils. An angry Foeger disputed the results. Curiously, though, no one seemed to be concerned that the Sun Valley pupils, who received the slightly modernized Arlberg form of instruction almost universal among novices at the time, did not perform better than the skiers who learned with the heretical, minority Natur Teknik condemned by the ski instruction establishment.

In the absence of certainty about which was the best way for people to learn to ski, resorts promoted their own systems. A maddening sort of Balkanization reigned. A person could take a week's lessons at one resort, only to go to another place and be told that he or she had to start over again using that resort's learning method. As early as 1950, Ford Sayre in Hanover, New Hampshire, an advocate of higher standards for certifying ski instructors, pleaded with ski schools to recognize the possibility that someone else's system had merits, "so that the first lesson isn't wasted in telling the skier how badly he was taught at another school."[5] Ideally, a skier should be able take a lesson at Cannon Mountain, New Hampshire, for example, and continue to learn in seamless progression at Sun Valley, Idaho.

The Effort to Unify Instructors

Even before Sayre's complaint, there were attempts to bring order out of the disarray. In 1938, Canada's instructors had formed the Canadian Ski Instructors Alliance, whose unifying influence strengthened in the 1950s

---

[*]In later years, as regular skis shortened, the idea of graduating in length in learning to ski lost its appeal. In the 1990s, the term GLM was briefly revived as the Guaranteed Learning Method. It proved, at least, that the money-back salesmen of ski instruction were still around.

under the professional leadership of Mont Tremblant ski school director Ernie McCulloch. In the United States, however, amateur associations controlled instructor certification. Regional and politically divided, they were unable to agree on a national standard. Finally, in 1960, the professional instructors arranged to meet on their own. Seventy-five ski school directors and instructors convened at the Alta and Brighton ski areas above Salt Lake City, where they discussed the creation of a unified American technique under the aegis of a national organization, not unlike the teaching arm of golf's PGA.[6] The Professional Ski Instructors of America (PSIA) officially came into being the next year, in May 1961.

Paul Valar was the natural choice to be the new organization's technical chairman. Tall and thin, his moving body parts easy to observe, Valar demonstrated technique so flawlessly that ski schools around the country pored over sequence photographs of his turns, the better to imitate him. "The new technique," announced Valar, "is skis parallel . . . turning initiated by the lower part of the body . . . reverse shoulder, but at the same time natural . . . without frozen positions or exaggerated motion."[7] The newly organized PSIA wholeheartedly embraced short swing, quick turns down the fall line, taking its cue from Kruckenhauser's New Austrian Ski System (see previous chapter). PSIA was way ahead of the old regional associations, and American skiing was way ahead thanks to PSIA.

"Our aim is for everyone to ski with similar form," said Valar.[8] In countries like Austria at the time, leading ski school directors agreed on the system to be taught, then made such agreements binding by law. A ski school director who failed to follow the agreed system could have his license to teach revoked. Such an authoritarian approach was unlikely to gain acceptance in America, the Swiss-born Valar conceded. Therefore, he purred assurances that an American ski school would be free to stay in or out of the system, but he also warned that those who stayed outside of the American Teaching Method would suffer in the long run.[9]

Four years after Brighton, by the mid-1960s, it was hard to find in organized instruction much of the freedom or tolerance that had been vaguely promised by Valar. Prescribed movements in an official technique book, written by a coterie of officials, became the basis of certification. Instructors unable to imitate precise hand and leg movements flunked the exam, however skilled they might be at teaching. Resentment rose. In 1965, western instructors were angered that the PSIA didn't recognize French split rotation (see previous chapter). Dozens of resorts that adopted GLM found it puzzling that the national association of ski instructors didn't support it. They believed that GLM would attract new people to the sport, and that the need for short skis would augment their equipment rental revenue. Indeed, Killington's ski school and rental business grew and local innkeepers filled more beds after the resort advertised that it offered GLM teaching.[10]

Vermont's Austrian-oriented Stratton Mountain ski school opposed PSIA's American Method of up-unweighting the skis to pivot the turn. Pennsylvania's Roundtop Ski Area found itself embroiled in a controversy over which of two men it should hire as the area's first ski school director. One candidate intended to teach up-unweighting, the other down-unweighting. "Not one of our directors or shareholders knew the difference," said Roundtop founder Irv Naylor, "so we didn't think our patrons would much care. We were right, they didn't."[11]

The narrow, doctrinaire arguments about how best to teach skiing irritated the leaders of major western resort ski schools, particularly Bill Briggs at Jackson Hole, French teachers like Joe Marillac at Squaw Valley, and the Mayer brothers at Taos. Aspen Highlands ski school director Fred Iselin hated the pedantry of instructors who insist there is only one way to ski. The good skier, he said, "is able to make variations of turns. You make a float turn, you make a swing, you make short turns and long turns, you jump over a mogul, you do a little wedel where it's justified."[12] Iselin mocked skiers who make only "little itsy-bitsy turns . . . techniques that only work on packed, easy slopes." At the time he had in mind wedeln, but he could have been talking about skiing's later obsession with carving.

A Swiss and a natural comic, Iselin produced an instruction book in collaboration with A. C. Spectorsky,* the editor of *Playboy Magazine*.[13] He believed that teaching people to ski is, at its best, a subtle blend of pedagogy and entertainment. At resorts, instructors were expected to mingle socially with guests after skiing.

PSIA had a different agenda. It wanted to build a profession to teach skiing, not cuckolding and drinking cocktails with students. Radiating *gravitas*, it encouraged the idea that the modern instructor should work regular hours like a lift operator. What mattered now was that you could go to a ski school almost anywhere, be taught competently, and find

---

*Spectorsky was not the only brilliant editor of a general magazine whose curiosity about the sport led to the writing of a learn-to-ski book. Little known among the accomplishments of Sir Harold Evans, the founding editor of *Conde Nast Traveler* and former editor-in-chief of Random House, is that he and a team of *London Sunday Times* editors and graphics people in 1974 produced *We Learned to Ski*, one of the most readable ski instruction books ever published.

yourself placed in a class suited to your ability, building on similar skills learned in a ski school elsewhere. But then instructors found themselves facing a fresh challenge—revolutionary new theories about how people learn sports.

Mind Tricks

No era offered more fertile ground than the 1970s for a revolution in learning theory. Tens of thousands of people were flocking to guru Werner Erhardt's EST seminars. The nation was in ferment over holistic thought and self-awareness. Esalen in northern California was a "metaphysical Grand Central Station, where anyone could choose the best train for his or her next personal destination."[14] Sports psychologists gathered at Big Sur for earnest discussions of the impending revolution. Neurologists were learning more about the brain's functioning. The left hemisphere was found to be verbally oriented, computer-like, and responsive to language. The right side processes spatial, visual, nonverbal input. People were found to possess a thought-oriented self, and a feeling-sensitive self.

The use of pop psychological techniques to improve ski performance first surfaced when it was revealed that Jean-Claude Killy had employed yoga to increase his power of concentration. In a 1968 experiment, the Swiss national team employed Jungian psychotherapist Raymond Abrezol to teach its racers techniques of mental preparation. Under Abrezol's guidance, a racer was instructed to focus on positive previsualization. "You take the course with tremendous speed," Abrezol repeated to a subject who was lying on a couch, his eyes closed. "With great confidence, you are absolutely in control. You know you are making a winning time!"[15] Racers would rise from the couch suffused with confidence. Prior to Abrezol, the Swiss hadn't won a single medal in Olympic and World Championship in ten years. Four years later they won seven medals at the Sapporo Olympic Winter Games, including three golds. As word of their training secret spread, more teams began to hire professional psychologists to enhance their coaching.

Professor Stefan Kruckenhauser also sensed that change was in the air. Austria's principal *skilehrer*, who in the 1950s had promoted the wedel revolution (see previous chapter), fifteen years later was aggressively promoting a different way to teach beginners. Kruckenhauser gathered thousands of sequence photographs and films of the crude uninstructed

Kids Teach Adults. The natural, untutored movements of children on skis led international instruction authority Stefan Kruckenhauser to promote the idea of a universal, rudimentary, open stance turn made by beginners. The unconscious way that children learn to ski partly inspired Tim Gallwey's popular Inner Game approach to teaching in the mid-1970s. *Photo by Barry Stott*

way that children ski. From the images, he concocted a simple, feet-apart, parallel turn that novices would learn on 4- and 5-foot skis. It was called the open turn (*offener schwung*), and later called *schwups*. It resembled the primitive turn instinctively made by children, who learn simply from watching and assimilating, and for whom verbal instruction is superfluous. But adults are full of rights and wrongs, of dos and don'ts that need words of remedy from professionals. In the environment of commercial instruction, adults would have to learn the child-like *schwups* with verbal input from paid instructors.

"Children learn faster because they don't think they know anything to begin with," said Tim Gallwey. "They don't have preconceived ideas about the right way to ski."[16] Gallwey was a California tennis teacher and the author of the runaway best-selling book, *The Inner Game of Tennis*. Grave, quiet spoken, a Harvard graduate, he resembled nothing so much as a priest who might have strayed into a sports clinic. Gallwey's central thesis was that the greatest enemy of learning the backhand or the serve is a mind cluttered with concepts and artificial performance goals. In skiing, learning's enemy is listening to second-by-second instructions of what to do with the knees, ankles, arms, and hips. Instead, skiers should

It's In Your Head. A couple of dozen ski schools in the 1970s adopted a mental approach to teaching—Inner Game, Skiing from the Head Down, Centering, Yoga, and more. The student was asked to visualize the turn in his or her mind. By the mid-1980s, such ski schools had dwindled in number, but their influence left a permanent mark not only on the teaching of recreational skiers, but also on the coaching of racers. *Photo © Jerry Leblond*

focus on mental images of how they want to ski and of how a successful, technically correct turn feels. Gallwey backed up his thesis with a book, *Inner Skiing*, paralleling his tennis book.

Many of the nation's ski school directors initially welcomed the shift away from over-verbalized lessons. Colorado's Copper Mountain started a program to make students feel the motions of skiing before they even put on skis. Standing in their boots, they were led, through kinesthetic feedback, to feel the shin and thigh pressures associated with pressuring the edges and with angulating and transferring weight. Pacific Northwest instructor Tim McKee created deep powder workshops based on the inner game. He pointed out how easily a skier tires on a long deep powder run requiring fifty or more turns. Legs tighten, breath is short. To reduce fatigue, he advised, you should listen carefully to the skis. By focusing on the lovely hissing of the skis slicing the deep snow and the gentle "whummp" of the turn in soft powder, your thighs and knees relax, you breathe easily. Effort gives way to relaxation.

An outpouring of books about alternative ways to learn the sport appeared in the 1970s. In addition to Gallwey's *Inner Skiing*, there was *The Hidden Skier*, written by the blond, personable freestyle star Corky Fowler.[17] His co-author Chris Smith, who had developed Hidden Skier Workshops, touted the notion that hidden within each of us is a talent, an individual style of skiing. In another book, *Skiing from the Head Down*, published by Lippincott, two psychologists presented skiing as a total mind and body experience, founded on principles of behavioral psychology and Eastern philosophy.[18] Yet another book, *Ski With Yoga*, emphasized the need to stay in shape mentally as well as physically.[19]

Perhaps the best known of the alternative teaching books was *The Centered Skier*.[20] The author, Denise McCluggage, an athletic, opinionated former race car driver and writer, was already interested in the application of yoga, tai chi, Zen, and the martial arts to skiing prior to Gallwey's appearance on the slopes. McCluggage's centered skiing, in fact, had a center. It was a point just below the navel. By controlling the skis not from the head and shoulders, but from the body's physical center, a skier could divert mental energy away from fear and misgivings, claimed McCluggage.

Horst Abraham, an Austrian native who trained instructors at the Vail resort, enthusiastically endorsed the thrust of inner game teaching. "The ski lesson becomes a meaningful experience, rather than a sequence of mechanical linkages," said Abraham, who had trained under the demanding Kruckenhauser and also had completed the rigorous French National Certification for instructors.[21]

Obstacles confronted the mental approach to ski teaching, however. For one thing, instructors who tried it discovered that they had difficulty in persuading adults to enter into a childlike trance. Skeptical students wondered why, "I'm paying all this money—and the instructor isn't telling me anything." Sugarbush ski school director Sigi Grottendorfer observed that his students, even though they were progressing, believed that he had no interest in their progress.[22] At Mount Snow, director of skiing Norm Crerar—who would one day head Interski, the international congress of ski instruction—worried that pupils might not grasp the inner game approach. "So just for the hell of it," Crerar reported, "I gave the whole lesson in Swedish, a language that no one in the class spoke. Everybody suddenly realized what the new idea was all about."[23] But it wasn't easy to rid instruction of verbal content. "Technical questions still are asked and must be answered," commented one inner skiing critic.[24] More was needed than a vague psychosomatic notion of skiing dynamics. There are practical details that govern how someone skis. The skier must understand how gouged running surfaces, incorrectly adjusted release bindings, and complexly adjusting or poorly fitting boots can interfere with learning. And safety is crucial. Skiing resembles sailing and climbing in that the participant must learn rules for avoiding injury, even fatal injury. A Zen-like silence doesn't really address the student's need for factual information. The physical insecurity of skiing has no counterpart in tennis or golf. Skiers don't stand securely on a flat surface, moving arms and legs. Rather, they must learn how to coordinate feet, legs, and upper body while accelerating down a mountain in the direction of a tree or a cliff. Fearful beginners instinctively lean into the hill, just as the novice climber intuitively clings to the rock instead of holding his body away from it. If a skier leans into the hill, the skis' edges won't grip. Is it simpler for the instructor to explain why in words? Or to demonstrate it wordlessly?

By 1984, the popular-psychology approach to ski teaching dwindled from more than twenty programs at various resorts to a handful. The Inner Game and other schools disappeared. The Professional Ski Instructors Association unceremoniously fired Horst Abraham, concluding that his ideas were too abstract. As director of Training and Education for the Professional Ski Instructors of America (PSIA), he had rewritten PSIA's American ski teaching manual. In place of a formal progression of turns—so long a fixture of ski teaching—his new American Teaching Method (ATM) advocated the learning of universal skills, such as edging, pressure control, and rotary action to turn. In an odd twist of fate, skiing's loss of Abraham's talent was U.S. industry's gain. With his knowledge of how people learn and how they overcome barriers to learning, Abraham went on to become a successful consultant to major corporations, including Motorola, Price Waterhouse Coopers, the U.S. Army, and Merrill Lynch.

Do Women Learn Differently?

The new psychological emphasis in ski teaching led to the question of whether women learn differently than men. In the early 1970s, the rising awareness of feminism created by Betty Friedan and others began to foster doubts in the minds of women skiers. Feminist critics claimed that the sexist environment in ski school was so bad that women were more likely than men to drop out of the sport. Hence arose the idea that segregated schools might expedite their learning. The pioneer of special instruction for women was Elissa Slanger, who in the winter of 1975 organized a five-day ski week, "Woman's Way" at Squaw Valley, California, in which women instructors, not men, did the teaching. It was one of the earliest adult women's programs in any sport. An ex–New Yorker, Slanger was the first woman examiner to be appointed by the Far West Ski Instructors Association. Slight of build, with a neat, short coif of hair, she set about convincing the world that conventional ski schools were not addressing the needs of women. She believed that a woman's different physiognomy—the tendency to be knock-kneed, for example—requires special attention. Besides, women ski and learn differently from men—not necessarily better or worse, but differently. Thus women err in using men as models when they learn to ski, claimed Slanger, who later trained as a clinical psychologist. She launched a traveling series of what she called "Woman's Way Ski Seminars," and wrote a book.[25] Subsequently, Jeannie Thoren and ex-racer Kim Reichelm launched their own women's programs. Perhaps they improved learning for women skiers. But the claim, repeated in the 1990s, that sexist attitudes were driving women out of the sport, was inaccurate. Indeed, a study by Jim and Joy Spring found women slightly *less* likely than men to drop out. And when they did quit skiing, it was usually for the same reasons given by men: lack of time and expense.[26]

Influence of Racing on Teaching

The setting in which people learn to ski has varied little over the years. Ungainly tip-crossing neophytes are herded into classes of eight to a dozen students. After a day, or perhaps five days, they emerge skilled enough to achieve what they want: to descend the mountain on pleasant trails while enjoying the scenery and the company of friends. Relatively few skiers elect to perfect their technique in advanced lessons. Even fewer are coached in racing, which is puzzling since racing over the years generated most of the techniques that instructors have come to teach—for example, counter-rotation, turn anticipation, starting the turn early on the edge of the outside ski, varying pressure along the length of the ski in phases of the turn. Why not teach racing skills to all skiers?

The vast majority of recreational skiers, however, are the equivalent of golfers remaining forever on the practice tee, or tennis players lobbing the ball back and forth across the net. They can ski proficiently, even elegantly, when they're able to choose anywhere to make a turn. But it's a different matter to go fast and turn at specific points, again and again coming down a slope, as a racer does going through gates.

In one of the earliest efforts to stimulate people to learn racing skills, Sun Valley in 1966 cordoned off a special slope, not too steep, dedicated to timing recreational skiers as they made runs through easy open gates.[27] The setting was the equivalent in golf of an easy par-3 layout. In reality, of course, skiing had no par. The absence of a handicap rating like golf's inspired me in 1968 to conceive of a program that would do just that: the National Standard Race, Nastar (described in chapter 9). Within three seasons, seventy-eight ski areas were staging weekly—sometimes daily—Nastar races.

The creation of Nastar raised the question: Why not incorporate it into ski schools as a measure of student's progress, complementing the instructor's assessment of the student's skills? Recreational racing lessons would train skiers to perform what might be called "the must-do turn," the ability to avoid another skier or a tree quickly. They would promote skills like gliding, skidding, drifting, pivoting, rebounding, absorption, and stepping, as well as carving, in order to get specifically from point A to point B. Such lessons would be attractive to better skiers, whose reluctance to buy traditional lessons is behind the statistic that only one in ten skiers enter ski school in any winter. At PSIA, only coach Willy Schaeffler was convinced that the organization, already famously resistant to innovation, should get behind Nastar. As it had with GLM, PSIA rejected Nastar and racing as a measure of skiing skill. It was odd, because the ability to race is considered so important in France, Switzerland, and Austria that instructors cannot gain certification without it. But not in the United States. (Well, not forever. In 2004, one PSIA division, the Rocky Mountain instructors, overcoming internal opposition, voted to make racing performance a condition of certification.[28])

Warren Witherell, in his 1972 book *How the Racers Ski*, was scathing in his criticism of the teaching establishment. "Watch a group of instructors at a certification exam," Witherell acidly noted. "They're incredibly self-conscious and constrained."[29] In contrast, he said, a racer's upper-body movements are naturally relaxed. It was not the kind of skiing he found among instructors, and especially among PSIA and its divisions, which did the certifying. They failed, in Witherell's judgement, by not emphasizing to students the primary importance of the ski as a tool for edging and pressure. "If you apply correct edge angle and pressure to a ski," wrote Witherell, "the ski itself will provide most of the turning force."[30] In a good ski school, he insisted, students would learn that railed edges (not flush with the ski's base) make it difficult to initiate a turn. They would learn the importance of tuning running surfaces. A competent ski school would insist that students who are knock-kneed or whose legs are bowed be equipped with underfoot wedges and canted boot shafts. So neglected was knee-to-boot alignment, claimed Witherell, that America was populated by "thousands of perpetual stem turners, who don't need lessons, they need wedges to flatten their skis in a natural stance."[31] No one, he later insisted, can ski properly without aligning the tibia properly over the ski.[32]

A Seasonal Profession

Through clinics, instruction manuals, and rigorous certification standards, PSIA and the regional instructor associations fostered advances in teaching the sport. But they were unable to advance the economic conditions of their members much. As late as 1994, only 7 percent of instructors made more than $10,000 a year from ski teaching.[33] For the majority it remained a part-time occupation. Outside of the big Rocky Mountain resorts, instructors in 1994 typically made only $2,500 from ski teaching, while making $78,000 from their main occupations as engineers, salesmen, contractors. In Austria, by comparison, two-thirds of instructors made enough money from full-time teaching in winter to support their families for half the year. The difference may lie in the fact that European ski schools typically are owned cooperatively by the instructors. American ski schools are typically owned and operated by the resorts, which operate them as profit centers. The ski school as pure business center takes little responsibility for certification and standards, while focusing on the bottom line, paying as little as possible in salaries and benefits, and charging customers whatever the traffic will bear.

Notwithstanding these difficulties, the modern ski school came to produce large numbers of competent parallel-turn skiers. The average man or woman on the slopes in 2000 skied a more proficient turn than the average skier in 1960, the consequence of the changes in equipment and technique described in the previous two chapters. The progress occurred in chicken-and-egg fashion. Manufacturers created new products such as fiberglass skis, elevated binding platforms, and canted boots, encouraging skiers to discover techniques to take advantage of the new technology. Or it happened the other way around. Racers experimented with new techniques to ski faster, which induced manufacturers to alter the design of gear so that they could execute a new technique better. Whatever, racing drove the agenda.

III

Alpine Competition

7

The World of Alpine Racing

The great medal winners—Sailer, Killy, Stenmark,
Girardelli—and how the World Cup changed
the measure of what it is to be a champion.

Success in ski racing is a matter of finding the shortest distance to the finish line from the starting gate, and skiing it at the highest velocity. The best line through the gates isn't necessarily the shortest; it also must be a line that delivers the most speed. Conversely, someone who skis at higher speed in a section of the course may lose to a racer who finds the shorter line. The difference may be a result of a minute action or a tiny variance of line, difficult for spectators, and even coaches, to observe. For periods from 50 to 130 seconds, the racer needs the leg strength of a weightlifter and the eye-foot coordination of a soccer player. He must possess a lightning-quick reactivity and a subtle feel for the snow. He must make rapid judgments at high speeds, and have the courage to face bodily injury at any moment. Skis and boots are as important as tires and engines are to race car drivers. Important are powers of concentration and of memorizing—retaining a mental image of the best route down a course created by forty or fifty gates. Technique becomes so embedded in the racer's muscle memory that he is able to focus on tactics—psychological and strategic. An unrelenting determination ... mental toughness ... is involved in each race.

Racing Before the World Cup

The racer who has won the greatest number of alpine gold medals—male or female—is Christl Cranz. Between 1934 and 1939, the German schoolteacher set a World Championships record, capturing twelve gold medals, plus one Olympic gold. A pre-war national—dare one say, National Socialist heroine—Cranz seldom lost a race in which she stood up, sometimes by margins as great as 10 seconds.

The first North American to cross the Atlantic and win a race in the Alps was Canada's George Jost. He did it in 1933 at the International University Ski Championships at St. Moritz, an amateur affair that attracted competitors from England, Italy, Norway, Switzerland, Austria, Germany, Yugoslavia, and Jost's own McGill University. He achieved his victory with a controversial technique of sitting back and riding on the seat of his pants in order to brake his speed. No one had seen such a ridiculous tactic before in a ski race, and the absurdity and ugliness of it in-

The World Championships, the Olympics, the World Cup, and the Combined

The FIS Nordic World Championships (cross-country and jumping) were conducted annually from their inception in 1924 until the outbreak of war in 1939. The Alpine World Championships (downhill and slalom), first held in 1931, also were staged annually until 1939. Following World War II, from 1948 until 1984, the World Championships were held every second winter, in even-numbered years. Starting in 1985, they took place in odd-numbered years, so that they no longer were held in conjunction with the Olympics, and a medal in the Olympics no longer counted as an FIS World Championship medal. The change arose out of a change in the Olympics, whereby the Summer and Winter Games no longer were conducted in the same year.

The World Championships and the Olympics were limited to three alpine disciplines—slalom, downhill, and giant slalom—until 1987 when the Super G and the alpine combined were added.

The Combined

The first FIS World Alpine Ski Championships in 1931 awarded medals only in downhill and slalom. From 1932 to 1939, the combined title was added, based on a statistical computation unknown to the author. The only thing about the alpine combined title that has remained constant over the years is that the result is based on a downhill race and a slalom race.

At the 1936 Winter Olympics, the alpine combined was the only result that counted—there were no separate Olympic medals for downhill and slalom.

The 1948 Winter Olympics and World Championships awarded medals for the best combined result of the slalom and downhill, but then the

furiated Arnold Lunn, who was serving as chief of race. Lunn wanted to disqualify Jost, but he was unable to find any rule expressly forbidding it. During the same winter, Jost, who was a member of Canada's Red Birds Ski Club, also won the Roberts of Kandahar downhill at Mürren.

After the war, the Fédération Internationale de Ski (FIS), short of funding and media support, decided not to stage its World Alpine Championships annually, as it had done before the war. It would hold them every second winter. When they coincided every fourth year with the Olympic Winter Games, the medals would count jointly; that is, if a racer won an Olympic gold medal, it was also an FIS World Championship gold medal.

title was dropped in 1950 and 1952 on the grounds that a third medal event, giant slalom, had been added. However, the alpine combined title resumed in 1954. Computation of the result was based on a mathematical formula of FIS points so arcane that only a few officials understood it. Starting in 1996, to aid public understanding, the combined result was simplified into a simple addition of the times of one run of downhill and two runs of slalom.

Since 1982, separate slalom and downhill races have been held for racers who want to try for a World Alpine Championship Combined medal. Separate combined races were introduced to the Olympics in 1988. Starting in 2005–2006, the World Cup calendar included Super Combis (SCs): a short downhill and one run of slalom raced on the same day.

World Cup

The 1968 Olympic and 1970 World Championship results counted for World Cup points, but afterward they no longer did. The reason for the change was that in the Olympics and World Championships a nation cannot enter more than four competitors in an event. The limitation deprived some racers of the opportunity to earn World Cup points. Eliminating the Olympics and the World Championships from counting toward World Cup points, however, diminished the World Cup, the equivalent in automobile racing of excluding Monte Carlo from the results of the Grand Prix. In juggling the point formula, the FIS also ruined any chance of comparing the performances of racers from year to year, impoverishing the sport's history. Fans and journalists today can't directly rate, for example, Hermann Maier's 1998 World Cup points against the 1967 points of Jean-Claude Killy. The basis for their calculation is totally different.[a]

The Greatest? Skiing like a cy-
clone, looking like a matinee
idol, Austria's Toni Sailer totally dominated alpine racing
between 1956 and 1958, winning races by margins as great
as five and six seconds. Sailer
was the first man to win all
the alpine skiing gold medals in a single Olympics. *Fri-
schauf-bild, Innsbruck*

St. Moritz, Switzerland, hosted the first post-war Olympic Winter
Games in 1948, only three years after Hitler had immolated himself in
Berlin. The St. Moritz games excluded German competitors and were
modest in scale. French racer Henri Oreiller won the downhill and the
slalom.

In 1950, the FIS World Alpine Championships were held at Aspen,
the first held outside of Europe (see chapter 3). The star was Italy's Zeno
Colo—the Alberto Tomba of his day—who won the downhill and the
giant slalom, a new competition, halfway in speed between slalom and
downhill.* In 1952, in the Olympics at Oslo, Norway, Stein Eriksen won
gold and silver and, two years later at the 1954 World Championships, he
won two gold medals, plus the alpine combination title, which is awarded
to the racer whose combined performance in slalom and downhill rates,
on paper, is the best.

The first skier to win all of the alpine races in a single Olympics was
Toni Sailer. The Austrian pulled off his Olympic gold medal hat trick at
the 1956 Winter Games with the explosive power of a fullback. The margins by which Sailer won his gold medals seem staggering: 3.5 seconds in
the downhill, a mind-boggling 6.4 seconds in the giant slalom, and 4 sec-

---

*The first giant slalom competition was held in Italy in 1933.

onds in a slalom set with a marathon ninety gates.* At the 1958 World Championships, Sailer almost repeated his Olympic hat trick, placing first in both downhill and giant slalom, and second in the slalom, and winning the FIS alpine combined gold medal. With jet black hair and a movie star's face, the handsome, six-foot poster-boy went on to act in films and, later, in television mini-series. Sailer's record makes him arguably the greatest champion in alpine ski racing history.[1]

In 1960, the Winter Olympics moved to the United States, where Canada's Ann Heggtveit won the slalom gold medal and the U.S. women two silvers at Squaw Valley. At the 1962 World Championships, at Chamonix, France, Austria's Karl Schranz dominated on a new kind of ski incorporating fiberglass and epoxy. The 1964 Olympic Winter Games, at Innsbruck, Austria, were notable for producing the first medals won by American men in alpine skiing, by Billy Kidd and Jimmie Heuga (see chapter 9).

In 1966, the FIS World Alpine Championships were not scheduled, as they usually are, in February. In a choice never since repeated, they were held in August in the southern hemisphere. At Portillo, Chile, France's racers won a record sixteen out of twenty-four medals. In the entire period from the end of World War II until Portillo, Austrian skiers had won more than sixty Olympic and World Championship alpine medals. The French defeat of Austria—historically alpine skiing's super-power—was not just a disappointment. For Austrians, it was a national disgrace. "It was Austerlitz all over again," wrote Europe's leading ski journalist, Serge Lang, in his typically florid style. "The great phlegmatic stuffed buffaloes of the Holy Teutonic Alliance were outflanked, surrounded, hectored, out-thought and picked serenely apart by the French. Honoré Bonnet played the part of Napoleon."[2] (Bonnet, the French head coach, did look remarkably like Bonaparte.)

Man Wins Women's Gold

The Portillo championships gave rise to one of the strangest stories in modern sports. The women's downhill gold medalist was nineteen-year-

---

*The time margins by which Sailer won can't be compared directly to later years, when speeds in races became greater. At the 1956 Olympics, his gold-medal winning time in the single-run giant slalom was 3 minutes. At the 1972 Winter Olympics, gold medal winner Gustavo Thoeni took 3 minutes 9.6 seconds for *two* runs of giant slalom! Sailer's winning margin of 6 seconds, however, was superior to Thoeni's 1.13 seconds.

old Erika Schinegger. The Austrian racer's life story came to be told in the book *Mein Sieg Über Mich*.[3] Intimate and honest, the autobiography pulled back the curtains on growing up as a young racer in the Alps, and on life in the glass house that is the ski champion's world. More important, it raised the tantalizing question of what defines gender in sports: the actual gender of the athlete, or the psychological and physical context in which the athlete competes?

Schinegger was born on a farm in Austria's Kaernten mountains on June 19, 1948—delivered by a country midwife who announced to the family after a cursory examination, "Congratulations, a girl!" Erika grew up to be a powerful skier, with curly brown hair, worn like a sloping straw pile, and with a deep voice. In the 1966 World Alpine Ski Championship downhill in the Andes, Schinegger catapulted herself down the steep course and beat France's Marielle Goitschel by an eighth of a second. Austria named Schinegger "Athlete of the Year." Her ski supplier Franz Kneissl presented her with a gold and diamond brooch. Her hometown promised her the gift of a building lot. She bought a Porsche. A young farmer mailed her a letter proposing marriage. Yet Schinegger was beset by doubts. She had never menstruated nor developed breasts. In training runs, she was often as fast as the men. "Anyone who out-skis me cannot be a woman!" protested a suspicious Karl Schranz, who turned out to be clairvoyant.

Prior to the 1968 Olympic Winter Games, athletes for the first time were required to take a gender test. When the results of the Austrian ski team's saliva tests came back, the examining urologist exclaimed, "I'm going crazy. There's a man racing on the ladies' team!" It turned out to be Schinegger. But if the reigning women's world downhill champion wasn't a woman, what was she? An abdominal incision soon gave the answer. Inside were male sex organs that had failed to descend during the mother's pregnancy at birth. After months of painful surgery, Erik Schinegger emerged from the hospital in men's clothes. At twenty-one, back at his home in Agsdorf, Erik became a ski instructor and fathered two children.

The FIS never took the 1966 downhill title away from Schinegger. It remains in the record book, as if there had been a tie for first place with Goitschel. FIS President Marc Hodler concluded that "the borderline between male and female is very thin. During the 1966 World Championships, Schinegger functioned as a woman."[4] The Canadian Academy of Sports Medicine thought similarly. "Individuals raised as females, who are psychologically and socially females from childhood," the Academy concluded, "should be eligible to compete in women's competition regardless of their chromosomal, gonadal and hormonal sex."[5]

The Invention of the World Cup

The Portillo World Championships were notable for another historical event—the announcement of a new annual competition, the World Cup of Alpine Skiing. Until 1967, no specific champions of alpine skiing had been crowned in the years when there were no Olympics or World Championships. Nor was there a season-long competition to determine who were the best racers. The only available measure was a complex system of seeding points introduced by the FIS in the 1950s. A principal purpose of the FIS point system was to regulate the starting order in races so that the better competitors would be assured of a good snow surface to ski on. FIS points were derived mathematically from performance in past races. The lower your points, the better you were, and the earlier was your starting position. The higher, or worse, your FIS points, the later you started and the more likely you coped with a course that was chewed up with ruts and the chatter marks left by the edges of prior competitors. Skiers world-wide were ranked by their FIS points.

The momentous shift to a popular way of measuring a season's results began in the winter of 1966 in Europe, with the creation of Challenge l'Équipe. The Austrians called it the Europa Cup. Skiers accumulated points in a series of races, and the winner at the end of the season was the racer with the largest total. Journalist Serge Lang, influenced by his reporting on the classic stage bicycle races of the Tour de France, saw it as the beginning of something much bigger: a winter-long competition, in which racers would gather points in the premier races around the world. Lang and his fellow journalists liked the idea because the almost weekly changes in the standings would supply grist for stories and attract readers. Lang also believed, as did the competitors, that performance in many races over a whole winter was a fairer measure than the results of only three Olympic or World Championship races.

Lang was a formidable figure, who appeared even more massive than his 240 pounds and height would suggest. His head was square and massive, and his eyes tightened into slits when he was angry, but he had gap-toothed and friendly smile. Lang had a harsh guttural voice, while his laugh was a squealing "hee hee hee hee," punctuating ridiculous stories that he told with relish, usually about bumbling ski federation officials.

New Way of Measuring Racers. A combination of journalist and impresario, Serge Lang created the World Cup of Alpine Ski Racing in 1966. His point formula measured the season-long performance of racers. Here, Lang presided over the presentation of the crystal trophies and the Nations Cup silver vase in 1986. *Photo at World Cup finale, 1986, Bromont, Quebec, from the archives of* Ski Racing Magazine

He already had been a journalist for more than twenty years. He wrote his hundreds of reports of ski and bicycle races in German, Italian, and French, and already spoke remarkably good English that became better with the passing years.

At Portillo, Lang won support for his World Cup idea from the U.S. Ski Team's alpine director Bob Beattie, who saw that it would enable the United States to host international races every winter, not sporadically as had been the case. Finally, FIS president Marc Hodler, the multilingual Swiss lawyer (who thirty-five years later achieved fame exposing the scandal of Olympic site selection at Salt Lake) gave the green light to launch the circuit the next season. It was already August, so the first World Cup season would start in a little more than four months.

The point formula for the first World Cup season, in 1967, demanded intensity and skill in all three alpine disciplines. There were to be seven slaloms, five giant slaloms, and five downhills. A racer's points would be derived from his or her three best results in each discipline. It was a little bit like draw poker, where the player discards a low card in the hope of replacing it with a better one. If a skier placed well in a race, the points he or she earned would replace a previous lesser result. A World Cup competitor, however, could not earn more than 75 points for the season in any one discipline. The closer a racer came to attaining 75 points in giant slalom, for example, the fewer were the points he would realize by entering more giant slalom races.* To gain better standings in the overall World Cup, he or she would be forced to turn to downhill and slalom. The goal was to reward the all-round skier, not the specialist. Although fair, the first World Cup formula was not easily understood. The *New York Times'* ski correspondent, Mike Strauss, whose regular beat was horse racing, complained that it was "too complicated" for the average reader to follow.

Lang visited me in my office in Manhattan, on a hot August day, en route from the FIS World Championships at Portillo to his home in Switzerland. "*SKI Magazine* should be involved in the World Cup," said Lang. "Why don't you present a trophy?" I conceived of a team competition—albeit a statistical one—using the World Cup points accumulated by each nation's racers. Year by year, the standings would compare how the alpine skiing nations ranked in strength. The next day, Lang stopped by my office, where I explained my proposal. The team whose racers aggregated the most points by the end of the season would win a trophy, called the Nations Cup. "It's good," he said quietly—so quietly that I couldn't tell if he was unenthusiastic, or sorry that the idea of the Nations Cup wasn't his own.

The initial World Cup races of 1967 were staged at Mégève, France; Adelboden, Switzerland; Kitzbühl, Austria; Berchtesgaden, Germany; and Sestrieres, Italy. In March, the entourage of racers, coaches, officials, press, and their mountain of luggage and skis flew to the United States for the first North American races at Cannon Mountain, New Hampshire. A new star, Jean-Claude Killy, led the new season-long competition. Fifteen thousand people—the largest crowd yet assembled for an alpine ski race in America—thronged the steep bottom slopes at Cannon. Newspaper sports sections took away space from the Boston Celtics' pursuit of another pro basketball title in order to report on the new races. Killy did not disappoint. He won all three: the downhill, giant slalom, and slalom.

---

*When World Cup races multiplied in number, the limit of winnable points in a discipline was increased from 75 points to 125 points.

From New Hampshire, the World Cup entourage flew west to Vail and onto Jackson Hole, Wyoming, for the final races of the season. A small plaque bearing the name of FRANCE already had been screwed onto the wooden base of the slender silver Nations Cup trophy, so far ahead were the French racers in the standings. With France's total of more than a thousand points, no possibility existed for the Austrian racers to catch up. Something had been learned already. In its slow, gradual, winter-long accretion of points by dozens of racers, the Nations Cup had as much suspense as a tortoise race. (In thirty-three winters from its inception to the end of the twentieth century, the Nations Cup was won twenty times by Austria, eight times by Switzerland, five by France. No other nation has ever won it.)

The individual men's World Cup season also lacked suspense. At Jackson Hole, as expected, a joyful Jean-Claude Killy, twenty-four, won the overall title. His season's overwhelming 225 points not only were double the total of his nearest rival, but they were the maximum that could be won. The women's overall World Cup, by contrast, was contested closely. Canada's Nancy Greene and France's Marielle Goitschel entered the winter's last slalom race with the fiercely competitive, feisty Canadian only 21 points behind the Frenchwoman. After the first run, only a fraction of a second separated the two women. In the second run, Greene took every risk, twisting through the flags, her edges rasping on the icy snow. When she flashed through the finish in a low crouch, her time was 7/100ths of a second faster than Goitschel's. The outcome of a whole winter of racing had been determined by a margin no greater than the blink of an eye! With Killy's spectacular triumph and the spectacular women's finish, no one doubted but that the new World Cup would be a success in the years to come.

Greene entered the record books as the first woman World Cup winner. A year later, at the 1968 Olympics, she won the giant slalom gold medal and the slalom silver, as well as the FIS World Championship gold medal in the alpine combined. No North American woman racer has ever matched her overall World Cup record—an achievement often neglected because all the racers of the time were so overshadowed by Killy. Shortly after she retired from racing, Greene married her former coach, Al Raine. She is a short, intensely competitive woman, an original, out-of-the-box thinker, a non-stop talker. She didn't have her autobiography ghostwritten, she penned it herself. Canada honored her by creating the Nancy Greene League. Modeled after America's Buddy Werner League, it fosters youth interest in alpine racing through team skiing.

First Woman to win the overall World Cup title was Canada's Nancy Greene. She won it a second time in 1968 when she was also a gold medalist at the Olympics in France. No North American woman equaled her record in the twentieth century. *Photo at Cannon Mountain, New Hampshire, by Peter Miller (petermillerphotograhy.com)*

After the Greene/Goitschel shoot-out on the slopes, the racers headed for Jackson Hole's famous Cowboy Bar. As they walked into the bar's dim interior, the racers encountered a counter about half as long as a football field, manned by bartenders willing to fill orders for any drink they wanted, from margaritas to boilermakers. Within an hour, the place was a Cuckoo's Nest, jammed with intoxicated competitors, coaches, and officials. Many had bought or borrowed cowboy hats, and with their deep tans they looked as though they had just ridden off the range. Having spent childhoods watching American cowboy films punctuated with barroom brawls, the Europeans knew how to strut and posture for the occasion. Killy and his best friend, downhiller Leo Lacroix, stood facing one another head to head. One guy would raise a plate and pretend to smash it over the other's head. They did this half a dozen times, laughing hysterically. The party was the beginning of an end-of-season ritual that continued on the World Cup.

Greater? A youthful Jean-Claude Killy in an appearance at Vail, Colorado, in the 1960s. He became the second man to perform the Olympic hat trick, winning all three alpine gold medals at the Winter Games at Grenoble in his native France. In the same winter of 1968, he won the overall World Cup title for the second time. *Photo by Barry Stott*

Jean-Claude Killy

Killy was unlike any ski champion who came before or after him. He was a cerebral athlete, who could win a race with insights and a creativity that his rivals lacked. He enjoyed extraordinary peripheral eyesight, a shrewd, calculating Savoyard mind, and an internal clock wired through his feet to the snow, by which he could tell how fast he needed to go to win a race. His smile was brilliant and he possessed a wry, sophisticated humor that triggered in him a joyous laugh. Yet he didn't look especially like a winter athlete. His narrow face often appeared sallow, affected by the amebic dysentery and hepatitis he contracted during compulsory military service in Algeria in 1962. He often appeared as shy and reclusive. In an unusually frank interview, he once explained why champion racers, like himself, were shy and why they were poor candidates for intense romantic love. "If you want to do the extraordinary," Killy said, "you have to concentrate on one thing at a time. A way to do that is by being very shy and having only one way to express yourself—through ski racing."

In a remarkable confession, Killy added, "And, by the way, being in love makes it impossible to be a consistent winner in skiing."[6]

At first Killy had a go-for-broke style of racing, which led to crashes and inspired coach Honoré Bonnet to advise him that he could become a great champion, "once you arrange to cross the finish line."[7] Illness was responsible for his lack of success at the 1964 Winter Olympics at Innsbruck. It so weakened him that it led him, he claimed, to ski in a different, more efficient way.

At the August 1966 World Ski Championships in Chile, Killy finally reached the top. He won the downhill and the overall combined title, making himself at twenty-three the world's best alpine racer. The feat was nothing compared to what he did the following winter. In the inaugural 1966–1967 World Cup season, he won an astonishing twelve of the seventeen World Cup races, including all of the downhills. In effect, he won 71 percent of the competitions on the calendar. (No racer has ever matched the feat. While Sweden's Ingemar Stenmark and Austria's Hermann Maier hold the record for most wins in a season—thirteen—they were thirteen out of thirty-three races, or only 39 percent of the winter's World Cup races.)[8]

Killy saved his greatest triumph for the 1968 Olympic Winter Games held in the mountains above the city of Grenoble, on the western edge of the French Alps. He won the downhill by employing what seemed like a trick at the time—one that became a standard starting procedure. Killy pitched his upper body down the mountain while his feet remained behind the timing wand. In effect, his body was moving downhill before the clock started. Because of a waxing failure, his margin of victory in the downhill was close, only 8/100ths of a second. But in the giant slalom, his winning margin—more than 2 seconds—was decisive. The most memorable event of the 1968 Winter Games, however, was the men's slalom held on the final day. At Chamrousse, in the mountains above Grenoble, the course was enveloped in fog. Flags drooped limply on the slalom poles, stirred occasionally by a breeze that momentarily might allow a lucky racer to see where he was going. The unlucky ones, unable to find an upcoming gate, would be disqualified. In the second and deciding slalom run, the pea-soup fog persisted. Killy ran first, enjoying good light on the first ten gates. "But nearly halfway down," he said, "the fog was tremendous. I slowed almost to a walk. About one-third of the guys disqualified there."[9]

At the finish line, the crowd waited for Austrian champion Karl Schranz to come down. After eleven years at the top of the international racing circuit, Schranz owned only one Olympic medal, a silver. A native of St. Anton, he seemed always to have an air of cunning about him. His eyes darted about and his face somewhat resembled that of the knave on a playing card. He had an aggressive, stubborn way of contesting rules, seizing on any circumstance that might give him an edge in a race, or in life.. The crowd was shocked when he failed to show up at the finish line. Schranz claimed that a soldier, or an official, had crossed his path. He demanded another run. Officials consented. Schranz returned to the top and proceeded to record a combined time a half-second faster than Killy. But the jury determined that his original second run had been invalid. Killy won his third gold medal.

Not long after the winter of 1968 melted into springtime, Killy retired, and his focus turned to making money. The truth—damaging if the International Olympic Committee's advocate of simon-pure amateurism, Avery Brundage (see chapter 8) had known—was that Killy had chosen the lawyer Mark McCormack to be his sports agent before he retired from "amateur" racing. McCormack controlled the lucrative product endorsement contracts of golfers Arnold Palmer, thirty-eight, and Jack Nicklaus, twenty-seven. Now Killy, twenty-five, became the agent's third superstar. ABC televised a special about what it's like to be a champion (Killy), pursuing new challenges—parachuting, racing cars, dating starlets. He was paid handsomely to appear in ads, although it's unlikely the indifferent Killy made much of an effort to wash his hair with Clairol shampoo or drive to the corner *boulanger* in a Chevrolet.

With Killy out of the picture, Schranz was able to win the overall World Cup title for two winters in a row. The French team remained strong, thanks mostly to its formidable women's team. France won the Nations Cup for three successive winters, 1971 through 1973. But ski teams, like empires, rise and fall. The French Ski Federation suffered from the kind of political intrigue that periodically affects the governance of national ski teams. Georges Joubert was brought in as coach in an attempt to revive the flagging men's team. The racers—abetted by Killy—denounced his coaching. Joubert eventually quit in disgust, or was fired. After 1972, France never won the Nations Cup again.

Seeking the All-Round Skier

Following the early success of the World Cup, the season-long competition fell victim to its own popularity. Resorts clamored to host World

Cup races because of the publicity they would generate. Pressured by member nations, the FIS added more and more races to the calendar. The season became longer, with one race piled on another. Serge Lang was unable to resist the bloating of the schedule by ski politicos seeking to satisfy the narrow interests of resorts and national federations. The FIS eventually allowed the number of World Cup races per winter to swell from the original seventeen races to thirty and more. The expanded schedule—cluttered with races from the Alps to the Rockies, from Scandinavia to Japan—came to be perceived as tediously drawn out. The press, which had played a role in creating the World Cup, pushed for ideas to keep the public excited. Journalist-founder Lang, abetted by FIS officials, proceeded to graft on innovations, such as splitting the season into three stages, thinking it would heighten fan interest. Points were doubled for anyone scoring downhill and slalom points in the same weekend.

Having to compete in more and more races reduced the time available to train. A racer could either devote less training time to each discipline, or decide to focus on only one or two. Manufacturers tended to reward the specialists, handing out more money to racers able to win the gold medal in one type of race—downhill, slalom, or giant slalom. They offered little financial incentive for overall success, while they poured millions of marks, francs, and schillings into developing sophisticated vibration damping, sidecuts, and flexes to meet the specific demands of a single discipline.

The changes led to an outcome that Lang and the FIS least wanted. The new overall champion, unlike Killy and Schranz, was no longer a potential winner in all three alpine disciplines. In the decade of the 1970s, Italy's Gustavo Thoeni, who raced infrequently in downhill, and Sweden's Ingemar Stenmark, who raced downhill not at all, were able to win seven out of ten World Cup overall titles. No less than 73 percent of the World Cup races in the decade were slaloms and giant slaloms.[10]

Shy, silent, and undemonstrative, Gustavo Thoeni was from a high, remote pass in Italy's South Tirol, where he spoke the local German dialect. Slight of build, with a deceptively hang-dog look, he lived a simple life, shunning the spotlight. Yet he won as many overall World Cups, four, as Killy and Schranz combined. His most remarkable victory was at the 1974 World Alpine Ski Championships at St. Moritz, where he won the giant slalom and came back from a monstrous 2-second, first-run deficit to win the gold medal in the slalom. Whoever set the course for the second slalom run must have had Thoeni in mind, as a composer

The Killy Start. Italy's Gustavo Thoeni was overall World Cup champion four times and double gold medalist at the World Alpine Ski Championships at St. Moritz, Switzerland, in 1974. In winning the giant slalom, he gained precious fractions of a second by launching his body down the hill before his boot tops hit the wand to start the timer, an innovative idea credited to Jean-Claude Killy six years earlier. *Photo by Margery Maltais from the archives of* Ski Racing Magazine

might have in mind a certain tenor when he writes an opera. The way the slalom flags were arranged magically resonated with Thoeni's skiing. What he did in the flags was not to race, but to fly through them like Peter Pan. His edges never rasped on the hard snow. Rather they bit delicately, lightly as he spun a turn. It was as if the gates weren't there, but just Thoeni executing a beautiful dance down the hill. When he flashed through the finish line, the crowd on the hill burst into applause. It was not so much for his second gold medal at the Twenty-third World Alpine Skiing Championships, but for a ballet on skis, the likes of which no one had ever seen.[11]*

Stenmark made the shy Thoeni seem comparatively gregarious. The Swede spoke sparingly. Each sentence he uttered appeared to drain him.

*Such runs are rare, but they do happen. Benno Rybizka wrote in *SKI Magazine* about a similar run that took place at the 1936 Arlberg-Kandahar, involving Emile Allais, Heinz von Allmen, and Friedl Pfeifer, the three greatest skiers of the age. While Allais and von Allmen slashed and hacked their way down the slalom, Pfeiffer's winning run seemed to have been accomplished without exertion. "He came dancing down ... with grace and ease ... so effortlessly, that he seemed to be not trying," wrote a marveling Rybizka. "Smooth, elegant, nonchalant, as if he were in no hurry." Rybizka, *SKI Magazine* (15 January 1949): 9.

He had expressionless eyes, set in a strawberry complexion face. His neat thatch of rusty blond hair never seemed to need combing or brushing. He and Phil Mahre competed at the same time as America's John McEnroe battled repeatedly on the tennis court with another taciturn, emotionless Swede, Bjorn Borg. Like McEnroe/Borg, the Mahre/Stenmark rivalry was relentless. Of nineteen technical (slalom and giant slalom) races in which they competed in the winter of 1982, Phil and Ingemar each won ten of them. On eight occasions when one of them won, the other was second, so close were they in performance.

Stenmark's turns were textbook-perfect. His upper body was solid and quiet when he skied, and he had extraordinarily powerful legs. Jean-Claude Killy remarked that Stenmark had something not possessed by prior champions like himself: "A very strong lower back and super-strong buttocks, almost abnormal. It allows him to drive his turns with less work from his upper body."[12] What Killy saw was a precursor of the muscular athletes who would dominate racing in 1990s — notably, Alberto Tomba and Hermann Maier.

Stenmark was three time overall World Cup champion from 1976 to

Unmatched Record. No racer, man or woman, has come close to matching the eighty-six World Cup victories of Ingemar Stenmark in a career that spanned fourteen winters, from 1975 to 1989. The Swedish racer notoriously didn't compete in downhill, provoking calls for reform of the World Cup point formula. *From the archives of* Ski Racing Magazine

1978. His unwillingness to compete in downhill was not something that the founders of the World Cup had in mind when they launched the season-long competition. The system was supposed to produce an all-round winner, skilled in all three of the alpine disciplines. The FIS decided to expand on a briefly introduced 1975 innovation: statistical combined results aimed at forcing racers into entering both downhills and slaloms. The expansion of combined points, installed in 1978–1979, practically was designed to cut Stenmark off from winning further titles, removing from contention the man who would go on to win the most World Cup races, eighty-six, of any skier in the history of the sport.* It was as if baseball shut the doors to its hall of fame to Joe Dimaggio because he refused to bunt.

In 1979, Switzerland's Peter Luescher took the overall title despite winning only one actual race. Luescher's strategy was to compete in all three disciplines and to try to place respectably in every race. His overall victory was ridiculed, although it can be argued that it was no different from cyclist Lance Armstrong capturing his seventh Tour de France title while winning only one stage race. The scoring system was there to be exploited by anyone with the strategic sense of how to pursue it. In the 1970s, Thoeni and Stenmark exploited the large number of slalom and giant slalom races to dominate the World Cup. Phil Mahre, Pirmin Zurbriggen, and Marc Girardelli did the same with the alpine combined in the decade 1981 to 1990, capturing all ten overall titles, in part due to the fact that they won twenty-five of forty-one combined competitions during the period.[13]

For a downhiller like Franz Klammer, who electrified the world with his famously televised gold medal run at the 1976 Innsbruck Olympics, no strategy would allow him to capture the overall title. There were not enough downhills in which to win points. The Canadian downhillers had no chance either. But over a period of nine winters ending in 1984, they won sixteen World Cup downhills. With the exception of 1959 Hahnenkamm winner Buddy Werner, no North American man ever had captured a classic European downhill title prior to the arrival of the "Crazy Canucks." Canadians Ken Read, Steve Podborski, and Tod Brooker proceeded to win every single major European title, including the Hahnenkamm at Kitzbühel, Austria (the equivalent in skiing of the Masters in golf); the grueling, long Lauberhorn at Wengen, Switzerland; and the Critérium des Premières Neiges at Val d'Isère, France.

*The woman racer with the most World Cup victories is Austria's Annemarie Proell, who won sixty-two times.

Streaker! Franz Klammer was the world's best downhiller between 1974 and 1978, winning twenty-one World Cup races. He was most famous for his spectacular, careening Olympic downhill gold medal win above Innsbruck in his native Austria, which thrilled millions of television viewers in 1976. *Photo of Klammer preparing to forerun the U.S. men's downhill championship race at Lake Placid, New York, 1979, by Wayne A. Emerick,* Ski Racing Magazine

Crazy Canucks. Over a period of nine winters, from 1975 through 1984, the Canadian men's team won sixteen World Cup downhill races. Previously, North American victories in downhill had been rare. First winner among the "Crazy Canucks" was Ken Read. *Photo—Paul Morrison*

The Solution—Super G

Serge Lang, who found a way to direct the World Cup competition even as he reported on it for newspapers, thought long and hard about how to give the speed-skiers a better chance. He concluded that the solution lay in creating a competition somewhere between the high-speed one-run downhill and the two-run giant slalom. He called it the Super G—faster and with fewer turns than giant slalom, but with more turns than down-hill. His thinking paralleled what had happened fifty years earlier, when racing officials had sought a competition to bridge the gap between sla-lom and downhill. It took seventeen years before giant slalom was intro-duced officially as a separate alpine discipline in 1950. Lang's new race took only six years to reach fruition. The Super G was introduced in 1982, and by 1988 it was an Olympic event.

Lang's idea seemed to work. Marc Girardelli seized on the Super G to win five overall World Cup titles in the nine winters spanning 1985 through 1993, scoring seven Super G victories as well as winning com-bineds. Of medium height and modest, the soft-faced, soft-spoken Girar-delli at a young age had been pulled out of the Austrian national team's training program by his father, Helmut, who became his coach, manager, and marketing agent. The wily, chain-smoking senior Girardelli arranged for his son to ski for Luxembourg, the tiny duchy in the decidedly non-skiing countryside adjoining Belgium. Over sixteen winters, Girardelli started in no less than 423 World Cup races, a record. His feat of piling up points allowed Luxembourg to rank high in the Nations Cup men's standings, even though the team had only one racer and one coach: Gi-rardelli and his father.

Girardelli and Stenmark, who also was virtually a one-man team, offer a perplexing answer to the question, what makes a champion? While the well-oiled, highly sophisticated machinery of the Austrian and the Swiss national ski teams won well over half of all the World Cup races between 1980 and 2000, on the other hand Stenmark and Girardelli won a total of 132 World Cup races without either one belonging to a functioning national team.

Girardelli was not the only racer to find the change in World Cup point scoring rewarding. The title began to go to all-round skiers such as Switzerland's Pirmin Zurbriggen and Paul Accola, Norway's Kjetil-Andre Aamodt, and Lasse Kjus, whose two gold and three silver med-als in all five alpine disciplines at the 1999 FIS World Championships is a record for men. As a result of a 1992 change in the World Cup point system, a single victory came to be worth 100 points, and there was no limit on the number of points you could win in a single discipline. While downhill and Super G specialists enjoyed a better chance at winning the overall title, half of the scoring opportunities were still in slalom and giant slalom. Alberto Tomba, a consummate gate skier, while winning the overall title only once, was second or third on five occasions, a record.

Champion Racers Become Older, Bigger

Girardelli stands out because his five overall titles were never matched in the twentieth century. His coach-father's stern hardness bred a hardness in the son. Many coaches found him, mentally, to be the toughest racer on the circuit. He was able to confront and overcome the harshest, most difficult hill conditions, willing to endure any pain. In one fall, he twisted his lower leg so grotesquely that it was at a 180-degree angle to the upper leg. All four of his knee ligaments were torn. European doctors hoped merely that the nineteen-year-old prodigy would be able to walk normally again. Girardelli was flown to the Steadman Clinic at Lake Tahoe, California.* Somehow, Dr. Richard Steadman put his leg back together and miraculously, Girardelli was winning World Cup races again the following winter.

The success reinforced Steadman's reputation as an authority on the anterior cruciate ligament (ACL), which was emerging as skiing's most common serious injury. In another amazing feat of surgery, Steadman repaired Steve Mahre's injured ACL so that only two months after the operation he won the giant slalom gold medal at the 1982 World Championships in Schladming, Austria. A few weeks after the gold medal, Mahre again needed surgery. Steadman performed another operation, and, amazingly, within eleven days, Mahre was able to race and win again. Not for nothing was the good doctor voted into the U.S. National Ski Hall of Fame.

The new surgery prolonged racing careers. The average age of a top-ten World Cup male competitor, twenty-three in 1973, rose to twenty-eight and a half years of age in 2004, a 24 percent increase. For women, the increase was even greater. The average top-ten female World Cup

---

*Steadman in 1990 moved his clinic to Vail, the cost underwritten by entrepreneur George Gillett, who correctly envisioned the value to the resort of having a medical star practicing in its midst.

racer rose in age to twenty-six, six years older than in 1973.[14] Austria's
Stephan Eberharter retired after he won the 2004 overall World Cup at
the age of thirty-four, in contrast to Jean-Claude Killy, who retired in
1968 when he was only twenty-four. Toni Sailer and Killy were on top
of their game for four seasons, whereas Stenmark and Girardelli enjoyed
fifteen-year careers and the Scandinavians Lasse Kjus and Kjetil-Andre
Aamodt competed even longer. True, the later racers were attracted by
money—the increased amount of product endorsements and of cash
prizes that didn't exist in Killy's era of FIS racing. But without the advances in knee surgery, many would have been unable to continue.

Michael Walchofer didn't win his first World Cup downhill title until
2005 when he was thirty years old, six-foot-two-inches in height and
weighed 220 pounds. The classic racer used to be short, lean, and an-
gular, and raced slalom on 210-centimeter skis. By the mid-1990s, the
new racer resembled a weightlifter standing on stubby 165-centimer skis.
World Cup 2000 champion Hermann Maier, known as "The Hermana-
tor" because of his resemblance to Arnold Schwarzenegger, who acted in
the *Terminator* movies, was the poster child of the new-age racer—someone who had massive muscles to hold an edged ski against what was once
overpowering centrifugal force. Bulging torsos—inflated by weightlift-
ing and, in a few cases, the ingestion of steroids and god knows what
else—made a Billy Kidd of the 1960s look like the scrawny boy in the
original Charles Atlas kick-sand-in-his-face advertisement.

The slalom racer took on the appearance of an imperial Roman guard
with the introduction of the hinged pole (see page 105). Tracing the
shortest line down a course became a jungle-like battle with the poles.
To protect eyes and arms, a whole array of gear was created—football-
style helmets with nose and chin guards, special pole handles and gloves,
elbow and shin protectors. Italy's Alberto Tomba donned a hard helmet
for giant slalom so that he could use his head to knock the pole aside.
Slalom speeds ratcheted up, as open gates were set 50 percent farther
apart. A slalom that took sixty seconds to run in the early 1980s was
being run in fifty-four seconds or less by 2000.[15]

Skiers from a handful of European countries dominated international
alpine racing from the beginning. Austria, a nation with less than three
one-hundredths of America's population, has produced the world's top
alpine ski team in two out of every three winters since 1952. Tiny Liechtenstein has spawned two World Cup champions, Switzerland nine. Many
of the greatest racers are from Italy's minor German-speaking Süd Tirol
region, and from France's compact, mountainous province of Savoie. All

are stars in the European sports firmament, as famous as the superstars of soccer. They garner six-figure incomes from endorsing products and from cash prizes for winning World Cup races. The opportunity to make serious money as an FIS ski racer—openly, not under the table—began only in the 1970s. How it happened shook the Olympic movement to its core.

How Skiing Changed
the Olympics

*Skiing's leaders battled hypocritical under-the-table payments
to athletes, and exposed Olympic site-bidding corruption.*

From the very first Olympic Winter Games involving alpine skiing, the
sport played the role of rebel and reformer. In the end, the strong voice of
skiing opened the door to professional athletes competing in the Olympics, and to a more honest process for choosing games sites.

Friction between the International Ski Federation (FIS) and the International Olympic Committee (IOC) started as early as 1936. At the
Olympic Winter Games at Garmisch Partenkirchen, Bavaria—officially
opened by Adolph Hitler—the IOC decided, against FIS protests, that
ski instructors were professionals, and therefore ineligible to compete.
Austria and Switzerland withdrew their top alpine racers and, as a result,
the 1936 Olympic men's downhill and slalom were not of the first caliber.
The absence of so many of the fastest, most skilled skiers paved the way
for the winning of alpine skiing's two races by a German man.*

The situation didn't improve as the years progressed. IOC chief Avery
Brundage, a man obsessed with the idea of pure amateurism, specifically regarded alpine skiers as a cancer within the Olympics because of
the money paid to them by equipment companies to use their products.
Taking the helm of the IOC in 1952, Brundage, a Chicago construction millionaire and former Olympic Summer Games decathlon athlete,
determined to cleanse alpine ski racing, or possibly throw it out of the
Olympics altogether. He met his match in Sir Arnold Lunn and in International Skiing Federation (FIS) president Marc Hodler, who became
FIS President at the same time as Brundage took over the IOC. Across

---

*As an example of the caliber of competitor missing from the 1936 Olympic ski races, *SKI
Magazine*'s March 1951 issue reported, in a profile of Austrian coach Toni Seelos, that he had
forerun the slalom five seconds faster than Franz Pfnur, the gold medalist.

He Ruled Skiing. For forty-seven years—a record unmatched in any international sports governing body—Marc Hodler ran the International Ski Federation (FIS). A multilingual Swiss lawyer, he fought to persuade the International Olympic Committee to allow racers to receive money, compensating them for the long months of training when they couldn't hold a paying job. The FIS eventually won out, paving the way for professional athletes to compete in the once-amateur Olympics. *Photo, Vail, 1989, by Peter Miller (petermillerphotography.com)*

a span of the next twenty years, the men fought over ski racing's role in the Olympics.

The hypocrisy of alpine ski racers being paid, even as they swore they were amateurs in order to be eligible to compete in the Olympics, enraged Lunn, slalom's inventor. It was causing young people to commit perjury, Sir Arnold said. "Fake amateurism . . . encourages young athletes to think that there is no particular harm in telling lies."[1] Marc Hodler, for his part, contended that skiers differed from track and field athletes and swimmers. Skiing, he said, entailed costs for training beyond the reach of normal wage-earners. To train on distant glaciers in summer and race all winter, the racers had no opportunity to hold a paying job. They therefore should be compensated for "broken time"—time when athletes in other sports were able to hold down paying jobs.

Fighting the crusty, autocratic Brundage must have been a painful experience for Hodler. He hated public controversy, favoring deftly contrived agreements quietly arranged in private meetings. A Swiss lawyer from Bern, Hodler grew up skiing in Mürren, where Lunn had invented modern slalom. His thinning black hair framed a pancake-flat face, set atop wide-set shoulders. He had the Swiss manner of talking quietly with a reasonableness that could make a listener with a contrary viewpoint seem like a troublemaker. He was a tack-sharp linguist, who could make a speech in eight different languages.

Hodler headed the FIS for forty-seven years, a record tenure for the chief of any international sports federation. I occasionally interviewed him at the attractive resorts chosen by the FIS for its congresses—in Nice on the French Riviera, at Opatija on the Dalmatian coast of the former Yugoslavia, on the Mediterranean island of Cyprus, and in Bariloche on the Argentine side of the Andes. The congresses were engaging, entertaining meetings of people, whom Hodler thought of as "family." The FIS family was an idea dear to his heart. The family enacted regulations, such as the length of jumping hills, the size of commercial logos permissible on helmets, and the switch of giant slalom from a one-run to a two-run competition. If Hodler, the *paterfamilias*, smiled warmly at you, you felt good about belonging to his FIS. No one seemed to know how much money the FIS took in, nor how much it spent. Hodler refused even to share with FIS council members the decision about who might one day succeed him.[2] Committee members who wanted reimbursement for their expenses incurred in traveling to meetings would track down Hodler in a hallway. Smiling, he would extract a massive wad of Swiss francs or dollars from his pocket and graciously hand the amount due to the committee member. No one ever questioned Hodler's integrity and there was never a hint, as there was later with sports officials like IOC President Antonio Samaranch, of financial irregularities.

Among the highest-ranking IOC officials, Hodler was regarded as the unofficial leader of the Winter Games. On the other hand, Brundage, a competitor at the 1912 Summer Olympics, didn't care for the Winter Games. It wouldn't have bothered him at all if skiing, which he regarded as a professional sport, were dropped from the Olympics.[3] His pallid face radiating obdurate, imperious conviction, he believed that any alpine skier, even someone who'd been paid a paltry few dollars to teach the sport, should be banned from Olympic competition. But he was unable to muster sufficient votes within the International Olympic Committee to overcome a majority headed by Hodler. Nor did it help Brundage's credibility that he didn't complain about Scandinavian jumpers and cross-country racers who regularly earned prize money and perks.

For Hodler, the solution was to legitimize the payments that alpine racers were receiving under the table from manufacturers. He proposed that the skiers receive the money indirectly, through their national ski federations. In theory, it would leave the competitors untainted. They would have money for training, while their Olympic virginity remained intact. That was the theory. In practice, the top racers would continue to receive money privately from the makers of their skis and boots and bindings. "The top skiers are not so stupid as some people seem to believe," Serge Lang wrote in 1969. "The national federations will negotiate endorsements *and* the skiers will continue to get under-the-table money."[4]

The knowledge that the top alpine racers were receiving the illegitimate payments so angered Brundage that he spoke about it at the 1970 annual meeting of the U.S. Ski Association. It was as if a convention of doctors had invited an injured plaintiff to talk to them about malpractice. The IOC chief proclaimed that skiers were cheaters, and he repeated his demand that the racers of the 1968 Grenoble Olympics return their medals to the IOC.[5] Later, he said that Swiss star Roger Staub, France's Marielle Goitschel, America's Suzy Chaffee, and thirty-seven other skiers should be barred from the 1972 games in Japan.

It didn't happen. Brundage faced the obstacle of his own commercial doing. His IOC had sold television rights to the Sapporo Games to NBC for $6 million, partly on the premise that alpine skiing would be a star of the show. The TV networks needed to recover the cost of the expensive rights fees they were paying to the IOC by selling commercial time. Restaurant chains and car companies advertised their products between interviews with Gustavo and Franz, the medal winners. If Brundage had expelled the alpine racers from the games, he would have stripped the show of its stars, undermining—possibly violating—the IOC's own television contract. He was, as they say, hoist with his own petard.

In the end, Brundage was able to expel only one racer from the Sapporo Games. That expulsion became the single most riveting occurrence at the 1972 Winter Games, which began as noisily and angrily as they had ended in France four years earlier. At Grenoble in 1968, Karl Schranz had accused Killy and the FIS of stealing his slalom gold medal (see previous chapter). The rancor of 1968, as if fresh frozen, was now being served up as a blue plate special to journalists at Sapporo. In the new version, Schranz was still the centerpiece, but this time the villain was an eighty-four-year-old American autocrat who was denying the most famous ski racer, from the world's best known ski racing nation, his final chance, at age thirty-three, to win an Olympic gold medal. Schranz was paid well by the ski manufacturer Kneissl, in whose advertising he prominently appeared. How could Brundage and the IOC officials, he demanded, "understand the real-life situation of top racers and their problem of getting compensated for broken time, when these officials have never been poor?"[6] Schranz's comment, on the eve of the Sapporo Games, infuriated the IOC's millionaire American president. Under intense pressure from Brundage, the IOC voted 28 to 14 on January 31, 1972, to expel Schranz from the Winter Olympics. The expulsion shocked the sports world. Austrian newspaper headlines screamed in protest. The national ski team should quit and come home with "Karli." However, the reality was that Schranz wasn't especially popular among his teammates, and it was no surprise when the Austrian racers did not walk out with him, but left on the bus to go to their downhill training. Back in Austria, though, anger mounted. One official, who supported the IOC's vote to expel Schranz, found tens of thousands of bottles of beer sent back to the brewery he owned. Schranz flew to Vienna. Hordes of people lined the streets to welcome him home.[7] Not even President Kennedy had drawn such a crowd. The hated Brundage was burned in effigy.

In an attempt to appease Austria, the FIS promised to hold a separate 1972 World Alpine Ski Championships after the Olympics, in which Schranz would be eligible to compete. The federation later reneged on its promise. Schranz's expulsion did little to scare off the top racers. Six months after Sapporo, thirty of them were on the Island of Elba enjoying a two-week vacation at a luxury resort—all expenses paid by the Salomon binding company.

Schranz had competed aggressively for more than fifteen winters on the international race circuit, beginning in 1957 when he won the prestigious Arlberg-Kandahar competition at the age of eighteen. Sapporo was the end of his racing career. It was a very long time to remain on top in ski racing. Citing Schranz's longevity and victories, Serge Lang, just before he died, regarded him as the greatest of all racers, superior to Sailer, Killy, or Stenmark. Yet the fierce, ramrod-erect Schranz had to live with the fact that he had won only one Olympic medal in his career, a silver in 1964. After Sapporo in 1972, he retired. He signed on with Mark McCormack's sports management firm, International Management. There was talk that he and Jean-Claude Killy, in their retirements, would compete in head-to-head races, and that he would join Bob Beattie's pro circuit in America. Spider Sabich, who won the pro title in 1971 and 1972, loved the idea. "He's the perennial bad sport, and we need someone . . . to be a heavy." said Sabich. "Plus . . . he's controversial and he's colorful."[8] It didn't happen. Schranz's home town offered him enough inducements, including directorship of the prestigious Hannes Schneider Ski School, to remain in St. Anton.

Brundage would have felt vindicated had Schranz turned pro. A professional circuit, he believed, was where the alpine racers belonged. But the best of the Austrian, French, and Swiss World Cup racers weren't about to abandon the FIS World Cup circuit and rush into the corporate arms of American pro racing. After all, they were competing on a pro circuit of their own. On the FIS World Cup circuit, "*shamateurs*" were paid handsomely by equipment sponsors, and their costs of travel and training were compensated by their national federations. They could net more than if they were racing on the American pro circuit, where they would have had to pay their own expenses. Moreover, as skiers on their national teams, they were rewarded with part-time jobs, often as customs agents.

Schranz's expulsion from the Sapporo Games, far from indicating a return to the amateur ideal in the Olympics, turned out to be its funeral. It was a watershed event in the history of the Olympics. After the games of 1972, Brundage stepped down as IOC president. He was succeeded by (Lord-to-be) Michael Killanin, a genial Irishman who communicated well with FIS president Hodler. By 1974, Killanin engineered a revision of IOC athlete eligibility rules that were almost identical to what the FIS had long demanded. Olympic athletes could be paid the amount of money they would have earned during the period when they were training and competing. The IOC came to embrace the idea that athletes should not have to suffer financial deprivation in order to compete for medals. Their names and pictures could be sold for advertising, with the proceeds paid to them via their national associations. Thereafter, the way opened for national sports federations to do their own sports marketing. Limits on ski racers making money came to be replaced by limits on finding money to pay them. "We got rid of the lying," said Hodler.[9]

After Antonio Samaranch succeeded Killanin in 1980, the Olympic gates opened fully to professional athletes. Even a superstar team of millionaire professional basketball players became eligible to compete.

Choosing Winter Games Sites — Scandal, Politics

Paradoxically, while Brundage insisted on simon-pure amateurism for the athletes, he accepted the idea of Olympic host cities and sports federations selling lucrative sponsorships to multi-national corporations, such as Coca Cola and General Motors. It was not okay for athletes to wear commercial logos, but okay for a host city to display them.

Skiing exerts a powerful influence over the selection of the Winter Games sites. Ice skating and hockey arenas can be built anywhere, but the credibility of the alpine competitions requires that the host city be near challenging mountain terrain. The 1960 Winter Games at Squaw Valley, in retrospect, were ideal—in a remote mountain setting, and blessed by sun and fine snow. No squads of businessmen cajoled International Olympic Committee members to vote for the small California ski resort. Its owner Alex Cushing almost single-handedly won the campaign to host the games, even though his ski area had one chairlift, a rope tow, a single lodge, and a serious lack of public awareness of its existence.

How did he do it? "We won with a purely intellectual idea," said Cushing. "There was a need to return the Olympics to simplicity. It shows the power of an idea, particularly when we had nothing."[10] Cushing, who possesses a personality that swoops mercurially from icy aloofness to disarming charm, stumbled on the idea of hosting the Olympics when he learned that Reno was bidding to be the U.S. candidate for the 1960 games. He decided to make his own application. "It was a way to get publicity," he admitted.[11] Gathering assurances of financial and government support, the six-and-a-half foot Cushing, forty-one, won the approval of the U.S. Olympic Committee, and in a few months he found himself in Paris confronting the International Olympic Committee. The IOC was ready to rubber-stamp Austria's Innsbruck. (St. Moritz, Garmisch, and Karachi, Pakistan, were the other candidates.) As for Squaw Valley, a U.S. delegate went so far as to sneer at Cushing. "Who's going to vote for you? I'm not."[12] But the IOC's voting power came from a collection of oleaginous minor European nobility and third-country bureaucrats. They were enchanted by the thatch-haired, lantern-jawed Cushing, whose social training at Groton and the phony corridors of Park Avenue society perfectly equipped him for the task at hand. He played the IOC members like a violinist stroking a Stradivarius. He wined and dined them. He made an impressive last-minute plea for their votes. Finally his persistence and panache won. In a narrow 32 to 30 ballot, the IOC chose the tiny California ski area over the city of Innsbruck. Skeptics predicted disaster. "Cushing," warned Avery Brundage, the crusty IOC chairman, "you're going to set back the Olympic movement twenty-five years."[13] Brundage believed that only a major city could host the games properly. As it happened, the next three Winter Olympics were hosted by the cities of Innsbruck, Austria, in 1964, Grenoble, France, in 1968, and Sapporo, Japan, on the northern island of Hokkaido in 1972. The French and Japanese governments poured billions into building roads and infrastructure around Grenoble and Sapporo, leaving taxpayers to grumble for years about the cost.

The next U.S. bid to host the Winter Games also came from a city, Denver. After first promising nearby ski sites, the organizers were forced to admit that the ski competitions in 1976 would have to be moved to sites more than two hours distant from the Olympic Village in Denver. The nordic competitions would be in Steamboat Springs; Beaver Creek would host the alpine events. The idea of locating competitions a hundred miles distant from the host city was unprecedented in Winter Games history.[14] Feeling betrayed, IOC members favored taking the games away from Denver. They didn't have to act. Colorado taxpayers did it for them in 1972. By approving an amendment that forbade the spending of state tax money on the Olympics, voters effectively withdrew Denver from the Winter Games. For one thing, they didn't care for the environmental impact on their state from the development surrounding the Olympics. Nor did they like the inept way in which the organizing committee, often short on facts and solutions, had promoted Colorado's candidacy.[15]

Whether it was Denver's failure, or the monstrous cost of the 1968 Grenoble and the 1972 Sapporo Games, the trend to large-scale urban Winter Olympics slowed for a while. The IOC sensibly shifted the 1976 Games back to Innsbruck, where facilities from the 1964 Games could be re-used. When Lake Placid succeeded in winning the 1980 Olympics, it was mostly because other cities didn't want them. Such an infusion of publicity and money normally would be expected to restore the flagging economy of almost any rural backwater. The Winter Olympics merely left Lake Placid a slightly gentrified tourist town in continuing search of wintertime affluence. Grey Sarajevo in Yugoslavia won the 1984 Games. Eight years later, much of the besieged Bosnian capital and the skiing venue on Mt. Bjelasnica were destroyed in the ethnic warfare that ravaged the former Yugoslavia.

The desire of cities to host mega-games is puzzling. Comparable to the notion that a sucker is born every minute is the quadrennial prediction by politicians—encouraged by audacious, avaricious developers—that the Winter Games will bring lasting benefits to any city that bids for them. Whether it was Sarajevo, Lillehammer, Nagano, or Grenoble, most Winter Olympics have wound up costing taxpayers a mountain of money and they have left behind questionable lasting benefits. To host the 2002 Winter Games, Salt Lake City required $1.3 billion in highways

Last of the Small Winter Games. At the 1980 Winter Olympics at Lake Placid, New York, ceremonial balloons rise into the sky against a backdrop of the Adirondack Mountains. The lure of sponsors, soaring television rights, and the alleged need for massive infrastructure caused the Winter Games to shift to larger urban sites. Bribery entered the site-selection process, shaking the Olympic movement to the core. *From the archives of* Ski Racing Magazine

and infrastructure, yet its downtown is only slightly less nocturnally moribund than it was before.

Bigger municipalities became Olympic sites not because they were better for the athletes, but because cities, not winter resort towns, have the financial resources to generate more money for the IOC and the international sports federations. They also have five-star hotels, which comfort-seeking IOC members and VIPs insisted on.* Cities could float multi-million dollar bonds to fund mega-amenities. Official sponsor and television network revenue paid off the bonds. Urbanization intensified commercialization.

When it was realized that the selection of the sites was infected with corruption, it was the International Ski Federation's leader who publicly blew the whistle. Marc Hodler became the number-one contact for the

---

*In 1991, IOC vice-president and FIS president Marc Hodler, to the embarrassment of the ski community, was quoted during a Salt Lake City press conference, as saying that the availability of five-star luxury hotels for the IOC and VIPs would be a factor in selecting sites for the Olympic Winter Games.

press in exposing the corruption involved in the IOC selection of Salt Lake, and possibly other cities, as sites of the 2002 Winter Games. Hodler knew whereof he spoke. The FIS recently had exposed its own failure to detect the bribes offered to its voting members by cities bidding to host the FIS World Alpine Ski Championships. But that wasn't all. Hodler was bitterly irked by the IOC's insistence on holding the 1998 Winter Games at Nagano, Japan, known for its poor snow conditions and an inadequate downhill course. Why had Nagano been chosen? Why Salt Lake four years later? When it was clear that vote-buying was involved, as it had been in skiing's own championships, Hodler spoke in his capacity as chairman of the IOC's Coordination Commission for Salt Lake. He exposed the IOC's wound to the media in order to be certain, in the glare of publicity, that President Samaranch would not find a tactical opening to evade reform, and because, as he said, "that when there is fear and disgrace, revolutions become possible."[16] Once again, a skier had revealed a shabby deception within the Olympic movement. First it had been the hypocrisy of condemning under-the-table payments to athletes. Then it had been the IOC's concealment of the venal Olympic site selections. Both crises led to reform of the Olympics, thanks to skiing's influence.

9

Racing in America

The rise of the U.S. Ski Team, Nastar, ski academies,
and professional racing.

Alpine racing was central to the culture of American skiing during the
sport's most rapid expansion before the 1970s. Ski clubs formed around
the agenda of competition. The ski magazines were filled with previews
and results of Olympics and World Championships, and lively athlete
profiles. Andrea Mead Lawrence, Buddy Werner, and Billy Kidd were
among the heroes. Robert Redford built a film career partly on the success of a movie set in the world of racing.

Women Racers Led the Way

Before 1970, when no man from the United States or Canada had ever
won a gold medal in Olympic and World Championship alpine racing,
women had already won eight. In 1948, Gretchen Fraser was the first
American to win an Olympic medal in alpine skiing. Andrea Mead Lawrence was the second.

Andy Mead grew up in Vermont's Green Mountains between Killington and Rutland. Her parents owned the Pico Peak ski area, where
she scooted up and down the mountain just about every winter day of
her childhood. She joined the U.S. Ski Team before her fifteenth birthday, making her the youngest U.S. Olympic ski team member in history.
The team was headed for St. Moritz, Switzerland, site of the first Olympic Winter Games held after World War II. In the slalom, Sun Valley skier
Gretchen Fraser, whom the press labeled "housewife" and who was thirteen years Mead's senior, shocked the alpine nations by winning the gold
medal. Mead managed to place eighth. In the 1952 Olympics, four years

Double Gold. In 1952, Andrea Mead Lawrence, a nineteen-year-old recently married American, shocked Europeans by winning two gold medals at the Oslo Winter Olympics. Her double win stood as a North American record for at least another half-century. It was closely matched in 1958 when Canada's Lucile Wheeler won two gold medals at the World Alpine Ski Championships. *Photo courtesy of Kästle Ski Company and Andrea Mead Lawrence*

later, it was a different story. By then, she was considered America's top woman racer, appearing on the cover of *Time Magazine,* and precociously, at age nineteen, she was the bride of Dartmouth racer David Lawrence.

The 1952 Winter Games were held outside of Oslo, Norway. Andrea skied the one-run (at the time) giant slalom race so smoothly and efficiently that she won by 2.2 seconds. She had her first gold medal. Winning a second gold medal came less easily. She fell and failed in the downhill. In the slalom, her first run was almost a disaster when she hooked a tip on a gate, forcing her to scramble back up the hill. Amazingly, she made up the lost time in the second run, and America had its first Olympic double gold medalist in skiing—a record that Andrea could still claim entering the twenty-first century. It was the climax of her racing career. The 1950s were an era when home-making and babies were uppermost in a young woman's mind. About the time that the gold medals were draped around her neck in Oslo, Mead Lawrence became pregnant, and in January 1953 she bore the first of five children in a span of seven years. Even though pregnant again in 1955, she won every race she entered, although unable to travel to Europe.

Mead Lawrence's prospective successor on the ski team was Jill Kinmont, an eighteen-year-old skier from Mammoth Mountain. The strikingly beautiful Californian, with short blonde hair and a pretty turned-up nose, appeared on *Sports Illustrated*'s January 31, 1955, cover. The day after Kinmont saw herself on the cover, she suffered a catastrophic fall in a race at Alta, severing her spinal cord at the level of her lower neck. She would never walk again (see page 260).

Prior to her accident, Kinmont had been linked romantically to two of America's most colorful racers of the 1950s, Dick Buek and Buddy Werner. Mad Dog Buek was a man who feared no hill, found no speed too fast. Green-eyed, wiry, with long brown hair, he performed crazy aerial stunts in his biplane. In 1953, he motorcycled into a car, rupturing his spleen, shattering a knee, mangling a leg, and taking 250 stitches. A year later—bent and twisted—Buek raced in the U.S. nationals, schussing hellishly down Aspen Mountain—wearing a cast on his mangled leg. Scoring the fastest time, he earned the title of 1954 U.S. national men's downhill champion!

Buek adored Kinmont. She, aware of Buek's wild, reckless lifestyle, was skeptical of his marital suitability. Her attention turned to a boy her own age, eighteen-year-old Buddy Werner, a rising ski star from Steamboat, Colorado. Buddy and Jill, until her accident, were the glamorous teenage champions of the U.S. Ski Team.[1]

By 1970, North American women had amassed twenty gold, silver, and bronze World Championship and Olympic medals. Quebec's Lucille Wheeler won two gold medals and a silver in the women's 1958 FIS World Alpine Ski Championships. Canada's Ann Heggtveit, 1960, and Nancy Greene, 1968, were Olympic gold medalists. The first two North Americans to win World Cup races were not men, but women—Greene and Kiki Cutter of the United States. While 45 percent of the skiers on the slopes are women, in North America they've won 75 percent of the Olympic and World Championship medals awarded for alpine racing.

Why were the U.S. and Canadian women more successful in international competition than the men? One theory holds that the girls grew up in a society that subordinated women less than did European society, and so they were more assertive and competitive. They also may have been more successful than the boys because neither the girls nor their parents were concerned that dedication to racing would lead to the loss of a college education, robbing them of future income and status. American boys were expected to go to college, and the academic obligation put them at a disadvantage against European men, who dedicated themselves to racing as a vocation.*

Struggle of the Men

The obstacles facing American racers before and after World War II were formidable. Funds to compete in Europe were meager. The budget for sending the entire U.S. Ski Team to the 1956 Olympics at Cortina d'Ampezzo, Italy, was only $37,500. Racers Ralph Miller, Brooks Dodge, and Tom Corcoran were released from regular military duty so that they could train for the Olympics. Families and wealthy skiers often functioned as philanthropies, underwriting the expenses of individual racers. The U.S. Ski Team would hire a coach—more like a manager—for a period of several months before an Olympics or an FIS World Championships. The job was temporary, and professional coaching experience wasn't necessarily required.

Despite these challenges, North American men performed respectably. In 1950, Jack Reddish placed fourth in the slalom at Aspen. At Oslo in 1952, Bill Beck was only two places away from a medal in the downhill. Brooks Dodge was the fourth best skier in the alpine combined at the 1954 World Championships. Buddy Werner placed fourth in the slalom and fifth in the giant slalom at the 1958 World Championships. At the 1960 Winter Olympics at Squaw Valley, Tom Corcoran was one place away from a bronze medal in the men's giant slalom. Brooks Dodge lost out on a medal in the disputed 1956 Olympic slalom, in which his Dartmouth teammate, Japan's Chick Igaya, placed second. (Dodge and U.S. Ski Team coach Bobo Sheehan officially complained that Igaya had missed a gate.)

Like many champions—Jean-Claude Killy, Ingemar Stenmark, the Mahre twins—Dodge grew up at the bottom of a ski mountain, just as champion golfers are likely to grow up within walking distance of a golf course. In Dodge's case, the mountain was Mount Washington, in New Hampshire. Dark-haired and handsome, he was canny and perceptive. He understood the aerodynamic drag created by loose clothing before European racers did and had the idea of hiring an Austrian tailor to make trim, more tightly fitting pants for the U.S. Ski Team. Rather humorless,

*After 1980, American male racers came to resemble their European counterparts in making ski competition a full-time career.

he never attracted the public adulation that the charismatic Buddy Werner did when he succeeded Dodge as the U.S. Ski Team's top racer.

The pre-eminent American skier of his era, Werner in 1959 won the world's most difficult downhill, Kitzbühel's Hahnenkamm, the only American to do so in the twentieth century. The winter before, Werner won the Lauberhorn combined downhill and slalom at Wengen. A leg fracture prevented him from competing in the 1960 Winter Olympics at Squaw Valley. Tom Corcoran wrote of Werner:

> He was a symbol. To the racers—junior and senior—of this country, he represented all that is good and wholesome in the sport. In Europe, where his popularity bordered on mystique, he was an ideal emissary for America. With the exception of the Olympics, where a medal always eluded him, there was hardly an important race in the world that he had not won. His skill was exceeded at times by his raw courage. He rode a faster ski and held a tuck longer than the others. There was only one Buddy Werner. You never confused him with another skier.[2]

Almost all of the U.S. Ski Team members were college students, and at times the team seemed almost indistinguishable from Dartmouth's.[3] For North American men, time spent to earn a university degree was believed to exceed the value of a world championship medal. It was a view supported by Corcoran, himself a Dartmouth grad. He advised any racer who'd dropped out to return to college. "If you procrastinate," wrote Corcoran, "you'll end up a plain ordinary ski bum with a wife and kids, a few laughs and no race or academic record to show for the time you've wasted."[4] Corcoran rejected the notion that academics were an obstacle to success in racing. "Racers may not need as much time to train as they think they do, if their training time is used to the fullest. An hour of intense practice is better than a week of fooling around—and most independent racers (not studying at college) do a lot of fooling around."[5]

Most people disagreed with Corcoran. The notion that a young man or woman could train and race and attend lectures on campus and take exams was as unrealistic as supposing that an Austrian skier could regularly milk his cows and tend bar in his *Gasthof* while winning at venues from Kitzbühel to Stowe. Two decades later, no college students would be among the Olympic medalists on the most successful of all U.S. Ski Teams—at Sarajevo in 1984.

Two changes in the early 1960s ultimately transformed the culture of North American racing. Racers, with or without a college degree, could find post-career jobs as equipment reps, coaches, and instructors, remaining in the sport. And the top racers migrated to the West, or developed there. Both changes coincided with the rise to power of Bob Beattie.

Bob Beattie Takes Charge

"From the time I was a kid, I wanted to coach sports," said Beattie.[6] As an education student at Middlebury College in the 1950s, he was mentored by the college's beloved ski coach, Bobo Sheehan (father of professional golfer Patty Sheehan). When Bobo was named coach of the 1956 U.S. Olympic Ski Team, Beattie took over the Middlebury team's coaching. A year later, he became head ski coach of Colorado University (CU), his salary subsidized by also coaching football. The western colleges at the time offered athletic scholarships on a scale unmatched at the eastern snow-country colleges, with the consequence that young men serious about competing now began to migrate to Beattie's CU. Or they headed to Denver University (DU), where Willy Schaeffler coached. The two men feuded bitterly. It especially irritated Beattie that Schaeffler's DU could win the National Collegiate Athletic Association's (NCAA) championships—a four-way competition involving nordic as well as alpine skiing—by stacking his team with imported Scandinavian jumpers and cross-country skiers. Nevertheless, Beattie coached CU to NCAA championships in 1959 and 1960, interrupting a string of DU wins.

Beattie's success caught the eye of an important U.S. Ski Association volunteer official, Dr. Bud Little, a Helena, Montana, physician. In the fall of 1961, Little hired him to be the national team's first full-time head coach. Beattie continued to serve as CU's coach for another three winters, further bolstering the belief among racers that Colorado was the place to go if you wanted to earn a berth on the U.S. Ski Team. The shift of power to Colorado angered the New England ski establishment. The U.S. Eastern Amateur Ski Association in 1967 authorized spending $50,000 to strengthen its racing programs; the Vermont legislature considered spending $50,000 to develop better skiers in the state's schools. (The bill didn't pass.) Neither initiative halted the westward migration.[7]

Few figures in athletics have held sway over their sport in such diverse ways over so many years as did Bob Beattie. He became skiing's combination in a single person of Vince Lombardi, Pete Rozelle, and Howard Cosell. In the 1960s, after he became the men's coach and alpine program director of the U.S. Ski Team, he helped to create the World Cup of Alpine Skiing, ensuring that the world's best racers would come annually

Coach, Czar. Few figures in athletics have held sway over their sport in such diverse ways over so many years as did Bob Beattie—coach of the national ski team, co-founder of the World Cup, television commentator, ski team fundraiser par excellence, czar of pro racing, National Standard Race Commissioner. *From the archives of* Ski Racing Magazine

to North America. He later caused the National Standard Race (Nastar) to spread to 120 ski areas. When he controlled professional ski racing in the 1970s, he gave the pro circuit national visibility. For at least twenty years, on ABC sports and ESPN cable, he was television's best-known ski commentator. History will judge Beattie to be the most important seminal figure in the development and promotion of organized ski racing in America. Yet coaching—his chosen profession—produced for him mixed results.

When he took over the U.S. Ski Team, Beattie wanted his racers to be tough. And tougher. He subjected them to football-style drills designed to drive them to exhaustion. This was a different kind of regimen from the past, setting a higher standard of physical condition required for a member of America's national ski team. But there was more. Beattie made it clear—wearing his football coach's hat—that he wanted above all to win. The racers needed always to do better. Often, better was not considered good enough. Did the intensification of training produce success? At the 1964 Winter Olympics, the first two men's races—downhill and giant slalom—produced only doubts. The best result was a fifth place by Werner.* Beattie had to worry about the possibility of failure

---

*Werner died without ever winning an Olympic or World Championship medal. Two months after the 1964 Olympics, when he was skiing near St. Moritz before the cameras of movie maker and skiwear manufacturing scion Willy Bogner, Jr., Werner and German racer Barbi Henneberger were swept to their deaths in an avalanche.

right up until the final day of the games when the men's slalom took place. On the rock-hard, icy course, Billy Kidd enjoyed the fastest first run. Jimmie Heuga, with bib number 24, raced so well that he earned the third starting position in the second run. They were set up for a shocking achievement. The two came in second and third behind the gold medal winner, Austria's Pepi Stiegler, who would soon emigrate to Jackson Hole, Wyoming.

With Kidd's silver and Heuga's bronze, Beattie understandably felt vindicated. Joyous, laughing, he wrapped his arms around the shoulders of his two young racers. It was the moment awaited since the end of World War II—the winning of America's first Olympic and World Championship medals in men's alpine skiing. Television and the press trumpeted the triumph. It was the acme of Beattie's coaching career. His physical, demanding approach arguably supplied the margin of improvement over the near-medal wins in the past by American men. The moment was portrayed as a breakthrough of American men's skiing, the sudden attainment of a higher level in international racing. In slalom it was. In 1966, Jimmie Heuga was fourth in the World Championship slalom, and in the 1968 Olympics the U.S. placed three men in the top ten—the best slalom performance by any nation. Whether Kidd's and Heuga's 1964 medals were a genuine breakthrough, though, is arguable. It was more like a continuum of the sporadically satisfactory U.S. results in men's alpine skiing that endured from the end of World War II until 1980. (After the silver and bronze of Innsbruck, a full sixteen more winters elapsed before an American male skier won another Olympic medal! That was in 1980 when Phil Mahre won a silver in the slalom at Lake Placid.)

The American women racers laid down a somewhat better record. At the 1964 Innsbruck Olympics, Jean Saubert won two bronze medals, while disavowing any connection between her performance and Beattie's coaching.[8] At the 1966 World Championships, America's only medal was a bronze by Penny McCoy, daughter of Mammoth Mountain's Dave McCoy, who almost single-handedly mentored an entire generation of great American women racers. Most of the girls on the 1966 U.S. Team were McCoy protégés.

Olympic double gold medalist Andrea Mead Lawrence, who kept in touch with the racers by reporting on the 1964 ski events for ABC television, thought Beattie insensitive to women, and she found little to like in his coaching. "Beattie's approach was demoralizing," said Lawrence. "He beat up on the racers. He didn't raise them up, he knocked them down."[9]

In his on-hill coaching, Beattie, like his star racer, Kidd, saw the arms as the key to a successful turn. By stretching the outside hand around and forward and keeping the inside hand low, the racer's shoulders, hips, knees, and ankles automatically fall into the correct position. He called it the Dynaturn. Simplifying the use of the hands, Beattie said, freed the skier to focus on terrain and gates and see the best possible line to go fast. It was hugely useful advice for any racer to follow. The trouble began when Beattie gave the impression that the Dynaturn was a startling universal technique. Dave McCoy, whose own children were on the team, charged Beattie with oversimplification. "Skiing is a continually changing thing," said McCoy. "We all have different physiques and different instinctive technique approaches to getting down the mountain. Part of coaching is finding the right words, seeing each skier separately, and helping him develop further in the way natural to him. This is what Beattie's method can't do."[10]

One reason for America's inability to match the performance of state-subsidized European ski teams, insisted Beattie, was that the U.S. team lacked sufficient money for training and travel. He persuaded the U.S. Ski Association to undertake the raising of an unprecedented $450,000 for the 1965–1966 season. It would be the second-largest development budget for any amateur sport in the United States, and a monstrous increase over the previous budget for a non-Olympic season, 1962–1963, when the ski team was forced to get by on only $33,000. "After Defeat, $450,000!" was the headline over an October 1965 column in SKI Magazine.[11] Yet despite the infusion of money, the U.S. men's team failed to improve, prompting the acerbic ski-pole manufacturer Ed Scott to suggest that he write a column, "After $450,000, Defeat!"

If such a column really had been published, Beattie would not have been amused. He was notably prickly about criticism. Beattie's arguments invariably were reinforced by a reddened face and raised voice. He was a master, like John McEnroe, of the controlled tantrum. The Beattie tantrum was actually a powerful negotiating tool—and exactly what U.S. skiing needed. He forced European officials, as no one had been able to do before, to listen to American demands, such as realizing a fairer basis of determining the precious points needed to gain better starting positions. He was a guy whom it was impossible to ignore.

Under Beattie, the post-retirement career goals of racers changed. Ski team members once had studied for a profession, such as medicine or engineering. The new racer had a potential future in the ski industry. Going into trade, so to speak, was no longer regarded as a career misstep.

The change can be measured in a couple of examples. Tom Corcoran went to the Harvard Business School, while Jimmie Heuga sold boots for the equipment importing firm, Beconta. Ralph Miller, a 1956 Olympic downhiller, went to Harvard Medical School, while Billy Kidd became Director of Skiing at Steamboat. As in Europe, operating a ski shop or promoting a resort became a desirable post-racing career. Beattie caused young American racers to perceive the national ski team as a door to opportunity, not just an interruption of college or a career dead-end. He brought fresh vigor to American coaching. He understood the importance of developing grass-roots talent. Admirably, he didn't scurry into corners evading blame for failure. He elevated public awareness of racing. The U.S. Ski Team began, for the first time, to raise money, not in the thousands, but in the tens of thousands of dollars. He created the Buddy Werner League, modeled after Little League baseball, aimed at identifying promising young racers.[12]

How to Find Young Talent?

The Kidd and Heuga medals of 1964 were presented as confirmation of the idea, encouraged by Beattie, that medals justify a strong, centrally funded and controlled national ski team. But neither Beattie's coaching nor his successful fundraising produced any more men's medals in 1966 at the World Alpine Ski Championships, nor in 1968 at the Olympics. And while the U.S. team eventually ranked third in the 1969 and 1970 Nations Cup standings, thanks to its women's squad, it was a weak and distant third, far behind the mighty French and Austrian teams. At this point, the coach himself may have begun to have doubts. After he retired in 1969 and turned to television work and the development of pro racing, Beattie asked, "Is a national team really the most effective way to bring the United States to the top of international racing? The question," he wrote, "sounds strange coming from a coach like myself who spent nine years trying to develop a strong national team."[13] But he believed there had to be another way. He suspected that national programs put a lid on new ideas. The remedy, Beattie suggested, was to disband the national team and to decentralize. He preferred swimming's model of success in creating Olympic medalists through autonomous programs such as the one at Santa Clara, California.

Are champions developed locally, or through powerful national programs? History offers no clear answer. But, as with the Santa Clara swim

Ski Academies. After 1970, many top U.S. Ski Team racers came from the
ranks of students attending specialized academies where they can train and
race while achieving a high school diploma. *Photo of Rowmark Ski Academy,
Utah, from the archives of* Ski Racing Magazine

team, the key is to identify talent at an early age. In 1970, at Burke Mountain, Vermont, Warren Witherell founded the nation's first ski academy
(see chapter 5). Witherell was aware that the historic obstacle to recruiting young American racers, especially males, is the worry that their education may suffer. He saw that the agenda of the conventional high
school didn't allow aspiring young racers the time openings they needed
to train. A ski academy—combining education and skiing—would create, he believed, the base of talented athletes needed to make America
competitive in racing. Similar schools catering to youngsters with athletic ambitions, funded mostly by the state, existed in Europe. Witherell's was a riskier proposition—a private school with parents paying fees,
supplemented by hoped-for philanthropy. He succeeded. Within a couple of years, ten Burke Academy students or graduates were members of
the U.S. Ski Team. Eventually the school that Witherell founded spawned
more than twenty similar academies across the United States.[14]

National Standard Race

Another approach for identifying young racing talent came to involve
Beattie himself. For many years, resorts such as Sun Valley, Mont Trem-

blant, and Stowe conducted standard races for guests. A participant could compare himself to others who had been in the race, but not directly to someone who wasn't in it. By contrast, a consistent 10-handicap golfer knows that on any day, on any course, he's likely to play ten strokes better than a 20-handicapper. Why not create the equivalent of par in skiing? In the winter of 1967, I conceived the national standard race, to which I gave the acronym "Nastar," copying the idea from a formula used in grading French ski instructors.[15] Times in a race were converted into percentage differences. Instructors from around the country would be brought together at the beginning of the season and rated against the top national racers of the time. Equipped with percentage ratings, they would then go back to their home resorts as pacesetters.

It would work as follows: If pacesetter Klaus at Mount Snow was originally 3 percent slower than the nation's fastest racer, and a Mount Snow guest was 20 percent slower than Klaus, then he or she would be about 23 percent slower than America's fastest skier would have been if he'd skied the Mount Snow course that day. Presto! The skier would have a 23 handicap. The sport of skiing could enjoy the equivalent of golf's par! A skier would know that on any slope anywhere, skiing through a couple of dozen gates, on a surface that could be sticky or icy, it didn't matter, his or her rating would be valid. If he had a 23 Nastar handicap, he would be 7 percentage points better than a guy with a 30 rating. The possibilities seemed limitless. You could make the results of races around the country equivalent to one another. You could take two equally rated skiers and put them in an exciting head-to-head race. You could have a competitive experience on a 300-foot vertical Michigan hill equivalent to one at a Rocky Mountain resort. Nastar was launched at eight ski areas in the 1968–1969 season.

At first, U.S. Ski Team director Bob Beattie didn't support Nastar, since he was busy concocting his own five-year, multi-million dollar Buddy Werner League aimed at identifying young talent. But a year later, no longer with the ski team, Beattie took over the operation of Nastar under license from *SKI Magazine*. Unfortunately, there was still no chance of tying Nastar closely to ski youth development because Beattie was temporarily *persona non grata* at the U.S. Ski Team. The team missed an opportunity. Fifteen winters later, prodded by Beattie, who was now also pro racing impresario and a national sports television commentator, Nastar grew to 135 areas, attracting a quarter of a million recreational racers each winter. Nastar clones sprouted in Canada, Scandinavia, Switzerland, and Australia. In liftlines and in base lodges could be heard the excited voices of thrilled intermediate skiers who had raced for the first time in their lives. Children boasted about winning a bronze pin. Gradually the U.S. Ski Team began to track the Nastar handicaps of sub-teen racers, looking for future Billy Kidds and Bode Millers.

The U.S. Ski Team Spirals Downward

In 1969, Earl Walters, a Salt Lake contractor, exploited the United States Ski Association's fractious, regionally dominated political structure to wedge his way in as its president. At USSA, the governing body of the ski team, Walters conducted a furious housecleaning, firing a slew of coaches and staff members.[16] He especially alienated Beattie, who was the head alpine coach *and* the team's best fundraiser. Beattie quit, or Walters fired him. The distinction is immaterial. Walters verified the observation that when it comes to the volunteer governance of amateur sports organizations, cream rarely rises to the top. Walters' alienation of former supporters and his absence of fundraising skills left the ski association virtually bankrupt.

USSA temporarily hired Don Henderson, ski coach at the private Holderness School in New Hampshire, to lead the U.S. Ski Team to the 1970 World Alpine Ski Championships at Val Gardena, Italy. The women's squad was talented and youthful. It was a period distinguished by racers such as the Nagel sisters—Cathy and Judy—the Cochran sisters—Barbara Ann and Marilyn—Kiki Cutter, Susie Corrock, Suzy Chaffee. The men's team, with little depth, was inconsistent at best. The exception was Billy Kidd from Stowe, Vermont. Not for nothing did Tom Corcoran correctly predict that Kidd, while a less exciting racer than Buddy Werner, would come to win more races because he was a shrewder competitor.[17]

Of medium height and slightly built, Kidd, twenty-six, won races by exercising a mental alchemy that enabled him to transform every apparent difficulty into what he convinced himself to be an advantage. An optimistic attitude is especially helpful to a ski racer, who faces odds as discouraging as those faced by a baseball batter. In forty or fifty gates, the racer is prone to a mare's nest of errors: turning too far from the inside pole of a gate, taking too low a line, hooking a tip and falling. Faced by so many negative possibilities, the racer's most valuable weapon becomes indefatigable optimism. For Kidd, no single factor counted as much in the starting gate as the conviction that everything—the snow, the course, and the weather that day—was in his favor.

Billy the Kidd. Celebrated as the first American male skier to win an Olympic silver medal, Billy Kidd's arguably greater achievement was winning the World Championship combined title six years later in 1970. He celebrated at the finish line of the Val Gardena downhill in the Italian Dolomites. *Photograph by Neil Leifer*

Kidd needed all of that optimism at the 1970 World Championship. After eight injury-ridden years on the international race circuit, his slim body was in agony. His back hurt so badly that he scarcely could bend over to buckle his boots. In the downhill, he was basically good for only two runs—the nonstop training run and the actual race. For most racers, it would have been a devastating disadvantage *not* to have practiced on Val Gardena's Saslonch downhill. No, said Kidd, the snow was too sparse to make it worthwhile for training runs.

"I was also fortunate," he reflected, "in that I had great new skis."[18] A less positive racer would have anticipated difficulty in adapting to new skis just before a race. Kidd thought only that his new skis must be better. At Val Gardena, he placed fifth in the downhill, he won the bronze medal in slalom, and together with his giant slalom result, he earned the lowest FIS points of all the racers in the World Championships. His gold medal in the alpine combined was the first such victory by an American. It was arguably a greater triumph than his silver medal at Innsbruck in 1964. On the cover of *Life Magazine,* he appeared over the caption, "America's first gold medal winner . . ." —erroneous in that *Life* ignored gold medals previously won by American women racers.[19]

After Val Gardena, in the summer of 1970, Earl Walters failed to win re-election as USSA president. Willy Schaeffler was named as the new alpine director. Schaeffler had been a four-event champion before World War II in Bavaria, and he brought impressive credentials to the job of directing the ski team. He had spearheaded Squaw Valley's preparations for skiing at the 1960 Olympics. He coached the Denver University Ski Team to thirteen intercollegiate championships. He had been a co-founder of the Professional Ski Instructors of America and presided at the first International Congress of Ski Instruction (Interski) held in the United States, at Aspen in 1968. He helped the Kennedy family launch the Special Olympics for handicapped athletes.

At the ski team, Schaeffler was driven by his belief that the cure for an anemic, poorly motivated, inconsistent bunch of racers was an old-fashioned dose of European discipline. Dealing with American youth was not a new experience for Schaeffler. When Ethel Kennedy needed help in managing her unruly children, she frequently brought him in to dispense discipline and advice. It did not yield much in the way of initial reform, but years later Bobby Kennedy, Jr., after he had ridden himself of alcohol and drugs, told me of his admiration for Schaeffler.[20]

Tough, with skin and muscle stretched tautly over his bones, Schaeffler was determined to rid the team of its laxness. In Schaeffler's view, many of the U.S. Ski Team's male skiers—raised in comfortable, middle-class surroundings and nurtured by a doctrine of youth's infallibility—didn't understand the sacrifices needed to win at the highest level of international competition. Routinely accepted by European racers, the sacrifices of time, dedication, and discipline weren't attractive to rebellious American kids emerging from the turbulent society of the sixties. Californian Spider Sabich so resented Schaeffler's regimented coaching that he quit the team and turned pro.

Unfortunately for Schaeffler, his often angry, impatient reign did not overcome the men's team resistance to self-improvement. Over three winters, 1971 to 1973, he achieved no more success with the young American racers than he did with the feckless Kennedy brood. He left the team. He did remain influential in the International Ski Federation, though. He wrote a piece about an FIS experiment to use a single pole for slalom racing, rather than two poles forming a gate. He thought that while the single pole would allow racers to go faster, there would be a loss of sophistication in course setting. Among his accomplishments was the invention of the Willy Bag. For many years, in international races, the falling racer's principal protection against injury was straw bales placed along the edges of course. But if it rained or if snow melted on the straw and then froze, the bales were like blocks of ice—a source of injury, not protection. Schaeffler had the idea of eliminating the freezing by placing the bales inside waterproof plastic bags. In a later safety improvement, the straw was replaced with foam inside what became known as the Willy Bag. It saved lives.

One of Schaeffler's rare satisfactions as alpine director, before he left the ski team, came at Sapporo in 1972, when Barbara Ann Cochran won the gold medal in slalom. Petite, blonde Cochran was one of four siblings—the others were her sisters Marilyn and Lindy and brother Bob—who became successful members of the national team. Neither Schaeffler nor his young colleague, women's coach Hank Tauber, could take much credit for it. The Cochrans all had been coached by their father Mickey on a rope tow hill in back of the family's house in Vermont, where the kids could race daily through the gates.

Was it possible that sensitive paternal nurturing might be better for young Americans than iron-handed European coaching? Something was going on that appeared to work better than the Schaeffler formula. Mickey Cochran—like Dave McCoy before him and like John Caldwell, who was the father of a couple of U.S. Ski Team cross-country racers (see chapter 10)—seemed to be demonstrating that if a man is good enough to take a narrow base of athletes, namely his own children, and raise them to be world-caliber racers, then wouldn't he be the right guy to coach the rest of the U.S. Ski Team? Indeed, why not? From the inception of the World Cup in 1967 to the end of the twentieth century, three families—the Cochrans, the McKinneys at Mount Rose near Lake Tahoe, and the Mahres at White Pass, Washington—accounted for roughly half of all the victories recorded by American racers. With an athletic talent pool of twenty children, they produced eleven U.S. Ski Team members. The Cochrans alone won five gold and three silver medals in Olympic and World Championship alpine skiing. Tamara McKinney's accomplishments include being the only American woman ever to win the overall World Cup trophy, in 1983. Tamara McKinney was one of seven in a family "so self-contained that it was almost a separate culture," wrote her biographer Nick Howe.[21] She and her siblings were schooled at home by their mother, who also taught skiing at Mount Rose. Tiny Tamara

Nurture or Nature? Tamara McKinney is seen at the beginning of the 1983 season when she went on to become the only U.S. woman to win the over-all World Cup title. She came from one of three U.S. families that produced five gold and three silver medalists in Olympic and World Championship alpine skiing. *Photo of World Cup race at Kranjska Gora, December 1983, from the archives of* Ski Racing Magazine

was the youngest, forever chasing her older brothers and sisters on skis. For her, life on a traveling ski team was not so different than growing up in a skiing family. Competing against teammates is similar to competing against siblings. If the coach occasionally favors one, you don't get upset and leave the family. McKinney raced on happiness, Howe observed. Her skiing was instinctive, not cerebral. While she never won an Olympic medal, she accomplished what many racers regard as a larger achievement, the overall World Cup title, reflecting the ability to perform consistently over a whole winter and to master more than one discipline.

Tamara's brother Steve McKinney—at Portillo, Chile, in 1978—became the first man to ski faster than 200 kilometers per hour (see chapter 11). Perhaps the love of speed is genetic, but there's no arguing the importance of family life in fostering disciplined, focused racers. And so the ski team hired Mickey Cochran, sire of champions, to succeed Schaeffler as head coach.* It was like going from TV's *Firing Line* to *Mr. Rogers.*

---

*Competing in Alaska in 2004, Mickey Cochran's grandson, Jimmie Cochran, won the national championship titles in slalom and giant slalom.

A genial, soft-spoken, rotund engineer at IBM in Burlington, Vermont, Cochran, forty-nine, started his reign in 1973 by announcing disquieting news. He said that he had no interest in ski politics or administration, and wouldn't take responsibility for them. He wanted only to coach athletes. But managing the ski team demanded political skill in negotiating with foreign teams and the International Ski Federation—a Machiavellian adroitness alien to a Green Mountain boy like Cochran. To no one's surprise, before the 1974 winter was out, Cochran was gone. Gone too was amateur U.S. Ski Association direction of the ski team. A group of reformers and businessmen led by W. Bradford Briggs had taken over the team's budgeting and fundraising in the summer of 1973.[*]

From a kind of human genome project, the team's coaching went to methodical direction. Cochran was replaced by Hank Tauber, an up-state New Yorker from a European family. Tauber had the advantage of speaking fluent Schweizerdeutsch, the phonetically challenging German dialect that is virtually the language of the inner circle of the International Ski Federation. Cautious in action and word, he was acculturated to the often bizarre politics of the FIS and the U.S. Ski Team. Tauber led the team to the World Championships at St. Moritz in 1974. No American, man or woman, placed in the first five in any event. Andy Mill was twenty-eighth in the downhill. It happened to be the year that his future wife, Chris Evert, won the ladies' singles at Wimbledon. The U.S. men's team fell to eighth place in the annual Nations Cup standings. Over a stretch of winters from 1974 to 1978, which included an Olympics and two World Championships, the United States failed to win a single medal in downhill, slalom, or giant slalom. Tauber had inherited a team that was young and unformed, its veterans having fled to Bob Beattie's pro tour.

Professional Racing Takes Off

After departing the U.S. Ski Team, Bob Beattie—divorced and remarried to Kiki Cutter, the first American woman to win a World Cup race—had launched his own company. He began by taking over the operation

[*] The committee-laden, political structure of the dues-paying U.S. Ski Association was becoming less suited to operating the ski team, whose budget grew to be larger than that of the USSA. The ski team effectively was put under the direction of a corporation, U.S. Ski Team, Inc., capable of receiving and spending funds raised by the U.S. Ski Educational Foundation, a creature of USSA. The team's governance underwent further separation from USSA in 1980 with the creation of USST and a U.S. Ski Team board of trustees, many of them wealthy businessmen.

of Nastar and of the almost moribund professional racing circuit. Beattie immediately raised pro skiing's fortunes through his dynamic promotion and media contacts. He was a skilled announcer. He understood the need to cater to television's needs. He increased prize money, with the results that racers competed for cash prizes on a scale not seen since the race-for-money California miners a hundred years earlier. By recruiting American racers, he enhanced pro racing's attractiveness to sponsors and to television.

One attraction of the pro racing format was that the spectator and television viewer could easily see the distances separating racers as they spun down the side-by-side courses.[22] No such spectator perspective exists in the traditional ski race. In earlier days, differences among racers might have been spotted more easily. Stein Eriksen once led a single run of slalom by 5 seconds. In the 1956 Olympics, the average gold medalist won by a margin of 3.5 seconds.[23] But by the time of the 1964 Olympics speeds had accelerated, and the average margin separating gold from silver had shrunk to less than three-quarters of a second.

Without the aid of video replay, it's almost impossible to judge what causes one racer to fall behind the other. But in pro racing, the spectator could spot the difference, as two skiers burst out of dual starting gates and shot through the flags, down parallel courses of equal length over a couple of fabricated bumps. Time-increasing errors are easy to spot. The slower racer is eliminated, the winner goes on to the next heat. The trouble was that if sixteen pro racers were competing, spectators had to watch as many as sixty short heats before the event winner emerged. The repetitive format, in short, was scarcely more exciting to watch than the FIS's one-at-a-time format, in which one racer after another makes similar turns on a single course. The FIS, on the other hand, offered a calendar of races that were more varied, challenging, and credible. It offered the three disciplines of downhill, giant slalom, and slalom. And its top "amateur" racers were better than those on the U.S.-based professional circuit, whereas in most sports, the opposite is usually true.

In the first two seasons of Beattie's pro circuit, 1971 and 1972, Billy Kidd and Spider Sabich successively won the Pro Skier of the Year trophy.*

* Sabich was shot to death at his Starwood, Aspen home in March 1976 by actress Claudine Longet. The killing was described by some as a firearms accident, by others as manslaughter provoked by jealousy. After convicting her of the killing, the judge sentenced Longet to thirty consecutive days in the Pitkin County jail, to be served at a time when it would not impact her three children.

The brief American dominance ended in 1973 when Jean-Claude Killy won. After Karl Schranz retired, he and Killy were scheduled to compete head to head in pro races, but the series of encounters never took place. "Perhaps," snickered Killy, "Schranz is too old to race and does not want to risk embarrassment."[24] Killy did return to racing briefly, competing on the American pro circuit, where he won $68,625 in the winter of 1974.

After Killy's final retirement from racing and after Spider Sabich's murder, the pro circuit came to be dominated by a couple of Austrian racers of little prior accomplishment. Few Americans, or even Europeans, had heard of Andre Arnold and Bernard Knauss. Most people assumed these guys were racing in America because they hadn't been good enough qualify for the Austrian national team. Arnold and Knauss could not have cared less. The two won no less than eight season titles. Knauss's million dollars in cumulative purses over eight seasons, adjusted for inflation, is the largest ever won by a ski racer, FIS or pro.

When Beattie brought his head-to-head, race-for-money racers to Europe in 1972 for the first of five seasons, the FIS began to fear that his pro tour might threaten its world-wide hegemony over racing—that World Cup racers would quit the FIS tour to make more money as pros. But it didn't happen. Although cash purses for winning had not yet been introduced by the FIS, its racers—with under-the-table payments from equipment firms and the cost of travel and training paid by their national federations—enjoyed a more assured income than a pro paying his own expenses.

In 1981, Beattie quit as the pro tour's organizer and impresario. He regarded the racers as ingrates. He had worked for eleven years on their behalf, while claiming to have made little money personally from the pro circuit. Over the next few winters, the pros dispersed, competing on regional circuits. Organizers scrounged among banks and car companies for scarce sponsor dollars. One of the regional tours was run by Ed Rogers, a gritty Maine restaurant owner. Rogers cobbled together a reborn national circuit, the U.S. Pro Ski Tour. He found partners and sponsors and convinced a rapidly rising new cable network, ESPN, to televise the head-to-head competitions. Eventually, though, he ran out of sponsors and channels willing to carry the races, which had experienced dismal audience ratings. In 1996, Rogers sold his pro racing enterprise. Two years later, exhausted of money, enthusiasm, and public interest, the thirty-six-year-old circuit died.

Inspiring Comeback of the U.S. Ski Team

The U.S. Ski Team throughout most of the 1970s was disappointing. The team fell from third place in the 1970 Nations Cup standings to as low as eighth place in 1977. Did its widely publicized lack of success cause kids to lose interest? Or was the team less successful because kids were seeking ways other than skiing through flags to prove they were good skiers? A rude lifestyle change was sweeping the sport. Guys with long hair on ultra-short skis extended the psychedelic rebelliousness of the tumultuous sixties with a new culture of freestyle (see chapter 12). Phil Mahre recalled what it was like at the U.S. Ski Team when he first joined it at the age of sixteen. "It had to do with the times . . . a generation of kids in the late sixties and early seventies who experimented with drugs. Racers fought with the team coaches over dress, hair length, diet, anything."[25] They complained of being away from home for most of the winter. They lacked concentration.

Not so the Mahre twins—Phil and Steve—who were raised in a family and a place as distant from hippy culture as a mountain cabin is from Greenwich Village. As youngsters, the boys grew up without TV. They attended regular public school in Yakima, Washington. They did their homework on the hour-and-a-half bus ride from school. By the time the Mahre boys reached home in the afternoon, their only entertainment was to play in the snow. Making the varsity basketball or football teams wasn't an option. Nor was a special ski academy, where classroom work is scheduled around race training. For the Mahre family, a ski academy was financially out of the question, anyway. Phil and Steve were unimpressed by the academies, even if they themselves hadn't had the experience of attending one. A ski academy, they said, is a poor substitute for a parent, "who's better able to supply a child with a notion of what's right and wrong and how skiing is supposed to fit into his life."[26]

Phil and Steve came to record thirty-five World Cup victories between them—more than half of all the World Cup competitions won by American men in the thirty-three years from the World Cup's inception to the end of the twentieth century. No American male, before or since, raced with Phil's consistent success. In the winter of 1982–1983, he placed in the top three in seventeen out of eighteen slalom and giant slalom races. In a span of three winters he won three overall World Cups and twenty-seven competitions. Most remarkable of all, he did it while competing against the most accomplished technical skier who ever

Top U.S. Ski Racer of the 20th Century. Born and raised at a small ski area in eastern Washington, Phil Mahre rose to win overall World Cup title in three successive years, 1981 to 1983. He did it while vanquishing Ingemar Stenmark, holder of the record for most World Cup races won. Phil and his twin brother, Steve—lifetime rivals and companions—won the slalom gold and silver medals at the 1984 Winter Olympics. *Photo, Vail, 1982: John C. Russell*

raced, Sweden's Ingemar Stenmark, the man who won a record eighty-six World Cup races. Phil was overall World Cup champion—the best alpine skier in the world—for three winters in a row, 1981, 1982, and 1983. Moreover, he led the most successful national team in U.S. skiing history! In 1982, America's Bill Koch won the World Cup of cross-country skiing (see page 199). In 1983, Phil and Tamara McKinney both won the men's and women's alpine titles.

The U.S. women's team that included McKinney also numbered among its members Christin Cooper, who won three Olympic and World Championship silver medals, and the gold medalists Debbie Armstrong and Diann (Roffe) Steinrotter. The U.S. women's good fortune was to have as head coach Michel Rudigoz, a combination of athletic trainer, psychologist, Solomon, den mother, and happy-time coordinator. Like the charismatic coach Honoré Bonnet, from whom he learned and whom he even physically resembled, Rudigoz understood that when a competitor reaches a high technical level, the coach's work is to attend to his or her psychological needs. Rudigoz was able to shape a group of stubborn, headstrong skiers, who nevertheless treated one another with respect and consideration. Like the Canadian men's downhill team (see chapter 7), the U.S. women's team thrived on collaboration and togetherness.

Competitors within a Team: The Paradox

A ski team is unlike a football, basketball, or baseball team. It is mostly an organizational infrastructure. Coaches cordon off slopes, set training courses, do timing and video. The team supplies its racers with travel and accommodations, medical care, training camps in the Southern Hemisphere and on glaciers in summer, course setting, and hill preparation. But individual success in a race doesn't depend on other team members performing well. The racer stands alone in the starting gate. The most frequent failing of both racers and team officials is to neglect or abuse the delicate symbiosis of individual and team. When the racer is selfish and overweening, he forgets why he needs the team. When coaches and officials believe they're in control, they forget that the organization's purpose is simply to create an environment for the individual to succeed. The aim should not be to teach an individual how to get along with the team; the aim is to teach the team how to get along with the individual.

The Mahre twins trained mostly by themselves. Critics accused them of not devoting enough time to competing against other team members, and therefore of not raising the bar for them. Wrong, said the twins. The problem was that the rest of the team didn't get out of bed early enough to be up on the hill to train with them. How could they set the pace if the guys didn't show up? The Mahres and downhiller Bill Johnson often chafed at the U.S. Ski Team bosses. "The ski associations and coaches," said the Mahres, "are forever trying to concoct foolproof programs to bring up kids to be champions. But a kid won't be a winner if he doesn't want it. A racer must have strength and belief in himself to be successful. A program that attempts to rub out that initiative won't work."[27]

"The Ski Team knocks me down," Bill Johnson said in 1984. "I fight back. They knock me down again. I fight back again."[28] A one-time teen-aged California car thief, Johnson possessed a natural bullet-shaped upper torso. The way he held his tuck in downhills—especially on the flat where races are won and lost—made him one of the most aerodynamically efficient gliders of all time. He was gifted with cerebral and physical brilliance and an inborn rebelliousness so great that it's difficult to conceive an organization able to contain him. He brazenly predicted victory at the Winter Olympics at Sarajevo in the former Yugoslavia, bragging to the Austrian downhillers that they shouldn't bother to show up at the starting gate, the gold medal was already his. Johnson made good on his boast. He did win the 1984 Olympic gold medal. But he never won an international race again. (In a quixotic attempt to return to racing in 2001, Johnson suffered a traumatic brain injury.)

The Mahres believed that it's impossible to program an athlete in such a way as to guarantee medals in a race. A single mistake in slalom— a small unanticipated patch of ice, one gate taken too wide, another attacked at the wrong angle—may represent the fraction of a second separating winner from loser. The Mahres knew this. But the rather disheartening way in which they proclaimed it during the 1984 Olympics caused the media to report that they weren't trying hard enough to win. The publicity especially irritated alpine director Bill Marolt, coming on top of another decision that upset U.S. Ski Team supporters at home. The team's coaches had agreed on a certain level of results that racers must achieve in races before the Olympics. Without the necessary results, a team member wouldn't get to race at Sarajevo, even if a starting position was open. Marolt backed the coaches and shouldered the blame. But it angered donors and volunteers, not to say the Mahres as well, that the team's policy would deny younger racers the chance to gain the tough, pressure-cooker experience of competing in the Olympics.

Failure, and Success Again

At the 1984 Games, the Mahres shocked everyone by winning the slalom gold and silver medals on the next-to-last day of the games. They retired after Sarajevo. So did Marolt. The U.S. Ski Team slid back to ninth place in the Nations Cup, the measure of national performance in alpine skiing. Not a single man or woman placed in the top six at the 1988 Calgary Olympics, giving credence to those who criticized the team for having kept younger racers out of the Sarajevo competitions. The team became a champion of fund-raising, not of racing. One chief executive marketed the U.S. Ski Team as part of "an attractive life style."[29] To quantify success, officials at headquarters in Park City focused attention on the medals Americans won in other snow sports—freestyle, snowboarding, disabled skiing. Alpine coaches came and went. Politics trumped accomplishment. John McMurtry was put in charge of a development program that spawned champions Picabo Street and Tommy Moe.[30] By the time they won their medals, McMurtry was rewarded by being fired.

Picabo Street turned out to be the greatest woman speed skier yet produced by the United States, with nine career World Cup downhill victories and an Olympic gold medal in Super G. She grew up in a skiing family that appeared to be emotionally on a bobsled ride much of the time. It's hard to know if Street spent more time training herself, or training her adoring father in anger management.[31] The family lived near Sun Valley, Idaho, on the edge of poverty until their tomboy, high school dropout daughter's racing success brought endorsement and prize money that virtually lifted Picabo and her parents from rags to riches. She possessed a fearless, reckless disposition and a coarse tongue, which contrasted with her pink-and-freckled child-like complexion. After she won six World Cup downhills in 1995 and the season title, Street brought ski racing into the mainstream of big-time commercial sports when Nike

Ski Team Diversifies.
While U.S. international competitiveness in traditional alpine racing dwindled after 1985, the national team succeeded as medal-winning opportunities expanded in freestyle, snowboarding, and handicapped racing. Amputee Diana Golden won a gold medal in the 1988 Paralympics and ten World Championship disabled skiing gold medals. *Photo of Diana Golden at the 1987 National Handicapped Ski Championships. George Marcelonis/Attitash Mtn. Photo*

Future Champion. The focus on cultivating junior ski racers paid off for the United States in the 1990s, notably with a freckled teenager Picabo Street from Sun Valley. Her Olympic Super G gold medal and her nine career World Cup downhill victories earned her a mega-dollar sponsorship deal with Nike. *Photo by Ben Chidlaw, Ketchum, Idaho, from the archives of* Ski Racing Magazine

gave her a reputed million-dollar agreement. For the first time, a skier was included in the world-famous pantheon of shoe-endorsing all-star athletes, including Michael Jordan, André Agassi, Nolan Ryan, and Jackie Joyner-Kersee.

In 1996, the team got what it needed. Marolt, who had become the highly successful athletics director at the University of Colorado after leaving the ski team, returned to it as president and CEO in 1996. The team's focus veered from marketing back to coaching athletes. In a staggering proclamation, Marolt announced that the U.S. racers would become the "best in the world." At first, he could not reverse history, and only a few individual Americans were able to rank among the world's best. But in the winter of 2004–2005, Marolt's boast about the best in the world began to look astonishingly credible.

The U.S. Alpine Team climbed to an unprecedented second place in the Nations Cup standings, better than its previous peaks in the 1960s and early 1980s. The women consistently began to win World Cup races. Bode Miller accomplished what only Jean-Claude Killy and Marc Girardelli had done—winning races in all of the alpine disciplines in a single winter. He also led the 2004–2005 World Cup standings from the beginning to the end of the season, a feat accomplished only twice previously,

European Celebrity. Home-tutored in New Hampshire's White Mountains, Bode Miller flashed into ski racing history with his 21st-century performances in the World Championships and World Cup. *1998 U.S. National Alpine Championships, Jackson, Wyoming, Photo by Heather Black for* Ski Racing Magazine

by two of the most famous men who ever raced, Ingemar Stenmark in 1978 and Karl Schranz in 1969.

Miller was a celebrity at home, unlike most North American champions who were better known in Europe: Tamara McKinney, Picabo Street, Daron Rahlves, Buddy Werner, triple World Cup winner Phil Mahre. Walking down New York's Park Avenue, they hardly would be recognized by their fellow citizens. They rarely appeared on national television, their names were not emblazoned in headlines on newspaper sports pages. Alpine racing is a minor sport in America. The athletes have never been drawn from basketball's or football's base of millions of hungry inner-city kids. The skiers were from a relatively tiny base of dedicated families and communities linked to the mountain environment, willing to finance their training as youngsters. They competed abroad for most of the winter, and when they did come home to race, spectator crowds were sparse. For financial support, they relied primarily on voluntary fundraising, not government grants as in Europe. Given these limitations, over more than a half-century the achievements of North American racers were commendable, even prodigious.

IV

Diversity:
New Disciplines,
Old Ones Restored

10

Cross-Country

Spurred by a public trend toward fitness, cross-country skiing soared in popularity. How and why it happened.

The decade of the 1970s spawned a surprisingly tough asceticism in a society known for its indulgence of soft, easily achieved pleasure. Guilt about a bad war (Vietnam) and bad politics (Watergate) gave way to guilt about bad diet and bad physical condition. People turned to arduous jogging, distance running, and bicycling outdoors. Chains of franchised health clubs opened. At home, nutrition-obsessed folks began to eat specially prepared health food and to drink bottled mineral water. From a sport scarcely known in the sixties, jogging grew to 15 million participants in the decade of the seventies. Tennis racquet sales doubled between 1971 and 1973. Cross-country skiing, hitherto a little practiced sport, soared in popularity, and by 1972 one out of every four pairs of skis sold in the United States was for gliding across the snow, not storming down a lift-served slope.

The wintertime image of men and women in knickers following a trail through the woods, stopping for a snack of gorp (Granola, Oatmeal, Raisins, Peanuts), was perfectly suited to the new American Puritanism. Cross-country skiers also felt a sense of brotherhood. In his book *The Complete Book of Running*, Jim Fixx noted a similar elitism among runners. "Every one of them feels—and in fact prides himself on it—that he and his fellows are fundamentally different from other people.[1] (A similar clannishness existed among alpine skiers in the 1950s, and it resurfaced rebelliously with snowboarders in the late 1980s.)

The attraction of cross-country was threefold. Sports medicine experts verified that it surpassed all forms of exercise in promoting cardiovascular fitness and in putting to work the body's main muscle groups. Second, cross-country was cheaper than downhill skiing at a time when

Return to Nature. The revival of cross-country skiing in the early 1970s re-awakened skiers to the pristine natural environment of winter. following trails deep into fir forests, hushed by the snow-blanketed trees. *Photo by Ken Redding for Stott Shot*

prices for lift tickets, gasoline, and other goods were escalating. Third, cross-country embraced the natural environment. Alpine skiers, it was said, had forgotten the true appreciation of nature in winter; rather they were seen as yo-yoing up and down crowded slopes, ears bombarded by music blaring from loudspeakers, riding lifts whose chairs now occasionally bore paid advertising signs. By contrast, cross-country skiers, by returning to the sport's Nordic heritage, re-discovered an awareness of the pristine natural environment in winter. They followed trails deep into silent, commercial-free fir forests, hushed by the snow blanketing tree branches and the ground.

I vividly remember a night when I skied on a track winding over a Vermont golf course. A full moon washed the snow-covered fairways in an eerie pallor, and the Green Mountains were etched in jagged black lines against the sky. The landscape looked as it might during a solar eclipse. I added a few dabs of klister wax to the running surface of my cross-country skis, and glided onto the trail. The night temperature had transformed the wet snow to tiny ice granules, which acted like ball bearings on the skis' running surfaces. I lunged over my poles and pushed off. Whoosh! My skis glided for 50 feet along the level fairway. Nothing resisted their sliding. Two smooth ruts, machine-groomed into the snow, guided my skis as if I were on a railroad track. As the grooved tracks made it unnecessary to direct the skis, I was able to gaze up at the winter stars and the alabaster full moon as I coasted along the surface of the snow as if in a dream.

The Commercial Touring Center Arrives

The first American resort to offer organized cross-country skiing was the venerable, exclusive Lake Placid Club, in New York's Adirondack Mountains. So that its rugged members could try the obscure new sport, the club imported forty pairs of skis and poles from Norway for its inaugural 1904 season. The shaped hickory skis, as narrow as 70 mm at the waist, with iron toepieces, could be used not only for cross-country, but also later for telemarking, jumping, and skijoring—being towed at high speed by a horse or Model T automobile.

In 1922, Jackrabbit Johannsen (see page 11) decided to move his family to Lake Placid from suburban Pelham, New York. Johannsen was perfectly suited to the vigorous sports environment of the exclusive Lake Placid Club, where he recruited Norwegian instructors to teach skiing. In January 1923, accompanied by the club's two ski pros, Ornulf Poulson and the Marquis Nicholas degli Albizzi, in temperatures down to 28 degrees below zero Fahrenheit, he climbed to the summit of Mount Marcy, a 3,000-foot vertical ascent.[2] His life was consumed with cross-country skiing. After he moved to the little village of Piedmont in the Laurentians in 1930, he began to lay out the 80-mile Maple Leaf Trail, which afforded perhaps the earliest opportunity outside of Europe and Scandinavia to ski from inn to inn over a succession of days. The work of clearing the trail progressed over several years. The old man created maps and guide books, for which he was paid by Sweet Caporal cigarettes. No one seems to have felt conflicted by the infusion of tobacco money into cross-country skiing. A trailside rest was often an excuse for a smoke.

Information about specially mapped trails and locations in the United States progressed nicely in 1962 when Rudi Mattesich, an expatriate

Austrian mapmaker and former fencing master who had migrated to Vermont, published a guide to eastern cross-country skiing, and founded the Ski Touring Council to promote the sport.[3] So far, though, no one had determined that cross-country skiing—informally practiced for years on hiking trails and across farmers' fields and golf courses—could be made into a recreation that people would pay to access, as alpine skiers did commercial ski areas. Johannes von Trapp had the idea in 1968. Tall, with a lean, animated face and a partiality for green loden jackets, Johannes is the Baroness Maria von Trapp's youngest child. It was above Stowe, in the never-filmed sequel to *The Sound of Music*, that his father Baron Georg von Trapp and the family's former governess Maria had settled following their emigration from Austria in 1943. When Johannes wasn't singing with his older siblings in concerts around the world, he was home-schooled. He went to Dartmouth and later studied at Yale's illustrious school of forestry. As it happened, the twenty-eight-room Trapp Family Lodge possessed several hundred acres of forested upland. Challenged by what to do in winter to balance the lodge's robust summer income, Johannes blazed and cut a network of trails through the woods, and then charged guests and anyone else who cared to pay for the experience, to ski on them. He recruited an instructor from Norway to teach them the technique of kicking off one ski and gliding on the other. Guests could ski to a hut in the woods, bringing lunch.

The success of his new cross-country center provoked young von Trapp to wonder if he couldn't franchise the idea. He had the idea of systematizing a package of products and services, which he would sell to urban golf courses across America, enabling them to generate revenue by turning themselves into cross-country centers in winter. In Boston, he enthusiastically presented his idea to the Arthur D. Little management firm. After first endorsing it, Little concluded that most of the golf courses in the business plan didn't have sufficient snow to cover two months of operation. True, there were enough customers nearby. But in the locations chosen, there wasn't enough snow.

In his third winter, 1971, von Trapp hired a witty, story-telling outdoorsman by the name of Joe Pete Wilson to run his fledgling touring center. Wilson picked up on his boss's idea of fostering a chain of commercial touring centers, and after one winter, he departed the Trapp Lodge and in 1973, with a friend, started North American Nordic, a chain of a dozen centers. One was in Stowe, another in Manchester, Vermont, another in Franconia, New Hampshire. His problem was the opposite of the Trapp-Little plan's: While his North American Nordic centers were located where there was snow, there weren't enough people living near them. He eventually down-sized his operation to the Adirondacks, at Keene, New York, where he operated the Bark Eater Inn. There the wisecracking Wilson presided over his guests' dinners like a rustic Jack Paar hosting *The Tonight Show* in a log cabin. Later, he wrote a cross-country ski book with William Lederer, co-author of the better known *The Ugly American.*[4]

The sport grew rapidly in the early 1970s. When the first North American directory of touring centers appeared in 1975, it contained the names and descriptions of no fewer than 213 places where people could ski on prepared tracks.[5] Few of the sites had existed a half-dozen years earlier. Such was the booming popularity of nordic touring that it now took thirty-two pages of 8-point type to list all the places. By 1978, *SKI Magazine's Guide to Cross Country Skiing* listed no fewer than eighteen books and fifteen films about cross-country.[6] Icons of the sport's new popularity appeared everywhere. Italian movie star Sophia Loren was seen cross-country skiing in France with her family. Smirnoff and Wolfschmidt used cross-country as a backdrop for vodka ads. Jean-Claude Killy took up the sport. Eager promoters advertised that almost anyone was capable of being a cross-country skier. "If you can walk, you can ski," it was said.

It was untrue. The two actions are totally different: The walker *steps* from one foot onto the other; the cross-country skier steps hard and propels himself with a thrust off of one foot, and *glides* on the other foot. The scooter-like kicking and gliding action must be learned; it's not natural, like walking.

A Revolution in Skis, Boots, Bindings, Poles

Kicking and gliding, or the diagonal stride, steadily improved. As in alpine skiing, technique and equipment progressed in tandem. By the end of the twentieth century, the typical cross-country ski was shorter, less than one-quarter the weight and half as wide as the ski used by the explorer Fridtjof Nansen to cross Greenland 110 years earlier.[7] The greatest progress came in the 1970s. Ski poles—of critical importance because they are part of the cross-country skier's propulsion system—were made drastically lighter around 1970 when lightweight fiberglass and aluminum shafts began to replace heavy tonkin shafts. The heavy and air-resistant webbed pole basket, designed to prevent the pole from plunging into the snow, was replaced gradually by lighter constructions and streamlined shapes. As in alpine skiing, racers led the way. After 1974 they began to move faster and endure longer distances as a result of lighter and more responsive skis, no longer made of wood, but of fiberglass and featherweight cores. The next great step ahead was the invention of boot-binding systems. Until 1976, the cross-country boot was held in place by toe sidewalls and a bail in front that clamped down on the lip of the boot sole.[8] Then it was discovered that the racer's stride could be improved radically by extending the boot's plastic sole like a snout, and clamping it down at a point farther ahead of the toe. It eliminated the sole friction caused by the binding sidewalls, and allowed the skier to extend his leg farther in the stride without lifting the ski tail. The new boot toe was custom-designed to work with the binding toe; the two had to be purchased as a combination.

Manufacturers introduced ever more specialized kicker and running waxes, drawing attention to the way that an ideal touring ski should work. With the correct wax and a flex matched to body weight and leg strength, the skier should be able to press the ski down so that the specially waxed or patterned zone underfoot makes contact with the snow in a manner that enables him to push off and propel himself forward without back-slipping. Following the kick, pressure is released from the kicker zone, the ski recovers its camber (tip-to-tail arch), and should glide easily on its smooth front and tail sections, which are coated with a wax designed purely to promote sliding on the snow. The problem for a long time was that cross-country skiers had difficulty buying ideal skis— that is, skis suited to their body weight and skill. A person might have bought a ski whose flex underfoot was too stiff to enable him or her to press the pattern or kicker wax down on the snow. The tortured skier not only back-slipped desperately on hills, but was unable to kick off the ski for forward propulsion. Or the ski's flex was too soft. The rough, patterned underfoot section was pressed too easily into the snow, with the consequence that the ski failed to glide efficiently. Ski shops, with rare exceptions throughout cross-country's rapid growth after 1970, had a hit-and-miss record of supplying recreational touring skiers with skis suited to their body weight, strength, and skill. To inventory a range of known flexes, they claimed, was too complex and expensive.[9]

The simplistic notion that walking was the only skill necessary to become a cross-country skier arose from a slick marketing view that people were unlikely to buy a product or pursue an activity that appeared to be complex. Waxing for cross-country was seen as just such a bother. The skier had to read temperature and snow condition charts and mess around with sticky, messy, tar-like substances. What was needed was a waxless, idiot-proof ski. An attempt in this direction occurred in the early 1950s, when an Austrian company briefly made a plastic ski with a running surface formed of tiny steps (the high point or riser facing backwards), to prevent back-slipping. In the mid-1960s, a Yankee inventor named Bill Bennett picked up on a similar idea. He designed a pattern formed like fish scales, embedded in the ski's running surface. Bennett's idea, however, was that such a ski would glide faster because the little fish scales broke the surface tension of the moist snow. Skiers who tested it in Chile found that Bennett's ski slid well if not spectacularly, but it was disconcertingly noisy. Before Bennett's idea was abandoned, an interesting piece of information developed. Cross-country ski racer Mike Gallagher eyed Bennett's ski when it was being tested, and saw that it resisted sliding backwards. It didn't go notably faster forwards, but it didn't go backwards at all!

For a few winters the world heard no more about the fish scale bottom until Bill Danner, a tall, husky graduate of the Harvard Business School, arrived on the scene. Danner was looking for a new business idea to apply to the fast-growing sport of skiing. He was one of an oncoming new breed of professionally trained executives, destined, it was believed, to succeed the ex-racers and the 10th Mountain Division veterans who pioneered the modern ski industry. By 1970, sales of cross-country skis were starting to take off. The main obstacle retarding the sport's growth, in Danner's not so humble opinion, was that people had to know how to wax. The fish scale running surface required no knowledge of waxing. Danner and his friends bought Bennett's old patent and formed a company, Trak, Inc., to make no-wax-necessary cross-country skis.[10] An idea originally intended to speed skiers downhill allowed millions of cross-country skiers to go uphill more easily!

The fish scale or step pattern was imposed in the area in front of and under the skier's foot, where "kicker" or climbing wax normally was applied. The smooth leading edge of each little scale glided, while the sharp rear edge gripped on the snow if you pressed down on the ski and kicked off it. At least, that was the idea. In fact, the early fish scale pattern didn't slide nearly as well as the waxes that had been used for generations. The skis were noisy, and they seldom performed well for either climbing or gliding. Inexperienced skiers who bought the early models condemned themselves to a disappointing experience. But, gradually, as more sophisticated patterns evolved and ski flexes improved, the non-wax surfaces performed better. Chemists every year created waxes that were more efficient and easier to apply, if not by casual recreational touring skiers, certainly by racers and the fast-growing number of participants in long-distance competition.

Marathon Mania

In 1967, the first open-invitation, mass-start North American ski marathon took place in the Ottawa River Valley, northwest of Montreal. The Canadian Ski Marathon and the Gatineau 55 race emulated Sweden's 53-mile long Vasaloppet, begun in 1922, and Norway's annual Birkebeiner. The Canadian races caught the attention of Tony Wise, a World War II veteran who owned a ski area at Cable in the remote hill country of northern Wisconsin. In 1973, Wise launched a 55-kilometer cross-country race, borrowing the name Birkebeiner, which literally means "birch legs." The Norwegian race commemorates the 13th-century winter rescue by the king's scouts of the infant royal son, whom they bore over the mountains on skis. For protection against the cold and snow, the scouts wrapped birch bark around their legs.

Held each February, the Wisconsin Birkebeiner was soon attracting as many as nine thousand competitors. Wise was a deceptively effective promoter. He had a rather owlish face. Speaking rapidly but softly, he could have made a case history at his alma mater, the Harvard Business School. No amount of money was sufficient to lavish on his remote Telemark ski center in Wisconsin, and if Wise didn't have enough of his own, he was not shy about using others'. He eventually built a monstrous, trapezoid-shaped sprawl of a building incorporating a 200-room hotel, a Colosseum sports complex that included a skating rink and four indoor tennis courts, gourmet restaurant, bars, convention rooms, two ballrooms, heated pools, a ski area base lodge, and 55-foot fireplace—the largest such construction at any ski resort. His method of financing the enterprise was ingenious. When Wise was unable to pay his bills, he confronted the government or the banks with demands that they extend or forgive his loans, or he would have to shut the place down. They invariably caved in if only because the ski center was the local economy's linchpin. Wise eventually ran out of people to borrow from. Unable to repay $8 million to six hundred creditors and the federal government, he was forced to sell his beloved resort in 1987. The monstrous Colosseum was gradually dismantled and sold for scrap.[11]

Before his demise, Wise had the idea of an international program that

Mass Marathon. The Wisconsin town of Hayward pioneered the first cross-country ski marathon in the United States. Its 55-kilometer Birkebeiner came six years after Canada introduced a mass participation ski marathon in the Ottawa River Valley region in 1967. Telemark Wisconsin ski area operator Tony Wise successfully fostered the idea of an international racing circuit, the Worldloppet, combining marathons in fourteen countries. *Photo of the 1980 Wisconsin Birkebeiner from the archives of* Ski Racing Magazine

would link his Birkebeiner race with the one in Norway, with the Canadian Ski Marathon, and with six other races, or "loppets," in nine countries around the world. He called it the Worldloppet. When a competitor completed each race, he would have his result stamped in a special passport. A skier who completed all of the loppets around the globe would receive a special medallion. The Worldloppet, launched in 1979, became a surprising success, and Wise's original circuit expanded to fourteen countries, including Russia, Canada, Japan, Australia, Finland, and Czechoslovakia. In 2004, about eight thousand people had Worldloppet passports, and eighty thousand cross-country skiers participate annually in the fourteen marathon races that comprise the international circuit.[12]

Bill Koch: Medal Winner, Skating Pioneer

America's emergence as a competitive cross-country ski racing power, while it lasted only from 1975 to 1984, originated in the 1960s at the progressive Putney School in southern Vermont where John Caldwell was a mathematics teacher. A crusty outdoorsman, Dartmouth graduate, maple syrup-maker and original thinker, Caldwell had been a Nordic combined competitor on the U.S. Ski Team at the 1952 Olympics in Norway. More notably, he wrote *The Cross-Country Ski Book*, which ultimately went into eight editions (between 1964 and 1987), eventually selling a half-million copies, greater than any specialized ski book ever published in the United States. The book made Caldwell a significant mentor—in print, at least—to tens of thousands of people who took up the sport. He combined his skill in teaching and his Nordic knowledge to quickly gain a reputation as America's most talented, native-born cross-country coach. Caldwell trained six high school boys—three of them his own sons—who were so good that they were able to win against seniors and college racers. Taking note, the U.S. Ski Team named him as the national cross-country coach in 1966. He went on to coach teams at two Olympics and two world championships. Not surprisingly, several of his racers, including his son Tim, came from Putney, where he had mentored them. One of them was Bill Koch.

Of medium height, Koch was ruddy-cheeked with dark sideburns that descended to his jawbone. He was serious, introspective, and life had not been easy for him. His parents divorced when he was eight, and his father suffered manic depression. Nothing about Koch's physical build suggested that he was an extraordinary athlete. But as soon as he stepped onto skis, you saw something special. He kicked the propelling ski in his stride with an explosiveness that made European trainers go to their slow-motion cameras to record it. And he was easily the best and fastest glider on downgrades. He also was ignited by an inner drive so great that if officials could have magically divided and distributed it, it would have been enough for the entire U.S. team. He trained fanatically. Even as a youngster at school, he didn't take the school bus; he raced it home on foot or on skis. The intensity of his training was legendary. "He kept training logs that were like novels," recalled U.S. coach Mike Gallagher.[13] For every hour Koch planned to train, he spent two hours in advance thinking about it.

Koch's moment of fame came at the 1976 Winter Olympics at Innsbruck, Austria. His chances of mounting the podium to receive a medal didn't look especially promising. Cross-country ski racing is dominated by Europeans—Norwegians, Finns, Russians, Germans, and even Italians. At three Olympics between 1956 and 1964, Sweden's Sixten Jernberg won five gold medals and two silvers. Later, in the 1980s, the sport was dominated by Norway's Odvar Braa and Sweden's Gunde Svan, and in the 1990s by Norwegian Bjorn Dahlie, who won eight gold medals in three Olympics, the most ever won by an athlete in the Winter or Summer Games. The record for the greatest number of World Championship and Olympic medals by a skier belongs to cross-country racer Raisa Petrovna Smetanina. The short, slender Russian woman raced in the 1974 FIS Nordic World Championships at age twenty-two, and eighteen years later, at age forty, in the 1992 Olympics, where she narrowly missed winning a bronze medal. In between, she collected a total of eighteen medals — half of them in the individual races and the other half in team relay competitions.

The chances of an American cross-country skier winning even a silver medal in the 1976 Olympics therefore were slim. But on the trails at Seefeld, the lovely, unspoiled alpine village in the beautiful high country that lies between Innsbruck and Garmisch-Partenkirchen, Koch did it. In the prestigious 30-kilometer race, he placed second. No American had ever won an Olympic medal in cross-country skiing before (or since). It was a heroic performance and, just as important, it was televised. Koch's medal put cross-country ski racing on the American sports map. A national Bill Koch League was created to encourage youngsters to pursue the sport.

Koch (or Kochie, as he's known to friends and teammates) now found himself pursued by phone calls and requests for endorsements. Naturally reclusive, he was unable to deal with his newfound fame. At the age of twenty-two, he temporarily quit racing. Then, surprisingly, he returned. "In the spring of 1980," he recalled, "I entered a Swedish 30-kilometer race on flat terrain, organized with the idea of setting a world speed record."[14] Koch found himself overtaken by experienced loppet skiers doing something he hadn't seen competitors do deliberately for a whole race. They propelled themselves by skating off one ski and leaving the other ski to glide in the track. For Koch, it was an epiphany. He saw the competitive edge that skating might give to a racer in conventional races. During the winter of 1982, the second season of the cross-country World Cup, which was modeled on alpine skiing's winter-long World Cup circuit, Koch skated frequently. Success followed success as he piled up World Cup points. In the last race, in the gorgeous Alpi di Suisi above Val Gardena, where the Dolomite mountains spear the sky like gothic cathedral towers, he earned the final points that won him the season-long World Cup title (see page 181). He was the season-long top cross-country skier. And he nearly repeated the feat in 1983.

Skating Pioneer. America's Bill Koch shook the tradition-bound Nordic world when
he skated instead of classically kicking-and-gliding his skis to win the 1982 World Cup
title. A half-dozen years later, Nordic competition came to be split into two catego-
ries—classic (stride) and freestyle (skating). *Photo of the 30-kilometer race at the 1980 Winter
Olympics, Lake Placid, New York,* © *Bob Woodward*

Part of what made Koch's skating technique possible was the wider,
flat surface being created by the ever-larger, powerful machines used to
set parallel tracks for the skis to run in. Mechanized track setting probably originated with the Oslo Forestry Department in the late 1950s, although the idea is so obvious that it may have occurred simultaneously
in other countries around the same time. A tractor, snow cat, or snowmobile hauls a specially weighted sledge with steel runners that cut perfect
parallel tracks 12 to 18 centimeters apart in the snow. As the area on each
side of the track progressively widened, it allowed racers to skate. Norwegian officials wanted to ban skating, believing that if the technique were
allowed to spread, it would be unfair to clubs lacking the money to buy
grooming machines; rural kids, skiing narrow trails in local woods, would
be at a disadvantage.[15] They also saw skating as a corruption of the sacred
striding movements of cross-country skiing. And so, wherever there were
FIS races, Norwegian officials created logistical and legalistic barriers to

skating. Their opposition was finally overcome in 1987, when the FIS essentially split the sport in two, creating separate events: freestyle or skating, and classic kick-and-glide.

Touring Centers Become Mini-Resorts

By 1980, most touring centers offered machine-set tracks and color-coded marked loops corresponding to trail maps. They had shops that sold and rented gear. They offered instruction and snacks. *Cross Country Ski Magazine*, which reached 150,000 readers in 1983, listed 380 places where they could go, up 78 percent from eight years earlier. A skier typically paid between $3 and $5 for a day's use of the trails. Some centers boasted illuminated tracks for night skiing. They guided skiers on nature tours and to outlying huts. The centers offered child care, sauna, showers, and a room to change out of sweaty clothes. Cross-country skiing even spawned the Nordic equivalent of alpine skiing's Vail—the mega touring resort At Royal Gorge near Lake Tahoe in California's Sierra Nevada, John Slouber began in 1971 to build a cross-country ski resort that eventually came to encompass 9,000 acres, more than 300 kilometers of groomed trails, a spacious day lodge, overnight lodging, trailside cafes, 15 kilometers of snowmaking to ensure skiing in case of drought or thaw, and four surface lifts for skiers wanting to practice turns, or perhaps for lazier, tradition-flaunting guests who wanted to enjoy touring without the exertion of climbing.

Royal Gorge's massive amenities were matched on the other side of the continent in Quebec by Parc du Mont-Sainte-Anne, which developed well over 200 kilometers of trails through forests of spruce and birch, overnight huts, World Cup racing facilities, and a virtual village as its center. Mont-Sainte-Anne is about 45 minutes drive from Quebec City, above the banks of the historic St. Lawrence River. A couple of hundred miles south, in the White Mountains, the environmentally conscious community of Jackson, New Hampshire, cleared 160 kilometers of groomed trails linking twenty inns. At Craftsbury Common in Vermont's Northeast Kingdom, Russell Spring developed a sort of Nordic Club Med, packaging a week of lodging and ski touring.

At Lone Mountain Ranch near Big Sky, Montana, Nordic-loving guests, overnighting in rustic elegance, were pampered with gourmet dinners and on-trail lunches. At Lake Placid, the demands of hosting the 1980 Lake Placid Winter Olympics amplified an already sprawling network of trails in the Mount Marcy region of the Adirondacks. Alpine resorts, such as Copper Mountain and Keystone, and Sven Wiik at Steamboat, operated large touring centers. At Vail, Steve Rieschl in 1978 directed the largest cross-country ski school in the Rockies, pioneering lessons in how to do a telemark turn.

Reprise of the Telemark Turn

A small elite group of skiers went back a century in time to rediscover a classic turn done by angling one ski ahead of the other. Some regarded the re-adoption of the telemark with skepticism. After all, skiers had happily abandoned it when heel-hold-down bindings allowed them to ski parallel. But the famed climber Yvon Chouinard disagreed. He believed that telemarking's emergence was a result of alpine skiing becoming less thrilling. "As a sport matures, it doesn't necessarily get better," wrote Chouinard. "The answer is to upgrade the challenge. When basketball players are all seven feet tall, raise the height of the basket. When the thrill is gone from alpine skiing, free up the heels and reinvent the telemark turn."[16]

In telemarking redux, participants bought souped-up gear that looked like classic 1930s alpine gear—higher boots held in place by cable bindings and heavy-duty cross-country touring skis mounted with steel edges. They even raced though gates. To ensure that they made correct telemark turns, judges had to be posted along the course in order to pe-

Return of the Telemark. A half-century after it was abandoned, the classic telemark turn enjoyed a revival in the 1970s. A turn once necessary to change direction became an option involving the creation of specialized new skis, boots, and bindings. *Photo by Barry Stott*

nalize or disqualify any competitor who cheated by making a turn with skis parallel.

Dick Hall pioneered the revival of the telemark in Vermont, in the early 1970s. Hall believed that telemarking was needed to restore skiing to what it was before it split into cross-country and alpine. Both had lost their way, in Hall's view. Alpine skiers had locked down their heels and abandoned going uphill. Cross-country skiers were on skis so narrow you could only point them like arrows down a groomed track. The droll Hall created NATO, the North American Telemark Organization, whose mission was "to achieve world peace through cross-country skiing."[17] Each winter, he staged an event where a hundred or more laughing skiers joined hands in performing a mass telemark turn.

A Mass-Participation Sport Reverses Direction

Warm or snowless winters followed one another in the early 1980s, an early indication of the devastation that global warming would wreak on the sport. An absence of natural snow could not be remedied by machine-made snow. Unlike concentrated downhill slopes, cross-country ski trails extend over miles, making it cost-ineffective to manufacture snow. Without natural snow, hundreds of thousands of participants were unable to use the cross-country skis stacked in their garages. They didn't need a cross-country periodical either. *Cross Country Ski Magazine* and similar magazines disappeared. Purchases of long, skinny skis fell from a half-million pairs annually at the end of the 1970s to less than one-third of that number by the end of the century.[18] In occasional winters when snow did return, the sport failed to recover its former popularity. For this the suppliers of equipment and clothing bore some blame. Young designers and marketers developed products derived from racing—skintight suits and skating skis. They lost sight of the larger market of folks not enthused by the idea of squeezing their middle-aged bodies like sausages into tight suits. The loose, comfortable clothing and stylish knickers preferred by veteran skiers disappeared from store racks. The traditional diagonal stride was also no longer chic. The authentic cross-country skier was now expected to skate vigorously with exhausting bursts of energy. Not surprisingly, tens of thousands of people who'd learned to love the sport in its less strenuous era backed off or continued informal, less frequent outings in the woods or on golf courses.

The sport didn't lose its hard-core enthusiasts. Young athletes—Bill

Koch wannabes—were attracted by the speed and energy of skating. By the end of the twentieth century, the speed in 50-kilometer races was twice as fast as eighty years earlier. Competitors were drawn to the fast-paced, short-distance sprint, and to the new pursuit race, in which the best competitor in one event—a classic stride race or, in the case of the Nordic Combined, jumping—starts first in the deciding event, pursued by the rest of the field. The new races transformed cross-country into one of the most exciting Olympic sports to watch. Indeed, after 1990, competitive cross-country changed more radically than did alpine racing. By 2003, the world championships of cross-country and Nordic Combined had almost doubled to nine medal events, from five in 1968.

Nordic skiers are responsible, over a hundred years, for notable achievements in winter exploration. When Norwegian Roald Amundsen employed skis to beat England's Robert Falcon Scott to the South Pole in 1911, his inspiration was Fridtjof Nansen. It was Nansen who had ignited the world-wide interest in skiing when he crossed the Greenland ice cap. In doing so, Nansen outlined a new extremity in human adventure: using skis to travel across difficult winter terrain, and then to go ever higher and faster.

11

Extremities

*Who went the highest, the fastest, the steepest. The story of
extreme skiing, speed-skiing, aerial stunts, and heli-skiing.*

Extreme skiers were once people who, having set out to go from point A
to point B on skis, amplified the adventure by accidentally falling down
an escarpment during a whiteout or getting caught in a snow slide. Mortal risk was a byproduct of going faster, reaching a higher place. But then
risk itself became the goal—deliberately leaping off cliffs, attempting
to ski in an avalanche, skiing in places where a fall meant certain death.
The use of skis to explore and climb snow-covered mountains escalated
from finding ever more difficult flanks and couloirs to ski down, then to
peaks so ferociously steep they had to be rappelled in places, and finally
to stunts having little contact with the snow at all.

It was Nansen's extreme risk in successfully skiing across Greenland
in 1888 that first inspired the use of skis to invade terrain previously un-
visited by men in winter. Nansen's equipment consisted of 7 foot 6 inch,
heavy oak skis and crude, ill-fitting willow-shoot bindings. Seventy-five
years later, in 1962, Bjorn Staib at the age of twenty-seven duplicated his
fellow Norwegian's crossing on skis. Aided by a dog-drawn sled laden
with supplies, Staib journeyed with a companion for 500 miles over ice
jams without radio, totally cut off from the possibility of rescue.[1] The two
men almost starved to death at the end. They had to destroy all but one of
their sixteen huskies, whose flesh they survived on. The mention of this
fact drew an angry reaction from people unaware that the more famous
Shackleton and his heroic crew did the same thing with their dogs in the
Antarctic in 1916. Like Nansen, Staib ultimately succeeded in making it
to Greenland's farther shore.

Nansen's exploit toward the end of the nineteenth century prodded the adventurous to climb mountains on skis. Shortly after his Arctic

exploit, skiers ascended peaks such as the Jungfrau in Switzerland and western Europe's highest mountain, Mont Blanc. In 1911, a French skier, using skis he brought back from Norway, pioneered what became the most famous alpine traverse, the classic Haute Route from Zermatt to Chamonix.[2] By 1920, ski mountaineers had conquered most of the main summits of the Alps. Like Nansen, they were aware of the ancient practice of attaching strips of fur pelt to the bottom of the skis for climbing: You could push forward on the skins, but the bristles prevented backslipping, and for the next hundred years ski mountaineers would continue to use sealskin and later synthetic variations of it for climbing.[3]

The first North American ski mountaineer, arguably, was Irving Langmuir, who climbed the highest Catskill mountains on skis in 1907, before going on to win the 1932 Nobel Prize in chemistry.[4] In 1931, Aspen pioneer Andre Roch and release binding inventor Hjalmar Hvam used skis in making an April summit climb of 11,245-foot Mount Hood. The following year, Erling Strom of Stowe and the Lake Placid Club, together with Minnesotan Al Lindley, employed skis for glacier-crossing during a successful ascent of Mount McKinley.

In 1964, the prodigious climber Fritz Stammberger, a printmaker and Aspen ski instructor, made a descent on skis from 24,000 feet in the Himalaya. In a story, "I Skied Higher than Any Man," Stammberger told of his agonizing, stormy climb of 26,600-foot Cho Oyu in Nepal.[5] The story was accompanied by a picture of two of his fellow climbers as they lay in a tent, slowly dying. The picture's publication brought down a hail of protest on Stammberger, who, critics said, should have been focused on saving lives, not on making a world record ski descent. In 1971, Stammberger accomplished a formidable first ski descent of Colorado's North Maroon Peak. The same year, Bill Briggs, the director of the Snow King ski school at Jackson Hole, using 210-centimeter K2 skis, descended the Grand Teton for 6,000 vertical feet, the most achieved in American mountains until that time.[6] The publicity emanating from Briggs's feat ignited interest across the United States in making first descents on skis.

The Rise of Extreme Skiing

The first hard-edged promoter of extreme skiing—or *ski sauvage*, as the French called it—was a Swiss, Sylvain Saudan. In a period between 1969 and 1974, Saudan made first descents of Alpine mountainsides so steep that, even with rope and crampons, they were formidable to ascend in winter, and looked impossible to ski down. Saudan was no shrinking violet, declaring himself "skieur de l'impossible."[7] With stringy long hair and extraordinarily broad shoulders for his modest height, he raised money to carry out his exploits by promising sponsors exposure for products employed in accomplishing them.

Saudan perfected a universal turn to get down couloirs as steep as 60 degrees and through treacherous breakable crust and gooey junk snow. Called "the windshield wiper turn," its pivot point was not the tips, but the tails of the skis.[8] Under the tips, often, was nothing but a void. A fraction of a second's lack of concentration by Saudan would result in a mortal fall into rocks or a crevasse below. Each turn had to be executed without error. Saudan likely made a thousand windshield wiper turns to descend, for example, the west faces of the Eiger and of the Mont Blanc near his home base of Chamonix. He made a ski descent of the precipitous north face of Oregon's Mount Hood. His concentration was so intense, observed Del Mulkey, who photographed many of Saudan's extreme adventures, that before a descent "you'd think he was in a trance."[9] Mulkey accompanied Saudan in 1972 on what they hoped was to be the first full descent of Mount McKinley on skis. McKinley may have the greatest vertical rise of any mountain in the world, since its base is only a few hundred feet above sea level. During the ascent, the Saudan-led group came close to losing their lives in a May storm. Winds blew at an estimated 150 miles an hour.[10] Saudan's ski boots, attached to his pack, were frozen like a block of ice. He could barely put them on. Starting from a point 800 feet below McKinley's summit and aided by the light of the midnight sun, he skied in two stages down to the snow line at 7,000 feet, for a record descent of 12,500 vertical feet.

In 1979, France's leading practitioner of *ski sauvage*, Patrick Vallencant, accomplished the longest, continuously steep (sustained 60 degrees) ski descent, from the top of 21,400-foot Yerupaja in the Andes of Peru. In a book about his conquests of the steep, Vallencant wrote floridly about the sensations he felt.

> On the steepest part of the mountain, about 65 degrees, my elbows graze the snow. Snow sprayed by (my ski) tips strikes my face. I bury myself in the violent happiness of my combat against the flanks of this towering, menacing mass—this Goliath. [Then] on the lower slopes of about 40 degrees . . . the going becomes easier. My heart is open and free, my head is clear—the light, the color of the lakes, the ice, all the beauty of the world is within the mad rhythm of my blood. It is in these moments that I see

inward and outward so clearly, and it is for this reason that I ski the very steep mountains."[11]

Skiing higher than any man attracted the ambitions of the kind of adventurer wanting to enter the *Guinness Book of Records*. One was the Japanese Yuichiro Miura, an adventurer and promoter in the mold of Sauden. Miura was a professional racer and the first man to ski down Mount Fuji. In 1970, he promoted the idea that he had skied down Everest. He did, but from the 26,200-foot South Col, not from the 29,028-foot summit. Miura wore a parachute and endured the last of his partial Everest descent being blown around like a rag doll at the end of a rope. What made the Miura expedition appear less heroic to observers at the time was that six sherpas and two guides died to make the boastful exercise possible, to say nothing of millions of dollars spent, and the need for almost a thousand people to carry it out.[12] (A beloved figure in Japan, in 2003, at the age of 70, Miura became the oldest person to climb to Everest's summit.)

In 1981, Ned Gillette, a Dartmouth graduate and a former member of the U.S. cross-country ski team, climbed and descended 24,757-foot Mustagh Ata in the Pamirs, crowning it the highest mountain ever skied from its summit.[13] His record was quickly erased, since during the same year Patrick Vallencant registered a descent from the top of 26,750-foot Broad Peak in Pakistan. Gillette, however, was accompanied by an adventurous young Vermonter, Jan Reynolds, who thus skied higher than any woman ever had. Gillette earlier used cross-country skis to traverse Ellesmere Island in the Canadian Arctic, and to trek around the bases of McKinley and Everest. (He was killed by bandits in 1998, while trekking in Pakistan with his wife, former U.S. Ski Team racer Susie Patterson.)

An obvious reward of skiing from Everest's summit is the satisfaction of knowing that no one in the future can possibly ski higher. In 1988, the South Tyrolean climber Hans Kammerlander took skis to the top of Everest, but he found it was impossible to ski on rocky sections where the wind had blown off the snow. Consequently, Kammerlander carried his skis down for much of the way. In 1992, Pierre Tardivel reported a ski descent from within 250 feet of Everest's summit. Total success finally came in 2000. After a solo ascent to the summit, a Slovenian, Davo Karnicar, put on specially designed 168-centimeter skis—short to enable him to negotiate narrow slits of snow—and descended Everest without rappelling or taking the skis off.[14] At least, that's what he reported. That a Slovenian should be the first to have skied down from the Earth's highest point, however, shouldn't be surprising. Slovenia's climbers are among

Extreme Skiing. Professional steeps skier and stunt expert Scot Schmidt appeared in no less than thirty-nine adventure films. The first competition judging the performance of skiers on difficult, steep terrain punctuated by rocks and cliffs took place in Alaska in 1991. *Photograph of Scot Schmidt, Aspen, 1990. John C. Russell*

the toughest and most courageous in the world. Five years before Everest, Karnicar and his brother skied from the summit of 26,000-foot Annapurna, considered, forty years earlier, to be one of the world's most difficult climbs.[15]

Extreme skiers came to tackle more difficult descents thanks to better designed gear. The Fischer ski company created a rugged fiberglass backcountry ski with aluminum edges. In 1976, Paul Ramer of Boulder, Colorado, began to produce and sell a sturdy alpine touring binding that allowed heel lift, while successfully holding the boot firmly in place during descent. Avalanche rescue improved with the more widespread wearing of Skadi transceivers, quickly giving rescuers the location of a buried skier.

The year 1991 saw the outstanding U.S. mountaineer Louis Dawson complete the project of being the first person to ski down every Colorado peak over 14,000 feet. The same year, the first World Extreme Skiing Championships took place in Alaska's Chugach range, formalizing high-risk, off-piste skiing as a competitive sport.[16] The winner on the first day was Jackson Hole heli-guide Doug Coombs. His run, which included leaping over precipitous bands of rock into a couloir, displayed the qualities that the judges were looking for—aggressiveness, fluid technique, air time, control, and an imaginative, difficult line. One of the judges was extreme skiing professional steeps skier and stunt expert Scot Schmidt, a super-star of the extreme, who appeared in no less than thirty-nine adventure films.[17]

Going Faster

Tuckerman Ravine, below the snowfields that go up to Mount Washington's summit, in the 1930s was a theater of early extreme skiing, its steep headwall the stage for the most audacious acts of skiing. Tuckerman is a cirque, a U-shape a half-mile across, and vertically an 800-foot-high wall of snow 60 degrees steep in places, rising to the skyline defined by the upper lip of the Headwall. Norway's Sigmund Ruud schussed it from the lip, after competing as a jumper in the 1932 Olympics.[18] His brother Birger Ruud did it after World War II, at the age of forty-four. Birger was an astonishing competitor, who had won the jumping gold medal at Lake Placid in 1932, and four years later, in the Garmisch Winter Games, the gold medals in both jumping and downhill—wearing the same pair of boots in both competitions—perhaps the greatest competitive combined skiing result ever recorded!

The Ruuds' schusses, however, don't stick especially in people's minds because of Toni Matt's famous schuss in the 1939 Inferno Race. Starting near the 6,288-foot summit, Matt, who was just nineteen years old, had planned to make check turns to slow his speed on the snowfields that lie above the precipitous Headwall. But he misidentified a gate above the lip. Judging that he wasn't going fast enough, he pointed his 7 foot 3 inch hickory skis straight down. He was never able to make another turn until he arrived at the floor of the Ravine and entered the Little Headwall and the Sherburne Trail below it. Later, attempting to explain what happened, Matt said of his amazing achievement, "It wasn't completely an accident because I planned to make turns. I just forgot how."[19] His winning time of 6 minutes 29 seconds almost halved the previous Inferno record set by Dick Durrance, who on this occasion came in a full minute behind Matt.

It's not known precisely how fast Matt was skiing when he was going full tilt down the face, but if he had the sense that his skis were barely touching the snow, he would have been approaching 100 miles per hour. At 110 miles per hour, a skier is more flying than skiing. Matt almost certainly was traveling at least as fast as Austrian Guzzi Lantschner, who in 1931 won the first speed trial at St. Moritz, where it was primarily staged as a ploy to promote the resort. Two years later, another Austrian, Leo Gasperl, hit an official 81 miles per hour. In 1949, future world champion Zeno Colo unofficially reached 99 miles per hour, and in 1955 America's Ralph Miller was clocked unofficially at 109 miles per hour at Portillo, Chile.

Unlike traditional downhill racing on longer twisting courses, where stamina is a factor, speed skiing's standard is streamlined simplicity: attaining a certain velocity. Official speed records came to be established on "speed traps"—sections of super-steep, carefully groomed surfaces with electric-eye timing. The two best-known tracks were above 10,000 feet—at Portillo, Chile, and on the glacier above Cervinia, Italy, a test known as the Kilometro Lanciato. The 100-mile-per-hour barrier was crossed officially at Cervinia in the winter of 1963, and later in the same year Americans Dick Dorworth and C. B. Vaughan pushed the record up to 106.52 miles per hour at Portillo.[20]

Vaughan later achieved fame as a skiwear maker. Dorworth contributed something more lasting. A gifted writer, he began to etch in the minds of tens of thousands of readers what it feels like to ski at velocities approaching those of skydivers freefalling through space. "In big speeds," Dorworth wrote,

> there is a continuous change of pressure from tip to tail of the skis. Continuous and violent. On a good run your body absorbs change and violence. On a bad run, it demonstrates them. Air pressure tries to push you over backward. If you break the tuck the pressure tries to rip your arm off. If you stand up, your back will hit the snow before the thought can come of what a mistake you had just made. No one on his back at 100 mph will ever after have contempt for speed.[21]

Throughout the 1970s, speed skiers pushed their bodies and courage attempting to break through skiing's equivalent of the four-minute mile—200 kilometers per hour, or more than 120 miles per hour. Finally, in September 1978, at Portillo, Steve McKinney pointed his skis down the 40-degree track and shot like a bullet through the timed section, hitting 200.222 kilometers per hour.[22] The barrier had been broken. In reflecting on what he'd done, McKinney made an observation about high-speed downhill racing that echoes the feeling of every competitor who has ever done it. "The faster my body travels the slower my mind seems to work," wrote McKinney. "What seems like an eternity . . . actually passes almost instantaneously until at the crescendo of speed there is no thought at all. Albert Einstein's theory of relativity holds that as the

Speed Skiing. World speed record breakers Steve McKinney and Franz Weber stage a head-to-head in 1982. The Darth Vader helmets were among several innovations created to reduce wind resistance. Slicing through the air, speed skiers travel faster than humans in free fall. *Photo, Les Arcs, France, by Peter Miller (petermillerphotography.com)*

velocity of an object increases, its internal time-frame slows. Our minds work in a similar manner."[23]

Amazingly, 200 kilometers proved to be no more of a ceiling than four minutes for the mile. Velocities continued to increase as the speed-skiers adopted wide, heavily damped 240-centimeter (about 8 feet) jumping style skis. They wore down-to-the-shoulders Darth Vader–like helmets that sliced through the air. With a stone grinder they "structured" the skis' running surfaces to reduce speed-sapping suction from the wet snow. Later, they applied a final wax surface of fluorocarbon costing a hundred dollars an ounce, Cera F. Skin-tight, wind-tunnel-tested suits reduced air resistance. Made of latex—oversize "condoms," they were called—the suits sped up the skiers, but they proved dangerous because of the terrible heat, up to 212 degrees Fahrenheit, from the friction generated by a fallen speed skier's body scraping along the snow's surface.[24] After a 119-mile-per-hour crash, Franz Weber took six months to recover from skin burns he suffered. The solution was clothing made of fire-resistant foam.

Speed skiing enjoyed modest success as a race-for-cash professional circuit, with as many as 350 international competitors. They included at least a dozen women. Women competitors came to achieve speeds above 230 kilometers per hour.

Purses reached as much as $20,000 or $30,000 per race. Half of the speed-skiing events came to be held at resorts in the French Alps, organized by the FSV (Fédération Ski de Vitesse). Two years into the twenty-first century, France's Philippe Goitschel—nephew of the famous Goitschel sisters of France's championship women's ski team of 1970—pushed the record above 250 kilometers per hour (155 mph), or 20 percent faster than the speed of a falling skydiver before his parachute opens.

The FIS in 1986 recognized speed skiing as a sanctioned amateur sport, and laid out rules, enabling it to be declared an Olympic demonstration sport at the 1992 Albertville Winter Games. It never made it to medal status, possibly because of the futility of records progressing by only tiny fractions of a second, or because of the obvious risk of fatality.[25] The cautious FIS mandated that the starting point for an event should be set so that speeds didn't exceed 228 kilometers per hour. In doing so, the FIS was imitating its own practice in ski jumping of shortening the in-run when there's a possibility that competitors may go too fast and out-jump the hill, injuring themselves.

Ski Flying

In classic ski jumping, competitors are judged for style and distance leaped. For a long time in Olympic and World Championship competition, jumping hills were designed so that the competitor could safely jump 70 meters (230 feet). In 1962, the 90-meter jumping competition was added. By 1992, 70 meters had become a relatively short distance, unworthy of an Olympic medal, and the 70-meter jump was replaced as a medal event by the 120-meter jump.

Not that men couldn't jump farther than 120 meters (393 feet). They could do so in the sport of ski flying. In 1969, the enlarged Yugoslavian ski-flying hill at Planica produced a jump of 541 feet. By 2005 at Planica, the distance had risen to 239 meters or 784 feet, more than the length of two football fields![26] Originally built in 1934, Planica is the oldest of a half-dozen ski-flying hills around the world. The only ski-flying hill in North America is Copper Peak on Michigan's Upper Peninsula, where the hill record is 518 feet. No ski-flying tournament has been held there since 1994, although the jumping tower is open to sightseers who can ascend to the top by elevator.

The ability of ski jumpers to soar farther increased after 1988 when they switched from maintaining their skis parallel during flight, to the technique of fanning the tips outward in a Vee configuration while arching the upper body over the gap between the skis. In this manner, the body and the skis act together as an air foil. Soon, it was found that even greater buoyancy and longer flight duration could be achieved if the jumper used longer skis in relation to his body size. The longer the skis and the taller he was and the less he weighed, the farther the jumper flew! By the beginning of the twenty-first century, jumpers were starting to look like virtual skeletons on skis, their grotesqueness an athletic embarrassment. One official worried about children entering a sport, "which requires dieting to a point of illness."[27] To attack the abuse, the International Ski Federation (FIS) in 2005 introduced a mathematical table that more strictly regulated ski length in relation to body height and weight.

Women, with their lower skeletal weight, are ideally suited to jumping, yet for a long time women's jumping was opposed by male officials who believed it too risky for females. But in the twenty-first century, when women began to reach distances only 10 percent less than top male competitors, the masculine wall of resistance broke. At Vikersund, Norway, in 2004, nineteen-year-old Lindsey Van from Park City, Utah, leaped 561 feet, and there's a good chance that women jumpers will compete at the 2010 Vancouver Olympic Winter Games.

Heli-Skiing

The use of ski-equipped Pilatus turbo-prop planes as a means to access liftless terrain was pioneered in the Alps in the 1950s by the Swiss Herman Geiger and the Frenchman Michel Ziegler. The switch to helicopters began as early as 1958, with two-passenger choppers doing the lifting in Alaska, at Gstaad, Switzerland, and Val d'Isère, France. "By helicopter," declared *SKI Magazine*, "it is possible to ski unbroken powder all day long without ever seeing ski tracks except the ones you make yourself."[28] In the winter of 1963, Alberta geologist Art Patterson, who was experienced in using helicopters for northern mineral exploration during summer, hired mountain guide Hans Gmoser to take him skiing in an area not far from Banff, Alberta. So that he and his friends wouldn't have to climb on foot, Patterson rented a helicopter and pilot. In 1965, chartering a helicopter himself, Gmoser led former Olympic skier Brooks Dodge and friends to the vast virgin powder slopes of British Columbia's interior mountains. So many skiers wanted to repeat Gmoser's and Dodge's experience that the idea of a heli-skiing vacation was born: To fly into a

Recreational Extreme Skiing. The willingness of skiers to spend more money and assume more risk took off in the late 1960s, with the introduction of commercial heli-skiing camps. Christin Cooper and Ken Read etched figure eights on Ruby Ridge, Colorado, in 1995. *Photo by John C. Russell*

remote lodge, stay there, and ski in deep, dry powder on trackless slopes over an area that would encompass a hundred Aspens. In 1968, Gmoser, an Austrian climbing guide who had emigrated to Canada in the early 1950s, built a cozy lodge with four eight-bed bunkrooms amid the spectacular Bugaboo peaks.[29] The new Lodge's windows looked across at the blue and white tongue of the Bugaboo Glacier whose surface, laced with moraine stone and crevasses, resembled the wrinkled carcass of an enormous gray whale, out of which sprouted the monstrous rock of the Marmolata Spire. The Lodge was a delightful, nostalgic throwback to the era of small inns. Guests dined at a common table, and sat around talking through the evening. Two years later, Gmoser had a competitor. Guide Mike Wiegele began to offer heli-skiing adventures in British Columbia's Cariboo and Monashee mountains.

In the early heli-skiing days, because of the chopper's size, the group of skiers and their guide typically were divided into two flights. Arriving on top and awaiting the arrival of the next group, skiers had time to relax and worship the pristine white wilderness. These untamed alps—the peaks stretching on and on—are as beautiful as any in Switzerland, yet superior because no human habitation intrudes. When the sun shines in the cloudless sky, it is like a king's crown gleaming against the background of a violet tapestry above a vast whiteness. In the distance, one could glimpse snow cascading like a waterfall down a cliff, then seconds afterward hear the sound of the avalanche's roar. In the foreground were the tracks of mountain caribou. A hole in the snow indicated the home of a hibernating grizzly. An eagle soaring overhead cocked his head and looked down, hunting a white ptarmigan, which was pecking for insects in the snow.

Years later, there was less time to sit around and contemplate the scenery after Gmoser introduced more powerful, larger helicopters capable of carrying a dozen skiers. More outfitters offered heli-skiing, centered around Revelstoke, British Columbia. Instead of 60,000 to 80,000 vertical feet of skiing in a week, clients in the new heli-skiing era wanted to do 150,000 and 200,000 feet. They competed to see who could record the most vertical, criticizing those who might delay them. Peacefully gazing at the scenery was a time-waster. Aggressive heli-skiing became a metaphor for a theme suggested previously: Superior technology to "benefit" skiers hasn't necessarily made the experience superior.

In 1969, just a year after the Bugaboo Lodge opening, Geoff Taylor, who had bought a week's heli-skiing trip with Gmoser's fledgling Canadian Mountain Holidays, died in an avalanche triggered after he dropped a short distance down a slope to take a picture of a group of skiers standing above. Taylor's death—the first recreational heli-skiing fatality—was one of more than fifty-four that would occur in British Columbia heli-skiing by the end of the century.[30]

Skiing Like James Bond

When a mountain could not actually be skied, there was always the possibility of descending it via the air. In 1973, Rick Sylvester slid on a snow-covered incline off the top edge of Yosemite's El Capitan cliff.[31] As he launched into vertical space, Sylvester arched his back in a beautiful dive, then opened his parachute and drifted down parallel to the face of El Capitan, his skis dangling uselessly in the air. While he didn't know it, he had rehearsed for his later role in the James Bond film, *The Spy Who Loved Me*. In the production of the movie, Sylvester skied off a 3,000-foot precipice on Baffin Island in the Canadian Arctic, employing the same parachute-assisted technique.[32] He pioneered several difficult Sierra ski descents, including a dangerously narrow cliff defile at his home base of Squaw Valley known as Sylvester's Slot and visible today by people riding on Squaw Valley's aerial tram.

Twenty-year-old Jeff Jobe was the first person to use skis to launch himself into the air on a hang glider. Before he did it on snow, Jobe had logged 200 hours of kite flying by water skiing behind a motor boat. In November 1970, at the Snoqualmie ski area outside of Seattle, his kite on his back and his skis pointed straight downhill, he sped off a ridge and into the air. Pretty soon he was selling kites to other skiers.* "It may only last another couple of years," he said in 1971. "I'm afraid someone without the necessary experience is going to get killed."[33] He was right. Among those who died hang gliding was Roger Staub, Vail's director of skiing. But Jobe was wrong in his pessimism about hang gliding's future. The sport grew as enhanced hang glider design made flying safer.

On skis and snowboards, kids after 1990 came to plunge down narrow chutes lined with rocks, simulating the extreme stars in movies and extreme-sport videos. The videos and pictures in magazines created a kind of pornography that furnished images to testosterone-charged young

---

*Technically, Jobe used a Rogallo Wing, developed for NASA. The sport of paragliding, according to the authoritative European magazine *Parapente*, was created by David Barish, who designed frameless soft chutes that NASA wanted for the astronauts. In the 1960s, Barish tested his paraglider designs at Hunter Mountain and other ski areas where I persuaded the owners to give him access for his tests in the summer and fall months.

Hang Gliding. Jeff Jobe in November 1970 was the first person to use skis to launch himself into the air on a hang glider, technically, a Rogallo Wing originally developed for NASA. "I'm afraid someone without the necessary experience is going to get killed," Jobe said. He was right. *Jeff Jobe photographed at Vail by Barry Stott*

men who hadn't yet gained respect for the rules of engagement out of bounds. They failed to realize that the one-quarter-inch strand of rope marking the ski area boundary separates a managed place, where conditions are safe and where hazards are mitigated, from a place where conditions are wild and unpredictable. During the winter of 1998–1999, avalanches alone killed thirty-six skiers and snowboarders in the United States, Canada, and in Europe. The European avalanche fatalities were almost double those of North America.[34]

Meanwhile, inside the ropes, an odd thing took place. In the 1970s, ski areas had removed kicker jumps from their premises and removed lift passes from any "hotdogger" caught attempting an inverted aerial. Then in the 1990s, the resorts reversed course. They began to spend hundreds of thousands of dollars to build terrain parks. They used special grooming machines to shape mountains of snow into halfpipes and jumps in order to offer young customers opportunities for the very risks that the resorts had deplored ten years earlier. Now every kid could be a freestyle acrobat!

How freestyle skiing rose, was rejected, then grew to become an Olympic sport is one of modern skiing's most intriguing, colorful stories.

12

Freestyle

How a generation of long-haired, pot-smoking acrobatic hotdoggers sought to liberate skiing from what they perceived to be its imprisoned past.

In the late 1960s, skiing began to assimilate the burgeoning long haired, hippie lifestyle that had entered virus-like into American culture. On the surface, it seems odd that a lifestyle could alter a sport. But skiing, as the pioneering instructor Otto Schniebs declared (see chapter 2), constitutes an ardent "way of life" involving attitude, language, friends, travel, clothes. Lifestyles, like fashions, change. In the case of freestyle, the change in the 1970s was seismic. It was a cultural upheaval—an Americanization of skiing in some ways as profound as the shift from Nordic skiing to Continental alpine skiing that occurred in the 1930s.

Within the period of a few winters, après-ski veered from the chorusing of traditional ski songs of Schniebs' era to wriggling on a dance floor under multi-color strobe lights. Skiers went from being college outing club members chug-a-lugging beer, to wild-eyed slope bashers smoking pot. The newcomers were an expletive-talking lot, not to be confused with the decent, law-abiding vacationing families pictured in resort ads. They aimed to reinvent skiing. On the slopes, they spurned disciplined technique. They trashed traditional forms of keeping the skis together, of leaning forward and weighting the downhill ski. Their sport, called hotdogging, was flamboyant, on-the-edge action, showoff skiing. No longer was performance defined by slalom flags, FIS seeding points, and levels of instructor certification. "You get ripped away from controls, from society, from washing your clothes, from taxes, from cutting your hair," said Mike Lund, who had run away from home at age fifteen and later joined the Sun Valley ski patrol.* "You're out there doing it. It's just complete freedom."[1]

"It's a rushed feeling, elating, creative," said bump and ballet skier John Clendenin, who had quit racing because he couldn't afford it.[2] Said another hotdogger, in an anti-rationalist evocation of late sixties generational rebellion, "I value learning something new, rather than a repetition of what my father did."[3]

Hot Dog!

Arms flailing, bodies hurling raggedly downhill, hotdoggers skied on the uphill ski and on the tails of their skis. People were now free to turn as they wished! Farewell to narrowly prescribed ski school forms! "I went off into the air and couldn't see anything," said Airborne Eddie Ferguson. "Then I saw the lake and the trees and the landing. I got into it like a bird. I wasn't part of the world anymore."[4]

Sensing somewhat belatedly the raw, unbuttoned spirit that had entered the sport's mainstream, *SKI Magazine* in October 1973 published a 28-page "Hot Dog" section bearing the headline, "The exploding world of hot dog skiing ... a look at the skiers, their way-out lifestyle and language, and how they're revolutionizing ski gear and technique!" Sequence photos showed how to do stunts, such as the "Back Scratcher," "Wheelie," "Mule Kick," and "Iron Cross." A dictionary of hotdog language included the terms "Gay Gainer" (two men flipping while they hold hands), "Boogying" (skiing the moguls all-out), and "Burned Out of the Scenery" (crashing in competition). The special section featured Airborne Eddie and acrobat Bob Theobald wearing the season's colorful new fashions. It was as if *Vogue Magazine* had employed a bunch of Che Guevara rebels to model Dior's latest clothes.

The special hotdog section might better have been initiated by Doug Pfeiffer, *Skiing Magazine's* editorial director, except for his publisher's fear that stories and pictures of pot-smoking, long-haired skiers might upset advertisers and parents worried about the possible moral undermining of their children reading the magazine. Pfeiffer was a pioneer of ski stunts,

---

*In 1978, Lund was charged with orchestrating an attempt to smuggle millions of dollars worth of marijuana from Colombia. To evade police, he changed his name to Lance McCain. For more than twenty years, McCain lived a relatively normal married life in various western states. In 2001 his refusal to make child support payments led to fingerprinting, which revealed to federal authorities the Mike Lund who had eluded them.

and had done more than anyone to engrave freestyle skiing on the public consciousness. A collector of early ski books, he understood that ski stunts weren't new. Ski jumpers were performing somersaults at the end of the nineteenth century. In 1920, a Dartmouth student was pictured in the *National Geographic* flipping off a jump at Hanover, New Hampshire. In 1929, Austrian-born ice skater Fritz Reuel wrote a book called *New Possibilities in Skiing*. Reuel proposed formal stunts, similar to ice skating figures, which could be performed on skis. In one figure, the skier made a turn on the inside ski, stretching the other ski out behind him, raised in the air. It became known as the Reuel. The author's name, pronounced "royal" in German, resulted in the later English misnomer, royal christie.

Inspired by Reuel, in 1956 Pfeiffer began to teach classes in "exotic skiing"—or what he called "monkey business"—at Snow Summit at Big Bear Lake in California's San Bernardino Mountains. Snow Summit was an innovative place, already the home to the first amputee ski school.* Now it was home to Pfeiffer's creative teaching. He'd come to Snow Summit from Squaw Valley, where Emile Allais had taught him the mambo—a danced series of turns with the upper body exaggeratedly leading the legs around in a turn that they never quite seemed to complete. Of medium height with limbs if not double-jointed at least capable of simulating a rubber band, Pfeiffer hated ponderous, overly serious ski teaching. Learning to ski should be fun. In 1958, he wrote his first book, *Skiing with Pfeiffer*. Containing ten pages of stunts, it could claim to be the first English-language book touching the subject of what would come to be known as freestyle. Pfeiffer demonstrated the "Flying Kick Turn," the "Outrigger" turn, and the "Crossover Kick." In the latter maneuver, the performer swung one ski around the other so that the feet were pointing in opposite directions, then with a kick extricated the standing ski to re-align itself to the other.

Vividly creative—his imagination perhaps stimulated by acute nearsightedness—Pfeiffer coined the names for stunts such as the "Deep-Crotch Christie" and "The Flying Sitz," the "Backscratcher" and the

---

*Snow Summit's program may have been the first amputee program in the United States, but it would be incorrect to call it the oldest because it was discontinued. Amputee skiing already was being taught in Europe, principally in Germany, when in 1952–1953 Bob Engelein, a returning Korea War vet who had lost a leg to cancer, vowed to help rehabilitate his comrades through skiing at Snow Summit. For a short period in 1953–1954, Doug Pfeiffer did the teaching. Pfeiffer would strap the heel of one foot to his butt to ski with them, to better understand and demonstrate the possibilities. One of Engelein's students took over the program, but after a couple of winters, it was dropped. Nearby Big Bear Mountain Ski Resort picked up the idea and continues to this day to operate a successful adaptive skier program.

Freestyle Innovator. Art Furrer impresses a pair of bunnies on the ski hill of the Lake Geneva, Wisconsin, Playboy Club in 1969. A Swiss native, Furrer introduced stunts such as the Butterfly, the Charleston, and a crossed-ski turn, the Javelin. *Photo, Lake Geneva, Wisconsin, by Barry Stott*

"Undecided Quersprung" (see Glossary). The "Hannes Jump" was a trick attributed to Hannes Schneider. The instructor starts with his skis across the fall line of the hill. In front of awestruck resort guests, he elevates himself on his poles, and jumps his skis around until they are pointing down the fall line and he descends the hill. The purpose of such an impressive trick—Tom Corcoran caustically remarked—was to enable an instructor to "assert his authority" over the class.

Pfeiffer soon had accomplices. In 1965, a rosy-cheeked, diminutive Swiss, Art Furrer, appeared on the American ski scene. Short, with a hoarse high-pitched voice and half-inch thick glasses, Furrer had a promoter's flair and the calculating mind of a Zurich banker. He announced that acrobatics on skis, by making people more agile, could improve their ability to ski better. His stunts included "The Butterfly," "The Charleston," the "Single Ski Christie." A crossed-ski turn, the "Javelin," later became a promotion for a new Hart metal ski that he endorsed. Furrer added to his repertoire at Bolton Valley east of Burlington, Vermont, where he was ski school director. He perfected the "360 Tip Roll" and the "Stepover." On the hill, readers began to show off stunts such as the "Worm Turn," the "Kick Out," and the "Slow Dog Noodle."

Ballet Arrives on a Moving Stage

The tricks were easier to perform on short skis, as Shortee ski evangelist Clif Taylor insistently reminded everyone (see page 112). Among short-ski users was Phil Gerard, a former choreographer who had been a star ice-show skater even when he was in his teens, and had hoofed in Broadway shows with the likes of Sammy Davis, Jr. In his ski version of show biz, Gerard designed stunts, or adapted gymnastic stunts, to be performed on a small, endlessly revolving carpeted belt called the Ski Dek by performers wearing stubby little skis. Gerard choreographed them to dance on skis—in effect, to do ballet. The moving indoor slope became the focal point of public ski shows that traveled from city to city in the fall, featuring Furrer, Stein Eriksen, and the racing stars Toni Sailer and Ernie McCulloch. A kind of jumping board was added to the Dek, so that the skiers could perform stunts such as the "Frog Kick" and the "Daffy," landing safely on an inflated mat at the bottom. Gerard appeared on the Ski Dek in 1966 on the nationally televised *Andy Williams Christmas Show*. The Dek took him in and out of bankruptcy. At one time, he engaged in a feud with David Schine, who controlled Ski Dek's marketing and who had been attorney Roy Cohn's partner on Joseph McCarthy's communist-hunting committee on un-American activities.[5] Cohn, it could be said, had migrated from political tricks to ski tricks.

Gerard himself mirrored the darker side of the hotdog culture. Gaunt, intense, with profuse jet-black hair framing an ashen face, he occasionally appeared wasted from a prior evening's surfeit of drugs and alcohol. But he was athletic and immensely talented. He was not alone in advancing the idea of performing to music, as figure skaters do. He coached blond, charismatic Suzy Chaffee, who, more than anyone, brought ski ballet into the public limelight. Suzy and her brothers (Rick raced on the U.S. Ski Team) grew up in Rutland, Vermont. Their mother had been an alternate for the 1942 U.S. Ski Team. Their father in the 1930s practiced stunts at Woodstock, Vermont's Suicide Six on short "goon" skis, made with upturned tips and tails. When the parents encouraged Suzy to learn ballet, she took the fruits of her indoor lessons out on the snow. As a teenager at nearby Pico Peak, paired with a male dancer on skis, she performed spinwheels and royal christies to music.

After she narrowly missed winning a downhill bronze medal at the 1966 FIS World Alpine Ski Championships, and after competing with the U.S. Ski Team at the Grenoble Olympics, Chaffee retired from racing

The Dead-End Sport.
Suzy Chaffee exhibited
athleticism and beauty
in popularizing ski bal-
let beginning in the
1970s. The sport was
tried as a demonstra-
tion sport at the Olym-
pic Winter Games in
1988 and 1992, but
never made it to medal
status. *Photo 1983 by
Barry Stott*

in order to focus on freestyle. She continued her ballet studies in New
York, where she also worked as a Ford model. Not only was Chaffee one
of the world's best women skiers, she was strikingly beautiful. At 5 feet 9
inches, she possessed an extraordinarily lithe body ideally suited for ballet. She starred in freestyle movies, notably *The Moebius Flip* and Willy
Bogner's *Fire & Ice*. She dated movie maker Bogner, the ski fashion heir,
among a number of celebrated men. She appeared in national advertising
for Seagram's, Dannon Yogurt, Revlon, and Chapstick lip balm (earning
her the sobriquet Suzie Chapstick).

Beneath the glitz of her brilliant sequined jackets and rhinestone head-
bands, she was a serious woman who cared deeply about women's rights.
She criticized the injustice of the U.S. Ski Team spending more money
on men than on its more successful women alpine skiers.[6] She lobbied
for the 1973 Amateur Sports Act to make athletics available to schoolgirls
and poorer youth. She helped to launch the National Sports Foundation,
aimed at establishing equal rights for women in athletics. Successful out-

side the sport and imbued with the new spirit of women's lib, Chaffee chafed at the piggish male chauvinism inside skiing. As the earliest and sometimes solitary female freestyle competitor, she competed directly against men, who resented it when music was played for her choreographed performances. Judges were stingy with points for creativity and gracefulness, Chaffee claimed, preferring to reward men for strength and degree of difficulty. Cash prizes for women weren't on a par with the men's awards. Yet Chaffee was better known to the American public than any of the male competitors.

The Flippers

Of course, there was one exception: the famous Stein Eriksen. Growing up in Norway, Eriksen had been inspired by seeing old films of Norway's Ruud brothers —Sigmund and Birger, both jumpers—doing somersaults. He trained in gymnastics as a youngster. Not long after winning the slalom, giant slalom, and combined gold medals at the 1954 World Alpine Ski Championships, Stein left Norway. He found his first job in far northern Michigan, where he was hired to head the ski school at Boyne Mountain—not exactly a glamorous big-mountain resort, but the highest bidder for his services. Stein wowed the Boyne crowds by regularly performing his aerial flip. Nothing matched the athletic excellence he brought to the act of making inverted aerials off a radically upturned kicker jump fashioned from hard-packed snow. He spread his arms wide in a layout, like the beginning of a swan dive, and ended in a forward roll, his hands grabbing his tightly tucked knees. His aerial somersaults were aided by the trampoline effect of his 215-centimeter skis, utterly different from the stubby, easier to deploy short skis worn by later hotdog aerialists. Stein eventually performed the stunt at every area where he was paid to be skiing director: Heavenly Valley, Sugarbush, Aspen Highlands, Snowmass. The first of Stein's serial employers, Michigan's Everett Kircher at Boyne Mountain, would have experienced no difficulty in proving to the Immigration and Naturalization Service that he'd been unable to find an American citizen capable of performing the services offered by Stein Eriksen. By common consent, there was no one in the world like Stein. He employed two principal body parts in skiing: his inside shoulder led the turn, and his lips parted in a dazzling smile. Skiing's most celebrated command of the 1950s, "Ski like Stein," was oxymoronic, since no one did. Blond, blue-eyed, erect as an ostrich, he was an absolute professional

Ski Like Stein! Stein Eriksen—his body forming a perfect comma—patented a turn unlike anyone else's. He also performed aerial somersaults and acrobatic turns at resorts where he was ski school director. Seen by millions in person and on film, he helped to inspire the freestyle acrobatic movement. *Photo by Fred Lindholm*

and perfectionist in everything he did, carefully enunciating his words with a Norwegian accent in a harmonica-like voice. He expected others to perform professionally and could be prickly and critical when they didn't. He worked assiduously on polishing his image. A friend of fifty years once defined Stein's life as "being Stein Eriksen." "Come Ski with Stein" came to be the advertising slogan of wherever he directed ski schools. Over the years, and past several marriages, he became a sort of institution independent of the gregarious, joking Stein some knew personally, who could be counted on to give fair-minded, generous credit to others who contributed to the sport. "I want to present the sport in the most graceful and beautiful way possible," he said. "That is my profession."[7] He accomplished it so successfully that he led hundreds of thousands of Americans to take up the sport and to love it as much as he did. And his aerial flips inspired other athletes to surpass him.

In Vermont, in the 1960s, Herman Gollner skied off a kicker jump into the air and performed the gymnastic stunt of a full somersault with a full twist. Outdoors, it appeared so complex that spectators experienced difficulty recalling exactly what they'd seen. Ski filmmaker Barry Corbet named it the "Moebius Flip," after the nineteenth-century German mathematician August Ferdinand Möbius, who created a surface having only one side and one edge by twisting one end of a rectangular strip through 180 degrees and attaching it to the other end.[8] The stunt was so spectacular that Roger Brown and Barry Corbet named one of their movies *The Moebius Flip* (see page 282).

The New Mogul

Freestyle, as showcased by Chaffee and by former champions on the Dek, helped to remove a prejudice among good skiers: Short skis could, after all, be used for more than teaching beginner classes or as a crutch for the timorous. With them, experts could perform formidable stunts and make dazzling descents. As the popularity of short skis grew, however, there was an unintended side-effect. A 185-centimeter ski makes a tighter radius turn than a 210-centimeter ski. It forms bumps that are closer together. In the early 1970s, slopes came to be pocked with choppy bumps.[9] Traditionalists, whose skiing was thrown out of sync by the new moguls, pasted their car bumpers with stickers announcing SHORT SKIS SUCK. To speed through them, the athletic skier needed rubber legs and a technique of rapid knee action and acutely wiggled turns. Or the skier skimmed from the crest of one bump to the next. Or he alternately slammed the bump with his rear end, porpoising the skis vertically up toward the sky. More often than not, the skiing looked less like linked turns and more like a series of linked recoveries from near-falls. Seeing blond wild man Bob Burns come down through a mogul run in 1969,

Bump Bashers. Scene at an early mogul skiing competition at Aspen in 1974, when long hair and short skis invaded the sport. *John C. Russell*

"changed my life as a ski filmmaker," recalled Dick Barrymore. "Burns's style was unlike any I'd seen before. Short and square with steel thighs . . . he attacked a field of moguls like Errol Flynn attacking a band of pirates. When he skied bumps, he sat down in a permanent 'toilet seat' position, with his arms high over his head, holding 60-inch-long poles."[10]

By the late 1960s, cinematography had become a significant catalyst of hotdogging's explosion. Burns starred in Barrymore's movies, Furrer in Roger Brown's *Incredible Skis*, and Gollner in *The Moebius Flip*. Brown's *Ski the Outer Limits* proclaimed that the oncoming freestyle wave beckoned people to express themselves differently on skis, that a fresh spirit reigned in the sport. Three strands of freestyle were emerging:

- Aerials, inspired by Stein Eriksen, and advanced by performers such as Herman Gollner and Tom Leroy;
- Ballet, advanced by Phil Gerard and Suzy Chaffee;
- Bump or mogul skiing, influenced by Bob Burns and others.

Formal Competition Arrives

In the mid-1960s, the undisciplined new sport of freestyle skiing began to take formal shape. Professional racers, in order to entertain spectators in the period before their dual, head-to-head giant slalom races, performed flips, mambo turns, royal christies, and leg-splitting gelandesprung jumps. Doug Pfeiffer did the commentary and judging. In 1966, promoter Marty Glickman persuaded Schaefer Beer to offer a $1,000 prize for the best stunt performance at an International Professional Ski Racing Association (IPSRA) race at Stratton, Vermont, making it the first freestyle competition to have cash awards.

At the same time, an event called the Ski Masters was started by ski instructor Peter Pinkham, head of the Eastern Slopes Inn at North Conway, New Hampshire, in January 1966. Judges assigned points to competitors for their skill in demonstrating ski school forms, such as the stem, stem christie, parallel, and wedeln. The maneuvers in Ski Masters were as formal as school figures in ice skating. An optimistic Pinkham predicted that style skiing would one day be an Olympic competition, similar to ski jumping, a sport judged for style as well as distance. However, the first Ski Masters at Mount Attitash threatened to accomplish the seemingly impossible: to make freestyle dull. "It was painful to observe grown, proficient skiers trying to show how well they could do a snowplow turn," recalled Tom Corcoran.[11] To spice it up, when something called the Junior Ski Masters was scheduled to be held at his Waterville Valley resort, he added bump and steep skiing.

Just as Corcoran had made Waterville a laboratory for the first Nastar races, he now made his White Mountains resort the creative venue for competitive freestyle. For help, he called on Doug Pfeiffer. Both men had grown up skiing in the Laurentians. In March 1971, they launched the first National Championship of Exhibition Skiing at Waterville. Chevrolet offered prizes of a $6,000 Corvette car, $2,000 in purse money, and $2,000 in expenses. Jean-Claude Killy served as one of the judges. Suzy Chaffee, the only woman entrant, cut stylish figures on 4-foot doubleended skis, wearing red, black, and white tights. Points were awarded for proficiency of skiing, for imaginative use of terrain, and for degree of excitement. In one continuous run, competitors started down through a steep mogul field, followed with aerial stunts off man made jumps, and ended on a groomed slope doing tricks and ballet maneuvers. It was an event in which American men could succeed immediately as they did not, at the time, in international racing. Americans were the world's best in freestyle if for no other reason than that Austrian, Swiss, and French skiers didn't yet know it existed.

Tragic Accidents, Clash of Lifestyles

Almost as soon as freestyle competition took off, it encountered turbulence. Early warning signals appeared at Aspen a few days before the Waterville/Chevrolet championships. The K2 Ski Company and filmmaker Dick Barrymore had staged a contest of mogul and hotdog stunts on Bell Mountain. Several thousand spectators lined the course. They drank jug wine, smoked pot, and were "getting it on with the contestants." Aspen Skiing Company president, balding autocrat Darcy Brown, was not pleased. Detecting the incense of marijuana rising from the slopes as he rode up the lift, Brown swore that such an event shouldn't be held again at Aspen.* That evening, another competition directed by Barrymore took place in the Red Onion bar and restaurant. It was a women's T-shirt contest promoting a freestyle film that Barrymore was making for the K2 Ski Company. On stage, a couple of women bared their breasts

---

*Brown held to his word and refused to endorse a hotdog event the following March. There wasn't much community support for the Skico embargo, and Barrymore and the contestants staged the second hot dog contest anyway on the ridge of Aspen's Bell Mountain. The Skico looked the other way.

for the benefit of onlookers, whose imaginations were insufficiently titillated by the other bra-less girls who had merely wetted their shirts.

There it was: nudity, drugs, shaggy long hair, behavior that flaunted convention. Freestyle had brought to skiing all the noxious things that conventional mainstream America feared. But then came something else—a sudden sense that freestyle competition was highly unsafe. It happened in the spring of 1973 at a Super Hot Dog Classic at Steamboat Springs, Colorado, where freestylers earned points for the quality of their takeoff, twisting and flipping in mid-air, and their landing. One competitor, Peter Hershorn, twenty-four, of Montreal, had announced his intention to perform a back layout with a spread going into a double somersault with legs tucked. Hershorn wanted his in-run to start 25 feet higher so that he'd have the speed he needed to complete his double inverted aerial. But the rules didn't allow it. He took off in the air, his layout was good, and he completed the first somersault. But partway through the second flip, Hershorn's insufficient takeoff speed caused him to close in too quickly on the packed landing surface. His head slammed the snow. His body slid limply down the hill, like a rag doll. A horrified hush fell over the crowd as it stared at the apparently lifeless Hershorn lying near the bottom of the landing. The contest was halted. Finally, an ambulance bore him off. Two days later, Hershorn awoke in a Denver hospital to learn that he'd broken two vertebrae and ripped his spinal cord. He would never walk again.

Hershorn had worked the entire previous summer with a gymnastic trainer in Aspen and a diving coach in Montreal, hitting the trampoline day after day. If a disciplined athlete could commit such an error, how many other accidents were waiting to happen on hills across America? The answer came quickly. A few days later, in a Rocky Mountain Freestyle Championship at Vail, a second competitor failed to complete a flip. Like Hershorn, Scott Magrino became a paraplegic for life.

Rocky Way to the Olympics

The tragic accidents didn't discourage enthusiastic new participants. Across the country, young skiers were boogying and going airborne. Pinkham's original Ski Masters bore fruit when the U.S. Eastern Amateur Ski Association in 1970 formed a Freestyle Committee to sanction competitions, define stunts, and codify rules. Competition spread to other regional divisions of the U.S. Ski Association. Former hotdog stunts were formalized and written up in rulebooks that were updated regularly. The United States Ski Association (USSA) began to hold its own national freestyle championships in 1975. In winter, kids practiced ballet, mogul skiing, and upright aerial stunts. In summer, they practiced on trampolines and on kicker jumps landing in water. At Steamboat Springs, Colorado, freestyle coach Park Smalley opened a freestyle center where he taught aerial acrobatics and ballet skiing on a moving deck in order to reduce the chance that future freestylers would suffer catastrophic injury.

While the amateur branch of freestyle was achieving slow, steady progress, professional freestyle was rapidly disintegrating. After 1975, the professional competitors split into two warring camps. On the one hand, there was Doug Pfeiffer's Chevrolet–*Skiing Magazine*, and the International Freestyle Skiing Association, which, according to Pfeiffer, had worked hard to build corporate sponsorships and more prize money, and to develop a national base of competitors. On the other hand, a group of dissident freestylers joined a Salt Lake City lawyer to form another association to promote their own exclusive welfare. Both associations eventually failed, and then the truly improbable happened. The professional circuit left the country of freestyle's birth and went abroad.

The cause of the exodus originated in a 1977 Vermont jury award of $1.5 million to injured skier James Sunday (see page 60) and because of an accident in the same year that rendered freestyler Dirk Douglas a quadriplegic. The National Ski Areas Association (NSAA) legal counsel advised the resorts to clamp down on freestyle, focusing primarily on banning inverted aerial stunts. The ski areas' opposition to inverted aerials seemed reasonable. They were just beginning to immunize themselves from accident litigation through skier responsibility codes. The areas worried that the sight of upside-down competitors spinning deliriously in the sky would tempt youngsters to try similar stunts. USSA, whose board included influential NSAA directors, went along with a decree banning inverteds. But the ban was devastating to the pros because the aerials were what attracted television, and television attracted commercial sponsors. No such ban existed outside the United States, so in 1978 a group of freestylers, led by champions Scott Brooksbank, Canadian John Eaves, and Germany's Futzi Garhammer organized a freestyle circuit that staged eight men's and seven women's contests in Yugoslavia, France, Austria, Italy, and Canada.

Perhaps the most significant event was not a competition, however. It was a demonstration of freestyle skiing orchestrated by moviemaker

Upside Down. Joe Kellie performs the Moebius Flip, a complex, spinning aerial maneu-ver, at the 1977 Australian Freestyle Carnival. The International Ski Federation approved such inverted aerials, but U.S. ski areas banned them until aerial freestyle competition neared acceptance as an Olympic sport. *Falls Creek, Australia, September 1977, Photography by Bill Bachman*

Willy Bogner at the opening ceremonies of the 1978 FIS World Alpine Skiing Championships at Garmisch Partenkirchen. Here, for the first time, scores of officials in skiing's conservative ruling body, the Interna-tional Ski Federation (FIS), saw sensational stunts being performed on skis. In front of national ski federations and Olympic organizers from around the world was evidence of a brand new kind of skiing!

In 1979, the FIS formally recognized freestyle as a skiing discipline. Ini-tially, freestyle was run by an FIS committee chaired by Canada's Johnny

Johnston. World Cup events in the United States and Canada, previously quasi-professional, were brought under the governance of the USSA and the Canadian Amateur Ski Association, the national associations officially recognized by the FIS. Former professionals were given the chance to reconstitute themselves as qualified amateurs.

Three kinds of competition were recognized: ballet, moguls, and aerials. But in the United States there was a problem. The FIS guidelines required that an aerial competition include the very flips and somersaults opposed by the ski areas. The USSA—under heavy pressure from lawyers, from its directors, from ski areas, and their insurers—allowed only upright aerials in its competitions. Consequently the USSA could not host FIS-sanctioned and World Cup events.

As the 1980s progressed, the ski areas' opposition to inverteds became less and less justified. The rising skills of athletes and coaches dramatically reduced the risk of accidents. There was a rapid increase in knowledge about how to construct kicker jumps, their angles and height, landing gradients and speeds. Of sixty-four thousand inverted aerials performed in World Cup events between 1982 and 1987, only two resulted in serious injury—one broken hip and one fractured vertebra.[12] World Cup competition organizers were willing to pay for insurance covering injuries, at no cost to host ski areas. Yet as late as 1986, when freestyle with inverted aerials was on the threshold of being declared a demonstration event at the 1988 Olympic Winter Games in Calgary, Alberta, NSAA was still fighting against them. One USSA official referred to the opposition of three NSAA officers as "a witch hunt."[13] The United States was out of line internationally with the sport that it had invented.[14]

In 1986, International Olympic Committee (IOC) president Antonio Samaranch effectively ended the dispute. He indicated to the FIS Freestyle Committee that freestyle had a very good chance of becoming an Olympic sport in 1992, and he gave his blessing to its inclusion in the 1988 Winter Games.[15] At Calgary there were demonstration competitions in moguls, aerials, and acro—the name given to ballet. Acro, however, eventually never made it to medal status.* A major reason, according to Howard Peterson who headed the U.S. Ski Association at the time, was that Marc Hodler, the FIS president and the IOC vice-president responsible for winter sports, witnessed a disappointing ballet competition

---

*Acro was a demonstration sport at the 1988 and 1992 Olympic Winter Games, then was discontinued. The last FIS World Championship of Acro (ballet) was held in 1999. Moguls became an Olympic medal event in 1992. Freestyle aerials were a demonstration sport at the 1988 and 1992 Winter Olympics, and became a medal event in 1994.

at the French ski resort of Tignes in 1988, and the unfavorable impression never left his mind.

Caution, Then Reversal

The opposition of ski areas to radical freestyle skiing coincided with a broad trend of cautiousness sweeping the country after 1970, reflected in the passage by legislatures of statutes to protect Americans from themselves. People were being ordered by law to buckle into seatbelts and to wear helmets when motorcycling. Diving boards were removed from public swimming pools. Cautioned by their lawyers, ski areas not only banned inverted aerial stunts. Many of them barred telemark skiers, snowboarders, and riders of skibobs (a kind of snow scooter) from riding on their lifts. The ski industry headed in a direction at odds with that of its young customers: It sought to make the sport less, not more, challenging. But in the late 1990s, bolstered by state skier responsibility codes (see page 62), the resorts reversed their legalistic obsession with risk. They opened special terrain parks full of jumps, moguls, and half pipes for young adventurous skiers and snowboarders to go airborne. It was a U-turn away from the past, and it came about as a new generation of youngsters, successors of skiing's hotdoggers, widened the vision of downhill sliding. They rode, not on two boards, but on one.

Snowboarding

A new sport, spawned by youth, passion, and rebelliousness, echoed an earlier era of skiing's own history.

Snowboarding's appeal is the rhapsodic sensation of banking against the turn's centrifugal force, like floating in gravitationless space. Projecting his feet outward from under him and tilting the board up on its edge, the rider hangs over the snow, like a bicycle racer leaning into a high-speed turn. Feet diagonally across the slope, arms flailing, the snowboarder introduced a fresh and welcome new sensation of descending a mountain.

In snowboarding's mushrooming growth in the 1990s, as in skiing's forty years previously, a grassroots spirit was at work. Teenagers, enthused by having their own sport, unique clothing and language, talked of shredding, bonking, and blunting.* Here was an echo of an earlier generation of young skiers who had talked of schussing, wedeln, and pre-jumping, and who formed a cult of special people. Tens of thousands of baggy-panted snowboarders served as a reminder that skiing's boom had once nurtured its own culture of youth and passion.

At first, ski areas weren't inclined to welcome their newly arrived rescuers. The resorts disdained the wildly colorful teenage riders of boards as much as they had the long-haired freestylers of a generation earlier. They even barred people wearing snowboards from riding the lifts. But the new invaders prevailed. Snowboarding rescued the ski areas in the 1980s just as their business was heading into decline.

Early Snowboarding

Hailed as new in the 1980s, the snowboard was not. In the 1920s, a device looking remarkably like one, the Skiboggan, took the form of a short

---

*To shred was to go hard and fast. To bonk was to hit a non-snow object hard. To blunt was to stall.

fat ski with a long, hinged wooden handle, which the rider grasped for stability. Later, in 1937, a Chicago native Vern Wicklund stood sideways on a snowboard-like sled, which he patented. In the 1960s, the popularity of surfing caused skiers to ask: If guys can ride waves on a board, why not surf across a sea of powder snow? The answer came on Christmas Day, 1965. Sherman Poppen, a Muskegon, Michigan, father, seeking to entertain his children after the plum pudding, nailed crosspieces onto two skis to make a single piece, which he called a "Snurfer." Grasping a rope attached to the tips, his children and neighbors used the Snurfer to slide down a snow-covered sand dune on Lake Michigan. When the run ended at the bottom of the hill (that is, the wave petered out), the rider stepped off the board, usually toppling onto the snow with howls of laughter or, occasionally, with howls of pain in the wrist or shoulder. Poppen, a practiced inventor, had the presence of mind to license the manufacture of his new snow-riding device to a hometown sporting goods company, the Brunswick Corporation. Brunswick perceived the Snurfer to be a plaything, like a hula hoop. The company sold tens of thousands as backyard toys for children.

The first picture of a snowboarder in *SKI Magazine* appeared in 1974.[1] It was not of a Snurfer, but of someone with one foot in front of the other, riding a device called a Winterstick, deep in Utah's powder-rich Wasatch Mountains. In all likelihood, the unidentified rider was Wayne Stoveken, who made boards that could be used for both water and snow surfing. Unassisted by a rope or handle, Stoveken was the first true snowboarder. At least, that's the view of Demetrije Milovich, a one-time Utah ski bum and admirer of Stoveken, who began in 1975 to sell the $80 Winterstick, fashioned by ski designer Mike Brunetto. Riders, who at one time included Robert Redford, could steer by body pressure and by moving their feet (in hiking boots) on the board, like surfers. The number of enthusiasts was small, and the Winterstick only worked well in powder.

Snow surfing, or boarding, needed a developer—the kind of obsessed entrepreneurial promoter who regularly has been attracted to skiing. In 1977, at Stratton Mountain, Vermont, twenty-three-year-old Jake Burton Carpenter began to manufacture a device resembling the Snurfer, on which he had ridden as a boy in the 1960s. The rider held onto a rope attached to the top of what Burton called a "Backyard Board." It cost $49. Traversing on it was almost impossible, although the rider could make passable wedel-like turns. For a more elaborate Backhill model that he designed, Burton added rubber straps that looked something like a water-ski foot piece.

To increase his production, Burton scraped together his own savings, a bank loan, and an inheritance from his grandmother—$100,000 in all—and converted a farmhouse near Stratton into a mini-factory capable of producing fifty wooden snowboards a day. It was a case of instant overcapacity. The first year, 1979, he sold only three hundred boards, the equivalent of six days' production. But sales doubled the next year to more than seven hundred boards, and they went on doubling. By the end of the twentieth century, Burton's privately owned, Vermont-headquartered firm, with operations in Austria and Japan, was the world's largest snowboard company.

Burton and the Culture Clash

Because I'd known Howard Head and Bob Lange, whose inventions revolutionized skiing, I drove to Stowe, Vermont, one summer day in 2001, in order to meet Burton. The man who midwifed modern snowboarding didn't much resemble his famously rebellious, baggy-panted teenage customers. He is neat, trim, polite, courteous to a fault. His vocabulary and manner of expression and evenly modulated voice appear to belong to someone raised in the affluent ex-urbs of northern Westchester or Long Island's south shore, where in fact he did grow up. He is lean, dark-complexioned, of medium height, with carefully groomed dark hair down the nape of his neck, crooked teeth, but with a kind of movie star athletic handsomeness. In his private life, he prefers to be known as Jake Carpenter. At the office, he is Jake Burton—his mother's family name and the one he uses for business. He may even have two *personae*. One Jake attended an exclusive prep school, the other non-conformist Jake was expelled from it. There is Jake the disciplined executive, and there's the Jake who runs a company where employees can bring their dogs to work. There is Jake the cool, calculating, youth-marketing strategist, and Jake the hotheaded believer in the right of teenaged snowboarders to access any resort.

"I didn't invent snowboarding the way Poppen did," said Burton. "No, I believe what Howard Head said about dogged persistence. If there's anything I give myself credit for, it's perseverance."[2] One of Burton's earliest commercial challenges was when skateboarding, a sport born on concrete, found its way onto snow. California skateboard maker Tom Sims began to shape snowboards different than Burton's, designed to make possible the kind of halfpipe stunts done by skateboarders on concrete.

Snowboard Pioneer. Few people have been so identified with the invention of a sport as snowboard maker Jake Burton Carpenter. "If there's anything I give myself credit for, it's perseverance," says Burton. In the decade of the 1990s, snowboarding rose to account for one of every three visits to ski areas. *Photo courtesy of Burton Snowboards*

They "were trying to simulate skateboarding on snow," according to Susanna Howe, the author of *(Sick): A Cultural History of Snowboarding.* An East-West rivalry emerged. The So-Cal skaters—seemingly lathered in perpetual anger—disparaged not only skiing, but also snowboarding as it had developed in the East; it was for dorks. Everything sucked, except their special way of snowboarding, whose origin was not in the mountains, but in the inner-city. Wild new magazines and videos enthusiastically celebrated the exploits of foul-mouthed bad boy Shaun Palmer, and flamboyantly, day-glo dressed Damian Sanders. In 1993, Lee Crane, the managing editor of *TransWorld SnowBoarding* magazine, described the scene. "Like their gang-member, skateboarding cousins, Yo-boarders tend to ride in large packs," wrote Crane. "They typically outfit themselves in baggy denim trousers and Paul Bunyan-size flannel shirts." Their favored music was punk, rap, and hip-hop. With eyes shut, you could identify a snowboarder on the slopes by his speech. *"Dude, I f____ing jibbed that f____ing stump and f____ing piece of s____ lift tower with the tail of f____ board. It was so rad, I nearly f____ing s____ in my f____ing pants. Then that lame-ass skier cut me off and I had to f____ing bail in the f____ing forest."*[3]

The language, the music, and the surliness were a problem if you happened to own a ski resort that was in the business of selling vacations to men and women, half of whom were older than thirty-five. Two out of three snowboarders were under twenty and predominantly male. Many ski areas—with the notable exceptions of Breckenridge, Colorado, and Stratton Mountain, Vermont—at first refused to sell lift tickets to them. The boycott made Burton both angry and skeptical. The resorts that banned snowboarding, he suggested, were bigoted—treating kids as if they were an objectionable minority. "To exclude young people from the mountain is wrong, negative, and shortsighted," he said. "It's terrible to hear people say, 'We don't want to be around kids.' Skiers who speak of 'f____ng snowboarders' give skiing a bad name."[4] Burton's criticism of obscene language by skiers, of course, was disingenuous . . . a supreme instance of the pot calling the kettle black.

While he was angry about the refusal of ski areas to admit snowboarders, Burton also found it ironic. "At the time we were lobbying to gain access to the areas and as they were complaining about snowboarder behavior, the National Ski Areas Association gave me a copy of Warren Miller's *Wine, Women and Skiing*. I read it. It described skiing's early days in the 1940s and early 1950s at Sun Valley. It was just like reading about snowboarders—young people living in the back of a van, counterfeiting lift tickets, eating free crackers topped with relish and ketchup at the condiment counter. I thought, 'Oh, my God, this is exactly the stuff that people are saying is so terrible about snowboarding.' The irony is that the people who gave me the book were once ski bums themselves. They lived that lifestyle. Now they were running the ski areas. And they wanted to throw snowboarders off the premises because the kids were behaving just like they once did!"[5] Burton's analogy was only partially correct. The rebellious early skiers were typically fun-loving college graduates bent on saving money. The snowboarders tended to be angry, subverting teenagers who made themselves authentic with self-mockery and a pride in dissing "the system."

The generational clash of snowboarders and skiers, Burton willingly conceded, helped his sales. Catering to the rebelliousness of his young customers, he said, was "to put snowboarding in a light that I think is appropriate."[6]

Earnest attempts were made, primarily by the ski community, to bridge the cultural gulf separating skiers and snowboarders. It wasn't easy—starting with vocabulary. All the world knows what happens when it snows, but to the snowboarder "snowing" meant "to go snowboarding." To skiers, the word "hotdog" brought up the image of the kind of guys who launched the freestyle movement in the 1970s. To snowboarders, "hotdog" meant a girl who rides fast and hard.

In an attempt to induce the sense of a common heritage, I conceived in 1995 of a competition called Snowmeister. It was not unlike the Nordic combined, in which competitors compile results in two different disciplines—jumping and cross-country—using different equipment. In the Snowmeister, a racer on skis was timed going head to head against a competitor on a snowboard, descending parallel, high-speed, giant slalom courses. Then the two switched equipment for another set of timed runs. (A skier is typically about 10 percent faster than when he rides a snowboard.) The grandly named First World Snowmeister Championship took place at Stratton Mountain, Vermont, in March 1995, with $25,000 in prizes, but the event was never repeated.[7] Later, the very idea of crossover—people both riding and skiing—was attacked by hard-core snowboarders, who regarded crossover as a betrayal of their sport.

In an attempt to tame the behavior of the snowboarders, a group of ski industry organizations in 1991 distributed a pamphlet, "Share a Chair," describing the commonalities of the two sports, such as steel edges and the same lift-ticket price. The pamphlet translated the long-standing language of the Skier's Responsibility Code (for example, "Avoid the skier below you") for snowboarders ("Don't run skiers down. If allowed, launch airs where you can see who may be in your way.").[8] The effort to bridge the gap mostly fell on deaf ears. Hard-core snowboarders were testosterone-charged young males resentful of skiers. The skiers, for their part, saw snowboarders as out-of-control torpedoes of potential injury.[9] They couldn't help feeling frightened at the loud noise of a snowboard approaching rapidly from uphill, being directed by a rider who half the time was blind-sided—that is, when traveling in one direction, the snowboarder must look over his shoulder to see what's ahead.

Rapid Growth

Snowboarders began to appear in real numbers on the slopes when boards and boots dramatically improved in design. Camber, metal edges, P-tex running surfaces, and two-footed bindings were introduced. In a repetition of skiing's development in the 1950s and 1960s, with each new equipment advance starting in the early 1980s, it became easier to practice the sport. Hundreds of thousands of people started to ride on snow for the first time.

"Without youthful snowboarders," said Burton, "ski areas would have become elitist, small, high-end, inbred. Half the business we brought to them came from skateboarders and surfers who wouldn't have taken up skiing. The other half came from people like myself who crossed over from skiing."[10] In the winter of 1984–1985, when it was rare to see a snowboarder on the slopes, skiers accounted for a total of 51 million visits to U.S. ski areas. By the winter of 2001–2002, when skier-visits totaled 54.2 million, snowboarders accounted for 16 million of the visits.[11] Without snowboarding, the resorts clearly would have suffered a punishing loss.

Burton confessed that when the potential for a mass snowboard market was largely a dream in his head, he suffered an accompanying nightmare: that the big ski manufacturers, Rossignol and Salomon, would begin to make snowboards before he could carry out his full business plan. He needn't have worried. The established companies initially failed to understand the culture of the new sport. They stood by passively as Burton and an army of pot-smoking, garishly dressed young entrepreneurs came to exhibit at the industry's annual trade show, sitting on beat-up sofas in booths decorated with graffiti, with the sales staff doing stunts on skate ramps. "We went from a fly on the windshield, to a nuisance, to a threat," said Burton. "They gave us a fifteen-year head start."[12]

The ski companies eventually did make snowboards, and for a while the market continued to soar, although not as much as promoters claimed. In 1994, the National Sporting Goods Association's estimate of two million snowboarders was a gross statistical exaggeration. For the number to be true, it was necessary to envision three people riding on every board that had ever been manufactured.[13] No matter. People who didn't know the difference between a jib and a bonk didn't want to hear about reduced numbers. Unrealistic investor expectation was in the air, and Wall Street exploited this new sporting-goods variation of the dot.com madness. In a 1994 IPO, Ride Snowboards raised $5.75 million on the first day its stock was traded. Its shares leaped from $2 to $35, before they plunged. Six years later, Ride was one of dozens of snowboard firms that went broke.

Soul-searching about Competition

In the 1990s, snowboarding was torn by differences over what it should be as a sport. As they floated across the snow switchstancing and hucking, snowboarders exulted in the freedom from rules and institutions that, as they saw it, had stifled the sport of skiing. Many in snowboarding, including for a while Burton, wanted it to remain a cool, kick-ass pursuit free of discipline. But snowboarders couldn't resist the human urge to compete, and competition inevitably brings rules and institutions. In 1989, 120 competitors from five countries formed the International Snowboard Federation (ISF) to oversee speed and halfpipe competitions.* Then came the urge to make snowboarding an Olympic sport.

The trouble was that the International Olympic Committee (IOC) did not recognize the ISF. The only way the IOC was prepared to recognize snowboarding was if the sport agreed to put itself under the jurisdiction of the Fédération Internationale de Ski (FIS), the governing body of the hated alpine skiing. It was as if a bunch of abortion rights advocates had to join a right-to-life organization in order to be recognized officially. In the United States, snowboarding would have to come under the yoke of the U.S. Ski Team, which is a member of the FIS, which in turn is recognized by the IOC. Submitting to U.S. Ski Team governance roiled influential snowboarders, including Burton. The ski team organized its teams of athletes in a centralized manner that irritated snowboarders. Like it or not, though, snowboarding went along, and that enabled snowboarders to earn medals at the FIS 1996 World Championships. Snowboarding was formalized as an Olympic sport at the 1998 Nagano, Japan, Winter Games, with competitions in giant slalom and halfpipe. Still, there remained rebels who resented the surrender. Norway's Terje Haakonsen—at one time the world's best halfpipe rider—thought so little of the FIS and the Olympics that he refused to participate in the 1998 or in the 2002 Olympics. Haakonsen regarded the IOC and its games as too commercial.[14] A quarter century earlier, the

---

*In 2002, the once free-spirited ISF ran out of money and ended its operations.

IOC ejected champion Karl Schranz from the 1972 Winter Games because *he* was too commercial.

By the end of the twentieth century, two million Americans were snowboarding.[15] Millions more took up the sport in every country that had snow. If they were not people who started on snowboards, they were people who switched to the new sport from skiing. Burton had been a skier in the 1960s. He remembered better than the ski companies that the passion of participants, not industry marketing, had driven skiing's growth.

V

The Culture and Business of Skiing

14

"The Industry"

Skiing is an odd little segment of industry better left to people who understand it and deeply care about it.　　　　　　　　　　　　　　*— Fortune Magazine*

Tennis players talk about their "sport," and golfers about "the game." Ski aficionados grow misty-eyed talking about the "industry." A dream of young skiers graduating from high school is to one day get jobs selling skis or designing new products. Editors of the national ski magazines talk not about the sport, but of the industry they cater to. It is almost a culture unto itself, producing over the years a special language of super-diagonals, offset edges, spoilers, canting, foam injection, sintered bases, and parabolic skis.

The interest of skiers in the industry came naturally. Ski, boot, and binding companies were at the epicenter of new equipment designs that allowed people to ski better with new techniques. The industry was filled with bright, enthusiastic individuals who wanted their clients to enjoy, as they did, the joyful experience of gliding and speeding on snow. As early as the 1930s, skiers socialized in shops and in places like New York's Madison Square Garden and the Boston Garden, where ski vendors and resorts exhibited. Following World War II, after their discharge from the Army, veterans of the 10th Mountain Division joined, or re-joined, the ski industry. Their idea of participating in the sport was to work in it. They managed shops, directed ski schools, ran ski areas, and designed and marketed ski equipment.[1]

Early Trade Shows

Trade shows, at which ski makers, importers, and wholesalers displayed their products to dealers, came to life in Europe after World War II, at

Grenoble, France, and Wiesbaden, Germany (and, later, at Munich). The first American trade show was held at the Hotel New Yorker in May 1953 in Manhattan.[2] Called the National Winter Sports Trade Show, it was organized by Andrew Squires. The following year, the trade show's dates were dictated by a newly formed organization, the National Ski Equipment and Clothing Association. In 1960, its unwieldy name was replaced by Ski Industries America (SIA). Ann Hasper and Doris Taplinger briefly managed the association. Women's skiing career successes typically have ended on the race course. They've rarely become the heads of resorts of ski schools, nor of ski equipment wholesaling and marketing companies. In 1963, SIA replaced Taplinger with Ralph "Doc" DesRoches, a Yankee and former Pennsylvania ski area operator. Taplinger started a parallel show across the street from the SIA show in New York, called The Snow Show, thanks to a window of opportunity created for her by SIA itself. The association excluded from its shows suppliers who hadn't been in the ski business for at least a year, and so Taplinger invited them to exhibit at her Snow Show.

Under DesRoches' vigorous, disciplined direction, SIA became a powerhouse in the sport. He firmly believed that what was good for the sport was good for the industry, and he cajoled his member firms to give generously to the U.S. Ski Team. A short, wide-set man with a stern face, DesRoches patrolled his trade shows like a policeman, reporting violations to his directors on a walkie-talkie constantly held in his hand. Woe to filmmaker Warren Miller if DesRoches caught him promoting his new movie in the aisles of the show without having paid an exhibitor's fee. The punishment was certain ejection from the premises. DesRoches had an unusual manner of expression, in which a first-person pronouncement, drenched in his Down East Maine accent, often was uttered in the third person, as when he would address someone by declaring, "Doc DesRoches says that no exhibitor can enter a competitor's exhibit."

Under DesRoches, SIA added shows in Chicago and the West Coast to its show in New York. A separate organization of western winter sports held trade shows. In Canada, at least two trade shows were staged each April. By the mid-1960s, big dealers and wholesalers were flying annually across the Atlantic to preview model lines at Europe's winter trade shows in Grenoble, Wiesbaden, and Munich. Vendors and shops exhausted themselves traveling from one show to the next, and exhausted their marketing budgets as well. By the time a U.S. skier shopped for a pair of skis, the manufacturer's suggested retail price was four times what it cost a European factory to make them.[3]

Annual Trade Show. Since 1975, the principal North American gathering place for equipment suppliers and retailers has been the yearly SIA trade show in Las Vegas, Nevada. The first ski industry trade show took place in New York City in 1953. By the twentieth century's end, almost a thousand exhibitors occupied a massive half-million square feet of booth space. *From the archives of* Ski Racing Magazine

A modicum of trade-show scheduling sanity arrived in 1975 when SIA downshifted to a single annual exposition, held in Las Vegas, Nevada. It drew 190 exhibitors and 11,000 attendees—principally the buyers from ski shops. When snowboarding began to boom as a business, the SIA show ballooned in size. By 1996, no fewer than 900 exhibitors occupied a massive 516,000 square feet of booth space in Las Vegas.

From Factory to Skier

The emergence of a formal ski industry, as a result of the trade shows beginning in the 1950s, spotlighted the process of getting ski equipment to the consumer. It was as complex as a Bach fugue and as prolonged as the gestation of an elephant. The timetable called for shops to have goods in racks and on their shelves early in the autumn, ready for skiers to buy them for the coming winter. So that the goods would be there on time, the European factories began in December of the previous year to press their overseas subsidiaries and importers to line up orders. Thus

On-Snow Shows. The effort by manufacturers to sell skis to retailers was ceaseless. At an on-snow trade show in the spring, dealers tested demo skis before choosing which models to stock for the following winter. *Stratton Mountain, Vermont, 1970s, Photo by Hubert Schriebl*

began the long wooing of the dealer. First, wholesalers and importer held regional January on-snow trade shows where the dealers could test the new models of skis and boots. Next came shows for special buying groups. They were an overture to the grand opera, the national trade show in March. Even after Las Vegas, ordering was not necessarily complete. The more-or-less final placing of orders took place in April. And if an order didn't come in, suppliers made further sales calls on recalcitrant dealers lasting into May. It was an annual ritual of product introductions and selling that persevered, almost unchanged, for thirty years.

When I first worked for *Ski Business* in December 1963, my desk was piled as high as a small alp with press releases, catalogues, and photographs from manufacturers and reports from correspondents. My job was to reduce the avalanche of information into the contents of a 200-page Show Issue previewing for retailers the products they would sell to consumers in the following winter of 1964–1965. The bases of skis featured polyethylene running surfaces—Kofix and P-Tex—introduced eight winters earlier. Johnny Seesaw's in Vermont was still offering laminated wood skis for $47.50. Boots had heel lacing that created a snugger fit above the ankle. Leather boots, with buckles not laces, sold for $60 a pair.

A releasable binding toepiece cost $9.95. Tapered aluminum poles were a very expensive $19.95. The body-hugging parkas and pants were spectacularly attractive.

The ski shop owner's task was to anticipate which models consumers would want to buy six months later, and then purchase and inventory correctly. Just when snow conditions were at their best, Louie of Louie's Bavarian Chalet wasn't in his shop where he might be profitably catering to clients. He was at the industry trade show in the Las Vegas Convention Center, trying to decide whether to buy three dozen pairs of triple-layer Gore-tex randonée pants for his opening sale the following September. The aim was to stuff the distribution system ahead of the season. In the minds of the suppliers, the customer was not the consumer, it was the dealer—as if General Motors thought its customer not to be the driver behind the wheel, but rather the car dealer. Even the advertising in consumer magazines was aimed at demonstrating a company's commitment to support its dealers in advance of the ski season. The industry advertised beginning in late August, and stopped advertising about Christmastime when people were just starting to ski. Typically, companies advertised their highest price—the suggested retail price—in defiance of the usual practice of luring customers with the lowest price.

The most prominent retailers of ski equipment and clothing before World War II had been the famous department stores, like Saks, Abercrombie & Fitch, and Filenes. They gradually gave up on skiing after the war, and for the next twenty years ski specialty shops reigned in downtown, the suburbs, in mountain towns, and at the ski area base where they were open in the winter, selling, renting, and repairing gear. The specialty shops employed staff experienced in installing safety bindings correctly, fitting boots, and repairing ski bases. In the 1960s, they began to encounter stiff competition from sporting goods stores like Hermans in New York City and Dave Cook's in Denver. The big stores were able to pressure suppliers to grant them lower wholesale prices, and they tended to put equipment on sale earlier. Both practices infuriated the specialty shops.

The principal defender of the specialty shops was the Head Ski Company. With its metal ski, Head was so dominant in the market in the late 1950s and early 1960s that two of every five pairs of skis bought by skiers in specialty shops were Heads. There were about seven hundred Head Ski dealers nationwide—all specialty shops. Head arranged it so that only one shop in a market area could have a franchise. Thus protected, the dealer could feel comfortable knowing his Head skis would not lose their value if he had to carry them as unsold inventory into the next season.[4] Head protected him further by generally refusing to sell to the sporting goods stores and discounters. And woe to anyone who discounted Head skis, or who resold them through another outlet! The penalty was to lose his franchise. The practice came under the scrutiny of the government in the middle of the 1960s, and the Federal Trade Commission issued a cease-and-desist order, restricting the exclusive dealerships that Head had established. The power of specialty shops thereafter weakened.

Prosperity Amid Turmoil

Despite a stagnant economy, skier purchases of equipment in the 1970s tripled, as people switched from metal to fiberglass skis and from leather to plastic boots, as well as taking up cross-country skiing (see chapter 10). In 1968, U.S. ski shops had sold about three hundred thousand pairs of mostly leather boots.[5] Seven years later, the Beconta Company alone imported a quarter of a million pairs of colorful plastic boots.[6] By the winter of 1978–1979, a million pairs of plastic boots were being sold to adult alpine skiers in the United States, and almost a half million more to cross-country skiers.[7]

Notwithstanding the buoyant sales, the ski industry entered a troubling period. In May 1970, the Dow Jones index fell to a low of 631. With inflation rising to a 7 percent annual rate, skiing added to its reputation as expensive. The increased power of the sporting goods discount chains to leverage prices left suppliers feeling pinched. They also had to worry about when the shops would pay them—if not by December 10, then maybe by January 10 of the following year, or as occasionally happened, never at all. A snowless winter could leave a terminal moraine of unsold inventory. Some shops dumped excess products at distress prices, scooped up the cash, and closed their doors. As late as 1987, when U.S. ski shops collectively were doing slightly in excess of $500 million in sales—an amount less than the revenues of the fledgling five-year-old Compaq Computer Corporation—they owed $50 million to suppliers on invoices more than ninety days overdue.[8]

A surprising number of companies seemed unable to establish long-term budgets that recognized the inevitability of winters with poor weather and low snowfall. Interviewing Las Vegas casino magnate Steve Wynn, who took off a winter to teach skiing at Sun Valley, I asked him

why—given his consuming interests in hotel management and skiing—
he hadn't bought or built a ski resort? "The ski business is like being a
one-crop farmer," said Wynn. "If it doesn't snow, you're ruined."[9]

Wynn's pessimism was not universally shared. A number of corporations entered the expanding sporting goods market by owning a ski company. Dunlop, a big name in American sporting goods in the 1970s, bought
a ski factory in Europe. Spalding purchased the Caber boot company.
After its acquisition of Head, AMF acquired Austria's Koflach boots and
Tyrolia bindings.[10] Beatrice Foods bought the Hart Ski Company. Kings-
ford, the charcoal briquette maker, bought Scott poles. Fuqua Industries
acquired the venerable A&T Ski Company. Fiberglass ski innovater Bill
Kirschner sold his K2 Ski Company to the Cummins Engine Company,
and later to Anthony Industries, the swimming pool company.[11] Product
brands changed ownership like seats in a poker game. When the Lange
Boot Company was about to go out of business in 1974, Laurent Boix-
Vives, the chairman of Rossignol, purchased it for himself.

European companies came to dominate the industry. Back and forth
across the Atlantic, they alternately gave their North American offices
more independence in marketing or they took it away. When the franc
and the mark strengthened in the 1970s, threatening to over-price their
products in North America, Rossignol and Bogner built factories in Vermont.[12] Later, when the dollar strengthened, the ski makers stopped production in the United States, and moved it to Slovenia and Spain where
labor costs were cheaper. The making of skiwear, once done by companies such as White Stag in the Pacific Northwest, departed U.S. shores,
as apparel companies outsourced the production of parkas and pants to
Asian factories. K2, the last company to manufacture skis in the United
States for the general market, moved its ski manufacturing to China
in 2002.

Austrian factories suffered badly. Kästle, Kneissl, Blizzard, and Atomic
had to be sold or went into bankruptcy. One cause of their decline may
have been the defeat of their family enterprises in the new global mar-
ketplace by the more sophisticated, publicly owned companies—Salomon and Rossignol in France and K2 in the United States.

Worldwide factory shipments of alpine skis cycled between 5 and
a little over 7 million between 1980 and 2000.[13] Then they fell to 4.1
million pairs in 2003 and 2004. The major cause was the steep drop in
Japanese purchases of skis, from a peak of 2.5 million in the winter of
1992–1993 to a half million pairs, as Japan's population aged and young
Japanese turned to electronic games.[14] In the United States, imports of

boots dwindled from a peak of 1.2 million pairs in 1988 to a level below 700,000.

How Many Skiers?

The national skier-visit count is the principal barometer of the sport's health—some think of it as the industry's gross national product. Newspapers pick up the statistic as soon as it's released each spring. Skier-visits were first measured in the winter of 1978–1979. A skier-visit is one skier or snowboarder participating one day at a ski area. Visits to U.S. ski areas hovered around the 50 million level from 1979 to century's end.

The industry hired consultants to tell it why the number of visits wasn't increasing. Market researchers analyzed the statistical results of phone surveys, mail surveys, and surveys of skiers standing in liftlines. They looked through one-way windows at earnest skiers participating in focus groups. It was by no means the first research done.

The earliest market research having any kind of scientific pedigree, in the winter of 1962–1963, projected the U.S. skier population at 1.5 million.[15] The study was conducted by Ted Farwell, a former Nordic competitor and graduate of Dartmouth and the Stanford Business School, with funding from the federal government. One percent of Americans skied, according to Farwell, and the sport was growing at an average rate of 16.7 percent annually. He also discovered, as did later researchers, that significant numbers of people drop out of the sport after sampling it.[16] Among people who skied less than five years, the dropout rate was higher. The leading reasons given for leaving the sport were having a baby, job demands, and expense.

Nevertheless, skiing's growth accelerated powerfully in the 1960s, so that it was not unreasonable to conclude that the number of skiers might double to three million before 1970. The skier population likely did grow by that much, but it was hard to prove because Farwell's statistical method, which started with a census of skiers standing in liftlines, came to be replaced by a different kind of research. By telephone to people's homes, a sample of respondents representing typical U.S. households were asked if they skied and how many days they had skied. The change in the research method generated much larger numbers than Farwell's. In 1976, the A. C. Nielsen Company upped the estimate to 10.5 million skiers and to 15.5 million in 1982. Simmons Research projected an astronomical 19 million U.S. skiers. In 1985, the National Sporting Goods Association placed the number of alpine skiers at 9.4 million and cross-country skiers at 5.5 million.[17] The statistics generated a number of ski area visits twice as great as the areas were counting physically in their lift-ticket sales. In short, the projections, made from very small samples of Americans contacted by phone, were inaccurate. From year to year, though, the research was at least useful in identifying trends, such as the aging of the skier population. And the industry gladly accepted the large numbers, perhaps because no one wanted to feel as if they were catering to a small market. It backfired in a way, however. The appearance of a sport large in size may have attracted more entrepreneurs than was good for the balance of the industry's supply and demand. Product over-supply induced falling prices. Nor did it help ski and boot makers that they continued to quote their highest price—the almost fictitious "suggested retail price." Or as filmmaker Warren Miller flippantly commented, "A special discount is the mystical amount subtracted from the retail price of any ski product after the normal markup has been doubled."[18]

Trying to Make the Sport Grow

Faced by a flattened growth curve, in the 1980s the industry came together in earnest meetings to preach the need to "grow the market." People taking up the sport seemed to be equaled by the number quitting it. Research was needed to determine what exactly was wrong and what was needed to fill the pipeline with new skiers. One memorable study, which at first glance seemed reasonable in its intent, sought to identify the demographics and psychodynamics of skiers, and then identify non-skiers having a similar profile. With this information, concluded an expensive consulting firm, the industry would be able to identify and successfully advertise to the heathen non-skiing segments of the population likely to want to take up the sport. It was all very scientific. Still, it's puzzling that anyone thought such an approach would work better than the existing system, involving no effort at all. Every year a half-million or more people took up the sport simply because their friends and families (similar demographics and psycho-graphics) introduced them to it.

Apparently it's not in the nature of Americans to accept the fact that something cannot be caused to grow. Leading management consulting firms, such as McKinsey, encouraged leaders of the ski industry to believe that a national marketing campaign would cause Americans to fill vacant rooms and chairlift seats and consume more of the capacity of factories to make skis and boots. In 1990, the industry committed more than $5 million for television and radio advertising and national promotions, and even more for the following season. The effort was regarded as so important that the industry's two leading associations, SIA and the National Ski Areas Association (NSAA), briefly merged in an organization known as the United Ski Industries Association. The resorts and manufacturers together decided to conduct a campaign fashioned after one that endeavored to persuade people to drink more milk. But it's an altogether different matter to persuade television viewers to jump out of their Lazy Boy chairs, strap two boards to their feet, and go to the top of a mountain where the temperature is zero degrees Fahrenheit, while exposing themselves to the risk of bodily injury. Besides, five million bucks of media spending doesn't make much of a dent in the American consciousness. In any event, the ski marketing campaign happened to coincide with a bad ski winter. Poor snow conditions were a discouragement that the most inspired TV spot could not overcome. The brief-lived United Ski Industries Association broke up.

Why didn't the industry accept the proposition that skiing failed to grow because it had matured as a sport? A leveling-off of participation is common to many sports. In-line skating (rollerblading) exploded in the early 1990s, then reached its maximum of around 25 million participants. Bowling alleys were filled with 40 million bowlers in 1999, the same number as ten years earlier. Tennis participation dropped sharply, then in the mid-1990s settled at a plateau of around 10 million players.[19]

After 1970, demographic trends distinctly did not favor growth for the ski industry. There was a decline in the population of youngsters who had once caused the sport to grow (see page 42) and a decline in local venues where they could go to ski (see page 60). In 1950, 55 percent of all Americans had lived in the snow belt of the Northeast and the Midwest; but by century's end only 42 percent lived there.[20]

Ski areas fought among themselves for share of the market as the population of downhill skiers skidded. They introduced discounted season passes, special coupons, and promotions. The inflation-adjusted cost of a lift ticket actually reversed course. Whereas the price of a daily ski pass had increased from an average of $8.52 in the winter of 1975–1976 to $20.37 in 1985–1986, outstripping the rate of inflation, the lift ticket's cost rose at about half the rate of inflation between 1986 and 2002, from $20.37 to $27.39.[21]

But what really rescued the industry from business disaster was snowboarding. A bunch of baggy-panted kids accomplished what America's leading management consultants, $5 million of TV advertising, and a boardroom of corporate suits had not. During the 1990s, when skiing was in decline, visits to resorts by snowboarders increased by 270 percent.[22] Snowboarding changed the face of what once was called the ski industry. So compelling was the change that in 1997, SIA changed its name from Ski Industries America to SnowSports Industries America. The U.S. Ski Association became the U.S Ski and Snowboard Association, and the Ski Writers Association became the North American Snowsports Journalists Association. The change in business dynamics, reflecting the vigor of snowboarding, can be measured in another way. In March 1997, the trade magazine *TransWorld Snowboarding Business* produced a monstrous 330-page trade show issue. Almost twenty years earlier, the 1979 trade show issue of *Ski Business* had also numbered more than 300 pages. But by the time the twenty-first century arrived, ski trade magazines were no longer being published.[23]

15

In Print

Books, magazines, and ski writers, and their struggle on publishing's slippery slopes.

At least 2,322 books about skiing were published in the English language between 1890 and 2002.[1] More than half are about alpine skiing. Technique and how-to-ski books (see chapters 5 and 6) were the most popular sellers for many years, quantitatively overtaken in recent years by an outpouring of where-to-ski guides. There is a small publishing industry built on 10th Mountain Division books, no fewer than thirty at last count. Skiing's literature—of uneven quality—includes fiction and nonfiction, biographies, and autobiographies of racers and resort developers.

Attracted to the Alps by John Ruskin's romantic mid-nineteenth-century sketches, and seeking mountains and snow for a winter vacation (see chapter 1), the British upper class were early readers of ski books. The publication in 1890 of Nansen's epic account of crossing Greenland on skis aroused huge interest in London, publishing's epicenter. Nine books and several magazine articles about the new sport appeared over the next decade. An 1895 article by enthusiast Sir Arthur Conan Doyle predicted that "hundreds of Englishmen will come to Switzerland for the skiing season in March and April."[2]

Ernest Hemingway—boxer, hunter, angler—managed to prove his manhood as a skier as well. He vacationed in Switzerland, in the Italian Dolomites, and at Schruns in Austria, a period of his life that he recalled with joy in *The Moveable Feast*.

> I remember all the kinds of snow that the wind could make and their different treacheries when you were on skis . . . Finally, towards spring there was the great glacier run, smooth and straight, forever straight if our legs could hold it, our ankles locked, we running so low, leaning into the speed, dropping forever and forever in the silent hiss of the crisp powder.[3]

Author, Slalom Inventor. England's Sir Arnold Lunn, credited as the inventor of slalom in 1922. He wrote about philosophy and religion as well as about skiing and mountaineering. "If Cardinal Newman had invented ice hockey, it would not have been more remarkable." *Photo courtesy of Elisabeth Hussey, longtime aide to Lunn*

In 1924, Hemingway wrote "Cross-country Snow," a wistful story in his Nick Adams series. He also wrote ski scenes into his famous *The Snows of Kilimanjaro*. Not long afterward, Thomas Mann wrote skiing into his 1928 novel *The Magic Mountain*. During the same period, Arnold Lunn was nearby in Switzerland concocting, with Hannes Schneider, the new alpine combined race, the Arlberg-Kandahar (see page 8). Skiing was Lunn's unpaid avocation. In fact, he was a working author. Of some forty books he wrote, half were about skiing and mountaineering, the rest about philosophy and religion. If Cardinal Newman had invented ice hockey, it would not have been more remarkable. In 1931, after Lunn's successful effort to induce the FIS to recognize alpine ski competition, he wrote *Difficulties*, with co-author Father Ronald Knox.[4] The book centered on Lunn's doubts about faith and Catholic doctrine. Knox must have been persuasive. In 1933, he instructed Lunn in the slalom inventor's conversion to Roman Catholicism.

Skiing's unreligious purpose, Lunn said, was "to increase the sum total of fun."[5] Lunn's commonsense wisdom, quintessentially British and amateur in spirit, inevitably was overwhelmed by the serious-minded professionals and bottom-line oriented businessmen who later came to invade the sport.

In 1951, a young, freshly crowned Queen Elizabeth knighted Lunn for his contributions to skiing and to Anglo-Swiss relations. In 1960, Sir Arnold met William F. Buckley, Jr. The pundit, Catholic apologist, and *National Review* publisher described Lunn in his 1997 book, *Nearer, My God.* "Lunn stood about five feet ten inches," wrote Buckley. "His hair was thick, unruly, and white. His face was a totally weather-beaten red . . . He spoke with animation and laughed a cackly laugh after every sentence or two, almost always provoking in his listeners similar laughter."[6] For several winters, Buckley and his wife used to visit Lunn and his wife at Mürren where Lunn had invented slalom. Buckley had taken up skiing in middle age, and he wrote one or two pieces on the sport.

The Publishing Scene in the 1950s

A flurry of learn-to-ski books just after World War II were authored by ski pros such as Otto Lang, Benno Rybizka, Taylor Micoleau, and Fred Iselin. Jay Laughlin, an owner of the Alta ski area and the founder of the highly influential *New Directions Press* in New York, publisher of Ezra Pound's poetry, found time in 1947 to bring out the English translation of Emile Allais' *How to Ski by the French Method.*[7]

The most readable and hilarious account of what it was like to live in ski country just after World War II is Frankie and John O'Rear's *Chateau Bon Vivant,* concerning the couple's madcap operation over thirteen winters of the Devil's River ski lodge at Mont Tremblant, Quebec. Disney bought the film rights, and made a dreadful movie, *Snowball Express,* that scarcely resembled the book's plot or characters. The O'Rears went on to help moviemaker John Jay write *Ski Down the Years.* Filled with photographs of the sport's pioneers, it remains the best pictorial account of the sport from the 1920s through the 10th Mountain Division ski troops and up to the 1960s.

The book that best captures what it was like to ski and race in the 1950s is *A Long Way Up*—an honest, detailed biography of Jill Kinmont, written by E. G. "Red" Valens, and fictionalized in the 1972 movie, *The Other Side of the Mountain.*[8] The main protagonists are so extraordinary that they seem almost fictional—a beautiful young princess (Kinmont) who is pursued romantically by wild Mad Dog Buek and by America's premier racer of the late 1950s, Buddy Werner. After her paralyzing fall in a 1955 race (see page 162), Kinmont's grief multiplied. In 1957, Buek was killed when practicing a power stall in his plane over Donner Lake.

Seven years later, Werner was suffocated in a Swiss avalanche. Kinmont spent the remainder of her life bound to a wheelchair.

Andrea Mead Lawrence, famous as the winner of two gold medals at the 1952 Oslo Winter Olympics, was stunned by the succession of woes suffered by Kinmont. She likened the story of *A Long Way Up* to a powerful Greek tragedy. Her own book, *A Practice of Mountains*, a collection of autobiographical reflections, is not the typical boilerplate as-told-to-account of a champion athlete. While Lawrence writes well about racing, much of the book is philosophical, drawing quotations from Plato, William Blake, Balzac, Carl Sagan, and Chateaubriand. It's an odd, exotic book, surely one of the most cerebral ever written by an athlete.

Oakley Hall stands out as ski fiction's most expert lecturer, if not most elegant writer. His descriptions of racing, whatever they lack in verve, made up for it in authenticity. "I checked my zippers and my helmet," observes the protagonist in Hall's *The Downhill Racers*. "I exhaled hugely to get the carbon dioxide of shallow breathing out of my lungs . . . In the slot I fanned my goggles in and out, set my poles. At the count of five I began to flex my knees. Go."[9] At Squaw Valley, Hall held seminars for writers, and himself wrote *The Art and Craft of Novel Writing*. One of his novels, *The Pleasure Garden*, concerns volatile, intense characters working at a new ski resort that suspiciously resembles Squaw Valley in the 1950s. Hall's greater commercial success, *The Downhill Racers*, was a page turner, mixing love, unplanned pregnancy, money, and schussing. The novel captures the aura of racing after Mead-Lawrence and Kinmont. Hall sold the film rights to the Paramount Studio. Published in 1963, its plot was all but discarded in the making of the 1970 movie (see next chapter).

An Explosion of New Titles in the 1960s

The very fine writer James Salter composed the screenplay for *Downhill Racer*. The sixties arguably produced the best prose about a sport that often has lacked the panache of golf and flyfishing literature. Irwin Shaw and John Updike, both skiers, included skiing in their fiction. Their writing, and that of John Cheever, Art Buchwald, and Gay Talese, appears in *The Ski Book*, a splendid anthology created primarily through the efforts of Morten Lund.[10]

Publishers flooded book stores and ski shops with ski books. *SKI Magazine's 1965 Annual* listed no fewer than thirty-six different titles in print at the time. Half of them were about technique and learning to ski, including books by triple gold medalist Toni Sailer and instant parallel advocate Walter Foeger, and a smorgasbord of versions of the best way to ski, including the Austrian technique and the American technique.[11] *America's Ski Book*, published in 1966, was an almanac that included instruction, racing, a resort guide, a history of the sport, and explanations of equipment.[12] Four years later, Harper and Row produced *SKI Magazine's Encyclopedia of Skiing*, filled with text from the magazine and hundreds of statistics, dates, and facts.[13]

Shift in Reading Interest

America's Ski Book and the *Encyclopedia of Skiing* proved sufficiently popular that they were updated in revised editions until 1984. Since then, information on such a scale hasn't been widely available, a void that partly gave rise to the idea of the book you are holding in your hands.

How-to-ski books peaked in popularity in the 1970s, then declined as people turned to video for their off-the-slope lessons. Ski book publishing came to be dominated by guides with pictures and maps of resorts and where to go cross-country skiing. No fewer than 250 new or revised editions of where-to-ski books were issued by publishers during the decade of the 1990s.[14]

The principal publisher specializing in ski books in the 1990s was Mountain Sports Press, an offshoot of *SKI* and *Skiing* magazines in Boulder, Colorado. It issued a dozen lavishly illustrated histories of ski resorts—Vail, Stowe, Mammoth Mountain—subsidized by the resorts celebrating themselves. A kind of literary counter-attack then took place. At the beginning of the twenty-first century, two angry books attacked the big resorts for their environmental impact. A remarkable transformation took place in ski literature. A couple of generations earlier, in *Chateau Bon Vivant* and *The Pleasure Garden*, the O'Rears and Oakley Hall had evoked the close bond among skiers; in 1984 Martie Sterling captured it in her wonderfully amusing *Days of Stein and Roses*, a memoir of running a boarding house in Aspen with guests and friends.[15] By contrast, the ski books of the twenty-first century were about the disappearance of community and a toxic invasion of the mountains by impersonal ski corporations. No joy of skiing is celebrated in 2002's *Downhill Slide*. The author, Hal Clifford, mourned the loss of the old-time intimate ski town. He attacked "the Wall Street imperative continuous growth ... in towns and environments that are ill-prepared to withstand such pressure."[16] In *Powder Burn*, about the 1998 mountain-top arson at the "glitzy ski resort" of Vail, author Daniel Glick described a day of skiing in which "wealthy patrons expect patrolmen to put their ski boots on . . . and phone to make restaurant reservations . . . A few C-notes get you VIP first tracks down the mountain after a stellar snowfall."[17] It was a different world than the innocent one viewed by Franky O'Rear thirty-five years earlier, when she described her reason for wanting to live near a ski area: "We lay back on our skis in the midst of a dazzling panorama of snow," enthused O'Rear, "with vast sparkling slopes and high peaks thrusting skyward. (Then) we were on our skis, racing through plumes of deep powder snow to the valley floor below."[18]

The Early Ski Magazines

Although it can't be categorized as "oldest continuously published," *SKI Magazine* certainly has the most extended lineage of any U.S. ski periodical. In 1935, Seattle journalist Alf Nydin had the idea for a national periodical, and he called it *SKI Magazine*. He published his first issue in January 1936. The next season, Nydin changed his new magazine's name to *Ski Illustrated*, sprucing it up with graphics and color. He also apparently sensed that if he wanted to ascend into the big leagues of publishing he needed to move *Ski Illustrated* to New York City. The title *SKI* was abandoned. The opportunity to use it was seized briefly in 1941 by magazine writer David Judson (later, a ski area operator and a founder of the National Ski Areas Association). Judson published only three issues, then sold *SKI* back to *Ski Illustrated*, and left to join the 10th Mountain Division. In 1948, Bill Eldred purchased *Ski Illustrated* along with two other magazines, *Western Skiing* and *Ski News*, and combined them under the single title, *SKI*.* Eldred's first issue, November 1, 1948, carried a disparaging account by Jay Laughlin of the rabid nationalism he found at the Winter Olympic Games at St. Moritz, entitled "International Racing Spews Discord."[19] The article was impressive in anticipating the jingoistic triumphalism that would come to pervade the Olympics (see chapter 8). Laughlin was among the numerous friends of the socially

---

*Between 1939 and 1943, *Ski Illustrated* continued to be published out of New York, although it suffered from the loss of European ski equipment and resort advertising because of the war, and moved its publishing base to Concord, New Hampshire. It kept its editorial and advertising offices in Manhattan. The author is grateful to ski historian Kirby Gilbert for this information.

The Ski Magazines. The oldest U.S. magazines for skiers are *SKI* and *Skiing.* After 1972, the publishing field came to be fractionated by special-focus periodicals such as *Powder* and *Cross-Country Skier.* Snowboard magazines arrived in an avalanche starting in 1988. *Photos: John C. Russell*

well-connected Eldred, who established his magazine in Norwich, Vermont, across the Connecticut River from Dartmouth College.*

Eldred labeled his first issue Volume 13, No. 1, most likely because he wanted to make it clear that *SKI* was the descendant of Nydin's original magazine, and therefore older than *Rocky Mountain Skiing*, a large-format, news-oriented magazine launched in Denver the same winter by 10th Mountain Division veteran Merrill Hastings. An opinionated bulldog of a man, Hastings had a reputation for occasionally stimulating advertising sales by communicating in advance to a resort or equipment company the possibility of a negative story appearing in his magazine's pages. Yet Hastings had a sound, visceral sense of what skiers wanted to read. He was aided in the endeavor by Doug Pfeiffer and by a couple of professional editors who successively managed for a few years to endure his abrasive management: Bil Dunaway, who would go on to own the award-winning *Aspen Times*; and Bob Parker, who would help to build the new ski resort of Vail.

Skiing and *SKI* faced competition from *Sports Illustrated* when it first published in 1954. Unlike today's magazine, which virtually ignores the sport, the *SI* of the 1950s featured tips on how to ski better, on racing, fashions, and profiles of well-known skiers. Ezra Bowen, the son of the novelist Catherine Drinker Bowen, served as *SI*'s original ski editor, aided by a young Morten Lund. Fred Smith, who created *SI*'s swim-suit issue, wrote extensively about skiing. (Later, Dan Jenkins reported on Olympic and World Championship racing, and William Oscar Johnson—over twenty years, between 1970 and 1990—came to write as many articles about skiing as had all of the rest of *SI*'s staff combined.)

Publishers, broadcasters, advertisers, and their families were hearty members of the ski community. They celebrated skiing as a sport and they regarded the people who built resorts as bringing good into people's lives. Ski scenes regularly appeared on the covers of *The New Yorker*, the *Saturday Evening Post*, and *Playboy*. The general interest magazines carried pictures and stories of new resorts and of celebrities and families on the slopes. *Life Magazine* often went to a ski party. *Town & Country* featured pictures and snobbish accounts of the jet-set crowd at Sugarbush.

In the winter of 1958–1959, Arnold E. Abramson in New York City launched a new magazine for skiers, *Ski Life*. He did it partly as a consequence of having taken a winter vacation at the northern Quebec resort of Mont Tremblant, where ski school director Ernie McCulloch taught

---

*SKI Magazine moved across the river to Hanover, New Hampshire, in 1952.

him to ski. Excited by McCulloch's approach to instruction, Abramson encouraged him to write a book with how-to-ski photos by his wife Janet, an accomplished photographer. Back in New York, where he ran Universal Publishing & Distributing Company, Abramson published *Learn to Ski* by Ernie McCulloch in an inexpensive soft-cover edition. Quick sales of fifty thousand copies of McCulloch's book convinced Abramson of two things. "One, there's a big market of people out there who want to read about how to learn to ski. Two, they aren't being served by the existing ski magazines."[20]

An engaging, lively fellow, Abramson started *Ski Life* as a sister publication of *Golf Magazine*, which he had just launched. He brought a harder-edged, more commercial approach to magazine publishing than the American skiing public had seen before. A circulation veteran of the old Bernarr Macfadden stable of fitness magazines, he was expert at concocting covers with hard-sell lines.

Hi-speed secrets by McCulloch!

Rotate or reverse? When to use each and why.

Use a platform, turn better!

Better and *why* were Abramson's favorite words. It was a style of blurb writing that flourished in 48-point type on the covers of ski magazines over the next forty years. Although Abramson's *Ski Life* lacked *SKI*'s authority and its early issues were amateurishly executed, his circulation savvy made the magazine the newsstand leader in its field. *Ski Life* and his *Golf Magazine* and *Family Handyman* were the kind of special-interest magazines that in a few years would attract readers away from the general magazines like *Life*, *Look*, the *Saturday Evening Post*, and *Collier's*.

In 1959, John Henry Auran became *SKI*'s managing editor. The magazine's circulation reached 51,000.[21] Auran began to introduce provocative articles and headlines and big picture stories, and he jumped at opportunities to introduce sociological, historical, and literary references into ski writing. He created a stimulating magazine, but it wasn't enough. The magazine was struggling and owner Bill Eldred in New Hampshire was in failing health. Although he'd married into wealth, the conjugal arrangement apparently didn't help Eldred subsidize his publishing business. In 1961, he sold the magazine to *Ski Life*'s owner, Abramson. Thus America's oldest ski periodical was merged with its youngest.

Abramson moved the newly titled *SKI Incorporating Ski Life* from Hanover to the corner of Second Avenue and 42nd Street in New York. In Manhattan, the magazine's offices would be a cab ride's distance from dozens of agencies that created ads for ski equipment and clothing firms, and that made media placement selections for automobile and liquor companies wanting to reach skiers. *SKI*'s associate publisher in Hanover, David Rowan, wasn't invited to join the newly merged magazines ... fortuitous perhaps, because it enabled him to start *Ski Area Management*, a successful trade magazine for operators of ski resorts. In the process, Rowan helped to launch the National Ski Areas Association in 1962 (see page 61).

Ski Life's editor Martin Luray took over as the top editor of *SKI Magazine Incorporating Ski Life*, the merged magazines. Invoices were slow in being paid. Costs were contained in a vise-like grip. Seeking an escape from Abramson, Luray got in touch with a young publisher, Bill Ziff, who had inherited control of the Ziff Davis Company, which eventually came to publish fifty-five magazines, including *Popular Photography*, *Hi Fi and Stereo Review*, *Popular Boating*, and *Car & Driver*. Ziff especially liked to ski, so he didn't need much encouragement to buy *Skiing Magazine* from Merrill Hastings in Colorado, in 1964. Moving the magazine to New York and needing people to operate it, he hired most of *SKI*'s editorial and advertising sales people. I did not join the exodus, and Arnold Abramson named me editor-in-chief of *SKI*.

Editing *SKI Magazine* in 1964 was like arriving in the Klondike during the gold strike and finding a well-paid job editing an entertainment guide for miners. That year, retail sales of ski gear jumped ahead by 25 percent. Advertising pages increased. The magazine's circulation almost doubled between 1965 and 1970, as hundreds of thousands of baby boomers took up skiing. At *Skiing Magazine*, Ziff's newly installed editor Luray attempted to imbue the magazine with the slickness of Ted Patrick's award-winning *Holiday* at the time. But Bill Ziff wanted a publication that more closely fit Ziff Davis's stable of hard-core car, boating, and hi-fi magazines. *Skiing* should be a "magazine for serious skiers," Doug Pfeiffer told Ziff. Luray was removed from the editor's chair. Pfeiffer, who confessed to Ziff that he was "not a professional editor, I'm a ski instructor," was named the magazine's editorial director. John Jerome, who had recently joined *Skiing*, became editor.

A quiet, tall Texas native and an excellent writer, Jerome was soon creating wonderful profiles and features. But he disliked living in New York, and he was irritated by the incessant complaints from the ad sales people, including the publisher, about the magazine's product reporting.[22] He abandoned his staff job and moved to Franconia, New Hampshire, where he wrote fine books on topics as diverse as building stone walls and canoeing. Ziff, meanwhile, gave total authority over his magazines to publishers whose principal skill was selling ad space.

Skiing Magazine intensified its *gravitas* ("The Magazine for the Serious Skier") by recruiting as its new editor Al Greenberg, a veteran business journalist. Greenberg wrote at length and in excruciating detail about bindings. "Shim washers are supplied for installation under the toe unit to eliminate vertical clearance between the release pin and the lip of the front insert," explained a three-page 1969 article under the tantalizing headline "Gertsch 6D."[23] Greenberg became an industry authority and, to his very considerable credit, his support of experts such as Gordon Lipe and the injury-crusading Carl Ettlinger led to important advances in skiing safety, such as universal anti-friction pads and workshops for training the people who install bindings in retail stores.

SKI Magazine competed fiercely with *Skiing* for advertisers and readers. It broke the first stories on the Graduated Length Method of ski teaching, the pure carved turn, and the possibility that Jean-Claude Killy would win all three alpine gold medals in the 1968 Olympics. The magazine introduced multi-page portfolios of dramatic black and white photography of skiers in exotic mountain settings. Many of the pictures were shot by staff photographer Paul Ryan, an intense, stuttering, owlish-looking guy, who later became an accomplished cinematographer, working on several Robert Redford films.

The large number of raw novices—office secretaries, professionals cooped up in offices—who were entering the sport and who were potential readers, raised concerns about whether they were strong enough to ski. One confessed in a letter to *SKI* columnist Ernie McCulloch that she couldn't get back on her feet after a fall, and what could she do? Without cracking a verbal smile, McCulloch advised her to practice getting up off her living room floor wearing skis. Dr. Hans Kraus, who served on President Dwight Eisenhower's Physical Fitness Council, wrote about similar concerns. A Park Avenue back specialist who served as a volunteer ski patrolman on weekends, Kraus had helped devise the Kraus-Weber fitness tests, which revealed that most American children lagged behind European youths in strength and physical condition.[24]

In the 1960s, America's most popular home exercise program was the Royal Canadian Air Force 5BX Plan for Physical Fitness. The author of the little RCAF booklet, Dr. Bill Orban, adapted the 5BX plan for *SKI Magazine* readers.[25] One of his exercises involved extending the arms toward a wall and leaning forward toward it, keeping the legs straight while raising both heels off the ground. The idea was to enhance ankle mobility, which was important in skiing. Orban particularly recommended the exercise for women, whose Achilles tendons at the time were shortened from the constant wearing of high-heeled shoes.

Rambunctious, politically incorrect humor radiated from the pages of the magazines. There were cartoons and even comic strips. The editors of the *Harvard Lampoon* created a special section in *SKI*'s Spring 1966 issue, whose cover displayed a curvaceous girl skiing in a bikini. A busty Playboy bunny topped a column entitled *Sandy Kofix's Repair Shop*. "What's the cheapest way to have my name engraved on my new skis?" asked a fictitious reader. Answer: "Change your name to Kaestle."[26] The term "ski bunny" took on a double meaning when the Playboy Club introduced skiing on nondescript hills next to its resort clubs at Lake Geneva, Wisconsin, and Great Gorge, New Jersey. Although a woman historically is twice as likely as an American man to win a championship medal, editors were more likely to celebrate her success, not by a picture of her racing through the gates, but by stretching her supine body across a color foldout. Ski publishing was a hive of male chauvinism, partly arising from the fact that 80 percent of its subscriptions were sold to men. Whatever the reason, no woman to date has advanced to become the chief editor of a national ski magazine. *SKI* briefly published a diverting column of tips and advice for women, *Girls' Rules*, written by Abby Rand, a movie publicity agent and freelancer (see page 39). A short, firecracker of a lady who talked like a New Yorker and skied with the enthusiasm of a Swiss mountain girl, Rand would go on to write the first decent, comprehensive guidebook for Americans on skiing in Europe.

Gradually, the two principal national ski magazines came to smother their covers with crackling "sell-lines" to attract readers.

Dollar-saving tips for that big trip!
How to spot skiing errors and correct them
In this issue, the country's greatest ski teachers!
The steepest slopes in North America . . .

As a result of discovering the kinds of article that most attracted readers, *Skiing* and *SKI* became more homogeneous and formulaic, mirroring each another's content. Editors came and went, their tenure often short-lived. Bill Tanler served briefly as *SKI*'s executive editor. He left to start a newspaper in Jackson Hole, then launched *Ski Racing, The Ski Industry Letter, Ski Tech, Bicycle Retailer News*, and *WinterSports Business*. He was succeeded by Jim Spring, who later started skiing's leading market research firm, astutely based on his insight, gained as editor of *Ski Business*, that retailers were abysmally short of information about the details of the inventory they held in their shops. In 1971, from the *Saturday Review* came a bright, energetic executive editor, Dick Needham, who would rise to be *SKI*'s editor and who remained with the magazine for another twenty years.

New Magazines Launched

Assisted by youthful demographics driving the sport's growth, the number of readers of *SKI* and *Skiing* had grown steadily since Eldred and Hastings launched their magazines in 1948. By 1966, *SKI* had 136,000 paid subscribers and 68,600 newsstand buyers.[27] It would add another 75,000 subscribers in the next two years as the magazine published six rather than eight issues per season. It seemed to be a great success story, but the reality was that some of the circulation growth had come from the aggressive selling of subscriptions to marginally interested readers. The field agencies making the sales retained all of the money from the first year's subscription, generating no net revenue to the publisher. Abramson sold *SKI* in 1972 to the Times Mirror Company, a New York Stock Exchange company headquartered in Los Angeles. The publishing merger reflected a broader trend of mergers in the ski industry, whose growing revenues were attracting the attention of new-business strategists at corporations (see page 59).

The money-making prospects attracted smaller publishers, too. The year 1966 saw the creation of *Skiers' Gazette*—a sort of skiing *New York Review of Books*—with stimulating essays and needling assaults on the sport's commercialism.* Another alternative magazine for skiers, *Powder*, was launched as an annual in the winter of 1972–1973 by the Moe brothers, Jake and David. The Moes were determined to exploit what they claimed was conservative, timid reporting by the established ski magazines. "What pushed us was a real disdain for *SKI* and *Skiing*," said Jake Moe. "I mean, we'd pick up a copy of either and just say, 'Where is the essence of the sport?' There were all these Grand Marnier ads, Jim Beam ads."[28] At *Powder*, the Moes emphasized the visual allure of the sport. In each issue appeared collections of exotic black and white photos of the kind pioneered by *SKI* in the 1960s and which that magazine had dropped from its pages. The contrast of *Powder*'s pages with the increasing

---

*Skiers' Gazette was published between 1966 and 1972, and as *Mountain Gazette* between 1972 and 1979, when it ceased publication. The magazine was revived in the year 2000, achieving most of its claimed 65,000 circulation from distribution through gear shops and bookstores.

density of information in the traditional ski magazines was striking, and breathtaking to behold. But economics inevitably trumped art, and *Powder's* pages came to be encumbered visually with the very ads it deplored in the other ski magazines. At the same time, it was unable to achieve their larger circulation, and what circulation it had was not scrutinized by the Audit Bureau of Circulation.

The soaring popularity of nordic skiing in the early 1970s triggered more publishing activity. In Brattleboro, Vermont, Barbara Brewster launched the first cross-country ski magazine. And in the summer of 1974, in offices on Madison Avenue in Manhattan, I worked up the design for an annual newsstand publication, *SKI Magazine's Guide to Cross Country Skiing*. By 1979, the guide had swelled to 186 pages, including 65 pages of advertising for nordic resorts, apparel, skis, boots, and poles. Its successor, *Cross Country Ski Magazine*, unhappily, lasted only three winters. The reality was that Nordic participation already had crested in popularity, partly due to a succession of warm or snowless winters in the early 1980s (see page 203).

A Switch to Lifestyle

The year 1985 began a period of magazine publishing turbulence. After twenty years of ownership, Ziff Davis sold *Skiing* and most of its other magazines to the diversifying broadcaster, CBS. Within two years, CBS sold the magazines to Peter Diamandis, who quickly unloaded four of them—*Skiing, Field & Stream, Home Mechanix,* and *Yachting*—on Times Mirror. The transaction shocked many in the publishing industry, who wondered why Times Mirror would spend in excess of $150 million, including $25 million for *Skiing*, to buy magazines aimed at markets the company already was serving. *SKI* and *Skiing*, which had competed fiercely against one another for forty years, were now under the same owner.

If Times Mirror's idea was to monopolize the ski publishing market, its strategy was shaky. In 1987, when the company was plotting to buy *Skiing*, the New York Times Company already had embarked on the launching of a new magazine aimed at skiers, *Snow Country*.* The choice of the name, employing "snow," not "ski," proved prophetic.

---

*The title actually was taken from an earlier failed magazine launched in 1969 by the Golf Digest Company, about the time the company was purchased by the New York Times Company.

At *Snow Country*, shortly after being retained as the magazine's founding editor, I took a trip in the summer of 1988 to Colorado, where I was astounded by the amount of building in ski towns. Construction derricks were everywhere. New hotels, condominiums, and second homes filled valleys. Even if the sport of skiing wasn't growing, the place sure as hell was. "Why not make *Snow Country* a magazine about a place?" I asked. *Snow Country* could be edited, not so much as a special interest magazine about a sport that wasn't growing, but about a place that was. It could be edited as a regional magazine, like *Caribbean Life*, *Sunset*, *Arizona Highways*, or *New England Journal*. It would be about the mountainous region where people ski, take vacations, and, increasingly, come to live. Moreover, it would serve the publisher's decision to publish not only in winter, but also in summer when people don't ski. A magazine oriented to a place would be relevant in July in a way that a magazine strictly about skiing could not.

The first published ratings and rankings of North American ski resorts appeared in *Snow Country*'s September 1989 issue. The magazine recruited a thousand readers to fill in Report Cards, assigning numerical ratings to their experiences of taking lessons, snow conditions, dining, and accommodations. It weighed the scores of their subjective experiences at each resort with statistics of chairlifts and gondolas, vertical drop and acres of terrain, snowmaking acreage, and number of beds next to the slopes. The scores became the basis of the magazine's rankings. *SKI* responded in October with its own rankings. Both magazines rated Vail number one.[29] The coverage by wire services and newspapers caused public awareness of the magazines to soar.

The contents page of *Snow Country*'s premier issue listed articles about Lifestyle, Property, Travel, Buying, and Instruction. The magazine photographed fashions suitable for wearing in the place: snow country. Readers were introduced to unusual products made and sold by craftspeople living in snow country. Robert H. Boyle, the noted angler and *Sports Illustrated* writer, wrote a piece called "The Snow Country Fly," about the salmon fly attractive to mountain trout. There was a chart of recent selling and asking prices for second homes and condos. Skiing was beginning to morph into one of several "lifestyle" amenities offered to guests at four-season mountain resorts, causing editors and publishers to rethink what a ski magazine should be.

The shift to lifestyle content caused the magazines to reduce their coverage of the athletic core of the sport. In the early 1990s, a new editor at *SKI* eliminated "Ski Pointers" from the magazine's pages. For thirty years the short instruction tips had been the most intensively read information in the magazine. The decision was roughly the equivalent of *Ladies' Home Journal* dropping its best-read department, "Can this Marriage Be Saved?" In its June/July 2005 issue, published after Bode Miller spectacularly won the first World Cup title for America in twenty years, *SKI* covered his feat on two-thirds of a page, while devoting two pages to cooking steaks on outdoor grills. The great racing events and their heroes virtually disappeared from the pages of the skiing magazines. It was as unimaginable as if the U.S. Open and Pete Sampras and the Masters and Jack Nicklaus all vanished from the pages of tennis and golf magazines. But it happened in skiing.

While general advertisers were attracted to the lifestyle content, readers didn't necessarily follow suit. *Snow Country* failed to turn a profit and shut down in the summer of 1999. The circulation of the remaining ski magazines flattened. In 1966, people had bought 68,000 copies of an issue of *SKI* at newsstands and other outlets; in 2004, they bought only 14,777 copies.[30] Paid subscriptions to *SKI* and *Skiing* in 2004 were also lower than thirty years earlier, as the publishers decided it was more cost effective to halt spending on subscription mailings and rather distribute the magazines free to targeted skiers.[31] Attempts to attract young snowboarders as readers failed. Snowboarding teenagers and twenty-somethings preferred their own raunchy, irreverent 'zines, saturated with their own language and lifestyle.

Snowboard Magazines

Snowboard publishing, from the beginning, was dominated by Californians. The earliest reporting on the sport showed up in West Coast–based skateboarding magazines such as *Heckler*, and in surfing and teenage music rags. In San Francisco, the first magazine specifically for snowboarders, *Absolutely Radical*, was created in March 1985 by a visionary American-Chinese youth, Tom Hsieh. Hsieh published only one issue before switching the title to the more establishment-sounding *International Snowboarding Magazine*. It didn't help, as Hsieh lacked capital to sustain his vision. But he triggered an explosion. In 1987, Larry Balma and Peggy Cozins launched what is today the oldest continuously published magazine for snowboarders, *Transworld Snowboarding*. Balma and Cozins had been presenting snowboarding in a skateboarding magazine they published, but they found they could attract more readers and advertisers in a separate periodical, *Transworld*. Shortly afterward, the publisher of *Powder* and *Surfer* magazines launched *Snowboarder*. Soon, snowboard magazines swamped newsstands, sports shops, and any store counter proximate to where teenagers gathered. Among the titles were *Plow*, *Blunt*, *Fresh and Tasty* (for women), *Snoboard*, *Snowboard Life*, and *Snowboard Canada*. Within a span of ten years, snowboarding spawned a dozen magazines.

"Advertising was easy to sell," recalled Brian Sellstrom, a former McGraw-Hill vice-president, who became an owner of *Transworld*. "There were at least 240 companies selling brands of snowboard . . . produced by maybe 15 factories."[32] Inflating the boom was a Japanese craze for the sport so intense that importers and dealers, bolstered by a strong yen, were willing to pay the U.S. retail price to obtain snowboards to sell in Japan. But when the Japanese mania for riding collapsed in 1995, so subsequently did the number of snowboard companies, and along with them the advertising that had sustained the sport's multiple boutique magazines. Yet their decline was short-lived. By 2005, as many snowboarding magazines were being published as in 1995.

"Snowboarding is a completely image-based sport," said *Snowboarder* publisher Doug Palladini.[33] The snowboarding magazines served as bibles for teenagers whom the ski magazines had failed to attract after 1970. They celebrated the adventures and lifestyle of snowboarding's champions at a time when the traditional ski magazines turned away from profiling the sport's star athletes. "Skiing became like a commodity—it lost its culture," claims long-time snowboarding editor Lee Crane.[34]

How Newspapers Covered the Sport

One reason for the success of the special-interest ski magazines is that the sports pages of daily newspapers in the United States typically lack the kind of detailed information about skiing that appears in European newspapers. Swiss, German, and Austrian papers, and the French sports daily, *L'Équipe* and the Swiss *Der Sport*, devote far more coverage to resorts and racing than do American dailies. As a result, few skiers in Germany, Switzerland, and Great Britain find it necessary to subscribe to ski magazines, whose circulations remain at forty thousand or less, about one-tenth the size of their American counterparts.

American newspapers, with a few exceptions, haven't made a substantial investment in skiing coverage. The typical ski editor, writer, or columnist of a large metropolitan paper is a full-time journalist, taking time off from other beats at the paper to cover skiing sporadically during the winter months. As long ago as 1952, New York sports writer Bill Wallace cynically described the situation. "The daily newspaper ski writer has two tremendous advantages," said Wallace. "His avid public will read anything, and his boss has no idea what he is writing about."[35]

The top newspaper journalists who have written for the national ski magazines over the past fifty years included Tony Chamberlain of the *Boston Globe*, Archer Winsten of the *New York Post*, Don Metivier and Phil Johnson in upstate New York, Mitch Kaplan in New Jersey, Dave Irons in Maine, and radio announcer Stan Bernard in New York. At the *New York Times*, Janet Nelson and Barbara Lloyd succeeded Mike Strauss after he retired as the paper's skiing reporter. The best of the newspaper writers, such as Charlie Meyers of the *Denver Post*, wrote also for the ski magazines. Meyers brought vividly to life the disintegration of the pro racing tour in 1982. "As another long, hot summer moved inexorably toward a second lean winter, the sport with a death wish retraced its previous traveled path to self-destruction."[36]

Freelance writers for smaller local dailies and weeklies authored ski columns, receiving little or no compensation. Many worked in professions other than journalism. They joined the U.S. Ski Writers' Association and its predecessor, the Eastern Ski Writers Association (ESWA), founded in 1959. The organizations struggled unsuccessfully to come to grips with the irksome fact that their members were not just part-time freelancers seeking free ski passes, junkets, and even equipment, but also people doing resort public relations and handing out the favors.[37] If the perks seemed like they might compromise what the recipients wrote, it should not go without mention that similar favors were commonly bestowed on the editors of the ski magazines.

Roxy Rothafel of New Hampshire may have been the only ski journalist willing to put his livelihood on the line. In 1971, Rothafel's independently validated reports of snow conditions were so at odds with the glowing reports issued by Killington that the resort, irritated by his sightings of ice where it saw none, attempted to persuade the Schaefer Brewing Company to withdraw the beer advertising that supported Rothafel's radio program.[38]

Snow reports, up-to-date news, and facts about travel, resorts, and equipment began to become available to skiers at websites in the mid-1990s. The number of ski-related websites grew from a mere half dozen to an estimated fifty thousand in 2004.[39] Skiers now paid nothing to gain access to information they previously paid for when they bought newspapers and magazines. Within a decade, a whole new medium transformed the way skiers received information. And in a parallel development, the ski movie lecture was replaced by VCRs, DVDs, and cable television.

16

In Movies, On Television

From the movie lecture to the DVD, and how commercials came to clutter television's Olympic coverage.

In conveying the exhilaration of skiing, a thousand words have seldom proven to be as compelling as a picture. The sport was made for filmed imagery. Moviemakers from the beginning were attracted by the artistic potential of uniting speed, pristine white snow, and jagged peaks on the screen. Germany's Arnold Fanck was the first top-flight European director to take the motion picture camera out of the artificial confines of the studio and put it on the slopes. In 1913, Fanck filmed the first ascent on skis of the 15,300-foot Monte Rosa in the Alps.[1] After World War I, he joined with famed ski teacher Hannes Schneider to produce several action films. Fanck's 1920s black-and-white Bavarian confections, iced with preposterous plots and frantic chases down mountainsides, were the precursors of the flimsily plotted, thumbs-down ski movies churned out in later years.

Fanck employed a young German dancer and choreographer, Leni Riefenstahl, to act in his films. Observing him at work, Riefenstahl saw how scenes were framed, how sequences were cut, film spliced and overlaid. She learned the craft well. Impressed by her skill and beauty, Adolph Hitler in 1934 invited her to take charge of filming the Nazi Party's annual Congress, and then of the Olympics. The rest is history. Riefenstahl's powerful, imaginative work put a permanent imprint on the art of documentary filmmaking.

The sport invaded the glamorous world of the cinema in America, as well. Sun Valley in the 1930s glittered with Hollywood stars entertaining themselves on the snow—among them Claudette Colbert, Clark Gable, Norma Shearer, producer Darryl Zanuck, and director William Wyler. Thousands viewed skiing for the first time on the big screen in 1938 when Radio City Music Hall used a pre-feature movie-short *Ski Flight*, made by Jerome Hill, aided by Sun Valley instructor Otto Lang. The year of Pearl Harbor, 1941, saw the release of *Sun Valley Serenade*, which featured Olympic gold medalist Sonja Henie skating and skiing, except that the skiing wasn't done by Henie, but by a double: future slalom Olympic gold medalist Gretchen Kunigk Fraser (see page 160). The movie featured the song "It Happened in Sun Valley" and music by Glenn Miller's orchestra, and it was made primarily in Twentieth Century Fox's studios. The ski sequences, filmed at the Idaho resort, etched a vivid image of downhill skiing in the minds of the millions who saw the movie, which earned three Oscar nominations.

The Movie Lecture Circuit

In the years following World War II, the outstanding makers of movies aimed at entertaining skiers were John Jay and Warren Miller, and later Dick Barrymore. The three were virtual missionaries for the sport. Between 1940 and 2000, they came to produce more than 125 films for their own shows and for sponsors. They traveled across North America, personally projecting their films on screens in lecture halls, theaters, and high school auditoriums. It was an annual autumn rite. The ski movies were where you met old buddies missing since the previous winter. The filmmaker, who had spent *his* previous winter shooting action in mountains from New Zealand to New Hampshire, now dragged his weary body over from a nearby Howard Johnson inn to present the resulting images and the tomfool escapades he'd been engaged in. He sold the tickets, talked through a microphone to the audience, and often ran the projector himself. On occasion, he modified his narrations to take into account the way the audience was reacting to the film. The music, at least until 1950, came from records played on a turntable. But the voice was live and in person. The audience went happily home, infected with the desire to return to the slopes as soon as the first snow fell.

John Jay, a descendant of America's first Supreme Court chief justice, was a combination of patrician New England and skinflint marketer, who justifiably earned renown as the originator of the ski movie lecture. After making his first ski movies in the 1930s, he served during World War II with distinction in the 10th Mountain Division, where he produced training films for the ski troops. Jay's sly wit, like Warren Miller's later, was attuned to the hilarious pratfalls and the spectacular action

Golden Years of Movie Making. Starting in the Sun Valley parking lot, cinematographer Warren Miller spent more than a half-century producing movies, narrating them, and writing books and columns. His movie lectures, done before live audiences, came to be replaced by DVDs and televised films. *Photograph by Tim Petros*

on the screen. The profound influence of the two can be measured in a couple of ways. In 1950, at a time when thirty thousand people were subscribing to *SKI Magazine*, at least as many people attended Jay's film showings. In one year alone, Miller showed his film in 106 cities.

Miller eventually surpassed Jay in commercial success. Balding and ox-strong, Miller was blessed with the talents of artist, communicator, and cinematographer. His Hollywood, California, childhood had been tumultuous and painful. His father was an alcoholic, and as a boy he had no bedroom, rather sleeping in the hall. He survived childhood experiences that society typically blames for producing failure. Miller was blessed with a natural ability to draw, and after the war he hoped to work as an animator in Walt Disney's studio. Instead, he went to Sun Valley where, living in a trailer in the resort's parking lot, he drew pictures of his friends skiing. But drawing didn't excite him as much as moviemaking. Equipped initially with a rugged 16-mm Bell & Howell camera, he began in 1950 to emulate John Jay, shooting and editing an annual motion picture, and traveling to cities around the country. The shows became more numerous, audiences swelled. During the winter, he hired more cameramen to help him. He gradually expanded into making sponsored films for resorts and films about surfing and sailboarding. In order to have something other than popcorn to peddle at his movie lectures, he sold books that he wrote and self-published—among them *In Search of Skiing*, and *Wine, Women, Warren, and Skis*.

In 1960 another Californian, Dick Barrymore, joined the now competitive lecture circuit after quitting his job as a Los Angeles firefighter. Barrymore showed his films in Detroit, Denver, Seattle, and Vancouver, and in ski towns such as Aspen. "I've had two operations to remove polyps from my vocal chords, and my hearing is impaired from listening to myself talk," he recalled.[2] He filmed the 1966 World Alpine Ski Championships in Portillo, Chile, and the work made it onto ABC Television's Wide World of Sports—the sport's first appearance on TV's most prestigious sports program. ABC used it in winning an Emmy Award for the Wide World series. Barrymore's most famous escapade was to don a disguise and use false credentials to film, in 35 millimeter, the ski races at the 1968 Winter Olympics at Grenoble, France. It took monumental effrontery and intricate logistics to make it happen. Barrymore did it at the instigation of Robert Redford, who urgently needed images from the Winter Games to convince the Paramount studio to make the movie *Downhill Racer* (see chapter 15). Barrymore decided to milk the bootlegged footage further by including some of it in his own traveling ski lecture. In New York City, he did four shows a day for four days in a rented theater—1,140 minutes of live narrative and talking with fans. After the owners of the authentic Olympic film rights sued Barrymore, a New York judge ordered him to excise the footage from his lecture film. "It was the beginning of the worst year of my life," he recalled in his autobiography *Breaking Even*.[3] When Barrymore came to New York to show his next new movie, *The Last of the Ski Bums*, starring speed skier Ron Funk and Judd Strunk singing the title song, *Downhill Racer* was playing in theaters across the city. *New York Times* film critic Judith Crist praised Redford's movie, while panning Barrymore's.

Downhill Racer was a documentary-style portrayal of the shallow personality of a rebellious but ultimately successful Colorado ski racer, played by Redford, whose double in the action sequences was a twenty-three-year-old former University of Washington racer named Joe Jay Jalbert.*

---

*In the making of *Downhill Racer*, Jalbert not only doubled for Redford in the racing sequences, but also filmed superb footage of the action as he trailed the racers at high speeds, holding a heavy camera. Later, Jalbert became a formidable producer in his own right, making ski shows for videotape, syndicated television specials and documentaries, promotional films and commercials in Manhattan, and later in a studio on New York's Long Island. Jalbert

He Cared about Skiing. At his Utah ski resort, Sundance, Robert Redford endeavored to ensure that development didn't despoil the mountain environment. His disappointment with the way the movie *Downhill Racer* was promoted led to the idea of a film festival for independent filmmakers. *Photo, Sundance, Utah, 1975, by Barry Stott*

Over Redford's objections, Paramount marketed it as an action feature, then did little to promote it. Redford had conceived *Downhill Racer* as the first in a trilogy of films about the American mythology of success. He never completed the trilogy, but his discouraging experience with the studio led him to create the Sundance Institute at his Utah resort, and the Sundance Film Festival at Park City—both dedicated to independent filmmaking and to repudiating the kind of Hollywood represented by Paramount's treatment of *Downhill Racer*. Thus did a minor controversy over a movie about ski racing inspire one of the world's premier film festivals.

Unlike *Downhill Racer*, most ski movies made in Hollywood have suffered savagely negative reviews and the box office blues. Even famed

---

edited hundreds of hours of motion picture and videotape of the Olympics, a dozen World Alpine and Nordic world championships, and scores of World Cup races, pro races, and speed skiing, freestyle, and handicapped-skier competitions. His output included dozens of hours of racing on the sport's most famous courses—the Hahnenkamm, Lauberhorn, Bormio, Birds of Prey—a rich visual archive.

director Vittorio De Sica could not save *Snow Job*, a 1973 bomb from Warner Brothers that featured Jean-Claude Killy and his wife, Daniele Gaubert. The specialized ski filmmakers, notably Willy Bogner, Jr., typically offered a paltry story line, if indeed they offered one at all. Dick Barrymore's excuse for the absence of intelligent plot was that the aspiring ski moviemaker cannot plan ahead because of the uncertainty of mountain weather. Story lines and scripts, thought out in detail in the office, are thrown out after the first week on location. "With a normal motion picture," said Barrymore, "you shoot a film about a story. With a ski film, you make a story about the film you've shot."[4] The 1968 movie *Ski the Outer Limits* originally was supposed to be about the fundamentals of ski technique: gliding, edging, and turning. But when they came to edit the film, the producers Roger Brown and Barry Corbet changed it into a flashy exposition of the new sport of freestyle skiing.

A New Kind of Ski Movie

Ski filmmaking underwent a shock with the 1967 appearance of Brown and Corbet's *The Incredible Skis*, and a year later of *Ski the Outer Limits*. The films showed skiers doing royal christies and wiggling patented variations of wedel turns, hopping spectacularly through mogul fields and making sensuous deep powder turns.[5] World Cup downhill racers crashed, Roger Staub performed stunts dressed like a clown, and in two perilous, slow-motion sequences, Herman Gollner and Tom Leroy were seen somersaulting off a cornice overhanging the narrow, almost-vertical Corbet's Couloir at Jackson Hole. Not only was the action captivating. The filmmakers used powerful back lighting, super-slow motion, and multihued images of a single skier unfolding accordion-like across the screen. The sound track gave the illusion that the skiers were performing their action sequences, ballet-like, to music. In reality, Corbet—who loved Mozart, Prokofiev, and Bartok—cut the film to the music, not the music to the film.* The score is the best for any ski movie made, before

---

*Corbet's life, of which a high point was his thwarted summiting of Everest in 1963, was transformed during the production of *Outer Limits*. After he and Brown shot the film during the winter of 1968, Corbet broke his back in a helicopter crash while shooting another film at Aspen. By the early autumn—now a paraplegic and in a wheelchair—Corbet nevertheless edited *Ski the Outer Limits*. Corbet's Couloir at Jackson Hole derives its name from the fact that Corbet first pointed out, to the future ski area's disbelieving owners, the possibility of experts regularly skiing the super-steep slot when it's filled with snow.

The Psychedelic Look. With the combined advent of freestyle and narcotics, ski moviemaking veered in a new direction starting in the 1970s. *Photo by Peter Miller (petermillerphotography.com)*

or since. The effect was magical. It was also a statement: Skiing's limits had been extended. "The conquest of the useless no longer needed an apology," declared the film's rather pompous libretto.

Ski the Outer Limits, like Bruce Brown's award-winning surfing movie *Endless Summer* two years earlier, was irresistible to watch, and Brown and Corbet went on to make a half-dozen sponsored 30-minute films, with sound track in a regular movie format. Unlike John Jay and Warren Miller, they had no intention of going out on the road as lecturers. Skiers would come to see their work on television or as a result of the films being projected to audiences in theaters and at receptions held by the companies that put up the money for making them. Later they could be bought as videotape cassettes.

Lectures Replaced by Watch-Alone Videos

Ski movies on videocassettes—sold in shops, by direct mail, and with advertising—arrived in an avalanche starting in the mid-1980s. By then, Miller, a frugal and a ferocious worker, was aged sixty. After thirty-five years on the lecture circuit, and worn down by the effort of repetitive speaking and the marathon travel, he began to put his voice on a sound track. By the late 1980s, ski clubs could rent a Warren Miller movie but not Warren in person. Finally, you could buy or rent a videocassette of the year's new Warren Miller movie. It was no longer necessary to gather in a hall with fellow skiers. The sport lost a valuable kind of socializing.

In the wake of Miller, dozens of young wannabes trekked into mountain fastnesses to shoot ever more exotic ski and snowboarding action. The most outstanding talent belonged to Maine native Greg Stump. America's 1979 Junior National Freestyle champion, Stump had performed in Barrymore and Miller movies. He had worked for a while as a radio disc jockey, and so he had this brainstorm that he could update and re-invigorate the traditional ski movie with in-your-face rock music. He coupled the music with images of skiers such as Scot Schmidt and Glen Plake jumping off cliffs and whizzing down steep chutes. The images of extreme skiing in his 1988 film *Blizzard of Ahhs*, with its edgy camera angles, were an instant hit with teenagers.

In the 1990s, as Stump retired from ski moviemaking and headed for Hawaii, he had no shortage of successors. Steve Winter and two college buddies founded Matchstick Productions and produced their first video *Nachos and Fear* in 1991 on a budget of $2,000. They promoted it at the ski industry's annual trade show in Las Vegas, sleeping in a borrowed car in the Convention Center parking lot. The spirit of Warren Miller, who had made his first movie while living in the Sun Valley parking lot, had not died!

Miller's films became ubiquitous on cable television, particularly on local stations or closed-circuit TV at ski resorts. In all, 570 films bear his name. In 1989, he sold the business to his son, Kurt. The two had a falling out. The son wanted sound tracks that would appeal immediately to the hip-hop tastes of younger viewers. The father did not want to abandon the familiar format that had produced past success, although he did want to develop simultaneously a second format for the future. The fissure became total in 2000 when Kurt and his partner sold Warren Miller Productions to the publishing conglomerate, Times Mirror. Warren's voice was the only remaining connection to what was now a small enterprise within a large corporation.

Early Television

Television's relationship with skiing is as old as Olympic alpine racing. The earliest TV coverage of the Winter Games, producing faint screen

The Olympics Showcased the Sport. Television coverage, starting with Squaw Valley in 1960, put alpine, nordic, and freestyle skiing in front of millions, and brought millions of advertising-loaded dollars to the International Olympic Committee. Bob Beattie (right) and Jim McKay were commentators for ABC Television at the 1980 Lake Placid Winter Games. *From the archives of* Ski Racing Magazine

images, was achieved in February 1936, at Garmisch Partenkirchen, Germany.[6] In 1956, the Olympics at Cortina d'Ampezzo appeared live on Italian television. The 1960 Squaw Valley Games were the first Olympics seen live on American television. ABC Television originally had offered the International Olympic Committee (IOC) $50,000 for the rights to Squaw Valley. When the network backed out, CBS picked up the rights, "not out of any love for the Olympics," according to Roone Arledge, "but as a favor from Bill Paley (chief owner of CBS) to Walt Disney (the *de facto* stage-manager of the Squaw Valley Games)."[7]

Arledge liked what he saw of the 1960 Games and so, after joining ABC, he convinced the network to pursue the rights to the next Winter Olympics at Innsbruck. ABC won, paying $500,000. Jim McKay anchored the show, produced on videotape trucked to Munich and flown to London, whence it was satellite-fed to New York. The logistics came to be streamlined with advances in technology. Satellites speeded transmission and multiplied the countries that could receive programming.

The rights and advertising dollars soared in value. The IOC sold television rights to the 1968 Winter Games worldwide for five times more than what it had earned four years earlier. When Antonio Samaranch became president of the IOC, he and vice-president Dick Pound took advantage of the aggressive competition among U.S. networks to wring lucrative contracts from them. In 1980, IOC Winter Games rights grew to $21 million. By 2002, the price had soared to $738 million—thirty-five times greater than the 1980 rights.[8] The TV bidding frenzy was propelled not only by ice skating and hockey, but also, ironically, by the alpine ski racing once so despised by the IOC's former president, Avery Brundage (see chapter 8).

The sums paid by CBS and NBC far exceeded what foreign television broadcasters were willing to pay, nor did the IOC aggressively pressure the latter.* The U.S. networks came to furnish three out of every four dollars of the IOC's Winter Games television revenue. The only way the networks could pay the astronomical fees was to collect more from advertisers. The result was a misfortune for American audiences, whose television screens were now choked with commercials. Congressman Tom McMillen, a former pro and Olympic basketball player, was so appalled by what American TV viewers were forced to watch during the Olympics that in 1991 he introduced a bill in the House of Representatives that would have barred networks from interrupting live coverage with commercials.[9] In return, the networks would have been permitted to bid for the Olympic TV rights as a consortium, eliminating the savagely competitive bidding that had driven up their costs. One can only imagine the ferocity of the lobbying that scuttled McMillan's initiative.

Total television coverage of the Winter Olympics mushroomed to a total of 375 broadcast and cable hours in 2002.[10] The programming served to remind recreational skiers every four years that their sport is not just downhill skiing. It embraces a broad spectrum of athleticism: not only downhill and slalom, but also cross-country, aerial stunts, nordic combined, and biathlon. (A hybrid of cross-country racing and rifle shooting, biathlon is technically not a ski sport—it has its own governing body.) Ski jumping attracted the largest number of viewers. For years, ABC introduced its weekly *Wide World of Sports* program with a shot of Yugoslav jumper Vinko Bogataj careening sideways off the in-run trestle into a series of horrifying, ground-slamming, bone-crunching cartwheels. At first, when Bogataj soared into the air, the announcer cried,

*ABC paid $300 million for the right to televise the 1994 Winter Games, and NBC an estimated $613 million for 2006.

"The thrill of victory," then as the unfortunate fellow crumpled into a fence, the voice intoned, "the agony of defeat."

Franz Klammer's come-from-behind gold medal–winning downhill run at the 1976 Winter Olympics provided the most thrilling of the sport's most enduring images. On the steep Patscherkoefel downhill above Innsbruck, Klammer drove a line down the course that had him teetering on the edge of disaster, making turns that barely overcame the centrifugal force threatening to throw him off the trail. ABC director Andy Sidaris rated it "the single most exciting event in the history of sports television."[11] The taped voice-over of Bob Beattie and Frank Gifford calling the race was the best the duo ever made.

Because of its spectacular accidents, or accidental spectacles, ski racing inevitably attracted broadcast television executives. In the 1960s, when Bob Beattie was directing the U.S. Ski Team, he drew the networks' attention to World Cup racing. In the 1970s, Beattie's success in pro racing (see page 178) arose from contacts he had nurtured in the TV world. At ABC, it helped that he knew Roone Arledge. Beattie sold the television companies   broadcast and emerging cable   on the excitement of pro racing's format: a pair of racers going head to head down the hill on parallel courses. The TV viewer could see who was moving faster, an experience not possible with one-racer-at-a-time FIS slaloms and giant slaloms. At the event itself, the air crackled with the voice of commentator Greg Lewis, a contrast to the silence at the dull, staid FIS races, where no one thought it was worth commenting about what was happening. "Beattie was on the leading edge of change that took sports from being sports to being entertainment," says Lewis, who later called the action on NBC and other ski shows.[12]

From the mid-1960s into the 1970s, the networks routinely covered the opening World Cup races at Val d'Isère and the numero-uno downhill, the Hahnenkamm at Kitzbühel. Television cameras blanketed the biennial World Alpine Championships in Europe and World Cup races in the United States. Shows, billed as "virtually live," were carried a few hours after the races took place on weekends. The shows generated reasonably good audience ratings, because they didn't have to compete yet against the football and college basketball games that later came to invade television's January schedules.

The pivotal change occurred in 1979 with the advent of cable television and a fledgling sports channel, ESPN. Suddenly the television scene was crowded with sports, including freestyle skiing. The audience ratings for alpine ski races now were perceived as comparatively weak. Several

Appeal to Viewer? Head-to-head racing opened the opportunity for the spectator to see who is going faster and leading down the hill. But the format's repetitive format proved no more appealing than that of one racer at a time on the course. *Stratton Mountain, Vermont, Photo by Hubert Schriebl*

negative factors were responsible. In America, ski racing is a second- or a third-tier sport, not a national sport as it is in central European countries such as Austria, Switzerland, and Slovenia.[13] Ski racing was unlikely ever to attract viewers in the southern, football-loving, non-snow U.S. states, with athletes bearing unfamiliar names like Pirmin and Helmut. As Greg Lewis mercilessly described the bleak situation, ski racing looked to most Americans like "a bunch of people I've never heard of doing something I don't understand in a place I'll never go to."[14]

The weak TV ratings also could be blamed on the relatively short duration of the competition itself. For many years, the outcome of a typical FIS race was determined in less than fifteen minutes, a consequence of the top fifteen racers starting in the first positions. The typical televised football, soccer, baseball, or hockey game, by contrast, lasts for about three hours. It didn't help either that the sport's season was short, and that the competitions never appeared on a regular, familiar schedule. Skiers, who might have comprised the largest audience, were typically on the slopes when weekend shows aired.[15] The shows also lacked emotional excitement. On the small screen, seen moving at high speed, dodging and weaving through distant gates, their heads shrouded by huge goggles and helmets, ski racers supply little visible facial display of the aggression, elation, anger, and happiness that can be seen on the faces of tennis players and golfers.[16]

In the 1990s, a refreshing new post-production technology, Simulcam, allowed viewers to compare the images of two racers as if they were on the course at the same time. U.S. television producers used it sparingly, having little confidence that viewers were interested in the technical subtleties of racing. Besides, Simulcam cost money. No one was willing to spend more to cover an already expensive-to-televise sport such as downhill or Super G held in freezing weather over a mile of steep mountain terrain.

Televised ski racing also wasn't helped by the absence of compelling commentators who could match, say, the trenchant analysis of figure skating's Dick Button. Even when Bob Beattie was at the acme of his career as an announcer, more viewers regarded him as the worst ("Yells stupid things all through the race"), rather than the best announcer. Greg Lewis, one of the most widely employed ski commentators, was a name barely recognized by readers of *Snow Country Magazine*, which conducted a 1994 poll.[17]

Not surprisingly, live coverage of ski competitions—costly to generate and tricky to schedule because of weather—gradually disappeared from U.S. television screens. Live was replaced by delayed coverage or "edited live" tape. The delayed coverage did not irk all viewers. If the live event was a morning race in Europe, they wouldn't have been awake anyway. But American racing fans wanting to view an Olympic ski competition, live, had to drive north and watch it in Canada. During the Salt Lake Winter Games, the Canadian Broadcasting Corporation aired the competitions as they happened, from nine o'clock in the morning through out the day and evening, until three o'clock the next morning, with only two breaks for news. U.S. television, instead of drawing on TV's unique strength as a live medium, came to treat skiing in the manner of an evening newspaper, full of background features and taped, edited coverage carried a day or more after the event.[18] In the 1950s, TV had been an inspiring innovation. For the first time, masses of people could see events as they happened—football, baseball, tennis, and golf. With skiing, television went backward.

Notwithstanding these negatives, the number of hours of televised post-event skiing increased with the advent of cable television. The new medium had a voracious need for programming. The trouble was that the number of people watching each show grew smaller as the number of cable channels multiplied. By the twenty-first century, ESPN had given up on alpine racing, turning it over to the Outdoor Life Network cable channel, where a World Cup race came to attract a meager sixty thousand viewers.[19] A broadcast network show of a World Championships or World Cup race, televised a week after the actual event, might draw 1 to 1.2 million viewers. It was not enough for the network sales folks. If the races did get on television, it was often because the U.S. Ski and Snowboard Association made the commitment to buy the commercial time in advance and re-sell it to sponsors.

The greatest shock to alpine traditionalists, however, was the success of the Winter X-Games early in the twenty-first century. Television screens came alive, not with ski racers in tight-fitting suits slicing through gates, but with guys in baggy clothes doing aerial and halfpipe stunts on snowboards. A half-dozen riders raced at the same time down a course, emulating motor bikers engaged in dangerous terrain races. Soon, X-Game skiers were doing the same.[20] ESPN's third sports channel not only showered the events with hours of tape-delayed coverage, ESPN2 didn't have to negotiate the TV rights—it owned the games! The television audience was ten times larger than that watching traditional World Cup ski races on the Outdoor Life Network.[21] In Aspen in 2005, the Winter X-Games attracted twenty-five thousand spectators. Four months earlier, only a few hundred people had shown up to watch World Cup alpine races. The contrast was astonishing and, for some, saddening. Fifty-five years after Aspen hosted the first World Alpine Ski Championships in the Western hemisphere, traditional alpine racing couldn't draw a decent crowd of spectators. Nor was skiing itself any longer central to the culture of the new mountain resort town.

17

The New Ski Country

From sport to recreation to resort amenity.

Among the foremost reasons that people give for wanting to ski is the desire to be in a natural environment and to enjoy the mountain scenery.[1] The ideal view from a lodge window is of a snow-capped alp rising into a starry sky uncontaminated by lights. Splendid! But ever since the first building erected to accommodate skiers marred a pristine alpine skyline, skiing's relationship to the mountain environment has been ambiguous. The larger the resort and the greater its need for rooms, restaurants, and shops to accommodate guests, the more it intrudes on the ideal vision.

After 1960, the price of the infrastructure-served land at ski areas within walking distance of lifts multiplied, sometimes by a hundredfold. It no longer made sense to build a $2,000 cabin on a piece of land that now cost $100,000.[2] Two solutions emerged. One was to build bigger, fancier houses. The other was to stack affordable second homes in multi-storied condominium buildings. Both fell within the purchasing power of millions of U.S. families who enjoyed a remarkable 40 percent increase in their real income between 1959 and 1968. So began an historical progression in which the sport of skiing triggered the construction of whole towns in the mountains. Like sea coasts lined with marina villages, mountain valleys filled with condos and suburban-style malls. The greater the construction, the greater the impact on watersheds and wildlife. It was a story with little potential upside.

Concerns in Vermont and Colorado

One early manifestation of environmental conflict in the mountains was in 1964 when the Wilderness Act disallowed the building of a ski area on

Mt. San Gorgonio on federal land outside Los Angeles. Another was in 1966 when an obscure Vermont State Representative named Ted Riehle drummed up support for a statute to remove billboards marring the Green Mountains.[3] Even before it was enacted, Stowe lodge owners, led by Johannes von Trapp, voluntarily tore down their own billboards. They had come to believe that what was good for the appearance of the state of Vermont must be good for their own enterprises.

A not-in-my-backyard (NIMBY) anti-development sentiment was sweeping the Green Mountains. Vermonters were not pleased with the efflorescence of motels, restaurants, shops, and second homes rising in their open fields and valleys, purchased by out-of-state skiers wanting to own a place near the ski slopes. Vermont, they feared, might become "another Long Island or New Jersey, with aggressive Florida-type real estate selling practices."[4] In 1970, the state legislature passed the pioneering Act 250, requiring developers to address problems of construction density, sewage, soil, and air quality. Act 250 was unopposed by ski area operators, although they later came to resent the bureaucracy it spawned, a familiar byproduct of environmental legislation.

The concerns in Vermont were heard in Colorado. As early as 1965, Bill Janss, who was developing Snowmass above Aspen (see page 56), was alert to his new resort's environmental impact. "A recreational development is not a subdivision," said Janss. "The relationships among mountains, streams, trees, and man-made facilities are critical. The last thing you want is a city or a suburb."[5] But a couple of years after Snowmass opened in 1967, there came news of a nearby development that *would* resemble a suburban subdivision.

Mr. Hyde in the Mountains

Aspen Wildcat, on 6,500 acres next to Snowmass, was the first large-scale harbinger of a rapacious kind of development directly related to skiing. To spearhead it, Citibank and the Tishman real estate people recruited David McTaggart, a British Columbia contractor and former vice-president of a California ski area, Bear Valley. McTaggart was a remarkable guy, whose bizarre career would take him from being a Mr. Hyde of the mountains to a Dr. Jekyll of the oceans. He came to Snowmass after suffering a devastating financial loss in 1969 when his California lodge burned down after a gas explosion. Newly arrived in Aspen, he boldly announced that Aspen Wildcat would have condominiums

and homes for forty thousand people. Locals were astonished, horrified.
Doug Burden, an investor and Aspen resident and former U.S. Ski Team
racer, said that "what McTaggart was proposing outraged environmentalists and town and county commissioners."[6]

Undeterred, McTaggart opened a spacious office, spent $25,000 to
print a lavish coffee-table book promoting Wildcat, and even sponsored
a ski team, "The Aspen Wildcats," as he drove around town in his Mer-
cedes. When the project needed more money, he helped persuade plastic
ski boot inventor Bob Lange and his two brothers to invest a half million dollars each. After McTaggart exhausted all of the investors' money,
Wildcat collapsed, eventually replaced by something quite different, as
we shall see later. The Mr. Hyde of mountain ecology hastily departed
Aspen, and within a couple of years McTaggart re-appeared, this time
as Dr. Jekyll battling pollution. In 1972, he sailed into the southern Pacific in a boat named Greenpeace III, protesting atomic bomb tests being
conducted by France. It was as if McTaggart were seeking to make up for
the ecological wreckage he might have inflicted on the mountains.[7]

After 1970, Seismic Change

Just when Aspen Wildcat collapsed as a threat to the lovely high country, environmentalists were fighting a planned ski resort in California.
The Disney Company wanted to build a destination resort in the Sierra Nevada at Mineral King, next to the Sequoia National Park.* Disney envisioned Mineral King as having a half-dozen lift-linked bowls for
skiing, with lodges and underground parking. At first, the resort's prospects looked good. After all, Sierra Club founder and 10th Mountain
Division veteran David Brower once had supported it. But the new Sierra Club—no longer Brower's creature—categorically opposed Mineral King. Nor was it the only development the club would oppose.
Henceforth, the Sierra Club announced that it would be against every
ski expansion on public land. The momentousness of the opposition can
be best understood by the fact that half of the nation's skiing is done on
federal land administered by the United States Forest Service. More than
120 ski areas, including Aspen, Vail, and Mammoth Mountain, operate

---

*The Disney Company eventually did build something resembling a ski area—in 1995.
On 120-foot high Mount Gushmore, Disney's Orlando, Florida, amusement complex, bathing-
suited visitors slide down inner-tube flumes and a toboggan slide, and ride back up on a
chairlift.

under twenty- and thirty-year leases in the national forests.* The terrain occupies less than one-tenth of one percent of the 197 million acres of the national forests. Yet the Sierra Club was saying it would seek to halt the creation of future ski areas on public land.

"The idea cannot be countenanced!" editorialized *SKI Magazine* following a 1969 interview with the Forest Service's director of recreation, Richard Costley. He framed the outline of the debate, which continued to the end of the twentieth century and beyond. Costley said that most of the opposition (to Mineral King) came from a small group of militant wilderness people. "Their creed," he said, "is that more wilderness is *ipso facto* good. We don't necessarily agree. We are charged by Congress with developing a multiple-use program, and *one* of those uses is wilderness. Another is lumbering. Another use is recreation."[8]

While the Forest Service saw its mission clearly, the majority in Congress didn't agree. Legislators responded to an increasingly vocal environmental lobby by passing the National Environmental Policy Act (NEPA), signed by President Nixon in 1970. Thereafter, every proposal to build or expand a ski area in the national forests would be subject to NEPA review. Any party claiming to be impacted by the development had the right to be heard.

They were indeed heard. With NEPA's enactment, skiing entered a troubled era. Not even Nixon's successor, Jerry Ford, a passionate skier, was able to help. The U.S. Forest Service went from being an agency eager to promote uses of the national forests for skiing to an agency encouraging opponents of development to come to the bargaining table. Almost any ski area expansion could be stymied in a drawn-out public forum—a daunting prospect for anyone applying for a long-standing Forest Service permit to build or add terrain at a ski area. A typical Environmental Impact Statement, wrote Rigo Thurmer, covered "everything from socio-cultural impacts on an Indian Reservation 50 miles away, to the mating habits of native brook trout."[9] Investors feared that resorts on public land would run into costly, interminable public hearings. Funding for new areas dried up.

There was more.

Two environmentally related events in the early 1970s added to the negative outlook for future ski area growth. The oil embargo of 1972–1973 and consequent gasoline shortage highlighted tourism's vulnerabil-

*After 1986, the standard national forest ski area lease was lengthened to forty years at the request of ski area owners, who said that shorter leases impeded their ability to attract capital investment.

ity to energy shortages (see page 59). And in Colorado the same year, voters rejected the state's hosting of the Olympic Winter Games (see page 157). The mistrustful voters feared that along Colorado's roads and in the hills, the Olympics would promote unplanned growth in a state already suffering from lack of planning.

One Coloradoan alarmed by the grassroots concern in his home state was Senator Floyd Haskell, the chairman of the U.S. Senate Subcommittee on Public Lands and Resources. In 1977, Haskell proposed that ski areas should supply detailed information on how their expansions affect the environment outside their footprint on federal land. The actual permitting of ski areas on federal property itself should be subject to state and local government approval. To federalists and environmentalists alike, Haskell's proposal was repugnant. I was invited to speak about it, first at a meeting of regional government foresters, and then at the annual convention of the U.S. Ski Association (USSA), where I delivered an impassioned oration. "The National Forest belongs to all of the American people," I cried. "I'm disturbed that the Haskell bill . . . would enable state and local government to veto the use of federally owned land for recreation. A day will come when the psychic, health, and fitness needs of an urbanized society, access to the outdoor experience, will take precedence over our needs for wood and ore, the physical resources of federal land."[10] A couple of hundred delegates rose to their feet, cheering loudly. But I'd not been totally accurate. True, the national forests were owned by all Americans. Yet communities impacted by recreational development on federal land, as Haskell said, deserved to be heard. The trouble was that local government was doing a poor job of guiding secondary growth on private land, which it regulated through planning and zoning boards. If local government was inept, why should it be trusted, as Haskell proposed, to determine ski terrain expansion on federal land?

It wasn't all that Haskell wanted. He proposed that state and local governments be allowed to regulate lift ticket price increases at areas operating on federal land. He wanted the resorts to install inexpensive lifts and amenities for less-affluent skiers, notwithstanding the fact that skiers over the years had consistently shown a preference for chairlifts over T-bars and groomed over ungroomed slopes. The idea of a kind of Volkswagen ski area, Haskell should have realized, had no support in reality.[11] Most of the people, including myself, who testified in Washington before his subcommittee, opposed his bill, and it died a more or less silent death.

Haskell's much-publicized hearings caused the ski industry to worry that Congress could one day redefine the conditions enabling it to expand on public land. The concern became so acute that a Future of Skiing Committee, formed in 1977, decided that the industry needed a Washington office. The decision eventually led the American Ski Federation and Ski Industries America (SIA) to move from New York City to the nation's capital. It was a huge paradigm shift. Almost overnight, making deals with Congress and federal government agencies became more important to the ski industry than making deals with Manhattan-based advertising agencies and the PR departments of giant corporations to promote the sport.

Planning versus Laissez-Faire

By 1978, skiing for the first time had a voice in Washington, but for whom did it speak? There was little likelihood that tens of thousands of skiers could be persuaded to become willing lobbyists for every new resort that developers want to build. To begin with, most of them were already sympathetic supporters of environmental organizations. Many of the Sierra Club's members skied.

North American ski resorts frequently occupied the sites of former mining and logging towns. Tourism took the place of resource extraction. European ski resorts typically arose from a pastoral culture onto which tourism was grafted. Above Lech in Austria and Zermatt in Switzerland, over several centuries cows grazed in summer on what are now winter ski slopes crisscrossed with lifts. As early as a thousand years ago, Bormio, Italy—the site of the 2005 World Alpine Ski Championships—catered to Romans soothing their bodies in the mountain town's thermal waters. St. Moritz hosted winter tourists since the middle of the nineteenth century. While Austria, France, Switzerland, and Italy didn't supply envelopes of protection around their mountains comparable to the U.S. national forests, the valleys of the Alps were in some ways better protected. Many were saved from unbridled development by land-use precedents and by ownership that remained within families, generation after generation. In Canada, the protection was different. The government granted resorts the right to develop on public or "crown" land in return for submitting to rigorous land planning. Whistler Mountain in British Columbia was so planned in the 1980s—carefully and in phases.

It wasn't the way most U.S. ski resorts developed. From the beginning, the U.S. Forest Service wanted no buildings on government land, except for day lodges where skiers could eat and rest, and facilities to house machinery. What happened outside the permit area, however, didn't concern the federal government, whose doctrine was laissez-faire. The bed and commercial base for ski resorts after 1970 spawned an inchoate sprawl of condominiums and second homes. Mammoth Lakes in California's Sierra, Whitefish in the Montana Rockies, Lincoln and North Conway in New Hampshire's White Mountains are typical places affected by careless zoning.

If land use was neglectful, it was often because the ski resort owner sold adjacent land in order to finance his lifts and trail-cutting. In Wyoming, Paul McCollister, chief owner of the Jackson Hole Teton Village resort, wasn't able to guide his base development rationally because he'd sold off the land. In Colorado, the fledgling Vail resort sold lots to expand its lifts and trails.

Vail founder Pete Seibert, short of money in 1960, persuaded the government to reduce the level of funding that he had to have in hand before the Forest Service would issue him a permit. But it could be asked whether the government wouldn't have served the community's long-term interests better by not issuing a ski area permit until Seibert and Colorado's Eagle County had presented a plan to conserve open space and protect view-sheds in the Vail Valley. Perhaps. But Washington wanted no part of deciding how Colorado counties should sort out their land use problems. The Mountain West was known for its resentment of the widespread federal control of land. The lack of regulations and of sufficient capital to retain ownership or control of land, however, proved to be seeds that would sprout into weeds at the resorts.

At the flat, gravelly, desert-like 9,650-foot base of Copper Mountain, within sight of giant trucks climbing to Vail Pass on Interstate 70, plans called for hundreds of beds within walking distance of the lifts. Buildings would be required to have underground parking and employee housing. "Everything is joined together compatibly," said Copper's chief, Chuck Lewis, in *Ski Area Management* in 1972. "Our design manual is very complete. Anyone who sees it might say, 'Good Lord, they copied that from a shopping center.'"[12] And that was the problem. The place took on the look, not of a shopping center, but something more like a semi-vacant office complex in Kazakhstan. Multi-storied buildings were scattered about. If any architectural guidelines were in effect, they were not readily noticeable. With the flat real estate market of the 1970s, shops and hotel and condo developers shunned the place. Only at the beginning of the twenty-first century did the British Columbia–based Intrawest Company, developer of Whistler and renovator of Mont Tremblant, begin to reshape Copper into a cohesive resort village.

Before and After. Above, Colorado's Vail valley photographed as construction of the resort began in 1962. Below, the same valley at the beginning of the twenty-first century, four decades later. *Courtesy of Dick Hauserman*

At Steamboat Springs, where Mount Werner itself is a wonderful natural massif of slopes and glades, the base of the mountain came to look as though Sheraton, having succeeded with a hotel at O'Hare Airport, decided similar buildings would work at the bottom of a ski slope. The American Skiing Company built a hotel that reminded skiers of the office buildings to which they would return after their winter vacation. A decidedly unlovely row of shops removed the necessity to drive into town to buy a Ski Town USA T-shirt.

When Vail began its Lionshead development in 1970, the compact complex of bulky concrete condominiums and a pedestrian shopping mall had a promising look of modernity. Yet thirty years later, Lionshead wasn't working. To refurbish it, the Vail Resorts Company cleverly discovered a way to exploit the tax advantages of urban renewal. A thirty-year-old ski resort had to prove it was suffering from urban blight![13]

At Courchevel and Val d'Isère in the French Alps, thirty years after their construction, locals had come to dislike the flat-roofed "modern" buildings dominating the resorts, and they eventually got their revenge. In the 1980s, they began to mount classic, alpine-peaked roofs on the hotels and condos, embellishing them with wooden fascia and porches.[14] It was a repudiation of a style of architecture that no more belonged in the mountains than a lagoon filled with flamingoes. At the French resort of Flaine, the famous Bauhaus designer Marcel Breuer in 1968 designed austere, sleek, mirror-glassed buildings, described as "Brutalist Bauhaus" by the American ski lodge architect, Henrik Bull. Emile Allais, who laid out the trails at Flaine, established a ski shop and took up residence there. Curious, I asked him, "How do you feel when you walk outside in the morning and see those buildings?"

"Like I want to puke," he replied.[15]

A Few Good Places

What is a well-designed ski village? Allais once sketched for me the essence of how one should be laid out. "It's the same as a seaside resort," he said, "except the mountain and its trails take the place of the ocean. Here, you see," and Allais drew a long elliptical line on a table napkin with the stub of a pencil, "you have a common area, the beach *comme on dirait*, a flat or slightly downhill tilting space, where the trails, coming down from the mountain, terminate. Across, on the other side of the space, are restaurants, public areas, hotels facing the mountain. The streets of the resort village are like spokes in a wheel, bringing people to the beach."[16]

Aspen doesn't much resemble Allais' sketch. But the 1966 U.S. Secretary of the Interior, responsible for public land, liked it. "Why can't all ski communities look like Aspen?" asked Stewart Udall.[17] He was not alone. Aspen Institute founder Walter Paepcke and his friend, Bauhaus leader Walter Gropius, quite liked Aspen's grid-like arrangement of Victorian houses and brick buildings laid out in city blocks.

In Utah's narrow Little Cottonwood Canyon, only a mile below Alta, Snowbird is hemmed in by the steep ski-able terrain of the national forest on one side and the precipitous, avalanche-producing canyon wall on the other. The narrowness of the valley demanded that everything— multi-storied condos, hotel, and restaurants—be within walking distance of the lifts. Snowbird's buildings, while tall, are sunk in the canyon. They don't appear out of scale, but appropriate to their setting. The imprint on the land is relatively small. Cars are parked underground. Robert Redford, however, doesn't care for the look of the place.[18] The actor-director's own resort, Sundance, also in Utah's Wasatch Mountains, is dramatically different. With its subdued log buildings, Sundance was built in response to Redford's belief that "development that squanders natural beauty destroys the very thing that draws us to the mountains."[19]

Several model ski villages were developed between the mid-1960s and 1982—notably Beaver Creek in Colorado, Elkhorn at Sun Valley, Northstar at Tahoe and Kirkwood Meadows in California, and Waterville Valley in New Hampshire. Drawing on New England architecture, and with its walk-to Four-Ways center containing restaurant, bar, and meeting rooms, Waterville's design was sensitive to the surrounding forested valley in which it was built, although it missed Allais' condition of a resort bordering the bottom of the ski mountain.

To connect its village to the slopes, California's Northstar-at-Tahoe built a transport lift, one of the first in the United States. The village was designed in the early 1970s by Henrik Bull, who was inspired by Avoriaz, a spectacular pedestrian resort in the French Alps that is reached by cable car. "Our approach," said Bull, "was to create a pedestrian village where people walked past stores and restaurants, within easy reach of their condos."[20] Northstar's buildings were almost invisible from the highway. Eight-inch trees growing beside a doorway were saved. Parking was terraced into a hillside outside the village, a walk or a short and free bus ride away. Northstar even had the blessing of the same Sierra Club that was fighting Mineral King at the time.

Car-free Villages. Two examples of the use of high-rise hotel and condominium structures to limit the footprint of mountain development. Above, Snowbird in the Little Cottonwood Canyon outside Salt Lake City. At right, in the French Alpine resort of Avoriaz, reached by cable car, the Hotel des Hauts Forts as it appeared in 1968 not long after it was built. Both Snowbird and Avoriaz are pedestrian villages. *Photos courtesy of the resorts*

The Intrawest Corporation purchased Mont Tremblant in 1991, confident that here was a place, however cold, that could always guarantee snowmaking in a future beset by global warming. At Tremblant, Intrawest combined shops and condos in buildings reflecting the colorful architecture of Quebec townhouses. Founder Joe Ryan's original *habitant* cottages were collected in a verisimilitude of a tiny French Canadian rural village (see page 18). By contrast, French Canadians, whose motto is "*Je me souviens,*" did not remember, as the American Ryan did, their heritage when they built a government-subsidized ski village at Mont Sainte-Anne outside Quebec City. The place for a long time looked like a collection of American office buildings.

Conferences Address the Problem

In Colorado, from the Continental Divide westward on both flanks of Interstate 70, a weed-like spread of second homes and shopping malls, triggered by skiing, fanned out across the valleys. Ten years after the opening of Beaver Creek, Whistler Village, and Deer Valley—the last major ski resorts to be built in the twentieth century—land planners, government officials, ski area operators, and a few environmentalists from across North America sat down to talk about the impact on the mountain environment of skiing-triggered growth. Their conferences, unfortunately, began *after* the environmental impact, not *before*. The earliest, held at Vail in May 1991, started as an academic tourism conference. *Snow Country* and *Ski Area Management* magazines expanded it to include resort operators and environmental organizations. Several of the latter declined to attend, fearing the conference would whitewash the resorts. But more than three hundred people came, overfilling the meeting facility. In 1995, a Boom in Mountain Living Conference was organized at Keystone, Colorado, by the Pinchot Institute for Conservation.[21] The Institute is named for Gifford Pinchot, the creator with President Teddy Roosevelt of the national forests, future home of more than 120 ski areas. Pinchot's biographer, Char Miller, happened to be the keynote speaker at the Boom in Mountain Living Conference. Miller averred that Pinchot, who had battled western ranchers and loggers over their abusive grazing and watershed destruction at the end of the nineteenth century, would have been equally distressed by the urban sprawl enveloping mountain valleys at the end of the twentieth. Miller discreetly avoided mentioning that the sprawl didn't especially concern Pinchot's bureaucratic successors at his U.S. Forest Service nor, ironically, the board of his eponymous Institute.

Another speaker at the Boom in Mountain Living Conference was Andrea Mead Lawrence, a formidable athlete who carried her competitive spirit into the battle to save the environment. Lawrence had moved to Mammoth Lakes in California's Sierra Nevada, where she successfully ran for the office of supervisor of vast Mono County. There she became mightily worried about the threat to alpine scenery. Like most ski communities, Mammoth was under siege from developers. "God did not make the Sierra Nevada as a lot-and-block subdivision," Mead Lawrence said. "We shouldn't treat our mountain valleys that way."[22] To the ski community, it was a powerful statement, coming as it did from an Olympic gold medalist.

Who would take responsibility for what was happening along the periphery of the national forests? Terry Minger of the Center for Resource Management—which Robert Redford earlier had helped to launch—attempted to focus on a solution when he organized yet another conference, Sustainable Summits, in 1999. Environmental organizations wary of ski resort goals were in attendance. The conference found promising potential grounds for future agreement among experienced ski area planners and environmentalists. But the National Ski Areas Association, alarmed at the participation of organizations known for their past antagonism toward ski area expansion, ignored the conference's recommendations, and instead created its own set of "Environmental Principles."[23]

A Bitter Debate

The ski areas increasingly found themselves under attack. In Colorado, they were charged with threatening the health of elk herds, even though the elk population was increasing every year. Actually, an animal didn't need to exist for its habitat to be considered threatened by ski area expansion. Such was the case when environmentalists claimed that Vail's expansion in the 1990s would destroy the habitat of the Canada lynx, even though a native Colorado lynx hadn't been seen in the area since 1973. So lynx were imported. The animal's contrived residency thus became a substitute for collaborative discussion of what to do about space for recreation in the mountains and about the development it incurs.

Organizations such as Colorado Wild, High Country Citizens Alliance, the Vermont Natural Resources Council, and the Conservation

Law Fund portrayed the ski resorts as an industry unnecessarily imposing itself on a fragile mountain ecology. But a healthy environment needs a healthy economy to protect it, a fact ignored by the anti-resort agenda. In 1991, the Vermont Ski Areas Association found that communities whose economies and tax rolls were bolstered by the spending of visiting skiers generated five times more tax revenue, available for education and ecology protection, than did non-ski towns.[24]

In 2002, the Sierra Club published *Downhill Slide*, in which author Hal Clifford painted the big ski companies as villains in the steady deterioration of the mountain environment.[25] Clifford blamed Vail Resorts, Intrawest, and the American Skiing Company (see page 69) for just about everything from the invasion of public land by all-terrain vehicles to the human tragedy of undocumented, impoverished Latinos crossing the Mexican border to find jobs. He mourned the disappearance of ski communities once led by hearty folks who were there "to ski first, and make money second."[26] But the truth was that many of the pioneers whom he admired had come to work in real estate and to serve on planning boards that approved the subdivisions. As for the big ski companies, their activities paled in comparison with that of the hundreds of private developers choking mountain valleys with condos and shopping malls. At least the ski companies invested millions to supply skiers with more snow and terrain to enjoy. The property-turnover artists contributed nothing but sprawl. Their rabid, unplanned development was not taking place in comparatively small acreages in the national forests leased to the resorts, but it was on the ski resorts that the environmentalists focused the blame. Being singled out understandably irked NSAA, the resorts' trade association.

Real Estate Outgrows Skiing

In Aspen, as a result of protective zoning, real estate prices rose so rapidly and so high that workers no longer could afford to live anywhere near the place. David McTaggart's Aspen Wildcat never became a subdivision of forty thousand people. In a monumental piece of downsizing, a group of real estate developers, led by the actor Michael Douglas, subdivided the former Wildcat ranch into thirteen 500-acre homesites, selling for $5 million each.[27] By now, Aspen faced a different challenge. The town was filling with multi-million-dollar homes and with gawking tourists yearning to catch a glimpse of celebrities like actor Douglas.

Furries. Aspen street scene in the 1990s. Shopping became the second most popular activity of ski vacationers. Many decided to live in ski country, inspiring critic Myles Rademan to call them "Furries," or Frozen Urban Refugees. *Photo: John C. Russell*

Aspen realtor and developer Harley Baldwin bought the historic Collins Block building in the middle of town and transformed its basement into snobbish, members-only, high-end restaurant and nightclub, the Caribou Club. Previously, Aspen had been a place where celebrities and locals sat elbow to elbow at the Hotel Jerome's bar.[28]

Myles Rademan, a charismatic speaker and visionary, saw ski resort towns becoming lifestyle enclaves "where the unconscionably rich push out the filthy rich."[29] The dark-bearded Rademan served as town planner in Crested Butte, Colorado, and later in Park City, Utah. He contended that classic ski towns were morphing into four-season "amenity communities, small urban centers. We're not staying rural," he said, "and we're not doing a good job of managing growth. We're filling up the mountains with sprawl."[30] A resort community, Rademan said, had become a place "where people spend a year's salary to dress like a forest ranger, and where there are more real estate agents than dogs."[31] The yuppies of the 1970s were moving to ski towns and becoming what Rademan called "furries," frozen urban refugees.

The influx of people boosted the economy of the new ski country, however. Between 1978 and 1987, in the dynamic western U.S. counties where ski lift capacity was concentrated, retail sales, corrected for inflation, grew by 25 percent, and the number of hotel and motel establishments grew by 54 percent.[32] In the early 1990s, property sales in the Vail Valley grew by nearly 400 percent during a period when skier use of the adjacent slopes rose by only 43 percent.

For every dollar spent on lifts and trails for the 1999–2000 ski season, the ski resorts invested four dollars in real estate.[33] Among Americans with net assets in excess of $10 million, seven out of ten owned second homes, many at ski resorts.[34] By 2002, half of all the dwelling units in Colorado's Eagle, Grand, Pitkin and Summit counties were second homes owned by non-residents.[35]

Ford Frick, an expert on Colorado tourism and a relative of the one-time baseball commissioner, caught the essence of what was happening. In the late 1960s, he wrote, the goal of someone's ski vacation was to learn to ski like Jean-Claude Killy. "Mountain real estate was a place to rest up for the next day's 8 A.M. assault on the mountain."[36] But then came a more relaxed, sybaritic vacation style, popularized in beachfront and island resort villages. Alarmed by the warm-weather competition, ski resorts set about building or re-vitalizing their villages. "A simple formula emerged," observed Frick. "Design a vibrant pedestrian downtown. Stimulate a host of recreational, cultural, retail, and entertainment attractions, and sell the bed base to light-skiing baby boomers."[37]

The new Disney-World-full-service ski village was perfectly adapted to the needs of aging boomers—the people who, as youngsters, had generated the sport's explosive growth in the 1960s. Now Mr. Babyboomer had more après-ski time on his hands; thanks to high-speed lifts, he took only three hours to ski the same number of vertical feet that once took a whole day. Plenty of time to rest, drink, eat, and shop. He needed to assure his now non-skiing, fifty-plus wife that the place he had chosen for their winter vacation had a Ralph Lauren Polo shop. The full-service village was lined with real estate agents to show them condos and timeshares that they might purchase.

For all its conveniences, however, the kind of experience offered by such a contrived village is not the same as the experience of vacationing in a real ski town. A rapidly built resort, skewed to selling real estate, is not the same as a complex community steeped in skiing history. In the new ski country, the sport was no longer necessarily at the center of the community's culture. The snowy slopes rising above a ski town might be of little more importance than the gated golf courses surrounding it.

Changing Resort Focus. By the 1990s, skiing —once central to the culture of mountain towns—had metamorphosed into one of a four-season resort's amenities, such as golf. At Aspen, the Maroon Creek Club golf course nestles below the terrain of the Highlands ski area. © *Dick Durrance II 2001*

Land of Promise?

Before the 1970s, skiing was a sport. Then it became a kind of multifaceted recreation. In the early 1990s, it began to morph into a kind of discretionary wintertime activity. Ski clubs, which brought fourteen of every hundred people to ski areas, shifted to becoming organizations offering sports and adventure travel packages.[38] Skiing became one of several amenities, such as golf and tennis, offered by the resorts. The amenities lured people to own a second home—even a third or fourth home—in snow country. Four of America's twenty fastest-growing counties in the last decade of the twentieth century contained Vail, Breckenridge, and Telluride in Colorado and Park City in Utah's western Wasatch mountains, which had become a virtual suburb of Salt Lake City.[39]

For all the problems it engendered, the influx of people into the new ski country brought an upside. Tens of thousands of outdoor-oriented entrepreneurs, blue collar workers, and professionals who commute to work via computer, became full-time residents. In 1967, IBM had

The Future. Children
at Vail, 1977. *Photo by
Barry Stott*

believed that it could attract employees by locating its operations close to
ski country.[40] Thirty years later, the original IBM vision had altered. A
New York stockbroker moved to Sun Valley where he continued to ply
his financial trade, possibly from an IBM terminal. An urban émigré illus-
trator started a commercial ski lodge. People came once again to live near
the base of lifts and ski mountains, just as people once lived near community rope-tow hills. They are building homes, raising children, joining
clubs. Ski towns are re-discovering the importance of their skiing heritage. In 2003, three major new ski museums opened in ski towns.

The first few years of the twenty-first century have seen the revival of
visits to small and medium-sized ski hills. U.S. ski area visits now average
57 million per winter, about 10 million higher than fifteen years earlier.
The number of people buying season passes has soared. Kids are banking
halfpipe turns and leaping off jumps, as kids did forty years ago before the

legal profession temporarily laid its suppressive hand on the spirit of adventure. The resorts initially opposed demands from new cultures, such as freestyle, telemarking, and snowboarding. Now, they nurture them.

The truth is not complicated. Skiing succeeds whenever and wherever it sustains the primal experience that has forever attracted its lovers: rising up a mountain into the sky, gliding through a spruce forest hushed by snow, thrilling at the fast descent, floating through an ocean of weightless powder, and looking back at the tracings etched on the snow . . . stored remembrances of a passage through space and time.

Afterword

I have written *The Story of Modern Skiing* partly to support a nostalgic belief that skiing's past was at least as good as its present. Contrivance tends to contaminate. As the money involved in the sport has soared, and as resorts have layered on more material comforts, and as equipment makers have applied technology to ratchet up product performance and safety, the quality of the ski experience has changed. But has it progressed? The pleasurable sensation of the twenty-first century skier—conveyed up the mountain in a heated gondola, dressed in high tech clothing and gear—doesn't seem to me to surpass the adventure of scooting up the hill clinging to a rope tow in 1950. Today's fashions look no better than the wonderful skiwear worn in 1969. At the end of the twentieth century, Hermann Maier was thought to be the best racer of all time. Technically perhaps, but he was no greater a competitor than Toni Sailer in 1956 nor Jean-Claude Killy in 1968. Stein Eriksen's dazzling, feet-together turn of 1955 appears to me as elegant as the carved, feet-separated turn forty years later. Perhaps more elegant.

The physical challenges that attracted people to take up skiing challenged inventors to find technologies to overcome them. At each stage of progress, they devised products—easy to get in and out of bindings, warmth-retaining space-age parkas, faster lifts—that made skiing simpler and more comfortable. Yet the sport's spirit may have burned as brightly among shivering 1940s weekenders joyfully chanting ski songs next to a potbellied stove. Today, people pay a hundred dollars to ride on a cold, exposed horse-drawn sleigh to a log cabin that once cost nothing to sleep in. The sensation of muscling seven-foot skis through pristine deep snow is equal at least to the sensation fifty years later of skiing on snow groomed to a creamy substance.

The joy of sliding on snow is immune to progress.

Acknowledgments

Focusing as it does on the second half of the twentieth century, *The Story of Modern Skiing* draws heavily on published articles in the ski magazines that dominated the period—*SKI* and *Skiing* magazines, and the trade magazines *Ski Area Management* and *Ski Business*. I also depended on *Skiing Heritage* and www.skiinghistory.org, creations of the International Skiing History Association, which I served as president.

The work of writing *The Story of Modern Skiing* would have been difficult without the help of a small army of friends who possess records and memories of skiing's past, and who gave generously of their time to help me. Ski historian Morten Lund reviewed half the chapters in the book and furnished detailed factual corrections and perspectives that I came to include. Doug Pfeiffer was similarly helpful. Former *SKI Magazine* editors John Henry Auran and Dick Needham, *Snow Country*'s Kathleen James Ring, ex–U.S. Ski Team racer Robin Morning, and Tom Wallace and Greg Clark supplied me with valuable comments based on reading earlier drafts of the book.

Part 1: Just when you think you've discovered the first time a thing happened, the historian E. John B. Allen is there to tell you of an earlier instance. And so he was there to help me with chapter 1. Allen is the author of *From Skisport to Skiing, One Hundred Years of an American Sport, 1840 to 1940* and of a new manuscript on international skiing history before 1940, recommended reading for anyone who wants to understand in more detail how U.S. skiing developed before World War II. As for the wartime years, the story of the 10th Mountain Division can be found in at least a dozen fairly recently published books. Several key facts in chapter 2, "Skiing as a Way of Life," came from the historian Allen A. Adler and songster Bill Briggs. Chapter 3 contains crucial data about lift construction and new resort openings systematically gathered over the years by *Ski Area Management*'s founding publisher, the late David Rowan. They represent a sort of posthumous gift to skiing history by Rowan, who was a close friend. I'm grateful also to National Ski

Areas Association chairman Bill Jensen and Snowmass's Jim Snobble for reviewing chapter 3, and to Michael Berry, Cal Conniff, and attorney David Cleary for improving my reporting on ski area liability and skier responsibility codes.

Part 2: Chapter 4 on the "Revolution in Equipment" owes a great deal to long-time *SKI Magazine* equipment editor and ski industry historian Seth Masia, to ski business veterans Ian Ferguson, Nick Hock, and Paul Bussman, and to Wini Jones, whose knowledge of changes in skiwear design and fabrics is unsurpassed. In chapters 5 and 6, concerning technique and teaching, I was aided in both fact and recollection by Bill Lash, Ron LeMaster, Morten Lund, Doug Pfeiffer, and Weems Westfeldt.

Part 3: The extensive account of alpine competition in this book was inspired by fellow journalist Serge Lang, who invented the World Cup and the Super G race. Lang wanted to write such a history himself, but was unable to complete it before his life was cut short. His son Patrick, who followed in his father's journalistic footsteps, helped me with information on how the World Cup developed, as did Phil Mahre, the three-time World Cup winner, and Andy Wenzel, the 1980 champion. Hank McKee of *Ski Racing Magazine* and Matteo Pacor in Milan, Italy, supplied key statistics and analysis. Pacor's website www.ski-db.com is a treasure house of racing statistics. Former Olympians Tom Corcoran and Billy Kidd and coach Ernst Hager reviewed information on U.S. racing in chapter 9, where I also was helped by double gold medalist Andrea Mead Lawrence and former *Ski Racing* publisher Gary Black.

Part 4: Chapter 10 on cross-country skiing benefited from the guidance of Oslo-based Michael Brady, former U.S. Ski Team coach John Caldwell, silver medalist Bill Koch, writer Bob Woodward, and Johannes von Trapp. An earlier draft of chapter 12 was improved thanks to a critique by Doug Pfeiffer, "the father of freestyle." Howard Peterson, who ran the U.S. Ski Association, furnished important documents illuminating freestyle's transition to an Olympic medal sport. I'm grateful to snowboarding maestro Jake Burton Carpenter, *TransWorld Snowboarding's* Lee Crane, and Brian Sellstrom, whom I interviewed at length for chapter 13.

Part 5: Many people, including ski industry veterans Nick Hock, David Ingemie, and Jim Woolner, and trade editors Seth Masia and David Rowan, furnished information for chapter 14. For chapter 15 on books and magazines, Henry Yaple, compiler of the monumental *Ski Bibliography*, supplied the first accurate breakout that I've ever seen of ski publishing activity by decade. Filmmakers Warren Miller and the late Barry

Corbet helped me with chapter 16. Interviews that I conducted with Tom Kelly of the U.S. Ski Team, Jim Bukata of International Management, and TV commentator Greg Lewis improved my understanding of television's historical role in the sport. I thank town planner and speaker Myles Rademan, architect Henrik Bull, Vermont's Joe Parkinson, Colorado's Ford Frick, Terry Minger, and many others who have shaped my views about skiing's impact on the mountain environment.

Photography: The pictures for the book came through the generosity of the photographers, who waived their fees in the interest of being a part of ski history. You'll find their names alongside the pictures, but I need to repeat those whose magnanimity extended to supplying multiple images: Dick Durrance, Jr., Fred Lindholm, Kim Massie, Peter Miller, John Russell, and Team Russell's Lorna Pedersen, and Barry Stott who flew his pictures to my home so that we could review them together. Thanks also to Gary Black, Felix Magowan, and Mark Eller of *Ski Racing*, whose picture archive I invaded, and to the Red Birds Ski Club's Peter Flanagan for his photo research of early Laurentians skiing. I am grateful to Viera Gorelova of David Howell & Company, who assembled the maps showing the locations of historic resorts and competition sites in North America and Europe.

Finally, thanks to the ski luminaries who succumbed to my request for a few complimentary words to augment the book's sale: Billy Kidd, Jean-Claude Killy, Andrea Mead Lawrence, Warren Miller, and Doug Pfeiffer.

I'm especially grateful to Ellen Wicklum of the University Press of New England who saw, in a prior memoir I'd written, the possibility of a more complete, more serious, better researched book about modern skiing. Her championing of the book and her editing helped me immeasurably.

Book writing today entails an alliance of author and computer. When the former is ignorant of the latter's operation, help is needed and mine was furnished by neighbors and friends Jay Maller and Chris Davis. Pamela Clark introduced me to the arcane discipline of writing footnotes. My patient wife Marlies fielded phone calls, typed the entire index, arduously hand-penciled seven hundred folios, and endured my yelps of writer's frustration.

Notwithstanding the foregoing acknowledgments and the extensive notes at the end of the book, crediting sources of information (page 323), it's entirely possible that there are individuals whose help I have failed to record. Whoever you are, you can write me a memo of outrage at snowfry@verizon.net. Meanwhile, please accept my heartfelt thanks.

Appendix: Top World Cup and Olympic Racers

Top World Cup Winners
(Number of races won, as of end of 2005 season)

Men's Winners, Top 15

Racer	Wins	Downhill	Giant Slalom	Slalom	Super G	Combined
Ingemar Stenmark (Sweden)	86		46	40		
Hermann Maier (Austria)	51	14	14		22	1
Alberto Tomba (Italy)	50		15	35		
Marc Girardelli (Luxembourg)	46	3	7	16	9	11
Pirmin Zurbriggen (Switzerland)	40	10	7	2	10	11
Stephan Eberharter (Austria)	29	18	5		6	
Phil Mahre (United States)	27		7	9		11
Franz Klammer (Austria)	26	25				1
Peter Mueller (Switzerland)	24	19			2	3
Gustavo Thoeni (Italy)	24		11	9		4
Michael Von Gruenigen (Switzerland)	23		23			
Kjetil-Andre Aamodt (Norway)	21	1	6	1	5	8
Bode Miller (United States)	19	2	8	5	2	2
Jean-Claude Killy (France)	18	6	7	5		
Lasse Kjus (Norway)	18	10	2		2	4

Statistics courtesy of Matteo Pacor.

Women's Winners, Top 13

Racer	Wins	Downhill	Giant Slalom	Slalom	Super G	Combined
Annemarie Proell (Austria)	62	36	16	3		7
Vreni Schneider (Switzerland)	55		20	34		1
Renate Goetschl (Austria)	37	19		1	13	4
Katja Seizinger (Germany)	36	16	4		16	
Hanni Wenzel (Liechtenstein)	33	2	12	11		8
Erika Hess (Switzerland)	31		6	21		4
Michela Figini (Switzerland)	26	17	2		3	4
Anja Paerson (Sweden)	26	1	9	15	1	
Maria Walliser (Switzerland)	25	14	6		3	2
Pernilla Wiberg (Sweden)	24	2	2	14	3	3
Janica Kostelic (Croatia)	21			17		4
Tamara McKinney (United States)	18		9	9		
Nancy Greene (Canada)	14	3	8	3		

Statistics courtesy of Matteo Pacor.

Top Olympic Racers

Men's Alpine: Toni Sailer and Jean-Claude Killy are the only two racers to have won all the Olympic alpine medals at a single Winter Games. They did it when there were just three races—slalom, downhill, and giant slalom. The 1956 and 1968 games, where they won triple gold, were the only Olympics either skier competed in, so that Sailer and Killy never wore silver or bronze medals. Kjetil-Andre Aamodt of Norway and Alberto Tomba of Italy were also triple gold medalists, but in more than one Olympic Winter Games. Kjetil-Andre Aamodt is the champion of total Olympic alpine gold medals won: 7.

Men's Olympic Games, Top 30
(Number of medals won)

Racer	Total	Gold	Silver	Bronze
Kjetil-Andre Aamodt (Norway)	7	3	2	2
Alberto Tomba (Italy)	5	3	2	
Lasse Kjus (Norway)	5	1	3	1
Stephan Eberharter (Austria)	4	1	2	1
Toni Sailer (Austria)	3	3		
Jean-Claude Killy (France)	3	3		
Ingemar Stenmark (Sweden)	3	2		1
Gustavo Thoeni (Italy)	3	1	2	
Josef Stiegler (Austria)	3	1	1	1
Frank Piccard (France)	3	1	1	1
Hermann Maier (Austria)	2	2		
Markus Wasmeier (Germany)	2	2		
Hubert Strolz (Austria)	2	1	1	
Tommy Moe (United States)	2	1	1	
Othmar Schneider (Austria)	2	1	1	
Phil Mahre (United States)	2	1	1	
Stein Eriksen (Norway)	2	1	1	
Bernard Russi (Switzerland)	2	1	1	
Ernst Hinterseer (Austria)	2	1		1
Henri Oreiller (France)	2	1		1
Pirmin Zurbriggen (Switzerland)	2	1		1
Bode Miller (United States)	2		2	
Peter Mueller (Switzerland)	2		2	
Marc Girardelli (Luxembourg)	2		2	
Christian Pravda (Austria)	2		1	1
Andreas Wenzel (Liechtenstein)	2		1	1
Guy Perillat (France)	2		1	1
Arnold Molterer (Austria)	2		1	1
Benjamin Raich (Austria)	2			2
Heini Messner (Austria)	2			2
Christian Mayer (Austria)	2			2

Women's Alpine: Janica Kostelic of Croatia is the only woman to have won three gold medals at a single Winter Games. In 2002 at Salt Lake, there were five alpine competitions and, in addition to winning the gold medals in slalom and giant slalom, Kostelic won the gold in the Combined (requiring her to race in separate downhill and slalom races), and she won silver in the Super G. The women who came closest to matching Killy and Sailer's hat tricks were Germany's Rosi Mittermaier (1976) and Liechtenstein's Hanni Wenzel (1980), who each won two gold medals and a silver medal. Vreni Schneider won her medals at two different Olympics, in 1988 and 1994, as did others.

Women's Olympic Games, Top 30
(Number of medals won)

Racer	Total	Gold	Silver	Bronze
Vreni Schneider (Switzerland)	5	3	1	1
Katja Seizinger (Germany)	5	3		2
Deborah Compagnoni (Italy)	4	3	1	
Janica Kostelic (Croatia)	4	3	1	
Hanni Wenzel (Liechtenstein)	4	2	1	1
Marielle Goitschel (France)	3	2	1	
Pernilla Wiberg (Sweden)	3	2	1	
Rosi Mittermaier (Germany)	3	2	1	
Marie Therese Nadig (Switzerland)	3	2		1
Anita Wachter (Austria)	3	1	2	
Annemarie Proell (Austria)	3	1	2	
Christa Kinshofer (Germany)	3		2	1
Martina Ertl (Germany)	3		2	1
Perrine Pelen (France)	3		1	2
Annemarie Buchner (Germany)	3		1	2
Isolde Kostner (Italy)	3		1	2
Maria Walliser (Switzerland)	3		1	2
Andrea Mead Lawrence (United States)	2	2		
Petra Kronberger (Austria)	2	2		
Trude Beiser Jochum (Austria)	2	1	1	
Picabo Street (United States)	2	1	1	
Ossi Reichert (Germany)	2	1	1	
Nancy Greene (Canada)	2	1	1	
Michela Figini (Switzerland)	2	1	1	
Christine Goitschel (France)	2	1	1	
Hilde Gerg (Germany)	2	1		1
Diann Roffe Steinrotter (United States)	2	1		1
Christl Haas (Austria)	2	1		1
Brigitte Oertli (Switzerland)	2		2	
Penelope Pitou (United States)	2		2	

Cross-Country: Skiing's most prolific Olympic gold medalist is cross-country racer Bjorn Dahlie, who won eight gold medals over the course of three Olympics between 1993 and 1998, a record for any athlete, Winter or Summer Games. He came close to winning more, with four silver medals to his credit. Two of his gold medals were won as a member of Norway's Relay Team.

Notes

1. Genesis (pages 3–23)

1. Thorstein Veblen, *The Theory of the Leisure Class* (New York: Penguin Classics, 1994).

2. Ales Gucek, *In the Tracks of Old-Time Skiing: History of Ski Technique* (Ljubljana: Ski Instructors and Trainers Association of Slovenia, 2004).

3. Matti Goksoyr, "Skis as National Symbols, Ski Tracks as Historical Traits: The Case of Norway," in *Collected Papers of the International Ski History Congress,* ed. E. John B. Allen (Woodbury, Conn.: International Skiing History Association, 2002), 200. *Idraet,* in Norwegian, and *Idrott* (Swedish), meant outdoor physical exercise in which "strength, manliness and toughness" were the goals. By 1834 *Idraet* included the effort to perfect not just the body but the soul, ideally even to develop "the physical and moral strength of nations." E. John B. Allen, "A Brief History of Ski Jumping," *Skiing Heritage* (2006).

4. David Brann, "Russian Skiers: First Tracks in North America," *Skiing Heritage*, International Skiing History Association (June 2003): 23.

5. E. John B. Allen, *From Skisport to Skiing* (Amherst: University of Massachusetts Press, 1993), chapter 2. Among the substances employed by competitors to make their skis go faster were buttermilk, furniture polish, camphor, spruce oil, and candle wax. Spermaceti is a waxy substance extracted from the sperm whale.

6. The National Ski Association was renamed the U.S. Ski Association in 1960. It became U.S. Skiing in 1991, and was renamed the U.S. Ski and Snowboard Association in 1997.

7. John Fry, "Legacy, 1907," *SKI Magazine* (January 2005): 61, citing a Barnum and Bailey's poster of 1907.

8. Janet M. Davis, *The Circus Age* (Chapel Hill: University of North Carolina Press, 2002): *www.biblio.org/uncpress.*

9. Vergilio Dotta, "Die ersten Skis in der Schweiz," *Ski,* Jahrb. des SSV (1941): 96–97. Courtesy John Allen.

10. John Jay, John O'Rear, and Franky O'Rear, *Ski Down the Years* (New York: Award House, 1966), 30.

11. Wolfgang Lert, "The First Slalom," *Skiing Heritage* (December 1999): 7.

Zdarsky's slalom-type competition, called a Torlauf, was a race through eighty-five two-poled gates, held at Lilienfeld, Austria, March 19, 1905.

12. John Fry, "The Afghan Ski Connection," *SKI Magazine* (January 2002): 26.

13. E. John B. Allen, the ski historian, notes that "slalom" is derived from the Norwegian Slalaam, a descent around natural obstacles such as trees and rocks. The first such race cited by Allen was staged in Norway as early as 1879. Allen, *From Skisport to Skiing*, 7.

14. Edward Percy and Hugh Brodie, "McGill and the Birth of Football," *McGill News*, McGill University, Montreal (Summer 2005): 48.

15. *www.collectionscanada.ca/hockey/.* Although there are disputes about where ice hockey was born, the International Ice Hockey Federation endorses Montreal as the game's birthplace.

16. "Winter Sports in the Laurentians," *Canadian Pacific Railway Bulletin* 204 (1926–27): 21.

17. Allen, "The Mechanization of Skiing," chap. 7 in *From Skisport to Skiing*,

18. Roger Langley, "The National Ski Association of America," in *Skiing the International Sport*, edited by Roland Palmedo, (New York: Derrydale Press, 1937), 51.

19. McKenty and McKenty, *Skiing Legends and the Laurentian Lodge Club*, 55. The precise date when Alex Foster operated the first rope tow is uncertain, a consequence of Foster experimenting with prototypes beginning in 1930. The McKentys state that Foster operated the tow spasmodically in 1931, and opened it commercially in 1932. In his book, *I Skied the Thirties*, Bill Ball says that Foster opened in the winter of 1933. In 1932, the Swiss, Gerhard Mueller, also patented a ski tow using rope. A few years later, to the north in Ste. Agathe des Monts, North America's first platterpull was installed.

20. Morten Lund, "Fred Pabst: Skiing's First Empire Builder," *Skiing Heritage* (June 2004): 24.

21. Morten Lund and Kirby Gilbert, "A History of North American Ski Lifts," *Skiing Heritage* (September 2003): 19.

22. Story related to the author by Alex Cushing in August 1997, at his home in Newport, Rhode Island.

23. McKenty and McKenty, *Skiing Legends and the Laurentian Lodge Club*, 18.

24. Allen, *From Skisport to Skiing*, 173.

25. Lorenz Pfeiffer, "Germans, Donate Your Skis for the War against the Communists," in *Collected Papers of the International Ski History Congress* (2002), 221.

a. William Lederer, "At 96, This Rabbit's Still Running," *SKI Magazine* (February 1972): 70.

b. William L. Ball, *I Skied the Thirties* (Ottawa: Deneau Publishers & Co. Ltd., (no date), 49.

c. Brian Powell, editor, *Jackrabbit, His First Hundred Years* (Collier Macmillan Canada, 1975), 28.

d. Ibid. Erling Strom: 130.

2. *A Way of Life (pages 24–43)*

1. *SKI Magazine* (January 1953): 28.

2. Jeffrey Leich, "Nine Decades of Skiing in Tuckerman Ravine," *New England Ski Museum Newsletter* (Winter 1999): 6.

3. *International Skiing History Association Ski Song Book*, "The Elliptical Technique's the Best," 5. Composer unknown. Collected, edited, and published by Mason Beekley, Morten Lund, and Doug Pfeiffer. New Hartford, Conn. (March 1995).

4. "The Editor's Bookshelf," *SKI Magazine* (February 1954): 24.

5. Survey of Aspen Accommodations, November 26, 1948, courtesy of Ken Moore.

6. Sung to the tune of "Bonny Dundee," by W. R. Drysdale in the 1930s, courtesy Red Birds Ski Club.

7. E-mail from Ed Morrison of Morlarty Hat Co. to A. B. Lyons, July 18, 2005.

8. Ann Lyons Fry, "Ma's Place," *SKI Magazine* (Holiday Issue, 1966): 155.

9. Abby Rand, "The Rise and Fall of an Icon, the Lodge at Smuggler's Notch," *Skiing Heritage* (March 2001): 18.

10. Stowe-Mansfield Association, Inc., *Where To Stay—Mt. Mansfield, Stowe, Vermont, Winter Season of 1947–48*, Pamphlet.

11. Peter Crowley, "Why Did the Lake Placid Club Close?" in *The Lake Placid Club, 1890 to 2002*, edited by Lee Manchester (Saranac Lake, N.Y.: Adirondack Publishing Co., 2003), 30. Also, Ned P. Rauch, "Lake Placid Club: The Beginnings," 4.

12. Louise Arbique, *Mont Tremblant, Following the Dream* (Montreal: Carte Blanche, May 1999), 112.

13. C. David Heymann, *A Candid Biography of Robert F. Kennedy* (New York: E.P. Dutton, 1998), 54.

14. Morten Lund, "Skiing's Angry Man," *SKI Magazine* (January 1967): 121.

15. "Skiers Look at Themselves," *SKI Magazine* (November 1950): 21.

16. Morten Lund, in a letter to the author, June 2005.

17. Morten Lund and Kirby Gilbert, "A History of North American Lifts," *Skiing Heritage* (September 2003). The first two-seater chairlift, designed by Robert Heron, went into service in the winter of 1948.

18. Bureau of Labor Statistics, *Consumer Price Index*. The increase in the consumer price index for the fifteen years between 1951 and 1965 was 21.1 percent. In the fifteen-year period between 1978 and 1993, the average adult weekend lift ticket rose by 180 percent to $31, compared with a 122 percent rise in the price index.

19. David Rowan, "Air Guide to Europe," *SKI Magazine* (December 1955): 22.

20. John Fry, "The Season Ahead," *Ski Life Magazine* (December 1958): 44.

21. Ted Farwell, "The Skier Market—Northeastern North America," a study

of the winter of 1962–1963, done for the Area Redevelopment Administration of the U.S. Department of Commerce.

22. Edward A. McCreary, "Profile of the Skier, circa 1964," *SKI Magazine* (November 1964): 54.

23. Population Resource Center, "The Changing American Family," www. prcdc.org/summaries/family.

24. "My Favorite Ski Trail," *SKI Magazine* (Holiday Issue, 1968): 65.

25. "Kennedy Christmas," *SKI Magazine* (December 1965): 72.

26. Phone interview by the author with Harry Holmes (October 8, 2005).

27. "Is There a Skiing Establishment?" *SKI Magazine* (December 1964): 6.

28. Oleg Cassini, "Reminiscences of Mascara Mountain," *Snow Country Magazine* (Premier Issue, March 1988): 94.

29. Abby Rand, Traveler's Checks, "Super Buses," *SKI Magazine* (February 1966): 27.

30. Ibid.

31. "The Dazzling Dozen," *SKI Magazine* (Holiday Issue, 1967): 72. The other hot après-ski places were the Boiler Room of the Sun Valley Lodge, Idaho; Seven Levels at Jackson Hole, Wyoming; the Chalet St. Bernard at Taos, New Mexico; Galena Street East in Aspen, Colorado; Horse and Hounds in Franconia, New Hampshire; the Christiania at Mammoth Mountain, California; Hotel Dilworth in Boyne City, Michigan; and Villa Bellevue near Mont Tremblant in Quebec's Laurentians.

32. Ibid. The writing of a section of the un-bylined introductory text block was done by Ms. Doran.

33. Bob Bugg cartoon, *SKI Magazine* (Spring Issue, 1969): 75.

34. Abby Rand, "Girls' Rules," *SKI Magazine* (November 1965): 31.

35. Morten Lund, "The Anthony Is Coming," *SKI Magazine* (February 1967): 117. A New York business executive by the name of Chet Anthony went every winter weekend to Vermont where he didn't even bother to ski. Anthony slept until noon and spent all his time organizing the evenings for his friends, happily listening to their complaints about waiting in lift lines and about their instructors.

36. Extensive accounts of early Aspen skiing are contained in *The Man on the Medal*, by Dick Durrance co-authored with John Jerome (Glenwood Springs, Colo.: Durrance Enterprises, Inc., 1995); and *Nice Goin'* by Friedl Pfeifer, with Morten Lund (Missoula, Mont.: Pictorial History Publishing Co., 1994).

37. Leon Uris, "Heatherbedlam," *SKI Magazine* (February 1965): 63.

38. Morten Lund, "They're Beautiful!—The new Aspen Ski Bums," *SKI Magazine* (January 1970): 66.

39. Abby Rand, "How Good Are the Big Ski Clubs?" *SKI Magazine* (October 1974): 52.

40. Eric Schmitt, "Tally of Students Equals Number at Boomer Peak," *New York Times*, March 23, 2001, A17.

41. John G. Hubbell, "Skiing's Good Samaritans," *SKI Magazine* (December 1965): 138. The article also appeared in the *Reader's Digest* at the time.

42. National Ski Areas Association, "1997–1984 Fatality Rates," *Member Update* (December 1997/January 1998): 15.

43. Data provided by the National Ski Areas Association, Lakewood, Colorado.

3. From Rope Tow to Resort (pages 44–70)

1. "How Big Is the Rope Tow Industry?" *SKI Magazine* (November 1, 1948): 35.

2. Morten Lund, "Ernst Constam and His Marvelous Uphill Device," *Skiing Heritage* (December 2005).

3. Estimates vary of the number of ski areas in 1935–1936. The number seventy-eight in *Ski Area Management* seemingly was contradicted in later years by the magazine's founding publisher David Rowan, who revised the number down to sixty-six. What is certain is that for a mountain to qualify as a ski area it had to possess some kind of wire rope lift, a chairlift, J-bar, or T-bar, as well as rope tows. Bill Tanler, "A Decade of Growth," *Ski Area Management* (Summer 1966): 10; and Kirby Gilbert and Morten Lund, "A History of North American Lifts," *Skiing Heritage* (September 2003): 25.

4. "Starr's Circus," *SKI Magazine* (October 1955): 60.

5. Mary Eshbaugh Hayes, *The Story of Aspen* (Aspen, Colo.: Aspen Three Publishing, 1996), 82.

6. John Fry, "Alec's Valley," *SKI Magazine* (50th Anniversary Issue, January 1986): 59.

7. Robert Frohlich, *Mountain Dreamers— Visionaries of Sierra Nevada Skiing* (Truckee, Calif.: Coldstream Press, 1997), 46.

8. John Fry, "Legacy," *SKI Magazine* (March/April 2005): 34.

9. Morten Lund, "Killington, Vermont," *SKI Magazine* (December 1975): 126E.

10. Study conducted by the New England Ski Areas' Council, reported in *SKI Magazine* (Spring 1974): 21.

11. Bill Tanler, "A Decade of Growth," *Ski Area Management* (Summer 1966): 10.

12. The *National Ski Areas Association Membership Directory* contains the founding dates of ski areas.

13. Tanler, "A Decade of Growth," 10.

14. "Comparison of Ski Vacation Costs at 20 Resorts," *SKI Magazine* (October 1967): 83.

15. The 1956 skier participation estimate of 500,000 represents research done at the time by *SKI Magazine* associate publisher David Rowan in collaboration

with the Tuck School at Hanover, New Hampshire, where the magazine was based. The estimate of 1.5 million in 1962–1963 was made by researcher Ted Farwell of Sno-Engineering, Inc., of Franconia, New Hampshire, working for the Area Redevelopment Administration of the U.S. Department of Commerce (see chapter 14). The estimate of 3.0 million in 1968, double 1.5 million in 1963, is based on Farwell's calculation of 16.7 percent annual growth that was occurring in the 1960s.

16. John H. Makin, "The Present U.S. Expansion Outshines the 1960s," website of the American Enterprise Institute for Public Policy Research (February 2000). www.aei.org/publications/pubID.11221

17. Arthur R. Hunt, "Snowmaking is 50 Years Old," *Ski Area Management* (March 1990): 89. Hunt was one of the three engineers who invented and held the patent on the original snowmaking system.

18. *SKI Magazine*'s 1965 Annual Ski Area Guide listed North American areas with snowmaking. Only eleven ski areas west of the Mississippi had snowmaking at the time.

19. Morten Lund, "A Big New Ski Weekend," *SKI Magazine* (November 1968): 94.

20. Jeffrey R. Leich, "Technology of Alpine Resorts—Lifts, Snowmaking and Grooming," *New England Ski Museum Journal* (Spring 2002).

21. John Fry, "Deja-Ski," *SKI Magazine* (November 2002): 65.

22. Paul Pepe, *The Sleeping Giant—The Story of Hunter Mountain* (Hunter Mountain, N.Y.: Mad Box Publishing, 1993), 61.

23. "Metroski," *SKI Magazine* (December 1968): 62.

24. John H. Auran, "Meet Mr. Janss," *SKI Magazine* (December 1964): 111. Also, interview by the author with Harry Holmes, president of the Sun Valley Company from 1965 to 1973 (October 8, 2005).

25. Bill Tanler, "The Condominium: New Form of Resort Living," *SKI Magazine* (October 1967): 84.

26. Calculation made by the author based on Vertical Transport Feet per Hour statistics appearing in *Ski Area Management* between 1966 and 1997.

27. Ibid.

28. "That Was Some Winter," *SKI Magazine* (September 1974): 29. The tight supply of gasoline caused skiers to patronize near-city ski areas and fly-to Rocky Mountain resorts.

29. New England Lost Ski Areas, nelsap.org. In 2000, the website listed more than five hundred extinct ski hills, equal in number to all of the ski areas operating nationally in 2000.

30. "Lack of Sportsmanship," *SKI Magazine* (March 1953): 9.

31. "The $1.5 Million Verdict," *SKI Magazine* (October 1977): 39.

32. I. William Berry, "The Insurance Mess," *SKI Magazine* (November 1977): 68.

33. David Rowan, "Unified Trail Marking," *Ski Business* (Fall 1964): 18. Also, Bob Cram, "Skiing's New Colored Trails," *SKI Magazine* (October 1964): 75.

34. I. William Berry, "Warning: Skiing Beyond Your Ability May Be a Crime," *SKI Magazine* (September 1979): 62. By 2005, twenty-seven states had skier responsibility codes, per e-mail to author from Michael Berry, President, National Ski Areas Association, September 1, 2005. Many codes have been updated to include the activities of snowboarders and snow tubers.

35. Charlie Meyers, "Happy Days for Highlands," *SKI Magazine* (November 1985): 21.

36. Morten Lund, "Skiing's Angry Man," *SKI Magazine* (January 1967): 108.

37. J. K Galbraith, "The Pleasures and Uses of Bankruptcy," in *The Liberal Hour* (Boston: Houghton Mifflin Company, 1960), 169–77.

38. Phone interview by the author in June 2005 with Ted Farwell, specialist in mountain resort appraisals, Winterstar Valuations, Inc., Post Falls, Idaho.

39. The two outstanding books about the history of Vail are Pete Seibert, *Vail—Triumph of a Dream* (Boulder, Colo.: Mountain Sports Press, 2002); and Dick Hauserman, *The Inventors of Vail* (Edwards, Colo.: Golden Peak Publishing, 2000).

40. David Rowan, "1998 Lifts—A Year of Records," *Ski Area Management* (January 1999): 82. The estimate that four companies accounted for about one-quarter of lift ticket revenues is made by the author, based on "National Ski Areas Association Kottke" skier-visit numbers for 2004, Colorado skier-visits by resort, and information in the annual reports of the companies.

41. Statistic derived by the author from annual new lift construction surveys in *Ski Area Management*.

42. Tim Sweeney, "Small Areas, Big Comebacks," *National Ski Areas Association Journal* (June/July 2004): 26.

43. Kottke National End-of-Season Survey, May 23, 2002—projection of skier-visits prepared annually by RRC Associates, Inc., for the National Ski Areas Association, Lakewood, Colorado.

4. A Revolution in Equipment (pages 73–91)

1. "What to Look for in Basic Equipment," *SKI Magazine* (October 1958): 27. The earliest introduction of plastic bases for skis was by Attenhofer in Switzerland in the early 1940s, and by the Northland Ski company, which supplied skis with Permacite to the 1948 U.S. Olympic team.

2. Seth Masia in an e-memo to the author regarding skis in the collection of the Musée Dauphinois, Grenoble, France (December 2004).

3. Cited in John Fry, "Howard Head: Color It Black," *SKI Magazine* (50th Anniversary Issue 1986): 42.

4. Record of a conversation in Aspen in 1965 between the author and Roby Albouy, now deceased. Albouy at the time was *SKI Magazine*'s equipment editor, Fry the editor-in-chief.

5. Ian Ferguson, product manager and national sales manager for the Head Ski Company between 1961 and 1969, to the author, February 2005.

6. "Glass in Skimaking," *SKI Magazine* (November 1955): 50.

7. "Fiberglass Victory," *SKI Magazine* (November 1, 1966): 29.

8. Ed Scott, letter written to the author at the time of Scott's eighty-fifth birthday in 1986.

9. Ibid.

10. Ed Scott, "Letters," *SKI Magazine* (November 20, 1966): 53.

11. Advertisement in *SKI Magazine* (October 1961): 17.

12. Information furnished to the author by Paul Bussman. John Fry, *SKI Magazine* (September 2005): 50.

13. Cited in John Fry, "The Legendary Plastic Man," *SKI Magazine* (November 2000): 75.

14. Ibid.

15. Morten Lund, "The Empire that Exploded: Bob Lange and the Plastic Boot," *Skiing Heritage* (September 2001): 15.

16. John Fry, *SKI Magazine* (November 2000): 75.

17. Ibid.

18. Ibid.

19. Cubco advertisement, *SKI Magazine* (December 1957): 95. It was created by New York advertising agent Robert Launey.

20. Seth Masia, "Evolution of the Modern Ski Shape," *Skiing Heritage* (September 2005): 35.

21. John Fry, "Short or Long Skis," *Snow Country Magazine* (October 1992): 8.

22. Seth Masia, "Skis '84," *SKI Magazine* (September 1983): 23.

23. "All-Terrain Skis," *Mountain Sports & Living* (October 1998): 111.

24. Ibid: 104.

25. "His Turn is Better than the One that Won an Olympic Medal 25 Years Ago," *Snow Country Magazine* (March 1990): 25.

a. Klaus Obermeyer in a phone interview with the author, April 2003.

5. Technique: From Stem to Carve *(pages 92–107)*

1. Morten Lund, "A Short History of Skiing," *www.skiinghistory.org*.

2. The ruade disappeared from technique for a long time, but in 1992, the author published an article in *Snow Country Magazine* (March/April 1992, page 48) about how French instructor Dadou Mayer at Taos, New Mexico, was reviving Allais' kick turn as a way to get through mogul (bump) fields.

3. John Fry, "When Form Came First," *Snow Country Magazine* (October 1995): 76.

4. Brooks Dodge, *SKI Magazine* (October 1956): 32.

5. Toni Sailer, "Wedeln the Relaxed Way!" *SKI Magazine* (November 1957): 15.

6. Paul Valar reported that French instructors demonstrated split rotation at the 5th International Ski School Congress at Zakopane, Poland, in 1959. Bill Lash, *The American Ski Technique, 1964–1970*, a privately published booklet, January 2004.

7. Tom Corcoran, "Counter-rotation and Rotation: The Split," Starting Gate, *SKI Magazine* (November 20, 1966): 44.

8. Ernie McCulloch, "You Can Adapt to Wedeln," *Ski Life Magazine* (December 1958): 65.

9. John Fry, "A New Look at Turns—Interpreting a Study by Hugo Brandenberger," *Ski Life Magazine* (February 1961). 40. Also, *SKI Magazine* (December 1964): 62.

10. Georges Joubert and Jean Vuarnet, "Look, They're Sitting Back!" *SKI Magazine* (November 1967): cover and 109.

11. Georges Joubert and Jean Vuarnet, *How to Ski the New French Way* (New York: The Dial Press, 1967), 10. This book originally was published in 1966 under the title *Comment se perfectionner à ski*, by the French publisher, Arthaud

12. Ezra Bowen, "A Russian Solution to Ski Instruction," *SKI Magazine* (November 1970): 154.

13. "Moment of Truth on Skis," *SKI Magazine* (January 1967): 39.

14. Seth Masia, "Evolution of the Modern Ski Shape," *Skiing Heritage* (September 2005): 36.

15. John Fry, "Ski Schools, They're Teaching Us What We Want, But It Isn't Enough," *Snow Country Magazine* (November 1994): 141.

a. Phone interview with Herman Gollner, November 13, 2005.

6. New Ways to Learn (pages 108–24)

1. Hannes Schneider, "The Arlberg Technique," *World Ski Book*, ed. Frank Elkins and Frank Harper (New York: Longmans, Green & Company, 1949), 27.

2. Clif Taylor, "The True History of GLM," *Skiing Heritage* (March 1999): 7. Reproduction of an advertisement from a 1962 issue of *Look Magazine*.

3. Clif Taylor and Morten Lund, *Ski in a Day* (New York: Grosset & Dunlop, 1964). Morten Lund wrote the book with Clif Taylor, and included two pages on gradually increasing the length of skis to teach people to make parallel turns from their first day on the slopes.

4. Karl Pfeiffer, "Learning to Ski by the Graduated Length Method," *SKI*

Magazine (November 1966): 58. The first draft of the article, ghostwritten by Morten Lund, referred to the short-to-long ski progression as Graduated Length Technique. Pfeiffer changed it to Graduated Length Method, hence GLM.

5. Ford K. Sayre, "Tolerance," *SKI Magazine* (February 1954): 27.

6. John Fry, "East-West Summit Meeting on Skis," *Ski Life Magazine* (October 1960): 27. This article was cited in the authoritative, privately published *The American Ski Technique, 1964–1970,* a history of the early Professional Ski Instructors of America written by Bill Lash, in January 2004.

7. Fry, "East-West Summit Meeting on Skis," 77.

8. Ibid.

9. Ibid., 78.

10. Morten Lund, "Graduated Length Method Goes National," *SKI Magazine* (November 1970): 150.

11. Irving S. Naylor, *Ski Roundtop—40 Seasons of Winter Excellence* (Lewisberry, Pa.: Snow time Inc., 2003), 3.

12. Burton Hersh, "Gnome of Fortune," *SKI Magazine* (January 1965): 76.

13. Fred Iselin and A. C. Spectorsky, *Invitation to Skiing* (New York: Simon and Schuster, 1947).

14. "About Esalen," *www.well.com/www/suscon/esalen/esalen.html.* 2001.

15. Abrezol quote from *SKI Magazine,* additional publication information unavailable.

16. Timothy Gallwey and Bob Kriegel, *Inner Skiing* (Toronto/New York/London: Bantam Books, 1979), 45.

17. Morten Lund, "The Head Benders," *SKI Magazine* (November 1978): 207.

18. Ibid.

19. Ibid.

20. Ibid: 196.

21. Morten Lund, "Inner Skier Meets the Skeptics," *SKI Magazine* (December 1977): 127.

22. Sigi Grottendorfer and Martin Marnett, "Inner Skier: How Ski Teachers React," *SKI Magazine* (November 1975): 77.

23. Norm Crerar, "How Ski Schools React," *SKI Magazine* (December 1975): 93.

24. Sigi Grottendorfer and Martin Marnett, "Inner Skier: How Ski Teachers React," *SKI Magazine* (November 1975): 77.

25. Elissa Slanger and Dinah Witchel, *Ski Woman's Way* (New York: Summit Books, 1979).

26. John Fry, "Do Women Need Special Help?" *Snow Country Magazine* (December 1996): 222. The author drew on research by James and Joy Spring of Leisure Trends, Boulder, Colorado, in which 429 people who tried skiing were interviewed. Nine of every ten women and men, alike, said they would defi-

nitely or probably stay in the sport. Of the women, 8.5 percent said they would *not* continue, compared to 9.2 percent of the men.

27. Tom Corcoran, "Recreational Slalom," In the Starting Gate, *SKI Magazine* (October 1965): 15.

28. John Fry, "PSIA Instructors Adopt Performance Requirements," *Ski Racing Magazine* (November 2, 2004): 15.

29. Warren Witherell, *How the Racers Ski* (New York: W.W. Norton, 1972), 15.

30. Ibid.

31. Ibid., 58.

32. Warren Witherell and David Evrard, *The Athletic Skier* (Boulder, Colo.: The Athletic Skier, Inc., 1993), 19.

33. John Fry, "Ski Schools: They're Teaching Us What We Want, but It Isn't Enough," *Snow Country Magazine* (November 1994): 141. The magazine surveyed 121 ski schools employing 11,000 instructors and selling $50 million a year in lessons.

7. The World of Alpine Racing (pages 127–49)

1 In 1972, the Swiss newspaper *Zurich Sport* named Toni Sailer as the best skier of all time, based on the results of races in the Olympics and World Championships. Sailer was awarded 550 points, Jean-Claude Killy, 400.

2. Serge Lang, "French Triumph, Austrian Fall," *SKI Magazine* (October 1966): 70.

3. Erik/Erika Schinegger, Mein Sieg Über Mich [*My Victory over Me*]. (Munich: F.A. Herbig Verlagsbuchhandlung GmbH, 1988). See also John Fry, "Women's Champ Was a Man!" *SKI Magazine* (March/April 2001): 36; Morten Lund, "The Man Who Became Women's World Champion," *SKI Magazine* (December 1978): 88.

4. Interview with Marc Hodler by the author in 2001 for article in *SKI Magazine*.

5. The Canadian Academy of Sport Medicine Position Statement, 1997.

6. John Fry, "Roots," Interview with Jean-Claude Killy, *SKI Magazine* (November 1978): 209.

7. John Fry, "Bode Miller and the Pantheon of Ski Champions," *Skiing Heritage* (June 2005): 8.

8. Robert Seeger, ed., *Ski World Cup Guide, 1996–1998* (Basel, Switzerland: Biorama Sportpublikationen AG, 1998). Historical statistics of the World Cup of Alpine Skiing.

9. John Fry, interview with Jean-Claude Killy in Val d'Isère, France, February 8, 2001.

10. Hank McKee, statistician and writer for *Ski Racing Magazine*, official alpine information specialist at the 2002 Winter Olympics.

11. John Fry, "Sights and Smells of '74," *SKI Magazine* (September 1974): 4.

12. Fry, "Roots," 146.

13. Seeger, *Ski World Cup Guide*; Matteo Pacor, *www.ski-db.com*. After 1990, Marc Girardelli went on to win two more titles and seven more combineds. He, Phil Mahre, and Pirmin Zurbriggen hold the record for most combined competitions won: eleven each.

14. Matteo Pacor, www.ski-db.com/db/stats/moldest_podium.asp

15. Estimate by Herman Gollner, inventor of the screw-in slalom pole.

a. The author is grateful to Matteo Pacor, www.ski-db.com, for providing facts about the post-1980 alpine combined.

8. How Skiing Changed the Olympics (pages 150–59)

1. Sir Arnold Lunn, "The Selective Indignation of the Olympic Committee," in *Unkilled for So Long* (London: George Allen & Unwin Ltd., 1968), 68.

2. Bjorn Kjelstrom, FIS Council member, beginning in the 1980s, pleaded with Hodler to address the matter of his succession. Before he died, Kjelstrom gave copies of the correspondence to the author.

3. Robert K. Barney, Stephen R. Wenn, and Scott G. Martyn, *Selling the Five Rings: The International Olympic Committee and the Rise of Olympic Commercialism* (Salt Lake City: University of Utah Press, 2002), 82.

4. John Fry, "Ski Racing Will Test a Testy Brundage," *SKI Magazine* (September 1969): 181.

5. John Fry, "Brundage in Turmoil," *SKI Magazine* (September 1970): 154.

6. "Report from Japan," *SKI Magazine*, (March 1972): 59.

7. Miki Hutter, "All Hail Karli," *SKI Magazine* (September 1972): 66.

8. John Fry, "A Kick and Scratch Fight All the Way," *SKI Magazine* (Spring 1973): 59.

9. Marc Hodler in phone interview with the author, September 2003.

10. John Fry, "Alec's Valley," *SKI Magazine* (50th Anniversary Issue, January 1986): 64.

11. Ibid.

12. Ibid., 62.

13. Ibid.

14. "For 1976, a Scattered Olympics," *SKI Magazine* (March 1972): 84.

15. John Fry, "An Opportunity to Reform the Winter Olympics," *SKI Magazine* (January 1973): 9.

16. John Fry, "Olympicgate: Why It Happened," *SKI Magazine* (March/April 1999): 22.

9. *Racing in America (pages 160–86)*

1. E. G. Valens, *The Other Side of the Mountain* (originally, *A Long Way Up*) (New York: Warner Books by arrangement with Harper & Row, 1975).

2. Tom Corcoran, "There Was Only One Buddy," *SKI Magazine* (September 1964): 126.

3. The historic, dominating presence of the Dartmouth Outing Club in U.S. ski competition was covered comprehensively in a two-part article by David Bradley in *SKI Magazine* (January and February 1959.)

4. Tom Corcoran, "Don't Be a Dropout," Starting Gate, *SKI Magazine* (October 1964): 46.

5. Ibid., 45.

6. John Fry, "Bob Beattie and America's First Medals in Men's Olympic Skiing," *Skiing Heritage* (December 2003): 9.

7. Bill Tanler, "$50,000 To Halt the Racer Drain," *SKI Magazine* (November 1, 1966): 97.

8. Burton Hersh, "The Total Coach," *SKI Magazine* (February 1965): 70.

9. Andrea Mead Lawrence in an interview with the author, April 2003, at Mammoth Lakes, California.

10. Hersh, "the Total Coach," 69.

11. Tom Corcoran, "After Defeat: $450,000," *SKI Magazine* (October 1965): 43. See also Corcoran, *SKI Magazine* (October 1966): 54.

12. "Pre-Teen Bud Werner Leagues Set," *SKI Magazine* (November 20, 1966): 25.

13. Bob Beattie, "Let's Do Away with Our National Ski Team," *SKI Magazine* (November 1970): 30.

14. Peter Miller, "Is This the School of the Future?" *SKI Magazine* (December 1972): 64. In 1985, Witherell moved to Winter Park, Florida. He eventually returned to snow country in order to direct a ski academy at Crested Butte, Colorado.

15. John Fry, "What's Your Ski Handicap?" *SKI Magazine* (December 1968): 102. A complete history of Nastar, written by Jim Fain, can be found at www.skiinghistory.org/nastar1.html.

16. Tom Corcoran, "Après Beattie, Le Deluge," Starting Gate, *SKI Magazine* (September 1969): 58.

17. Tom Corcoran, "The Solitary American," Starting Gate, *SKI Magazine* (Spring 1966): 20.

18. "The New World Champions," *SKI Magazine* (Spring 1970): 51.

19. A reproduction of the *Life Magazine* cover (6 March 1970) hangs on a wall in Billy Kidd's Steamboat, Colorado, home.

20. The author had frequent discussions with Robert F. Kennedy, Jr., in the late 1990s when he served on the board of the Riverkeeper, an environmental organization. Its chief attorney was Kennedy, who resides in the town of Bedford, New York, where the author also lives.

21. Nicholas Howe, "Tamara McKinney—The Enigma, the Racer, the All-Time Winner," *Skiing Heritage* (Third Issue, 1997): 20.

22. See Friedl Pfeifer, *Nice Goin', My Life on Skis* (Missoula: Pictorial History Publishing Co., 1994). An illustration of the first side-by-side dual slalom appears on page 156. With two racers starting simultaneously, the two-course format was created by Friedl Pfeifer for the March 13–14, 1948, North American Downhill and Slalom Championships at Aspen.

23. Calculation of time differences are derived from 1956 Olympic race results, *SKI Magazine* (March 1956).

24. "No-Show Pros," *SKI Magazine* (February 1974): 22.

25. Phil Mahre and Steve Mahre, *No Hill Too Fast* (New York: Simon & Schuster, 1985), 174.

26. Ibid., 139.

27. Ibid., 183.

28. Peter Miller, "Being Bill," *SKI Magazine* (November 1984): 56.

29. John Fry, "America's Snow Sports Team," *Snow Country Magazine* (March 1996): 116.

30. John Fry, "Forgotten Youth," *Snow Country Magazine* (May/June 1994): 43.

31. Picabo Street and Dana White, *Picabo: Nothing to Hide* (New York: McGraw-Hill, 2002).

10. Cross-Country (pages 189–204)

1. Jim Fixx, *The Complete Book of Running* (New York: Random House, 1977), 251.

2. Godfrey Dewey contributed to a collection of essays about Johannsen, *Jackrabbit—His First Hundred Years*, ed. Brian Powell (Collier Macmillan Canada, 1975), 172.

3. "Cross Country People," *SKI Magazine's 1975 Guide to Cross Country Skiing*, published by Times Mirror Magazines: 8.

4. Bill Lederer and Joe Pete Wilson, *Complete Cross Country Skiing and Touring* (New York: W. W. Norton, 1980).

5. "Where to Go Skiing," *SKI Magazine's 1975 Guide to Cross Country Skiing*: 65.

6. Ibid., 24.

7. Fridtjof Nansen, *Paa Ski over Groenland* (Christiania, 1890), 125–26. Nansen's oak skis were 230 centimeters long, 9.2 centimeters wide at the shovel, 8 centimeters wide underfoot. His equipment is on display in the Holmenkollen Museum outside of Oslo. Information courtesy of E. John B. Allen.

8. Bob Woodward, "Naming the Norms," *SKI Magazine's 6th Annual Guide to Cross Country Skiing*: 8.

9. John Fry, "Cross-Country at Cross Purposes," *Snow Country Magazine* (January 1989): 4.

10. John Fry, "Cross-Country Goes Waxless," *SKI Magazine* (50th Anniversary Issue, January 1986): 172.

11. John Fry, "Legacy: 1972," *SKI Magazine* (October 2005): 77.

12. Ski Worldloppet, *www.worldloppet.com*.

13. Bruce Stoff, "Bill Koch Won't Quit," *Snow Country Magazine* (October 1994): 60.

14. Bill Koch, phone interview with the author, September 2003.

15. Michael Brady in an e-mail to the author (December 2, 2004).

16. Yvon Chouinard, "Climber's Bill of Rights," *Voices from the Summit*, The Banff Centre for Mountain Culture (2000): 98.

17. Andrew Nemethy, "Anything Goes—Dick Hall Has No Time for Telemark Snobs," *Snow Country Magazine* (March 1989): 37.

18. Seth Masia, www.snowindustrynews.com

11. Extremities (pages 205–18)

1. John Henry Auran, "Staib's Pole," *SKI Magazine* (November 1965): 152.

2. Chamonix Mountain Guide. www.chamonixmountainguide.com.

3. Roland Huntford, *Scott and Amundsen* (New York: G.P. Putnam's Sons, 1980), 168.

4. Louis Dawson, "Chronology of North American Ski Mountaineering and Backcountry Skiing," www.wildsnow.com/chronology/timeline.

5. Fritz Stammberger as told to John Henry Auran, "I Skied Higher than Any Man," *SKI Magazine* (December 1965): 82.

6. Dawson, "Chronology of North American Ski Mountaineering and Backcountry Skiing."

7. "He Broke the World's Vertical Record," *SKI Magazine* (September 1972): 42.

8. Morten Lund, "Is This the Foolproof Turn?" *SKI Magazine* (November 1971): 153.

9. Del Mulkey told this to the author during an extended visit to his home in Katonah, New York, in 1992.

10. "He Broke the World's Vertical Record," 40.

11. Patrick Vallencant, *Ski Extreme: Ma Plenitude* (Paris: Flammarion Parution, 1992).

12. Peter Cooper, "Attack of the Rising Sun," *SKI Magazine* (November 1971): 98. For a criticism of Miura's "stunt," see *SKI Magazine* (September 1976): 33.

13. Dick Dorworth, "Pain and Peril in the Pamirs," *SKI Magazine* (November 1981): 108.

14. MountainZone.http://ski.mountainzone.com/2001/freshtracks/everest/html.

15. Ibid.

16. John Page, "Extreme Affair," *Snow Country Magazine* (July/August 1991): 17.

17. Schmidt's first appearance was in Warren Miller's 1983 *Ski Time*. Later he was featured in Greg Stump's 1988 *The Blizzard of Aahhhs*. See Scot Schmidt, *www.gowithapro.com*.

18. John Holden, "Spectacular Schuss of Headwall Told by Amazed Witness," *SKI Magazine* (February 1954): 22.

19. Toni Matt, *Ski Down the Years* (New York: Universal Publishing, 1966), 169.

20. Ron Funk, "The Fastest in the World," *SKI Magazine* (February 1964): 120. Dorworth and Vaughan went through the timed trap in the same elapsed time, clocked to a hundredth of a second, recording a speed of 171.428 kilometers per hour.

21. Dick Dorworth, "In Pursuit of Pure Speed," in *The Ski Book*, ed. Morten Lund, Bob Gillen, and Michael Bartlett (New York: Arbor House Publishing, 1982), 87. Permission of the author.

22. Steve McKinney, "Getting Two — For More than a Decade, Skiers Have Sought to Break the 'Impossible' Speed Barrier of 200 Kilometers-per-hour. Here's How I Did It," *SKI Magazine* (March 1979): 33.

23. Ibid.

24. Peter Miller, "How Fast Can I Go?" *Skiing Heritage* (September 1999): 17. Also, Charles Plueddeman, "The Mechanics of Speed Skiing," www.speedski.com/PopularMechanics.

25. The author is unaware of official statistics of fatalities that have occurred in speed skiing. They are not numerous because of the even snow surface and gradients employed in speed skiing. The most famous fatality — Walter Müssner at Cervinia in 1965 — was described by Dick Dorworth, "Death the Companion," *SKI Magazine* (February 1978): 104.

26. Paul Robbins, "Nordic Roundup," *Ski Racing* (23 March 2005) www.skiracing.com.

27. John Fry, "Fly Boys," Fall Lines, *SKI Magazine* (December 2004): 36.

28. "By Helicopter to Virgin Snowfields," *SKI Magazine* (January 1959): 20.

29. John Fry, "The Attainable Dream," *SKI Magazine* (January 1969): 44.

30. The fifty-four fatalities between 1965 and 2000 were suffered by clients of heli-skiing services. Canadian Mountain Holidays, the largest heli-skiing operator, reported twenty-two deaths by avalanches, six in tree wells, one in a crevasse, and two the result of helicopter accident. The statistics do not include guides killed. Source: Martin von Neudegg, Canadian Mountain Holiday, Banff, Alberta.

31. Peter Miller, "The Outrageous Bunch," *SKI Magazine* (January 1980): 131.

32. Rick Sylvester, "I Doubled for James Bond," *SKI Magazine* (Late Winter 1978): 53.

33. John Fry, "It's a Plane, It's a Bird, It's SUPER JOBE," *SKI Magazine* (September 1971): 68.

34. Statistics of the Cyber Snow and Avalanche Centre, www.csac.org.

12. *Freestyle (pages 219–34)*

1. Peter Miller, "Cult, Philosophy, Sport, Art Form: Freestyle Skiing is American-made," *SKI Magazine* (October 1973): 49.

2. "Hot Dog: Grace, Daring, Pizzaz," *SKI Magazine* (October 1973): 42.

3. Miller, "Cult, Philosophy, Sport, Art Form, 48.

4. Ibid., 49.

5. Morten Lund, "Phil Gerard and His Wonderful Electric Skiing Machine," *SKI Magazine* (September 1970): 150.

6. Suzy Chaffee, "It's Time to Give U.S. Ski Team Gals a Break," *SKI Magazine* (November 1975): 7.

7. Remarks made by Stein Eriksen at the 2003 meeting of the International Skiing History Association, Deer Valley, Utah.

8. Gollner performed the "Moebius Flip" in the film *Ski the Outer Limits* made by Roger Brown and Barry Corbet (see chapter 17). Corbet, knowing of the mathematician, had the idea to name Gollner's spectacular acrobatic ski stunt the "Moebius Flip." Phone interview with Herman Gollner by the author, November 13, 2005.

9. "Guide to Getting Through the New Bumps," *SKI Magazine* (January/Holiday issue, 1974): 71. The article contrasted 1974 bumps with those typically found on the slopes in 1969.

10. Dick Barrymore, *Breaking Even* (autobiography of the ski filmmaker). (Helena, Montana: Pictorial Histories Publishing Co., 1997), 231.

11. E-mail exchange between the author and Tom Corcoran, August 2005.

12. Report November 14, 1987, by Whitey Willauer, president of USSA, to Dr. Bud Little and Hank Tauber, in connection with 1987 FIS Council meeting in Madrid, Spain.

13. Note March 4, 1986, by Whitey Willauer to USSA's executive director, Howard Peterson.

14. "Update on Freestyle World Cup Events in the United States," a 1983 report by Jim Palmquist to the U.S. Ski Association.

15. Report by Whitey Willauer to Dr. Bud Little and Hank Tauber, in connection with 1987 FIS Council meeting in Madrid.

13. Snowboarding (pages 235–43)

1. "The Year of the Snurfer?" *SKI Magazine* (November 1974): 43.

2. Author's taped transcript of interview with Jake Burton Carpenter, Stowe, Vermont, September 24, 2001.

3. Lee Crane, "A Board-Watcher's Field Guide, *Snow Country Magazine* (November 1993): 82.

4. Interview with Carpenter.

5. Ibid.

6. Ibid.

7. Mark Sullivan, "Master of the Mountain," *Snow Country Magazine* (September 1995): 196.

8. "Share a Chair," pamphlet published in 1991. A quarter of a million copies were distributed to ski areas, according to Roger Lohr who worked for Ski Industries America at the time.

9. A snowboarder is less prone to fatal injury than is a skier, according to Jasper Shealy, who has studied ski accidents for forty years. The reason is that the most common cause of a slope fatality is when a skier or snowboarder slides into a tree or manmade object. But when the snowboarder slides, according to Shealy, his or her body acts like a kind of sea anchor, dragging on the snow and bringing less kinetic energy into the collision. Phone interview and e-mail exchange in January 2004, by the author with Dr. Jasper Shealy, who since 1972 has been a leading researcher on the causes of injuries at ski areas.

10. Interview with Carpenter.

11. Kottke National End-of-Season Survey 2001/02 for the National Ski Areas Association, Lakewood, Colorado, p. 3. The survey estimated that snowboarding accounted for 29.2 percent of a total of 54.2 million visits to the nation's ski areas.

12. Interview with Carpenter.

13. John Fry, "Snowboarding by the Numbers," *Snow Country Magazine* (November 1995): 220.

14. Allen St. John, "I'm on the Olympic Team? Bummer," *New York Times Magazine* (January 27, 2002): 35.

15. Jim and Joy Spring of Leisure Trends, Inc., Boulder, Colorado, research in the 1999–2000 season.

14. "The Industry" (pages 247–57)

1. Richard Wilson, "They Made It Happen!" *U.S. Skiing and Men of the 10th Mountain Division* (December 4, 2000), seventeen-page list.

2. "Ski Newsletter," *SKI Magazine* (January 1953): 5.

3. Computation based on manufacturer's suggested retail prices for skis listed

in *Ski Business* (Spring 1965), and the dollar value of skis in the import statistics of the U.S. Commerce Department (1964). The four-times multiple of retail over factory cost remained more or less constant over the years.

4. William Hazelett in a letter to the author, January 2001. An engineer and a friend of Howard Head, Hazelett in the late 1940s experimented with making metal skis and successfully manufactured the Stowe Flexible Release binding.

5. Imports of leather, welt-sole boots (1967). U.S. Department of Commerce, *Skiing Trade News* (April 1968): 36.

6. James Woolner, Readers Respond, *Skiing Heritage* (March 2006).

7. Analysis of Alpine and Cross-Country Boot Sales for 1978/79, Ski Industries America.

8. John Henry Auran, "Shop Debt Hits $50 Million," *Skiing Trade News* (Fall 1987).

9. John Fry, "A Certifiable Ski Nut," *Snow Country Magazine* (October 1991): 109.

10. "Conglomerated Ski Co. Inc.," Ski Life, *SKI Magazine* (November 1973): 49.

11. Seth Masia, "The Selling of Skiing," *Skiing Heritage* (December 2005).

12. Ibid.

13. Evolution Marché Mondial du Ski—En Volume, Rossignol Ski Company, courtesy Richard Prothet.

14. James Brooke, "Japan's Ski Industry Stumbles on Age and Economy," *New York Times* (March 24, 2005): C6.

15. John Henry Auran, "The Farwell Report," *Ski Business* (Spring 1964): 35.

16. James Ross Edrys, "Who Is the Dropout?" *Ski Business* (Spring 1965): 189.

17. National Sporting Goods Association, Sports Participation (1994)—people older than seven years of age participating more than once during year; www.nsga.org/public/pages/index.

18. Warren Miller, "Mountain Speak," *SKI Magazine* (March/April 2005): 108.

19. National Sporting Goods Association, Sports Participation, 2004.

20. "A Population Perspective of the United States," Population Resource Center, www.prcdc.org, 2004.

21. C. R. Goeldner, University of Colorado Business School. For the 1986 to 2002 period, data is from Kottke National End-of-Season Survey, projection of skier-visits prepared annually by RRC Associates, Inc., for the National Ski Areas Association, Lakewood, Colorado, 2002/02. Between 1976 and 1986, the price of a lift ticket rose from $8.52 to $20.37, a 139 percent increase, compared with a U.S. consumer price index increase of 92.6 percent in the same period. Between 1986 and 2002, the price (yield to the ski area) of a lift ticket rose from $20.37 to $27.39, a 35 percent increase, compared with a U.S. consumer price index increase of 60 percent in the same period.

22. Kottke National End-of-Season Survey for the National Ski Areas Association.

23. Sean O'Brien, Editor, *Snowboard Business*, and Wini Jones, collector of ski trade publications.

15. In Print (pages 258–76)

1. A book here is defined as a publication of more than one hundred pages. Henry Yaple, *Ski Bibliography* (Woodbury, Conn.: International Skiing History Association, 2004), *www.skiinghistory.org*. Since Yaple completed his monumental work in 2004, the total of books published by now is greater than 2,322. The earliest books in Yaple's bibliography are Nansen's *The First Crossing of Greenland* and *The Snow-Shoe Itinerant* by the Reverend John Dyer, both published in 1890.

2. Arthur Conan Doyle, "An Alpine Pass on Skis," *Strand Magazine* (1895). Doyle and Arnold Lunn shared an interest in mysticism and attended séances together. Both came to be knighted.

3. Ernest Hemingway, *The Moveable Feast* (New York: Charles Scribner's Sons, 1964).

4. Arnold Lunn and Reverend Ronald Knox, *Difficulties* (London: Eyre and Spottiswoode, 1932).

5. Sir Arnold Lunn, *The Story of Ski-ing,* quoted in *SKI Magazine* (January 1954): 15.

6. William F. Buckley, Jr., *Nearer, My God* (New York: Doubleday, 1997), 52.

7. Emile Allais, translated by Agustin R. Edwards, photo-illustrations by Pierre Boucher, *How to Ski by the French Method* (New York: New Directions, 1947).

8. E. G. Valens, *The Other Side of the Mountain* (originally, *A Long Way Up*) (New York: Warner Books by arrangement with Harper & Row, 1975).

9. Oakley Hall, *The Downhill Racers* (New York: The Viking Press, 1963), 217.

10. Morten Lund, Bob Gillen, and Michael Barrett, *The Ski Book* (New York: Arbor House, 1982).

11. *SKI Magazine's 1965 Annual* (New York: Universal Publishing and Distributing Corp., September 1964).

12. John Henry Auran and the Editors of *SKI Magazine*, *America's Ski Book* (New York: Charles Scribner Sons: 1966).

13. Robert Scharff and the Editors of *SKI Magazine*, *Encyclopedia of Skiing* (New York: Harper & Row, 1970); third edition by Dick Needham, 1979.

14. Yaple, *Ski Bibliography*. From his massive database of more than seven thousand books and films, Yaple generously supplied the author with a statistical breakdown of published ski books, by topic, for the five decades 1950 to 2000.

15. Martie Sterling, *Days of Stein and Roses: A True Aspen Adventure* (New York: Dodd, Mead, 1984).

16. Hal Clifford, *Downhill Slide* (San Francisco: Sierra Club Books, 2002), 17.

17. Daniel Glick, *Powder Burn* (New York: Public Affairs, Perseus Books Group, 2001), 85 and 186.

18. Frankie O'Rear and Johnny O'Rear, *Chateau Bon Vivant* (New York: Macmillan, 1967), 7.

19. James Laughlin, "International Racing Spews Discord," *SKI Magazine* (November 1, 1948): 8.

20. Personal interview with Abramson, New York City, Winter 1958.

21. Statement of Circulation, *SKI Magazine* (November 1960): 8.

22. John Jerome, Interoffice Communication to Bill Ziff, Furman Hebb, and Bradford Briggs, May 17, 1967.

23. Al Greenberg, "Gertsch 6D," *Skiing Magazine* (February 1969): 72.

24. Hans Kraus, "Sounding Off," *SKI Magazine* (October 1965): 142.

25. William Orban, "5BX Exercise Plan for Skiers," *SKI Magazine* (October 1964). 149.

26. "Sandy Kofix's Repair Shop," *SKI Magazine* (Spring Issue, 1966): 46.

27. Statement of Ownership, Management and Circulation, October 1, 1966, *SKI Magazine* (January 1967): 121.

28. *Powder Magazine* (30th Anniversary Issue, December 2001), 67.

29. *Snow Country Magazine* (September 1989): 47; *SKI Magazine* (October 1989): 100.

30. Statement of Ownership, Management and Circulation, *SKI Magazine* (January 1967): 121.

31. *SKI Magazine*'s audited paid circulation, exclusive of sponsored subscriptions, in 2004 actually declined to a level below where it was in 1973 when paid circulation was 383,000. As many as 170,000 "subscribers" in 2004 were receiving *Skiing Magazine* as a result of distribution deals cut with "sponsors" and "partners." Audit Bureau of Circulations statement for six months ending June 30, 2004, 900 North Meacham Road, Schaumburg, Illinois.

32. Quote is from author's phone interview with Brian Sellstrom in Rancho Santa Fe, California, February 3, 2005.

33. Susanna Howe, *(Sick): A Cultural History of Snowboarding* (New York: St. Martin's Press, 1998), 104.

34. From transcript of phone interview by the author with Lee Crane, general manager, On-line, *Transworld Snowboarding*, February 4, 2005.

35. Bill Wallace, "Martinis for Lunch—Strange Secrets and Habits Are Confessed by Ski Writer," *SKI Magazine* (November 1952): 20. Wallace worked at the time for the *New York World-Telegram*.

36. Charlie Meyers, "Pro Racing: Bucks and Brinkmanship," *SKI Magazine* (October 1982): 158. Text reproduced courtesy of Charlie Meyers.

37. Janet E. Franz, *From Liftline to Byline: A History of the Eastern Ski Writers Association's First Forty Years* (Cherry Hill, N.J.: ESWA, 2003).

38. John Fry, Skier's Notebook, *SKI Magazine* (November 1971): 10.

39. The information about skiing on the web was furnished to the author by Seth Masia who created the Times Mirror website SkiNet in 1995. The sport's first web presence was engineered by former *Powder Magazine* editor Neil Stebbins for AOL in 1991.

16. In Movies, On Television (pages 277–90)

1. Arnold Fanck, *4628 Meter Hoch: Ski Besteigen des Monte Rosa* (1913).
2. Dick Barrymore e-mail to the author, October 11, 2005.
3. Dick Barrymore, *Breaking Even* (Helena, Mont.: Pictorial Histories Publishing Co., 1997), 171.
4. Ibid: 328.
5. "A Film to Dance By," *SKI Magazine* (December 1967): 102.
6. Robert K. Barney, Stephen R. Wenn, and Scott G. Martyn, *Selling the Five Rings: The International Olympic Committee and the Rise of Olympic Commercialism* (Salt Lake City: University of Utah Press, 2002), 54.
7 Roone Arledge, *Roone* (New York: Harper Collins, 2003), 67.
8. IOC television rights fees derived from the website www.olympic.org/uk/organisation/facts/revenue/broadcast.
9. Barney et al., *Selling the Five Rings*, 247.
10. USAToday.com reported shortly before the 2002 Olympic Winter Games at Salt Lake that NBC expected to collect $720 million in ad sales for 375.5 hours of programming on the NBC, MSNBC, and CNBC networks.
11. Jim Spence, *Up Close and Personal* (New York: Atheneum Publishers, 1988), 287.
12. Author's interview with Greg Lewis, Arrowhead Village, Colorado, February 2005.
13. German viewers in the winter of 2004–2005 could see 61 hours of alpine ski racing on broadcast television and Swiss viewers 209 hours, compared to a scant few hours in the United States and in France, according to Media Partners, Italy.
14. Interview with Greg Lewis.
15. Telephone interview by the author of Jim Bukata, former television executive with International Management responsible for skiing, February 4, 2005.
16. Interview with Greg Lewis.
17. Results of a poll conducted by *Snow Country Magazine* (January 1994): 60.
18. Bob Wolfley, reporting on the 2002 Salt Lake Winter Games at jsonline.com/sports, wrote that non-event coverage and commercials accounted for 42 percent of the first three days of NBC's coverage. Live event coverage was limited to 26 percent.
19. Phone interview by the author with Tom Kelly, vice-president for Mar-

keting/Communications of the U.S. Ski and Snowboard Association, January 27, 2005.

20. The idea of creating a ski race in the format of a motorcross race was first proposed by a group of Mission Ridge, Washington, skiers in a letter to *SKI Magazine* (December 1976): 22.

21. Interview with Kelly.

17. The New Ski Country (pages 291–309)

1. "Common Ground in the Mountains," survey conducted by *Snow Country Magazine* (October 1995): 70. See also "Vote for Better Scenery," *Snow Country* (January/February 1992): 9.

2. Allen I. Barry, "Pleasures and Pitfalls of Owning a Ski Cabin," *SKI Magazine* (November 1959): 74.

3. John Fry, "You're a Good Man, Ted Riehle," *SKI Magazine* (Holiday Issue, 1967): 8.

4. I. William Berry, with Morten Lund and Richard Sapir, "Lest Skiers Forget," *SKI Magazine* (Holiday Issue, 1969): 78.

5. John Henry Auran, "Meet Mr. Janss," *SKI Magazine* (December 1964): 111.

6. From longhand notes of the author made during a phone interview with Doug Burden, summer 2000.

7. David Brand, "Cutting His Own Path," *Time Magazine* (August 21, 1989): 44.

8. I. William Berry, "Lest Skiers Forget," 75.

9. Rigo Thurmer, "So You Want to Build a Ski Resort," *SKI Magazine* (December 1976): 149.

10. From "The Public's Right to Ski," address by John Fry to 69th Annual Convention of the United States Ski Association, Snowmass, Colorado, June 17, 1977.

11. Charlie Meyers, "Anyone for a Bargain-Basement Ski Resort?" *SKI Magazine* (January 1979): 86.

12. Barbara Wicks, "Who Is Chuck Lewis?" *Ski Area Management* (Fall 1972): 32.

13. Steve Lipsher, *Denver Post*, November 6, 2003.

14. John Fry, "The Boxes that Didn't Last," *Snow Country Magazine* (March/April 1991): 96.

15. Told by Emile Allais to the author in the course of an interview in the winter of 1984 at Vail, Colorado, for a profile of Allais that appeared in *SKI Magazine* (December 1984).

16. Ibid.

17. Handwritten letter from Stewart L. Udall, Secretary of the Interior, to the author, December 5, 1966.

18. John Fry, "A Friend of Skiing," *Snow Country Magazine* (October 1980): 4.

19. Robert Redford, "Warning of the Wasatch," *Snow Country Magazine* (October 1989): 54.

20. Henrik Bull, in a letter to the author, July 18, 2005.

21. William Oscar Johnson, "A Vision for the Mountains," *Snow Country Magazine* (September 1995): 58. The Boom in Mountain Living Conference was supported by a $25,000 grant from the U.S. Forest Service and an equal grant from the New York Times Company, publisher of *Snow Country*.

22. Ibid., 62.

23. John Fry, "Talking, Not Fighting," *Ski Area Management* (May 1999): 71.

24. Michel Beaudry, "The Limits to Mountain Resort Growth," *Ski Area Management* (July 1991): 40, 63. Beaudry reported on the national conference on skiing-triggered growth, held at Vail in May 1991. Rural Vermont communities, struggling with unemployment and poverty, were said to be generating less than $400 per capita in taxes, while ski towns of comparable size were generating $2,000 a year.

25. Hal Clifford, *Downhill Slide: Why the Corporate Ski Industry Is Bad for Skiing, Ski Towns and the Environment* (San Francisco: Sierra Club Books, 2002).

26. Ibid., 38.

27. The Mountain Ear, *Snow Country Magazine* (December 1992): 46.

28. David Colman, *New York Times*, January 31, 2005. Baldwin died on January 23, 2005. "Many people saw him as promoting divisiveness between rich and poor, we and they," commented Aspen mayor Helen Klanderud.

29. Michel Beaudry, "Will 'Ski' Resorts Be History?" *Snow Country Magazine* (January/February 1991): 7.

30. Kurt Repanshek, "A Prophet of Boom," *Snow Country Magazine* (September 1996): 58.

31. Ibid.

32. David Rowan, "Where Is the Growth?" *Snow Country Magazine* (July 1989): 28.

33. Nolan Rosall Associates, research conducted for the National Ski Areas Association.

34. Hubert B. Herring, *New York Times*, 2004. Sources: Elite Traveler, Prince Associates.

35. Northwest Colorado Council of Governments, www.nwc.cog.co.

36. Ford Frick, "A Village Too Far?" *Ski Area Management* (September 2001): 51.

37. Ibid.

38. Eric Vohr, *National Ski Areas Association Journal* (October/November 2005): 19. Also, Martin Forstenzer, *SKI Magazine* (February 2005).

39. John Fry, "Fast Times at Mountain High," *SKI Magazine* (September 2001): 74. County growth as measured by U.S. Census 2000.

40. IBM recruitment advertisement in *SKI Magazine* (November 1967): 137.

Glossary

acclimatize, acclimate. Adapt to a change in altitude, ideally done in stages to reduce physiological stress.

Alpine, alpine. When the A is capitalized, the word Alpine relates to Europe's Alps. In lower case, alpine may refer to anything mountainous like the Alps, and specifically applies to downhill skiing, as contrasted with nordic—cross-country and jumping. Downhill, slalom, giant slalom, and Super G are alpine competitions.

alpine combined. A downhill and a slalom race either held intentionally as a combined event, or the linking of two races on the calendar to produce a combined result. Result of a combined competition once was derived from mathematically computing FIS points. Today it is done by adding up the times.

angulation. A body position that enables the skier to edge the skis aggressively in traversing across the hill and in completing the turn. The upper torso is angled outward and down the mountain, at the same time as the hip and knees are angled into the mountain. Angulation was also known as the comma position.

anterior cruciate ligament (ACL). The knee ligament that connects the femur (thigh bone) with the tibia (shin bone) and prevents the forward movement of the tibia on the femur. The posterior cruciate ligament prevents backward movement of the tibia on the femur. ACL tears became a common ski injury after 1980 as a result of changed boot design, ski shape, and binding height combined with the skier's feet-apart stance.

anticipation. The skier's upper body anticipated the direction of the coming turn, acting as an anchor for the lower body to turn against. As the tension was released (muscles relaxed) and the skier "let go" of the old turn, the legs realigned with the upper body and started the turn.

arête (French). Sharp mountain ridge with steep sides.

Arlberg. A mountainous region of western Austria encompassing the classic ski resorts of St. Anton, St. Christof, Lech, and Zurs. Home of famed ski

The author is indebted to Seth Masia, to Doug Pfeiffer, to the editors of the Professional Ski Instructors of America Alpine Technical Manual, and to the glossary at www.snowboarding.about.com for help in assembling this Glossary.

teacher Hannes Schneider, who formulated the Arlberg technique, and of Stefan Kruckenhauser, who popularized wedeln.

Arlberg strap. A leather strap that was wrapped around the boot and attached to the ski to prevent it from running away when the binding released.

Arlberg technique. A series of movements taught in progression, starting with the snowplow and progressing to turns made with the skis parallel, developed by Hannes Schneider. See also **Arlberg**.

Backscratcher. While airborne, the skier's knees are bent so as to force the ski tips to drop sharply downward. The tails of the skis may even scratch one's back. Also called a Tip Drop.

backside. The backside of the snowboard is the side where the rider's heels sit. The backside of a snowboarder is the side where the rider's back faces.

bathtub. See **sitzmark**.

bear trap. A binding with fixed toe irons that did not allow release. The heel often was lashed to the skis with a leather strap, long thong, or lanière.

bevel. Modifying the edge of a ski so that it doesn't form a perfect 90-degree angle. The ski edge has two surfaces: the base edge contiguous to the ski's sole, and the side edge meeting the ski's sidewall. A beveled base edge is "softened" by about one degree—in effect it's recessed relative to the ski's running surface—so the ski rolls more smoothly on and off the edge. A bevelled side edge—sharpened to 1, 2, or 3 degrees of acute angle—can help a racer to hold a more aggressive line on ice.

biathlon. A competition among rifle-bearing skiers originating in the eighteenth century, which rewards skill in skiing cross-country and marksmanship. Results are computed in time. Minutes are subtracted for errant shots. Biathlon has a separate sports governing body recognized by the International Olympic Committee.

binding platform. In the days of carved "ridgetop" skis of hickory and ash, it was common to provide a flat, and usually slightly raised, platform at the ski's center for mounting the binding and boot. Beginning with international standards for bindings (see **DIN setting**), the binding mounting zone on the ski was defined as a flat platform or plate designed to anchor the binding screws. In 1989, World Cup champion Marc Girardelli began using the Derbyflex plate, a solid aluminum plate glued to a thick sheet of neoprene rubber, inserted between the ski and the binding. The platform provided an additional inch of leverage relative to the ski's edge for more edging power, and additional boot clearance so that the ski could be pitched onto a higher edge angle. The leveraging power from the elevated platform also leveraged the power of forces coming back into the knee from the snow. To reduce knee injuries among racers, the FIS limited the total "stack height"—the distance between the snow and the sole of the boot—to a maximum of 55 millimeters. A typical high-performance recreational binding today has a stack height of 45 millimeters; the ski itself may be about 15 millimeters thick.

blindside. In snowboarding, when the rider approaches or lands "blind" to the direction of travel.

boarder cross. Snowboarders race through turns and obstacles and jumps in heats of four to six riders, starting simultaneously. The term derives from a similar format used in motorcycling: motocross.

bonk. In snowboarding, to hit a non-snow object hard.

boilerplate. A glazed covering of solid ice on a trail, usually produced after rain or after wet snow freezes.

boogying. To ski the bumps all out—a 1970s hotdog skiing term.

canting. The process of making adjustments—primarily to bindings and boots—in order to improve the alignment of feet, knees, hips, and upper body. The alignment typically is done mechanically by a footbed in the boot and/or by adjusting the boot's cuff.

carving. Turning the skis by causing them to travel on edge with minimal lateral slipping or skidding. The tail of the ski is on a forward moving path that follows the tip of the ski. A pure carved turn, whether on skis or on a snowboard, is defined by its leaving a clean, elliptical track on the snow.

camber. The arch built into a ski from tip to tail. Camber was created to generate even pressure on the snow along the length of the ski. A "stiff" ski resists being de-cambered or pressed flat.

catwalk. Narrow road often built to enable wheeled machines to ascend the mountain in summer and snowcats in winter. Catwalks double as ski trails in winter, characterized by long traverses that link to another trail, a lift, or another section of the resort.

center line. A model created by the Professional Ski Instructors of America "for selecting appropriate movement patterns under a variety of circumstances."

chattering. Vibration and chattering caused when the ski's edges fail to grip on ice.

christie. A contraction of the word christiania, describing a turn made with the skis parallel (a parallel christie), as distinct from a turn made with the skis partially in a stem or Vee configuration (known as a stem christie), or a turn made wholly with the skis stemmed (known as a stem turn, snowplow, or wedge turn). In post-twentieth-century ski schools, the term christie may distinguish a skidded turn from a carved turn.

cirque. A bowl-like shape, typically at the head of a valley, created by a former glacier.

concave running surface. A frequent defect for many years in the manufacture and curing of fiberglass and plastic skis produced in molds. The concave ski's bottom resists turning. The defect is corrected by flat-filing or machine-grinding the skis to bring the edges down to the level of the running surface.

convex. The opposite condition of concave. A convex base feels unstable to the skier, doesn't track accurately, and sideslips on ice.

corn snow. Pellet-sized particles formed from repetitive thawing, refreezing, and recrystallizing of the snow. Corn snow has a texture that facilitates turning and causes skiers to feel as if they're skiing on ball bearings.

cornice. Overhang of snow and ice typically found on a high ridge. Dangerous skiing to the skier who stands for long on one, and an opportunity for the extreme skier to jump off one.

counter rotation. Simultaneously twisting the upper body in one direction (usually opposite to the direction of travel) and the lower body in another direction.

cross-country relay. See **team event**.

crossover. Swinging one ski around the other so that the feet point in opposite directions, then extricating the standing ski to re-align itself to the other.

crud, breakable crust. A condition in which the snow surface has frozen into hard crust over soft snow underneath; settling snow that has been cut up by skiers. When the skier's weight is sufficient to break through the crust, but unpredictably, the resulting condition is difficult to ski.

Daffy. An early freestyle stunt, the Daffy was a mid-air split—the skier extended one leg forward, the other rearward. If airborne long enough, the skier could sky-walk—that is switch legs fore and aft two or three times. The term Daffy originated in the idea of the stunt being daft, or slightly crazy.

damping. Quality in a ski that prevents it from vibrating excessively, a problem with early metal skis. Skis insufficiently damped are unstable and may not hold an edge on ice. An over-damp ski, on the other hand, feels heavy and sluggish, doesn't glide easily on wet snow especially, and tends not to rise to the surface in heavy powder.

deep-crotch christie. While traversing at a comfortable speed, the skier suddenly assumes a low crouch position. Taking advantage of this unweighting movement, he turns the skis toward the fall line while keeping the weight on the inside-of-the-turn ski and letting the outside one drift off as if about to do a gymnast's split. Once the desired new direction is obtained, a normal skiing posture is resumed.

DIN setting. Every binding has an adjustable release setting that determines the torque required to release the skier in a fall. Beginning in 1979, bindings used a standard scale to measure release values. The standard, DIN, stands for Deutsche Industrie Normen—German Industrial Standards. The number, usually visible in a tiny panel on the toepiece, theoretically represents the torque in decanewtons per degree to release the binding toe. The higher the number, the greater the force required to release. An expert recreational skier might set his binding at 8; a beginner, depending on weight and strength, much lower, say 3. The setting of the binding's heel piece is proportional to the toe setting at a ratio determined by the manufacturer.

down-unweighting. A lightening of the pressure of the skis on the snow made by a sudden dropping of the skier's body. See **up-unweighting**.

Fakie. In snowboarding, to ride backwards without facing the direction of travel.

fall line. Line down the hill that gravity would direct a rolling or falling object. The steepest or shortest line. A sequence of ski turns typically is made by a skier crossing back and forth across the fall line.

FIS. Fédération Internationale de Ski. The International Ski Federation, made up of almost a hundred national ski federations around the world, headquartered at Oberhofen/Thunersee, Switzerland.

Flying Sitzmark. In deep snow, with a modicum of speed, the skier launched airborne from between both poles, kicks the skis forward and vertical, typically in an X-configuration, and landed with his rear end first in the deep stuff, leaving a giant sitzmark in the snow.

four-way skier. One who competes in downhill, slalom, cross-country, and jumping. The four-way champion often is called **skimeister**.

frontside. The frontside of the snowboard is the side where the rider's toes sit.

grab. To hold the edge of the snowboard with one or both hands while airborne.

halfpipe. A vertical U-shaped structure sculpted from snow. Snowboarders and skiers use the opposing walls of the halfpipe to get air and perform tricks as they travel downhill. At ski areas, specially designed grooming machines are used to make halfpipes.

jib. In snowboarding, to ride on something other than snow, such as rails, trees, garbage cans, or logs.

garland. A traversing exercise used to develop skill in unweighting and edging the skis. The skis are alternately slipped downhill and run straight, without the skier making a turn.

gate event. Refers to a slalom or giant slalom race. A gate or technical skier specializes in slalom and giant slalom, in contrast to the speed competitions of downhill and Super G.

gelandesprung. A powerful jump off a bump or a built-up jump, executed by the skier using both poles and often spreading his legs in mid-air.

geschmozell, geschmozzle. A downhill competition in which all the racers started at the same time. The practice was abandoned for most of the twentieth century, but was revived with the popularity early in the twenty-first century of skier-cross and boarder-cross races.

goofy, goofy-footed. In snowboarding, riding with the right foot in front instead of the left foot, which is the normal stance

Graduated Length Method (GLM). A system of teaching in which the pupil progressed from shorter to longer skis.

hairpin. In slalom, two gates set vertically down the hill and close together.

heel side. The edge of the snowboard under the rider's heels.

herringbone. A technique for climbing the hill by putting the skis on edge in a Vee configuration, with the tips fanned outward. The skier walks up the hill on alternating feet while edging the skis to avoid slipping backwards. The pattern left in the snow resembles the skeleton of a fish.

high-back boot. See **jet sticks**.

huck. In snowboarding, to throw one's body wildly downhill. A huckfest is a gathering of snowboarders riding as hard and wildly as possible.

inside ski. In a turn, the skis describe an arc or partial circumference of a circle. The inside ski at the beginning of the turn is the one toward the circle's center, or the downhill ski. At the turn's conclusion, it has become the uphill ski.

IOC. The International Olympic Committee is headquartered in Lausanne, Switzerland. The IOC recognizes the FIS as the official governing body for the sports of skiing and snowboarding.

ISHA. The International Skiing History Association publishes a quarterly journal, *Skiing Heritage*, and operates the most extensive website about the sport's history. Its office is in South Burlington, Vermont; the subscription services are in Lakewood, Colorado.

jet sticks, Jet Stix. Beginning around 1966, the French introduced an aggressive style of slalom skiing called *avalement*, which depended in part on storing energy in the stiff tail of the ski, then releasing it for acceleration. To aid in loading the tail, racers began experimenting with ways to build up the back of their leather and plastic boots using tongue depressors, aluminum plate, fiberglass, duct tape—anything that fell to hand. By 1969, most boot manufacturers responded by offering plastic "spoilers" to build up the back of the boot. An aftermarket option was Jet Stix, a set of spoilers with a buckle strap that could be attached to any pair of boots.

kicker, kicker jump. Steeply built jump designed to hurtle the freestyle aerialist vertically into the air, making possible flips and various inverted aerial stunts. By contrast, the lip of a classic Nordic jump is designed to maximize the jumper's horizontal distance.

klister. An extremely sticky or tacky wax enabling cross-country skis to grip and glide on warm, wet, or frozen granular spring snow.

Kofix. One of the early brand names for a polyethylene laminate bonded onto the ski's base to form its running surface.

langlauf. German word for cross-country skiing.

lanière. Shorter version of the **long thong**.

long thong. A leather strap used by racers and good skiers until the 1960s to hold the foot securely on the ski and to strengthen the leather boot's lateral support of the ankle. As long as six feet and wrapped around the boot, the long thong attached to steel rings on the sides of the ski or was threaded through a mortise drilled through the wooden ski under the foot.

liftline. A line of skiers waiting to get on a lift. Long liftlines are synonymous with waiting a long time in the liftline. The term liftline may also refer to the cut through the trees where the lift ascends the mountain.

massif. A mass or group of summits.

mid-entry boot. A design usually incorporating an overlap lower shell to provide accurate shell fit, and a hinged upper cuff that opens wide for easy entry and exit. Mid-entry boots were aimed at intermediate skiers who wanted a more precise fit than was available with rear-entry boots, but who didn't want to wrestle with the stiff flaps of an overlap racing boot. See also **overlap boot** and **rear-entry boot**.

mogul. A bump formed as a result of skiers repeatedly turning in the same place.

moraine. Large mounds of boulders, rocks, and gravel ground up and shifted or left behind as a result of a glacier's movement. A terminal moraine appears at the end of the glacier; lateral moraines at its sides.

NSAA, National Ski Areas Association. A trade association of more than four hundred mostly U.S. ski areas, headquartered in Lakewood, Colorado.

NSPS, National Ski Patrol System. Association of ski patrolmen and women, headquartered in Lakewood, Colorado.

Nordic combined. The result of competitors racing cross-country and jumping. Distance and style in the jumping event and times in the cross-country event were converted into points. Beginning in 1968 in Norwegian meets, and then in the mid-1980s in international meets, the finish order in the jumping event established the starting order in the cross-country race. The first man crossing the finish line in the cross-country race wins the combined.

off-piste. Terrain that is not on a prepared slope. See **piste**.

outside ski. See **inside ski**.

overlap boot. The ski boot prevalent today. The foot is inserted as it once was into the old-fashioned boot—that is, through the top of the cuff. Overlap boots typically consist of a lower shell with overlapping flaps over the instep, which are closed tightly around the foot with over-center buckles (see also **rear-entry boot**).

piste. French word for trail or track or groomed slope.

platterpull, Pomalift. A stick with a round, flat disk is attached at its other end to a moving steel cable. To ride uphill, the skier inserts the stick between his or her legs, with the flat disk placed behind his or her derriere. The other end of the stick mechanically grabs the moving cable and the rider is pulled along the snow uphill. The platterpull is often called a Pomalift, after the name of its inventor Pomagalski.

Polish Donut. In freestyle, a variant of the Worm Turn. The skier, usually while traversing, suddenly sat down to the side of the skis, raised them sufficiently to clear the snow, and spun around in a full circle before continuing.

pre-jump. A technique for reducing the tendency to become airborne when confronting a bump or terrain irregularity. The skier jumps before reaching the bump or drop-off, skims over its top, and lands on the downhill side.

PSIA, Professional Ski Instructors of America. National association of certified ski instructors, headquartered in Lakewood, Colorado.

rappel. Descending a mountain on a rope using braking devices.

rear-entry boot. A plastic boot into which the foot was inserted through a "door" or flap at the back. The main shell was seamless and the rear flap was secured with over-center buckles or ratcheting straps. The advantage of the rear-entry boot was that it was easy and quick to get in and out of. The disadvantage was that the shell didn't close accurately around the foot. Aggressive skiers and magazine testers found the rear-entry boot inadequate for performance skiing, and it went from the most widely sold boot in the 1980s to one that is almost unavailable in shops.

reuel (royal) or flying christie. Moving in a traverse, the skier picks up the lower ski and angles it downhill toward the fall line. The turn is done with the weight entirely on the inside or uphill ski, the opposite of what is considered "normal" skiing. For greater spectator effect, the last ski to leave the snow is raised into various positions such as a T-position or back-scratcher. Named for the freestyle pioneer Fritz Reuel (pronounced "royal").

schuss, schussing. To ski without making turns or checking speed. From the German word meaning gun shot, rush, rapid movement.

scree. Rocky debris on mountainsides.

serac. A tower of ice, found among glaciers, and often spectacular in appearance.

shaped skis. Skis with an emphatic or exaggerated **sidecut**. Over a period of several years since the 1990s, "shaped" skis have come to be the norm and represent the bulk of current ski sales. Future technological advances could change this in unforeseeable ways.

short swing. A series of short, tight turns executed down the fall line. Called *wedeln* in German and *godille* in French.

shred. In snowboarding, to tear up the terrain.

SIA, SnowSports Industries America. Formerly Ski Industries America, a trade association of equipment and clothing manufacturers and distributors, headquartered in McLean, Virginia, near Washington, D.C.

sick. Expression for something radically good.

sidecut. The linear curved side shape of a ski that facilitates its turning when the ski is on edge. Sidecut or side camber causes a ski, viewed from the top or bottom, to resemble a wasp shape. It is wider at the tip or shovel of the ski, narrow at the waist, and flares again at the tail.

sitzmark. A term used to describe the depression in the snow left by a fallen skier.

skier cross. A giant slalom–type sprint with bumps and mounded curves, in which a half-dozen competitors start simultaneously (see **geschmozell**), and the winner crosses the finish line first. Top finishers from each heat move on to the next round. The event is patterned after motocross racing.

skier-day, skier-visit. One skier or snowboarder participating one day at a ski area. The skier-day is the most common measure used by ski areas to measure the volume of their business.

ski flying. Ski jumping on a jumping hill rated greater than 120 meters. On March 20, 2005, Finnish ski flyer Matti Hautamaki jumped 235.5 meters, a distance of 772.7 feet.

skijoring. A skier holding a rope is pulled along the snow by dogs, a horse, snowmobile, or four-wheel vehicle. Popular activity in the 1930s.

skimeister. German word meaning an all-round proficient skier in both alpine and nordic. A skimeister was the winner of a four-way competition involving slalom, downhill, cross-country, and jumping. See **four-way**. The term snowmeister was used in 1995 to describe the winner of a competition involving skiing and snowboarding.

slab. Layer of compacted or frozen snow that creates the potential for snow lying on top of it to avalanche.

Slow Dog Noodle. The skier rode up a steep side of a mogul to dissipate speed while assuming an exaggerated sitting-back position. At the crest of the mogul and while still crouching, with skis now balanced directly on the crest, the skier swiveled the skis. The slower the motion, the more perfect the execution.

snowplow, wedge. Going straight down the hill or making slow turns with the skis in a Vee configuration—tips pointed in, tails fanned out.

steepness, pitch. The gradient of a slope's steepness can be determined by two measures: degrees or percent. Percentage—the figure commonly used by ski areas—is determined by dividing the vertical height of the slope by its horizontal distance. For a hill that drops 20 vertical feet and projects out by 100 feet, the division yields .20 and the hill is said to have a 20 percent gradient, equal to a steepness of 11 degrees. A hill with a 60-foot drop and projecting out 100 feet has a 60 percent grade and a 31-degree steepness. A 100 percent slope is 45 degrees steep, dropping one foot for every horizontal foot. Beyond that steepness, snow has difficulty holding and only the most extreme skiing is performed. About 70 percent of the terrain at ski areas falls between 15 and 40 percent of grade, according to the ski area design consultant, the late Jim Branch.

stem, stemming. Technique for slowing speed. See **snowplow**, **christie**.

Super-Diagonal. A 1940s rubber strap that attached to hooks on the ski's sidewall and that stretched diagonally forward around the ankle to hold the boot heel firmly in place.

Switch. See **Fakie**.

switch stance. In snowboarding, to ride backwards with the tail of the board in front.

team event. The oldest team event in skiing is the cross-country relay race involving four competitors, with men racing a 10-kilometer leg and women

5 kilometers. In the Olympics and FIS World Championships, all members of the first, second, and third-place relay teams win medals. Beginning in 1982, team competitions were introduced in jumping and nordic combined.

technical racer. See **gate event**.

téléphérique. French word for an aerial tramway and cable car. Most téléphériques are jigbacks, in which two large cabins are suspended from cables; as one goes up, the other comes down.

telemark turn. The outside ski of the turn is advanced forward and is stemmed, with the knee bent, causing the skis to change direction. Requires use of bindings that allow the skier's heel to rise.

three sixty. An airborne skier doing a complete 360-degree rotation.

Tip Drop. See **Backscratcher**.

Tip Roll. The skier traversed the slope, and with both poles held close together, he suddenly jabbed them into the snow on the uphill side of the ski tips. Skier then vaulted with stiff arms, pivoting on the ski tips, and swung the skis in a 180-degree arc so they landed pointing in a direction opposite to the original direction of travel. In a 360-degree Tip Roll, the skis were whirled around in the air so as to land in the original direction of travel.

top-entry boot. See **overlap boot**.

torsion. The resistance of a ski to being twisted along its length. Skis with high torsional resistance (or torsional stiffness) set an edge into the snow more quickly, especially at the tip and tail. Skis with softer torsion set an edge into the snow less emphatically and can feel more forgiving.

Track! A verbal shout or warning by a descending skier to a person below. "Track left" indicates that the overcoming skier intends to pass the person on his or her left; "Track Right," on the right. The skier or snowboarder above is responsible for avoiding the person below.

tracking. Ability of a ski to hold a line in straight running.

transition. A change in ski terrain, as in going from a flat area to a steep pitch, or going from steep to flat.

turntable. A binding heelpiece that holds down the heel while allowing the boot to swivel when the toepiece rotates.

twin tip. Skis turned up at both ends. A snowboard's nose and tail are shaped identically, so the board rides equally well in both directions.

unweighting. Taking varying amounts of weight off of the skis to manipulate and control pressure. There are four types of "unweighting": (1) up-unweighting, produced at the end of the turn with a rapid upward extension of the body; (2) down-unweighting, produced by a rapid downward flexion of the body; (3) terrain-unweighting, produced by using the terrain to help unweight the skis; (4) rebound-unweighting, produced by the energetic force of the skis "decambering" at the end of a turn. Up-unweighting was the classic technique employed for years to get weight off the skis so that they could be twisted or pivoted in the direction of the turn. It allows a flattened ski to be steered more readily.

uphill ski. See **inside ski**.

vertical drop. The difference in elevation between the top of a ski run and the bottom; the difference in elevation between the summit of a ski resort and its base; or between the top of a specific lift and its base. A resort typically advertises its vertical as the elevation change from the top of its highest lift to the base of its lowest.

wedeln (n.), to wedel. See **short swing**.

wedge turn. See **snowplow, christie**.

windmilling. Flailing-about of a ski after the binding releases. At one time, skiers wore "safety straps" so that when a ski released it wouldn't take off downhill at high speed and become a potential source of injury to other skiers. The trouble was that the windmilling ski attached by the safety strap could seriously injure and cut the falling skier. With the invention of the safety brake—a double prong that snaps downward and prevents the released ski from sliding—the safety strap was no longer needed and the danger of windmilling was eliminated.

Worm Turn. At a slow moderate speed, skier headed straight down the fall line, lay back on the skis, rolled over like a log, then stood up to continue downhill.

Bibliography

Books and Periodicals

Allais, Emile, trans. Agustin R. Edwards. *How to Ski by the French Method*. New York: New Directions, 1947.

Allen, E. John D. *From Skisport to Skiing. 100 Years of an American Sport, from 1840 to 1940*. Amherst: University of Massachusetts Press, 1993.

————, ed. *Collected Papers, International Ski History Congress 2002*. Woodbury, Connecticut: International Skiing History Association, 2002.

American Ski Annual. The National Ski Association, Brattleboro, Vermont: Stephen Daye Press, 1942, 1949, 1956.

Arbique, Louise. *Mont Tremblant, Following the Dream*. Montreal: Carte Blanche, 1999.

Arledge, Roone. *Roone*. New York: Harper Collins, 2003.

Auran, John Henry, and the Editors of *SKI Magazine*. *America's Ski Book*. New York: Charles Scribner Sons, 1966. Second edition, 1973.

Ball, W. L. *I Skied the Thirties*. Ottawa: Deneau Publishers & Co. Ltd., no date.

Barney, Robert K., Stephen R. Wenn, and Scott G. Martyn. *Selling the Five Rings: The International Olympic Committee and the Rise of Olympic Commercialism*. Salt Lake City: University of Utah Press, 2002.

Barrymore, Dick. *Breaking Even*. Helena, Montana: Pictorial Histories Publishing Co., 1997.

Beekley, Mason, Mort Lund, and Doug Pfeiffer, eds. *The International Skiing History Association Ski Song Book*. New Hartford, Conn.: Beekley, Lund, and Pfeiffer, March 1995.

Brady, M. Michael. *Nordic Touring and Cross Country Skiing*, Third Revised Edition. Oslo, Norway: Dreyer, 1971.

Buckley, William F., Jr. *Nearer, My God*. New York: Doubleday, 1997.

Caldwell, John. *The Cross-Country Ski Book*, 6th edition. Brattleboro, Vermont: Stephen Greene Press, 1981.

Chouinard, Yvon. *Climber's Bill of Rights: Voices from the Summit*. Washington, D.C.: Adventure Press, National Geographic, 2000.

Clifford, Hal. *Downhill Slide: Why the Corporate Ski Industry Is Bad for Skiing, Ski Towns and the Environment*. San Francisco: Sierra Club Books, 2002.

Cohen, Stan. *Pictorial History of Downhill Skiing*. Missoula, Montana: Pictorial Histories Publishing Co., 1985.

Durrance, Dick, as told to John Jerome. *The Man on the Medal: Life and Times of America's First Great Ski Racer*. Glenwood Springs, Colorado: Durrance Enterprises, Inc., 1995.

Dyer, Reverend John. *The Snow-Shoe Itinerant*. Cincinnati: Cranston and Stowe, 1890.

Elkins, Frank, and Frank Harper. *World Ski Book*. New York: Longmans, Green & Co., 1949.

Evans, Harold, Brian Jackman, and Mark Ottoway, editors of the *London Sunday Times*. *We Learned to Ski*. New York: St. Martin's Press, 1975.

Fixx, Jim. *The Complete Book of Running*. New York: Random House, 1977.

Franz, Janet E. *From Liftline to Byline: A History of the Eastern Ski Writers Association*. Cherry Hill, New Jersey: ESWA, 2003.

Frohlich, Robert. *Mountain Dreamers: Visionaries of Sierra Nevada Skiing*. Truckee, California: Coldstream Press, 1997.

Frohlich, Robert, and S. E. Humphries. *Skiing with Style*. Truckee, California: Coldstream Press, 1999.

Galbraith, John Kenneth. *The Liberal Hour: The Pleasures and Uses of Bankruptcy*. Boston: Houghton Mifflin, 1960.

Gallwey, Timothy, and Bob Kriegel. *Inner Skiing*. Toronto/New York/London: Bantam Books, 1979.

Gamma, Karl. *The Handbook of Skiing*, revised and updated. New York: Alfred A. Knopf, Inc., 1992.

Gilbert, Martin. *A History of the Twentieth Century*, vol. 3, *1952–1999*. New York: William Morrow & Co., Inc., 1999.

Glick, Daniel. *Powder Burn: Arson, Money and Mystery on Vail Mountain*. New York: Public Affairs Perseus Books Group, 2001.

Gmoser, Hans. *Twenty-five Years of Heli-Skiing*. Butte, Montana: Earth & Great Weather Publishing, 1991.

Gucek, Ales. *In the Tracks of Old-Time Skiing*. Ljubljana, Slovenia: Ski Instructors and Trainers Association, 2004.

Hall, Oakley. *The Downhill Racers*. New York: Viking Press, 1963.

———. *The Pleasure Garden*. New York: Viking, Pyramid, 1966.

Hauserman, Dick. *The Inventors of Vail*. Edwards, Colo.: Golden Peak Publishing Co., 2000.

Hayes, Mary Eshbaugh. *The Story of Aspen*. Aspen, Colo.: Aspen Three Publishing, 1996.

Heymann, C. David. *A Candid Biography of Robert F. Kennedy*. New York: E. P. Dutton, 1998.

Howe, Susanna. *(Sick): A Cultural History of Snowboarding*. New York: St. Martin's Press, 1998.

International Ski Federation. FIS Official Bulletin, *World Ski Statistics, 1924–2003*. Oberhofen, Switzerland: International Ski Federation, 2004.

————. *75 Years of Skiing History in Stamps*. Oberhofen/Thunersee, Switzerland: Swiss Academic Ski Club and FIS, 2000.

Iselin, Fred, and A. C. Spectorsky. *Invitation to Skiing*. New York: Simon and Schuster, 1947.

Jay, John, with John and Frankie O'Rear and the Editors of *SKI Magazine*. *Ski Down the Years*. New York: Award House, 1966.

Johannsen, Alice E. *The Legendary Jackrabbit Johannsen*. Montreal and Kingston, Canada: McGill-Queen's University Press, 1993.

Johnson, William O., Jr. *Super Spectator and the Electric Lilliputians*. Boston/Toronto: Sports Illustrated Books, Little, Brown and Co., 1971.

Joubert, Georges, and Jean Vuarnet. *How to Ski the New French Way*. New York: The Dial Press, Inc., 1967. Originally published as *Comment se perfectionner à Ski*, 1966.

Killanin, Lord Michael. *My Olympic Years: Reminiscences of the IOC's President from 1972 to 1980*. New York: William Morrow & Co., Inc., 1983.

Lash, Bill. *The American Ski Technique, 1964–1970*, a privately published history of the early Professional Ski Instructors of America, January 2004.

Lawrence, Andrea B., and Sara Burnaby. *A Practice of Mountains*. New York: Seaview Books, 1980.

Lederer, Bill, and Joe Pete Wilson. *Complete Cross Country Skiing and Touring*. New York: W.W. Norton, 1980.

LeMaster, Ron. *The Skier's Edge*. N.p.: Human Kinetics, 1999.

Leocha, Charles. *Ski Europe*, 13th edition. Hampstead, N.H.: World Leisure Corp., 2002.

Lund, Morten, Bob Gillen, and Michael Bartlett. *The Ski Book: An Anthology of Ski Writing*. New York: Arbor House, 1982.

Lunn, Arnold, and Reverend Ronald Knox. *Difficulties*. London: Eyre and Spotiswood, 1932.

Lunn, Sir Arnold. *Unkilled for So Long*. London: George Allen and Unwin, Ltd., 1968.

————. *The Kandahar Story*. London: George Allen and Unwin, Ltd., 1969.

Mahre, Phil, and Steve Mahre, with John Fry. *No Hill Too Fast*. New York: Simon and Schuster, 1985.

Manchester, Lee, ed. *The Lake Placid Club, 1890 to 2002: A History*. Saranac Lake, N.Y.: Adirondack Publishing Co., 2003.

Matt, Toni. *Ski Down the Years*. New York: Universal Publishing, 1966.

McKenty, Neil, and Catharine McKenty. *Skiing Legends and the Laurentian Lodge Club*. Montreal, Canada: Price-Patterson Ltd., 2000.

Mergen, Bernard. *Snow in America*. Washington, D.C.: Smithsonian Institution, 1997.

Miller, Peter. *Peter Miller's Ski Almanac*. Garden City, N.Y.: Doubleday & Co., 1979.

Miller, Peter. *The 30,000–Mile Ski Race*. New York: Universal Publishing & Distributing Co., 1972.

Nansen, Fridtjof. *The First Crossing of Greenland*. London and New York: Longmans, Green and Company, 1890.

National Ski Areas Association Membership Directory. Lakewood, Colo.: National Ski Areas Association, 2004.

Naylor, Irving S. *Ski Roundtop—40 Seasons of Winter Excellence*. Lewisberry, Pa.: Snow Time Inc., 2003.

New England Ski Museum Newsletter (Journal). Various issues. Franconia, New Hampshire: The New England Ski Museum.

O'Rear, Frankie, and Johnny O'Rear. *Chateau Bon Vivant*. New York: Macmillan, 1967.

O'Rear, John, and Frankie O'Rear. *The Mont Tremblant Story*. Mont Tremblant, Quebec: Les Editions Altitude, 1988.

Palmedo, Roland, trans. *The New Official Austrian Ski System, From Walking to Wedeln*. Edited by the Austrian Association of Professional Ski Teachers. New York: A.S. Barnes and Co., 1958.

————. *The New National Austrian Ski System*. New Jersey: A.S. Barnes and Co., 1974.

————, ed. *Skiing the International Sport*. New York: Derrydale, 1937.

Pepe, Paul. *The Sleeping Giant—The Story of Hunter Mountain*. Hunter Mountain, N.Y.: Mad Box Publishing, 1993.

Pfeifer, Friedl, with Morten Lund. *Nice Goin', My Life on Skis*. Missoula, Montana: Pictorial History Publishing Co., 1994.

Pound, Dick. *Inside the Olympics*. John Wiley & Sons Canada Ltd., 2004.

Powder Magazine. Special 30th Anniversary Issue, December 2001.

Powell, Brian, ed. *Jackrabbit, His First Hundred Years*. Don Mills, Ontario: Collier Mcmillan Canada, Ltd., 1975.

Rosall, Nolan. *Economic Analysis of Ski Areas*, and selected Kottke Reports. Lakewood, Colo.: National Ski Areas Association, 1980–2005.

Scharff, Robert, and the Editors of *SKI Magazine*. *Encyclopedia of Skiing*, 3rd edition. New York: Harper & Row, 1979.

Schinegger, Erik/Erika. *Mein Sieg Über Mich* [*My Victory Over Me*]. Munich: F.A. Herbig Verlagsbuchhandlung GmbH, 1988.

Schranz, Karl. *Mein Olympiasieg* [*My Olympic Victory*]. Munich: F.A. Herbig Verlagsbuchhandlung GmbH, 2002.

Seeger, Robert, ed. *Ski World Cup Guide, 1996–1998*. Basel, Switzerland: Biorama Sportpublikationen AG, 1998.

Seibert, Pete, with William Oscar Johnson. *Vail, Triumph of a Dream*. Boulder, Colo.: Mountain Sports Press, 2002.

SIA SnowSports Annual Show Directory. McLean, Va: SnowSports Industries America, 2001.

Ski Area Management. Woodbury, Conn.: Beardsley Publishing Corp., selected issues between 1985 and 1998.

Ski Business. New York: Universal Publishing & Distributing Corp., selected issues between 1962 and 1966.

Ski Guide and Travel Planner, United States and Canada. Mark C. Borton, publisher. Old Saybrook, Conn.: Peak Productions, Inc., 1994.

Ski Life Magazine. New York: Universal Publishing & Distributing Corp., 1958–1961.

SKI Magazine. In 2005, publisher of the magazine was Time 4 Media, Boulder, Colo. Various issues published between 1948 and 2005.

Skiing Magazine. Denver, Colo.: Skiing Publishing Co., selected issues, 1960–1962.

Slanger, Elissa, and Dinah Witchel. *Ski Woman's Way*. New York: Summit Books, 1979.

Spence, Jim. *Up Close and Personal*. New York: Atheneum Publishers, 1988.

Sterling, Martie. *Days of Stein and Roses: A True Aspen Adventure*. New York: Dodd, Mead, 1984.

Street, Picabo, and Dana White. *Picabo: Nothing to Hide*. New York: McGraw-Hill, 2002.

Taylor, Dorice. *Sun Valley*. Sun Valley: Ex Libris, 1980.

Thoeni, Hans. *Hannes Schneider, zum 100. Geburtstage des Schipioniers* St. Anton, Austria: Hans Thoeni, 1990.

Valens, E. G. *The Other Side of the Mountain* (originally, *A Long Way Up*). New York: Warner Books by arrangement with Harper & Row, 1975.

Vallencant, Patrick. *Ski Extreme: Ma Plenitude*. Paris: Flammarion Parution, 1992.

White Book of Ski Areas. Robert G. Enzel, Publisher & Editor. Washington, D.C.: Interski Services, Inc., 1986.

Witherell, Warren. *How the Racers Ski*. New York: W.W. Norton & Co., 1972.

Witherell, Warren, and David Evrard. *The Athletic Skier*. Boulder, Colo.: Johnson Books, 1993.

Yaple, Henry. *Ski Bibliography*. Woodbury, Conn.: International Skiing History Association, 2004.

Zdarsky, Mathias. *Die Lilienfelder*. Skilauf-Technik, Hamburg: Verlaganstalt und Druckere A-G., 1897.

Websites

www.fisski.ch — Rules of competition.
www.nelsap.org — Lost Ski Areas of New England.
www.ski-db.com — Statistics of World Cup, Olympic, and World Championship alpine racing, edited by Matteo Pacor.
www.speedski.com — Speed skiing information.

www.skiinghistory.org—Ski history information of all kinds. Managed by Seth Masia.

www.sam.info.com—Information about ski area operations.

www.snowindustrynews.com—Ski industry news.

www.onthesnow.com—Ski industry news.

Index of Names and Places

A page number in *italics* refers to a caption. The abbreviation "fn" indicates a footnote, "n" an endnote.